parenting
gifted
children

*The Authoritative Guide From
the National Association for Gifted Children*

parenting
gifted
children

edited by Jennifer L. Jolly, Ph.D., Donald J. Treffinger, Ph.D.,
Tracy Ford Inman, and Joan Franklin Smutny, Ph.D.

PRUFROCK PRESS INC.
WACO, TEXAS

Library of Congress Cataloging-in-Publication Data

Parenting gifted children : the authoritative guide from the National Association for Gifted Children / edited by Jennifer L. Jolly ... [et al.].
      p. cm.
Includes bibliographical references.
ISBN 978-1-59363-430-8 (pbk.)
1. Gifted children. 2. Parents of gifted children. 3. Parenting. 4. Child rearing. I. Jolly, Jennifer L., 1972- II. National Association for Gifted Children (U.S.)
  HQ773.5.P35 2011
  649'.155--dc22
                        2010025251

Printed in the United States of America.

At the time of this book's publication, all facts and figures cited are the most current available. All telephone numbers, addresses, and website URLs are accurate and active. All publications, organizations, websites, and other resources exist as described in the book, and all have been verified. The editors and Prufrock Press Inc. make no warranty or guarantee concerning the information and materials given out by organizations or content found at websites, and we are not responsible for any changes that occur after this book's publication. If you find an error, please contact Prufrock Press Inc.

Prufrock Press Inc.
P.O. Box 8813
Waco, TX 76714-8813
Phone: (800) 998-2208
Fax: (800) 240 0333
http://www.prufrock.com

Contents

Part I: Nature and Assessment. 1
by Catherine M. Brighton

Chapter 1

Chapter 2

Chapter 3

Chapter 4

Part II: Characteristics and Development. 37
by Joan Franklin Smutny

Chapter 5

Chapter 6

Part IV: Programming Options 151
by Donald Treffinger

Part VI: Advocacy 323
by Tracy Ford Inman

Part VII: Twice-Exceptional Students 383
by James T. Webb

Chapter 41

Part VIII: Social and Emotional Needs 411

Chapter 42

Chapter 43

Chapter 44

Chapter 45

Chapter 46

Chapter 47

Chapter 48

Preface

CONGRATULATIONS. You are probably reading this book because you are a parent of a gifted child. You may be a grandparent, teacher, or other interested person. You may have been identified as gifted when you were younger and are searching for answers to questions you have about your giftedness. Regardless of your reason, you've come to the right place. For nearly two decades, *Parenting for High Potential* (*PHP*), the quarterly magazine published by the National Association for Gifted Children (NAGC), has provided practical advice to parents based on research and best practices in the field of gifted education. This book represents the best thinking of parents, teachers, and scholars who have contributed to *PHP*. All of the pieces are relevant to issues parents currently face or will encounter in the future. The pieces reflect the outstanding editorial skills of Jennifer Jolly, current *PHP* editor, and Donald Treffinger and James Alvino, the previous *PHP* editors, who shepherded them through the review and publication process.

The first two sections introduce readers to characteristics of gifted children and much of the terminology parents will encounter as they seek to understand how students come to be identified as gifted. Conceptions of giftedness have expanded, and readers will learn how giftedness can extend beyond intelligence and how intelligence can extend beyond a simple IQ score. Navigating educational assessment terminology and understanding how gifted children might function differently from other children can be confusing. These sections provide a clear, useful introduction to the field of gifted education. Because children's needs change as they grow and mature, the second section is divided by age. As many parents know, college planning is very different than contemplating preschool needs.

The third section of this book addresses the important issue of diversity and underrepresentation in gifted education. Unfortunately, many gifted students' talents go unrecognized, particularly students from diverse backgrounds. Even if they are identified, many underserved populations do not receive the educational opportunities they need to reach their full potential. According to a 2008 report by Wyner, Bridgeland, and Diiulio, almost half of children of poverty who enter first grade in the top 10% will no longer be achieving at top levels 5 years later. They simply are not receiving the services they need.

Parents face a variety of educational choices for their gifted child. Because each child's uniqueness renders some programming options more feasible than others, the fourth section provides an overview of programming options that range from educating children at home to early entrance to school and other acceleration options. Effective programs for the gifted involve a continuum of services that include many of the options described in this section.

The fifth section addresses the specific issue of family dynamics, including general parenting issues. Parents often wonder whether their children's development is on schedule, early, or late. When a child begins reaching developmental markers earlier than other children, parents begin considering the parenting and educational implications ahead. Most of us are not fully prepared to raise a gifted child. This section addresses many issues involved in parenting a gifted child.

The sixth section addresses the various advocacy roles parents must play. Every parent is confronted with questions of "How can I best help my child?" "When should I intervene on my child's behalf?" and "When should I just let events unfold?" Support for gifted children is an important role for parents; in many cases, parents are their children's sole advocates. Parents of gifted children can advocate for their children along a broad continuum of support that begins at home and ends on a national level. These can include:

- advocating for the child's personal performance by helping build his or her confidence,
- advocating for specific services for the child in the community and school,
- advocating for greater schoolwide services for gifted children in general,
- advocating for state support for gifted education, and
- advocating for national attention on gifted education (both legislatively and with the general public).

The final two sections of this book cover concerns related to subpopulations of gifted children and social and emotional issues. These include issues facing students who are gifted with learning disabilities or attention deficit disorders. It also covers a variety of social and emotional concerns that parents of gifted children will recognize.

Parenting Gifted Children: The Authoritative Guide From the National Association for Gifted Children is a comprehensive overview of what we know about meeting the parenting, educational, and social and emotional needs of gifted students. We often hear that gifted children are a national resource that needs to be cultivated and that they represent the best hope for the nation's future. The gifted child in your home may achieve great things in his or her life. However, this is not the reason his or her giftedness needs to be recognized and addressed. Future eminence is an unreasonable expectation to place on a 5-year-old child who is headed to kindergarten with some advanced skills. Although it is true that many innovative individuals may have been classified as gifted as young children, others did not demonstrate their exceptional gifts at an early age. We simply have not yet developed procedures to reliably identify future adult eminence in young children.

We identify and provide services for gifted children because it is the right thing to do. Young children who read early or grasp mathematical concepts before their peers may or may not be eminent writers or mathematicians later in life, but they will need to have their learning needs met when they enter school, and they will lead happier and more enriched lives when they are allowed to pursue their interests and talents.

The assistant at our pharmacy recognized this issue when she observed a 22-month-old girl reading words from a sign posted on her counter. "You're in trouble when she gets to school," the clerk commented to the child's parent. Even though the pharmacy assistant lacked training in education, she recognized the need for "something different" when the young girl began attending school. She also knew that the schools might not be receptive to recognizing that need.

This book helps all of us understand the importance of assessing and understanding gifted children's learning patterns and providing support that matches their learning needs. The important advocacy role everyone has is recognized. Each of us, parents, relatives, educators, and researchers, can be a part of the solution of ensuring that every child has an opportunity to reach his or her potential.

—Del Siegle, Ph.D.,
NAGC President 2007–2009

Reference

Wyner, J. S., Bridgeland, J. M., & Diiulio, J. J. (2008). *The achievement trap: How America is failing millions of high-achieving students from lower-income families.* Lansdowne, VA: Jack Kent Cooke Foundation.

Editors' Note

Parenting for High Potential was first published in 1996 as a resource for parents of gifted high-ability children who were members of the National Association for Gifted Children (NAGC). In the nearly two decades since the first issue was printed, many of the country's leading experts in various educational fields have covered some of the most pressing concerns and questions that parents face in raising gifted and high-ability children. *Parenting Gifted Children: The Authoritative Guide From the National Association for Gifted Children* represents the absolute best of the more than 350 articles that have been published since the inception of the publication with the intention of providing an enduring tome of information and guidance. Although this book is meant primarily as a guide for parents, it also could be a beneficial resource for those who work with gifted and high-ability children and their families, including teachers, administrators, counselors, and other educators.

Each article was selected for inclusion in this compendium after being considered against criteria developed to provide a collection of work that best serves parents and those who work with families of gifted children. Articles were specifically evaluated for the following:

- recognizing and developing children's strengths and gifts and talents (whether children are formally identified as gifted or not);
- providing parenting advice from a practical outlook;
- including information based on research but also emphasizing the implications for children and families;
- focusing on the needs of the reader and carefully defining terms without cumbersome jargon;
- offering print and online resources;
- promoting a collaborative relationship in home, community, and school; and
- presenting creative, new, and original perspectives.

Once the articles were selected they were grouped according to topic and then arranged by chapters. The chapters begin with the nature and assessment of giftedness and high ability followed by character-istics and development. Sections on diversity, programming options, family dynamics, advocacy, the twice-exceptional student, and social-emotional considerations follow. These chapters give the reader the option of focusing on one particular topic or gaining a holistic view.

Nearing its 15th anniversary, *Parenting for High Potential* continues to be a current and timely resource for parents and those profession-als who work with families. To find out more about how to receive this publication and for other parent resources go to the National Association for Gifted Children's website (http://www.nagc.org).

—Jennifer L. Jolly, Ph.D., Donald J. Treffinger, Ph.D.,
Tracy Ford Inman, and Joan Franklin Smutny, Ph.D.

PART I

Nature and Assessment

by Catherine M. Brighton

T HIS section of the text addresses some of the most central questions of importance to parents of gifted children:
- What is the nature of giftedness and talent?
- How can tests reveal (or inadvertently conceal) it?
- What can parents and educators do to maximize gifted potential?

A range of authors offer a variety of insights on these and other related questions and suggest concrete ways that parents and educators can play an active and informed role in the process of nurturing and advocating for gifted children. A brief glimpse into what to expect in the chapters that follow is offered. In each piece, note how the authors make the assumption that parents are partners with educators in the conversations about giftedness and talent. Authors also recommend that parents use this information to become better advocates for their children.

In the first chapter, Barbara Clark reminds us about the importance of keeping our own beliefs and assumptions about children's potential in check. In the discussion of how giftedness and talent is manifested, Clark offers some consideration for the genetic background of the child; however she makes a stronger case for a stimulating and nurturing environment as a more powerful force in the talent development process. She then offers specific ways in which parents and teachers can optimize the development and learning of young children.

Psychologist Robert J. Sternberg provides an alternative to the over-reliance upon traditional intelligence testing or using only an IQ score as the primary indicator of giftedness. Rather, he offers his theory of successful intelligence, whereby individuals identify and cultivate their strengths and figure out ways to compensate or correct for their relative weaknesses. Sternberg punctuates the explanation of his theory with a call to action for parents and teachers; research findings suggest that students who are offered instruction in ways that allow them to play to their strengths and minimize their weaknesses outperform those who were not offered such flexibility. In short, not scoring high on a traditional intelligence test can be overcome by considering strengths more broadly and playing to those strengths.

In the chapter, "Why Gifted Children May Not Test Well," Ben Paris examines issues surrounding testing and, in particular, the specific ways in which some children's scores may be negatively impacted. He identifies and describes seven major problems—lack of motivation, "overthinking" test items, perfectionism, overconfidence, sloppiness, excessive test anxiety, and the mismatch between a child's area of giftedness and the test being administered. While the path beyond these common pitfalls is often complex and requires specific time and attention to improve, he makes clear that "not testing well" is a challenge that can be overcome. As readers progress through the previous chapter, they may find the "Glossary of Terms Used in Educational Assessment" by Michael Freedman and John Houtz useful as a companion tool. This glossary outlines key terms used in the discussion of intelligence and assessment in a concise and readable manner.

As a set, these three pieces share several common themes. First, in each piece the authors make the explicit point that knowledge is power and this knowledge can make parents more effective advocates for their children. For example, Paris offers strategies for parents (and ultimately for the student) to move beyond the self-defeating belief that "I just don't test well," translate it into self-awareness of the problem, and use that knowledge to optimize his or her performance on a test. The glossary offered by Freedman and Houtz is a tool for parents to employ as they become acquainted with terminology and jargon associated with the testing and evaluation process. Again, knowledge is power and, in sum, can translate into more effective communication between the family and the school when testing is undertaken.

A second theme surrounds the difference between giftedness and talent as an educational label and how this impacts a learner's future. While Paris focuses on the immediate process of acquiring the gifted and talented identification, other authors approach this differently. Sternberg suggests that successful intelligence is a broader way to view a child's potential contributions and that it is the responsibility of parents and educators to help children find their areas of strength and figure out ways around their weaknesses. Parents can convey this by providing enriched environments in a variety of ways as described by Clark. The Sternberg and Clark pieces suggest that parents have important responsibilities to help children see talents as more than just a score on a test.

Third, in various ways, these authors make clear that the process of testing is an imperfect science. For example, Paris reminds us that there is no universal definition of giftedness and, as a result, tests may not be designed to test for the specific area(s) that are of interest to the family or school. Second, there may be a mismatch between the purpose of the test and the services delivered in the program.

Questions to consider as you read each of the pieces include:

- What do I need to know to be the best advocate for my child?
- What questions can I ask to become even more educated?
- How can I use the suggested resources to help further my knowledge base?
- Does my child's school district/school/classroom take a short-term (e.g., prioritizing identification) or long-term (e.g., testing concerns) view of giftedness and talent?
- How are my child's strengths (areas of giftedness) measured?
- What tests are being used to assess my child's abilities?
- If the test used is norm-referenced, what was the norming group for this test?

No Child Is Just Born Gifted: Creating and Developing Unlimited Potential

by Barbara Clark

I listened carefully as my graduate student described the activity he wanted to do for one of his term projects. He was very excited as he told about the research he planned using his baby son as the object of his study. "I have already put pictures of cats around his crib and he looks at them a lot," he said. "Yesterday I held the family cat where he could see it and he enjoyed that even more. Today I will print some large cards with 'CAT' on them and show them to him before I hold up the cat, then I'll show the cat, then the card again. Maybe I'll try to paste some of the printed cards next to the cat pictures in the crib. Oh, I got a very colorful book with pictures and words about cats I can read to him too. What do you think? Does that sound like an interesting way to build his visual/language connections?"

Observing what a little child is capable of is always exciting. Many of the limits we thought children had do not seem to be as absolute as we once believed. The more we study children, the more we discover that what is limited are our beliefs, not the children.

I agreed that my student could work with his son and report on anything that he observed that was interesting in the process he was planning to follow. From his explanation I assumed the boy was 12 to 18 months old. Although some early learning data was becoming available (then in the early 1970s), there was a lot to learn, and it was obvious that the baby and his father were enjoying the interactions.

At the end of his project he presented it to the class. Some of the results included tape recordings of his son saying some of the words he had introduced by cards, pictures, and books. Not until the end of the report was it that the stunning conclusion caught everyone by surprise. The baby, who I had thought would be 15 to 21 months old by the end of the study and who was so successfully engaged in early learning, was actually only 6 months old. He was only 3 months old at the beginning of the study. Had I known his age I would have been sure that what occurred would have been impossible. My beliefs would have limited this student and, more importantly, his son.

What are the limits we should expect in regard to learning and our children? What do we believe they could or should learn and when should they learn it? Is their potential dictated by their genes? Is this advanced and accelerated development we refer to as *giftedness* the result of rich experiences and good parenting, or are some children born that way? How can we know? What can we use for a guide?

Are Children Born Gifted?

The potential for giftedness or a high level of intellectual development begins very early in a child's life. Studies since the early 1970s consistently show that such development is the result of an interaction between the child's genetic endowment and a rich and appropriate environment in which the child grows. *No child is born gifted—only with the potential for giftedness.* Although all children have amazing potential, only those who are fortunate enough to have opportunities to develop their uniqueness in an environment that responds to their particular patterns and needs will be able to actualize their abilities to high levels. Research in psychology, neuroscience, linguistics, and early learning can help parents create responsive environments that allow their children to develop their potential to the fullest—that is, to *create giftedness.*

Giftedness Is a Changing Concept

Giftedness can now be seen as a biologically rooted label for a high level of intelligence, which indicates an advanced and accelerated development of functions within the brain that allow its more efficient and effective use. While old ideas of intelligence and giftedness generally were limited to analytical and rational thinking, giftedness really includes an interaction of all of the areas of brain function—physical sensing, emotions, cognition, and intuition. Broader concepts of intelligence and giftedness may be expressed through problem solving, creative behavior, academic aptitude, leadership, performance in the visual and performing arts, invention, or a myriad of other human abilities. High intelligence, whether expressed in cognitive abilities such as the capacity to generalize, conceptualize, or reason abstractly, or in specific abilities such as creative behavior, results from the interaction between inherited and acquired characteristics. This interaction encompasses all of the physical, mental, and emotional characteristics of the person and all of the people, events, and objects entering the person's awareness. Our reality is unique to each of us.

What Is More Important, Nature or Nurture?

An endless interaction between the environment and our genetic framework creates our intelligence, even our perception of reality. This process begins very early, as soon as the fertilized egg attaches to the wall of the uterus. As the cells divide and the fetus begins to grow, the environment already begins to exert a determining influence. One could not say from this interactive point of view which is more important—the inherited abilities or the environmental opportunities to develop them. Restriction on either nature (genes) or nurture (environment) would inhibit the high levels of actualized intellectual ability we call giftedness.

Our genes are not a limit, but provide a rough outline of the possibilities for our life. While genes provide us with our own unique menu, the environment makes the actual selection within that range of choice. Any reference to "high-IQ genes" must be seen as a misnomer because the discernible characteristics of an organism always depend on its particular environmental history.

Environmental interaction with the genetic program of the individual occurs whether planned or left to chance. By conservative estimates, this interaction can result in a 20- to 40-point difference in measured intelligence. Teachers and parents must be aware that how we structure the environment for children changes them neurologically and biologically. Without opportunities for appropriate challenge, talent and ability may be lost. From an overwhelming body of research, we must conclude that the development of intelligence includes both nature *and* nurture.

Who Are Gifted Learners?

At birth the human brain contains some 100 to 200 billion brain cells. Each neural cell is in place and ready to be developed, ready to be used for actualizing the highest levels of human potential. With a very small number of exceptions, all human infants come equipped with this marvelous complex heritage.

For example, two individuals with approximately the same genetic capacity for developing intelligence could be regarded as potentially gifted or as intellectually disabled as a result of the environment with which they interact. Although we never develop more neural cells, it is estimated that we actually use less than 5 percent of our brain capability. How we use this complex system becomes critical to our development of intelligence and personality and to the very quality of life we experience as we grow. Those who work with gifted children must acquire an understanding of the power of the interaction between the organism and its environment.

When the brain becomes more accelerated and advanced in its function through this interaction, the individual shows characteristics that can be identified with high intelligence. Some of those characteristics can be seen as the direct result of changes in brain structures. These changes continue to occur as long as appropriate stimulation is available. Over and over, brain research points to the dynamic nature of the brain's growth and the need to challenge the individual at that individual's level of development for growth to continue. Unchallenged, the individual will lose brain power.

Although each child will express giftedness in his or her unique way, behaviors often observed among these children include intense curiosity, frequent and sophisticated questions, an accelerated pace of thought and learning, complex thinking, often connecting seemingly disparate ideas, persistence in pursuing interests, and early development of language and mathematical skills.

Emotionally gifted children may show a heightened awareness of "being different," unusual sensitivity to the expressed feelings and problems of others, early concern for global and abstract issues, idealism and concern for fairness and justice, and high expectations for self and others. Gifted children often show an unusual asynchrony or gap between physical and intellectual development and a low tolerance for a lag between personal vision and physical abilities. Most interesting is the gifted child's early awareness and expression of heightened perceptions, preference for creative solutions and actions over predictable ones, and early use of hunches and best guesses.

The best way to identify high levels of intellectual development, or what we call giftedness, is to observe the child at play in a rich, responsive environment. During the early years, it is important to provide many opportunities for children to interact with interesting, novel, and unusual experiences that allow them to stretch just beyond their current ability level. All children must have experiences at their level of development because it is during early childhood that intelligence is nurtured and giftedness is developed. The most important challenge for teachers at home and at school is to stay just ahead of the child in presenting materials and experiences—not too far ahead and yet not too much repetition. Creating an environment and experiences that respond to the child with an appropriate balance of the familiar and new is the best way to provide for optimal development.

Provide for Early Learning

Parents are their children's first teachers, and they need to provide a rich, responsive environment and guidance based on the unique needs and interests of their children. You will be most effective when you create the appropriate emotional and social climate and are sensitive to your infant's unique personality and development.

Following are some activities to optimize development and learning based on observing your child's rhythms, abilities, and interests.

Beginning Very Early:

- Respond to your infant's signals and encourage attention and active involvement.
- Play games using lots of sensory activities—tickle, squeeze, rock and move, use different textures against the baby's skin, use lots of different sounds.
- Place mobiles and moving toys in and around the crib.
- Have a variety of patterned materials available for your baby to see.
- Talk to your baby during all caregiving activities.
- Show lots of affection; cuddle and pat.

Around 4 Months of Age or Before:

- Place an unbreakable mirror in the crib.
- Provide stacking toys and objects for throwing, banging, and moving.
- Play games with fingers and toes; play peek-a-boo.
- Talk to your baby and encourage your baby's use of words.
- Take trips around the community.
- Read books to your baby.
- Provide social interactions for your baby with adults and older peers.

By 10 Months of Age or Before:

- Provide a wide variety of toys and household objects for stringing, nesting, digging, pounding, screwing, and construction.

- Provide magnets, blocks, puzzles, books, and art materials.
- Play guessing games, matching and sorting games, finger games, circle games, and treasure hunts.
- Read to your child; make books of the child's activities— scrapbooks, color, and number books.
- Take neighborhood learning excursions; develop collections.
- Organize a safe physical environment that allows for a variety of sensory experiences and explorations.

Allow your child to dictate when and how long an activity lasts. By adding ideas and enthusiasm, parents introduce the world of learning to their child in exciting and pleasurable ways. Love of learning and discovery is a deep motivation for every child; all the parents need to do is encourage and respond.

The Importance of Parenting

Families have long-term effects on their children in many ways. They create the attitudes and expectations that allow high levels of development. Some of the most important parenting factors are articulating your beliefs about success and failure and your aspirations and expectations for achievement, teaching and modeling strategies for self-control and responsibility, providing a variety of language opportunities, and developing a close family environment.

As gifted children grow, they will require more complexity and more opportunities to nurture their rapidly expanding and curious minds. The following are a few activities parents can provide from kindergarten throughout their child's school life:

- Give your child access to new ideas and information by including him or her in discussions at dinner and during family conversations.
- Research ideas together; show your child how you gather information for your work and personal interests.
- Share your enthusiasms with your child.

- Provide choices and alternatives as much as possible and include your child in decision making whenever appropriate. As soon as children can understand the consequences of an action, they should be part of the decision.
- Model clear and open communication principles such as not blaming others, making expectations known, and identifying and speaking from one's own beliefs while accepting the beliefs of others. Help your child use these principles in communicating.
- See and use problems as opportunities for learning, and help your child do this in his or her life.
- Reduce tension for your child, as gifted children are known to put excessive pressure on themselves to achieve or to be "perfect" in what they attempt. Share your strategies for accepting less than perfection in yourself. Also, have flexible rules that change appropriately and with discussion, share the establishment of guidelines and goals, and acknowledge and point out strengths, as well as areas in need of development.
- Acknowledge your child's accomplishments even though everyone may expect him or her to do well.
- Help your child understand what giftedness is and the implications of this level of brain growth, including the responsibilities your child has to help nurture this dynamic process.
- Provide a safe place for your child to discuss problems. Listen without judgment as your child explores his or her feelings and possible solutions. There are many people who will not understand gifted children's intensity and the needs that relate to their advanced and accelerated brain processes. Your home may at times be the only place your child feels protected.
- Mostly, just enjoy living with your gifted child. Although it is a never-ending challenge, it is an unbelievable joy!

The newborn child is amazingly competent and able to learn. With love and careful attention, parents and teachers can provide the opportunities to optimize every child's potential and realize each child's giftedness. No child is just born gifted.

Chapter 2

Developing Your Child's Successful Intelligence

by Robert J. Sternberg

TIME was that when you wanted to know whether a child was gifted, you gave that child an IQ (conventional intelligence) test. That's what Lewis Terman did in his famous study of gifted children conducted at Stanford University in 1921. Terman did the same in a less well-known but equally important study done at the Hunter College Elementary School. In both studies, the mean IQs of the children fell in the 150s, scores achieved by only a small fraction of 1 percent of the population. What happens to people of such high IQ?

The results of these two studies—one done on the West Coast and one done on the East Coast—were practically identical. Most of the individuals identified as gifted became highly educated and professionally successful. Most of them were satisfied with their professional and other life accomplishments. But both studies yielded a similar puzzling result: very few of these ultraintelligent individuals became eminent in their fields, leading one set of researchers to wonder why so much intellect failed to lead to eminence. In short, IQ tests seem to have selected those who would be consummate adapters to the demands of society, but not those who would shape society—not those who would lead it into the future.

These results are not only unsurprising, but also predictable. IQ tests have always been intended to measure a person's ability to adapt to the environment. That's what Alfred Binet and David Wechsler, the developers of the two most well-known and widely used conventional tests of intelligence, contended. In symposia of psychologists who specialize in intelligence, dating back to 1921 and continuing on into the present, intelligence typically has been defined as the ability to adapt to the environment. Thus, at some level, IQ tests do what they were designed to do.

Conventional Academic Intelligence Quotient (IQ)

IQ tests work to some degree, but how well and why? These tests do not measure adaptability as well as we once thought. More importantly, in doing what they do, they may not only fail to identify our potential leaders, but actually derail them. Intelligence tests measure primarily two kinds of cognitive skills—memory and analytical reasoning skills. They do so using mostly verbal and quantitative items and sometimes figural (geometric) items as well. They are well-adapted to children who: (a) have experienced high-quality schooling in Western society; (b) speak English as their native language or have learned English well and have had rich exposure to English in the household in which they have grown up; (c) have had the experiences that middle- to upper-middle-class living arrangements typically afford children in Western society; (d) tend to think well in conventional, though somewhat narrow, ways (e) without questioning whether this thinking yields correct answers; and (f) think in this way quickly.

Children who meet these criteria are in a good position to excel in schools, which basically teach and assess achievement in ways that value the same attributes as are valued by conventional intelligence tests. There is nothing wrong with these attributes. They are, in fact, moderately associated with good school performance and weakly associated with various criteria for success in life. But there is a problem. Not all gifted children fit the "IQ-like" description of giftedness. As a result, certain children are identified and thus spotlighted as gifted—which they are—but giftedness in other children is being missed. Who are these other children who might become the next generation of leaders?

From IQ to Multiple Intelligence (MI)

Howard Gardner has proposed that we need to expand the range of cognitive skills measured to include *multiple intelligences:* (a) linguistic (reading a book, writing a poem); (b) logical-mathematical (solving math or logic problems); (c) spatial (fitting suitcases into the trunk of a car); (d) musical (composing or singing a song); (e) bodily-kinesthetic (dancing or playing football); (f) interpersonal (understanding others); (g) intrapersonal (understanding oneself); and (h) naturalist (making sense of the natural world).

This theory has the potential for widely expanding how we identify who is gifted. In general, high-IQ children would be expected to perform well on the first two or three intelligences, but not necessarily on the others. Conversely, children who excel in the other intelligences might not look particularly bright on an IQ test. Gardner's proposal is part of the answer to the limitations of IQ tests, but not the whole answer.

From MI to Emotional Intelligence (EQ)

Other researchers have suggested that to understand intelligence and who is gifted, we have to go beyond the cognitive to the emotional domain, to *emotional intelligence.* Basically, emotional intelligence is the ability to understand, regulate, and effectively channel emotions.

Is emotional intelligence important? It most certainly is. All of us know children who ended up on the wrong side of their teachers because of emotional outbursts or other examples of poorly regulated emotional behavior. The problem is not limited to children. I know a man who was an executive in a major firm, who on being informed that he was passed over for a promotion, called his boss to chastise him for his poor choice of a successor. The man not only lost the promotion, but also his job.

Although research evidence on emotional intelligence has been slow in coming in, the importance of this area of functioning is now more widely recognized. In order to adapt to the environment, people need to be effective not only in the use of their cognitive skills, but in the use of their emotional skills as well.

From EQ to Successful Intelligence (SI)

In some ways, emotional intelligence represents the opposite side of the coin from academic intelligence and perhaps multiple intelligence. One deals with cognitive skills, the other with emotional skills. Is there any way to combine these different kinds of intelligence?

One solution to this problem is what I call *successful intelligence* (SI). Successful intelligence is a person's ability to attain success in life, whether by personal standards or by others' standards. Successful intelligence is different in kind from the other types of intelligences because it is unique to each individual. Thus, one cannot graph a set of scores for successful intelligence the way one might potentially do for IQ, MI, or even EQ.

A person is successfully intelligent to the extent that he or she is able to figure out what he or she does more and less well, and then figure out how to capitalize on or make the most of the strengths, while at the same time compensating for or correcting weaknesses. People's strengths and weaknesses are as diverse as they are. Most people who attain success in their lives, however defined, are people who figure out who they are—what they have to offer themselves, others, and the world at large. They find ways of making the most of their diverse talents, and they find ways to live with their weaknesses.

The implication of this theory is that *the single most important thing a parent can do for a child is to help that child figure out his or her pattern of strengths and weaknesses.* This pattern may have little or even nothing to do with the kinds of talents recognized by the school. For example, my son, at 17, became a pilot; my daughter, at 16, was playing the oboe and the bassoon. Neither set of skills was particularly valued by the school. What matters is not so much what the school values, but what the child can turn into a lifelong pursuit. I was studying psychology independently as an adolescent in the days when almost no junior or senior high school offered psychology. My teachers were vaguely aware of what I was doing, but not terribly interested in it. I turned this interest into an adult career and a lifelong quest.

Successful intelligence involves a blend of many kinds of skills, but three are particularly important: analytical skills of the kinds measured by conventional IQ tests, as well as creative skills and practical skills — neither of which is measured by conventional tests. Children with high levels of creative and practical skills often are not identified as gifted and may even be seen as "problem children." The creative child may be viewed as contrary, the practical child as unmotivated. In a sense, these attributions are correct. Creative children do tend to be contrary, and practical children tend to be unmotivated by academic work that makes little or no connection to their daily lives. Instead of looking at these attributes as weaknesses, schools can view them as strengths if they teach and then assess achievement in ways that recognize these important skills.

My colleagues and I conducted a study in which we identified high school students for conventional (IQ-like) skills, but also for creative and practical skills. We then taught these children college-level psychology in a way that either allowed them or didn't allow them to capitalize on their strengths and compensate for or correct their weaknesses.

In other words, they were placed in a classroom that was either a better or worse match for their pattern of abilities. The crucial finding was that children who were taught in a way that recognized and rewarded their pattern of abilities significantly outperformed those children who were taught in a "one-size-fits-all" manner of teaching.

Schools can probably improve the achievement of many children if only they were to teach in a way that recognizes and capitalizes on students' strengths while allowing them to compensate for and correct their weaknesses.

What Parents Can Do

Here are seven strategies for helping your child develop successful intelligence:

- *Find the strengths and make the most of them.* The search can be frustrating. Often it means trying many different areas of pursuit, many of which lead nowhere. At times, you and your child may just want to give up. But think of how many potentially gifted children will never be identified because they and their parents never took the time to dig out their strengths. Finding the few areas of strength, or even one, that set your child apart is one of the best things you can do for your child. When it comes time for that child to apply to college, remember that the unusual strengths are what set young people apart from each other. Schools like Yale and Harvard can find lots of students with good grades and test scores. What they look for is the special something that makes one applicant stand out from the rest.

- *Think unconventionally.* When looking for strengths, think unconventionally. Strengths can be anywhere: academic areas, music, drama, fiction writing, metalwork, drawing, sculpture, archaeology, athletics, investing, fixing things, inventing, working with animals, entrepreneurship, sewing, gardening, or interacting with others. The main limit is in our imaginations in exploring various options.

- *Find the weaknesses and correct or compensate for them.* Children also need to know what they do not do well. Once you identify these weaknesses, then help your child correct them as much as possible or devise strategies of compensation. Many weaknesses make little difference to people's lives. My artwork is terrible, but I manage to get by quite easily without this skill. But if your child's weakness is in an area in which he or she must function—language, math, the sciences—then work to develop compensatory and corrective strategies.

- *Allow for mistakes and false paths.* The search for strengths and weaknesses and ways to deal with them will inevitably lead to mistakes and routes down false paths. As a society, we tend to abhor both of these outcomes. Learn instead to welcome them as learning opportunities. There is no better way to learn than from one's mistakes and from the false paths one has taken.

- *Find what is right for your child, whether or not it is what would have been right for you.* I cannot tell you how many college students I meet who are studying law, medicine, or business simply because it is what their parents want them to do. Ultimately, they may achieve some success in these fields, but usually not with the success they would have achieved had they followed their own interests and strengths. I never dreamed of my son's getting a pilot's license, nor was it something I had in mind for him. I'm not crazy about the bassoon. Nonetheless, I encourage my children to find the right path for *them*, not the path that might have been my wish for them to have taken.

- *Encourage sensible risks.* Finding the right path entails risks because many times people travel down the wrong paths first. Also, people will make mistakes while traveling down these paths—and even while traveling down the right path. Finally, the right path may not always be one that friends, school officials, or even some parents value. Children and their parents need to take the risk of finding what is right for them. Opportunities for sensible risk taking include summer programs, camp, semesters abroad, afterschool volunteer programs, internships, and the like.

- *Celebrate your child.* Successful intelligence is within everyone's grasp. It represents a very different idea from the conventional IQ-like notion. The question is not whether the strengths are there. The question is whether we can find them. Seek, and you shall find!

Chapter 3

Why Gifted Children May Not Test Well

by Ben Paris

"I DON'T do well on tests." Ever heard someone say this? Ever say this same thing about yourself, or your child? Many people believe that they (or their children) are much smarter than their test scores seem to indicate. Some of the time this is wishful thinking, but some of the people who say they "don't test well" have a valid point. Academic tests are designed to accurately measure specific knowledge and skills, but they aren't perfect. Sometimes tests indicate a higher ability than one actually possesses. Test takers don't complain about those mistakes. It's the flip side that brings the complaints: Sometimes the test's ability estimate is too low, and worse, some people consistently get test scores that underpredict their true ability. Not testing well can mean receiving scores that indicate less ability than one really possesses. This happens even to gifted students, and for some of them it happens repeatedly.

Typically, it's assumed that gifted students would likely do well on tests, and many do. But for other gifted students, part of what makes them who they are also makes it more difficult for them to succeed on tests. Based on 15 years of experience helping students succeed on standardized tests, I have seen patterns underlying poor test performance, including lack of motivation, overthinking, perfectionism, overconfidence and sloppiness, excessive test stress, and the administration of the wrong test. Provided are reasons why these performance inhibitors occur, along with suggestions for overcoming these barriers.

Lack of Motivation

For many, the greater barrier to success is a lack of caring about success. Of course, caring about success does not guarantee it; failure occurs for lots of reasons. Still, not caring at all usually guarantees failure. If a student is not motivated to succeed, that issue must be addressed before any other. Unmotivated students often ignore tutors, dismiss educational supplements, and gain little from the best enrichment programs.

All kinds of students lack motivation. Gifted students are no exception. Sometimes they lose motivation when they are bored and unchallenged. Others are so independent that they are uninterested in anyone's approval. Regardless of the cause, if motivation is an issue, it immediately becomes a priority.

Like many problems, lack of motivation is best addressed before it starts, but this is not always possible. Still, there are approaches to be tried:

- *Don't chase an unmotivated student.* Begging, pleading, and throwing resources at an unmotivated student results in nothing but frustration. This also can reinforce a situation in which the student does none of the work and shirks the responsibility for his or her behavior. Parents think that they need to try harder (or shout louder) to get their kid on the right track, but more effort or higher volume goes nowhere with a child who truly doesn't care.
- *Break the cycle.* Find out what motivates the student who is unmotivated about academic success. Everyone cares about something. Sometimes a student will have a special interest in one subject. Sometimes education is a means toward achieving independence. If nothing else, a student who is unmotivated to succeed in high school may want to get into an excellent college that offers a different environment. Having a reason to succeed is a good step toward actually wanting to succeed.
- *If you cannot discover anything in the academic world that motivates a student, you can try other rewards or punishments,* such as driving privileges or grounding him or her on weekends. However, this path is full of danger. Rewards and punishments

need to be reasonable, proportionate, and applied consistently. Unrealistic demands, unkept promises, and empty threats will destroy your credibility. Also, be aware that when a student achieves merely to get some external reward or avoid punishment, those achievements are quite fragile. Sometimes students need encouragement just to discover their own love of learning, but if that doesn't happen, then those rewards and punishments are merely postponing the moment of failure.

- *Be patient.* Motivation does not appear in one day, but once developed, it endures.

Overthinking

Gifted students are skilled at seeing things in different ways. They come up with possibilities that other people don't see. In most contexts, this ability is an asset. But on a test, particularly multiple-choice tests, coming up with a unique interpretation is a real weakness. Gifted students will bend over backwards to find arguments for all of the choices, whereas average-ability learners tend to pick their answer and move on.

Overthinking can be overcome. At first, it's hard to recognize the difference between making solid inferences and overdoing it. However, analyzing one's results after the fact can reveal a pattern. When taking multiple-choice practice tests, overthinkers should note when they are following the straightforward path and when they are going fishing. After the test, he or she should see how often the straightforward approach was correct. After a while, the overthinker will develop a sense of when he or she may be going too far.

Perfectionism

Gifted children often are highly motivated to succeed, and they frequently display great attention to detail. Typically these are good things, but when taken to an extreme, this can lead to perfectionism. The perfectionist is focused on answering everything correctly. On many tests, an obsession with avoiding mistakes is an advantage, but on timed tests this obsession can lead to disaster. On time-pressured tests the test taker has to move on to scoop up as many points as possible before time runs out. But perfectionists can't move on. They become obsessed with certain questions and devote too much time to answering them. Perfectionists do well on the questions they answer but often do not answer enough questions to score well. They have an even harder time with timed essay exams and often are so focused on writing the perfect essay that they wind up writing nothing at all.

There's no quick fix for perfectionism, but here are some suggestions:

- *The first step is to recognize that there is a problem.* Sound familiar? Usually a low score on a practice test makes the point, although sometimes the lesson needs to be learned through a low score on the real thing. One way or another, the student needs to learn that searching for perfection is doing harm.

- *Once the problem is acknowledged, new habits need to be formed.* Put the perfectionist in situations in which it is possible to do well even while making mistakes. Strictly timed practice on very time-pressured assignments can take the sting out of every little mistake. How many math problems can you solve in a minute? Can you write a good (but not perfect) short essay in 20 minutes? Succeeding on these tasks builds familiarity and comfort with the mindset required to succeed under imperfect conditions.

- *It isn't worth rewiring one's entire personality in the pursuit of a few good test scores.* Still, the benefits of overcoming perfectionism aren't limited to tests. If you're looking for greater change, consider putting the perfectionist in competitive situations. Sports or even card games can work this way. Students can mess up left and right and still win as long as they do better than their opponent. Activities that reward precision and practicality can help the perfectionist find a better balance. Playing the card game Bridge is a good option. The bidding stage appeals to the idealist, but the play allows you to win despite your mistakes.

Overconfidence

This is the flip side of perfectionism. Many gifted children are so used to succeeding without really trying that they are convinced that they can't possibly fail. Although the perfectionist does well on the questions he or she answers but doesn't get to them all, the overconfident/sloppy student will answer the hardest questions correctly but miss too many of the easy ones.

Here are some suggestions for addressing or stopping this problem before it starts:

- *Overconfidence is learned*, and so people who are consistently challenged are less likely to be overconfident in the first place. A child who always succeeds can be prone to overconfidence. Maintaining a proper balance both in school and at home is important. At school, children need challenging assignments or special projects. At home, parents can draw upon a wide variety of resources to find enrichment activities for their children. For example, the California Learning Strategies Center (http://www.learningstrategiescenter.com), Hoagies' Gifted Education Page (http://www.hoagiesgifted.org), and the National Association for Gifted Children (http://www.nagc. org) offer resources, information, and advice to help parents provide gifted children academic challenge.

- *If overconfidence cannot be avoided, start by recognizing the problem.* Sometimes a low score will be enough to raise the red flag. If that's all it takes to dispel overconfidence, then consider yourself lucky. Often, overconfident students brush off poor results by explaining why the test is stupid or why the teacher hates them. Try to address concerns in the cold light of reason. This can be tough, because the overconfident student is typically resistant to admitting flaws. Slowly demonstrate the real cause of some of the errors, emphasize that everyone makes some mistakes, and help the overconfident student find the better path him- or herself.

Sloppiness

While the overconfident student does not recognize the possibility of failure, others recognize this possibility but keep on making too many avoidable mistakes. This can have a devastating effect on one's score, especially on exams where one small mistake can prevent earning any points at all. There's a famous story of an engineering student whose exam answer was off by a minus sign. He got zero points for the question, so he asked the professor for partial credit. The professor told him, "It doesn't do any good to build a bridge upside down."

- *Sloppiness also is difficult to address quickly.* Analyzing one's performance is important, because the sloppy student's test score looks the same as the scores of students with much lower ability. If the student handles the toughest abstract algebra concepts with ease but blows the question by making an addition mistake, then sloppiness may be the issue. This sounds obvious, but people skip this step every day. A parent once came to me for SAT advice. Her daughter was getting low scores in math despite hours and hours of math tutoring. I looked at her results and told her to stop studying math. She already knew the math, she just needed to make fewer careless errors.

- *However, making fewer mistakes is easier said than done;* the issue is how to reduce them. Slowing down often helps. Students should learn to recognize the kinds of mistakes they are likely to make. Examining recent test results often helps uncover existing patterns. For example, the results of a math test can determine how many errors were caused by calculation errors or by not answering the question asked, as opposed to not understanding the content. The student who makes calculation errors should slow down and perhaps double-check. The student who does not answer the question asked should devote extra attention at the start of a new problem to make sure that he or she understands the task at hand.

- *Carelessness.* A student who understands all of the higher-order concepts but loses too many points because of simple calculation mistakes could have a disability. Initially, the leading explanation of careless errors is carelessness. But if the student makes a strong effort to concentrate and still fumbles away points, then testing for a learning disability may be appropriate.

Excessive Test Stress

Tests are stressful for everyone, but some people get so stressed out that they can barely function. Test stress has both physical and mental ramifications. Physically, the stressed-out student may experience an increased heart rate, excessive perspiration, and even shaking. Mentally, the stressed-out student may panic, experience a sense of impending doom, and an escalating cycle of negativity. Test stress can affect anyone, but gifted students who already are supermotivated in a high-stakes environment are more susceptible to excessive stress.

Dealing with test stress starts with recognizing its cause. Test stress is an overreaction to one or more real problems, such as not being prepared for the test. Often, test stress comes from fear, such as fear of the unknown, a low score, or the consequences of a low score. In most cases, preparation and practice can take the terror out of testing. Becoming familiar with the test can help to eliminate many of the unknowns.

Gifted . . . But in Something Else

Even gifted students may not be gifted in every way. Some are especially strong in math, language arts, or science. Even within math, some students are strong in abstract reasoning but average at simple calculation. Unfortunately, most academic tests are not designed to uncover which of many possible gifts the examinees possess. Instead, they typically measure ability in a restricted number of skills, and so a gifted child whose gifts are not measured by a particular test will have rather ordinary test results. For example, students who are highly creative but not especially good at calculation or reading comprehension often have unremarkable test scores.

If your child has gifts that aren't measured by an exam, consider seeking out a context where his or her gifts can be expressed. For example, the creative writer who doesn't do well in reading comprehension may not get into an honors English class, but there may be a creative writing class or supplemental program that will give that writer the chance to flourish.

Conclusion

The various reasons that many students do not test well have been addressed individually. But more often than not, several factors are in play. Some form nasty combinations, such as perfectionism and test stress. Some play off each other, such as being sloppy and unmotivated. Regardless of the combination, understanding what is going on is a great step toward addressing the problem and finding the appropriate solutions.

Students who don't test well get lower scores than they should, but in most cases there are concrete reasons for their low performance. More importantly, there are steps to help them achieve scores that are commensurate with their true abilities. Sometimes the improvement can be immediate. High achievers can quickly learn not to overthink or take more time to avoid sloppy mistakes. Other issues, such as motivation, take longer to address. But, in any case, the most important step is to understand that not testing well is a solvable problem and not a life sentence. A student who rises to many of life's challenges can handle this one, too.

Chapter 4

A Glossary of Terms Used in Educational Assessment

by Michael Freedman and John Houtz

*"When I use a word," Humpty Dumpty said in rather a scornful
tone, "it means just what I choose it to mean—neither more nor less."
"The question is," said Alice, "whether you can make words mean so
many different things."
"The question is," said Humpty Dumpty, "which is to be master—
that's all."* (Carroll, 1865/1974, p. 238)

WHEN talking with your children's teachers or other school
personnel, you might find that you're feeling a bit like
Alice in Wonderland. All professional fields have special
vocabularies, or jargon, but in education today there are
a great many new terms. And many of these terms are quite technical
and specialized, dealing with testing and other forms of assessment.

In response to many new laws, practices, and advances in research
and theory, there is additional jargon or new vocabulary that makes it
harder for you as parents—and for everyone else concerned—to keep
"on top" of things, to understand your children's school experience, and
to participate fully in your children's education. The purpose of this
article is to offer definitions and explanations of some "classic" terms
that you often will hear, and of several of the more recent measurement
terms that are finding their way into the world of education today. We
present the terms alphabetically, in the form of a glossary.

Ability and Aptitude. The terms ability and aptitude are closely related and often difficult to distinguish from each other. Ability, the mental or physical capacity to perform at a given level, is considered to be innate, therefore determined genetically. According to psychological theory, it may be described as possession of one or more of the multiple areas of intelligence that have been described by various theories and models. Aptitude may be described as the proclivity to excel in the performance of specific tasks (as in, "she has a real aptitude for drawing").

Accountability. Accountability in assessment refers to holding individuals or institutions responsible for the outcomes of instruction. For example, you might hear or read that "students are accountable for their school successes and/or failures," that "teachers (or parents) are accountable for the performance of their students (or children)," or that "school principals are accountable for the achievement of their schools."

Achievement. Achievement is a measure of the quality and or the quantity of the success one has in the mastery of knowledge, skills, or understandings. References to academic achievement, for example, usually involve performance in such areas as reading, mathematics, science, or social studies.

Achievement Test Batteries. Many schools test students using an array of subtests, in a number of academic content areas and at a variety of grade levels under a single overall test name. For example, a particular "Test of Basic Skills" might involve subtests of mathematical skills, language skills, and vocabulary.

Assessment. Assessment involves the process of "taking stock" of, or understanding, an individual's characteristics, status, or performance, and typically involves considering and interpreting information from several sources of data. It might involve, for example, observations, interviews, or other kinds of information. (Compare with evaluation and measurement.)

Authentic Assessment. Authentic assessment refers to the evaluation of students' work on activities that students engage in that approximate realistic or real-life tasks and performances, rather than answering traditional paper-and-pencil tests. Authentic tasks typically require complex work, problem solving, and integration of a variety of knowledge and skills brought to bear on a realistic task or challenge. For example, students might use grocery store ads, a shopping list, and a budget to spend as a realistic alternative to completing a group of arithmetic "column addition" exercises on a worksheet.

Competency-Based Assessment. This phrase indicates that students will be evaluated against some specific learning, behavior, or performance objective. This objective and/or the level of performance that represents "competency" is clearly established in the curriculum and represents an expected level of expertise or mastery of skills or knowledge.

Criterion-Referenced Testing. Criterion-referenced testing refers to evaluating students against an absolute standard of achievement, rather than evaluating them in comparison with the performance of other students. A standard of performance is set to represent a level of expertise or mastery of skills or knowledge.

Derived Scores or Standard Scores. Derived scores or standard scores transform raw scores (the actual number of correct responses) into values that allow us to compare one student's performance in relation to the performance of others of the same age or grade or to the highest possible score on a test. Common standard scores are z-scores, T-scores, percentiles, and stanines. Derived or standard scores are all computed by determining how far above or below the mean of all scores a student scores, and then representing the results using a standard scale.

Evaluation. Evaluation represents a judgment or determination of value (e.g., effective or ineffective, or below, at, or above grade level) that is placed on some performance.

Formative Evaluation. Formative evaluation refers to any form of assessment, such as quizzes, tests, essays, projects, interviews, or presentations, in which the goal is to give students feedback about their work while it is in progress, to help students correct errors or missteps, or to improve the work along the way to the final product. In contrast, summative evaluation is to make a judgment about a final product or about the quality of performance at the end of an instructional unit or course.

Grade Equivalent Score. A grade equivalent score describes a student's performance on that test in relation to a grade level and number of months during the year of that grade. (A score of 8.2, for example, tells you that your child obtained the same score on a test that an average student in the second month of the eighth grade would obtain.) Of course, if your child is in the fifth grade, that's very good, but if your child is in the tenth grade, that's not so good!

High-Stakes Testing. High-stakes testing typically refers to major state or national standardized school achievement tests administered periodically to students at various grade levels. The phrase "high stakes" is used to signify that these test results carry a great deal of weight among school personnel, government agencies, politicians, community leaders, and the general public. These test results often are used to make important decisions about students, teachers, and their schools, such as graduation, grade promotions or retentions, selection for highly competitive programs or schools, or staffing and budget decisions.

Intelligence. Over many years, the concept of intelligence has had many definitions. Intelligence has been defined, to cite several examples, as the ability to think conceptually, to solve problems, to manipulate one's environment, or to develop expertise. Some theorists have proposed that intelligence is mostly innate, inherited, or biologically based, and others have argued equally strongly that intelligence is influenced by one's environment. Issues regarding the nature and breadth of intelligence continue to be topics of lively discussion among theorists and researchers in several fields of study (including educational psychology, cognitive psychology, and sociology, for example).

Learning Objective. A learning objective is a specific statement that describes what the student is to learn, understand, or to be able to do as a result of a lesson or a series of lessons.

Learning Outcome. A learning outcome represents what the student actually achieved as a result of a lesson or a series of lessons. The success of lessons may be influenced by the students' prior knowledge, their effort and attention, teaching methods, resources, and time. Learning outcomes refer to the results of instruction, while learning objectives refer to the intended goals and purposes of lessons.

Measurement. Measurement is simply the process of assigning a number, or a score if you will, to some performance or product. Examples would include grading a test or a homework assignment in terms of number or percent of correct or incorrect responses.

Measures of Central Tendency. Measures of central tendency are quantitative (numerical) ways to describe the middle of a distribution of scores. Because most individuals in a given population tend to exhibit middle levels of competence or presence of a characteristic, most people tend to earn scores that are near the central portion of the normal curve (see definition below). There are three common measures of central tendency: mean, median, and mode. The mean refers to a numerical average of the scores. It is obtained by adding all of the scores and dividing their sum by the number of scores (e.g., scores of 100, 90, 80, 80 and 70 result in a mean of 84). The median is simply the middle score when all scores are placed in ranked order. The median in our example would be 80 because it is the third score counted in from either direction. The mode is the most often occurring score. In our example, the mode is 80 because it occurs more often than any other score.

Minimum Competency. Minimum competency is a judgment of the lowest level of skill or knowledge a student must have attained to be considered competent in that area. Minimum competency tests are often the focus of broad national educational efforts to improve education. It is important to note, especially for high-ability students, that minimum competencies do not represent an adequate standard or expectation of performance, nor do they imply proficiency in, or mastery of, the content or skill being tested.

Normal Curve ("Bell Curve"). The normal or "bell" curve is a common way of representing the distribution of scores for a particular competence or characteristic in a large population. Because most individuals of any population would exhibit "average" competence or presence of a characteristic, their scores appear in the middle area around the crest of the curve. Those who exhibit exceptionally high or low competence or very great or very small presence of a characteristic appear at either end of the curve's shape.

Norm-Referenced Testing (or Norm-Referenced Assessment). Norm-referenced testing refers to testing in which individuals' results are compared to some larger group (such as a national or statewide sample of students). Usually, "norm" or "normal" groups are those in which the students' scores are distributed in a "normal" (or bell-shaped) pattern. In these cases, an individual's performance is assessed in relation to where his or her score would fall under the normal curve.

Objective Test Items. Objective test items require the student to select a specific response to a question that can be graded as either correct or incorrect. They are easy to administer and score (and often can be machine-scored). Common examples of objective test items include true-false, multiple-choice, and matching questions.

Online Assessment. Online assessment is an assessment that is accessed on a computer via the Internet or a similar computer network. The assessment or test is read online and the responses are given online by selecting or checking a choice by clicking the mouse, typing a response, or perhaps even touching the computer screen with a special "pen," or speaking a response aloud using voice recognition technology. Online assessment also may be a vehicle for submitting a portfolio of student performances or completed assignments for the teacher to evaluate.

Percentile Ranks. Percentile ranks refer to an individual's standing in relation to the rest of the individuals in the norm or comparison group (i.e., others who are taking the same test). If your child receives a percentile rank of 90, it means that your child achieved a score equal to or better than 90% of the rest of the group with whom he or she is being compared.

Performance Assessment. Performance assessment refers to a system of evaluating individuals' abilities or achievements based on actual work or behavior. Performance assessment focuses on the student's ability to apply what he or she has learned to a realistic task—a problem or situation that might be encountered in real life.

Portfolios. Portfolios are collections of an individual's work. Some educators regard portfolio assessment as a better method of observing and evaluating what learners truly know, understand, and can do than tests and homework exercises, for example. In typical classrooms that employ portfolios, students keep their work (e.g., quizzes, test papers, creative writing, homework, book reports, project reports, art projects, etc.) in large folders, boxes, electronic files, or other storage containers. They may keep all of their work or, as is more typical and recommended as best practice, students (on their own or with their teachers' guidance) periodically select samples of their work to illustrate their best performances across a variety of activities. Students and teachers also may keep work samples of various degrees of achievement to illustrate growth in ability over time or to help identify and illustrate particular weaknesses or disabilities that require additional attention.

Power Tests. Power tests typically have no time limits or very generous time limits so that the individual has sufficient time to answer all questions. On a power test, the goal is to measure as much as the individual can do without the pressure of time limits. (Compare with "speed tests.")

Profile. A student profile often is used to describe a student's characteristics and learning needs, to help guide important educational decisions for a particular individual, or to guide individualized instructional planning. It may contain many different kinds of data (including test scores, observations, anecdotal records, samples of student work, or comments from cumulative records) that describe the student, the circumstances that prompted creating the profile, questions or problems requiring resolution, and suggestions for making desired decisions.

Range. The range of scores is the difference between the highest and lowest recorded scores. If the lowest score is 28 and the highest is 98, then the range is 70.

Reliability. Reliability refers to the degree of consistency or dependability of a test. A reliable test will produce similar scores and distributions whenever it is given to similar populations. Thus, if a student scored a 90 on an achievement test today, then, if the test is reliable, the student's score would not differ substantially if the test were taken again another day. Reliability also may mean that a student would earn similar scores on two different forms of a test, if tested at about the same time.

Rubric. A rubric is a chart or plan that identifies criteria for evaluating a piece of a student's work, be it an essay, test, a paper, or some other student production. The rubric offers a description of the qualities or characteristics of performance for several levels (such as beginning, intermediate, or advanced, or needs improvement, adequate, or outstanding) that the teacher or other evaluator may assign. The best rubrics offer the clearest details for each category of evaluation so that a student's products can be evaluated consistently. Rubrics may be "analytic" and "holistic." An analytic rubric specifies all the components of a perfect response and point values are assigned to each component. Although holistic scoring also identifies a model or perfect answer, point values are not assigned. Thus, holistic or global scoring is more subjective and may be less reliable than analytic scoring.

Speed Tests. Speed tests are tests with specific time limits. Such a test rewards individuals who can work fast to answer the test items. Students with disabilities may be exempt from time limits set for speed tests. (Compare with power tests.)

Standardized Tests. Standardized tests are instruments that are administered, scored, and interpreted in the same, prespecified way by all users. There are detailed instructions or rules for how a test is administered and scored. (One example of a well-known standardized test is the Scholastic Aptitude Test or SAT.)

Standards-Based. To put standards-based in front of such terms as instruction, assessment, testing, measurement, evaluation, and other terms typically means that whatever teachers teach and students do in class is evaluated against specifically written and adopted standards, or goals and objectives, of achievement, usually written and adopted at the state or national level.

Subjective Tests. Subjective tests refers to the approach used to evaluate or score the student's response to a writing prompt, an open-ended task or question, or a "free," unstructured response to a short answer or essay question. Unlike objective tests, in which the correct or incorrect answer selection is easily and quickly obtained, subjective assessments present a more difficult challenge to score and require considerably more time to read and to analyze carefully and equitably.

Validity. Validity is a term that describes how well a test, or a test item, measures what it claims to measure, accurately predicts a behavior, or accurately contributes to decision making about the presence or absence of a characteristic.

A Note of Caution

Any interpretations of the results of an assessment and any educational decisions should be made with the primary goal of understanding and doing what is best for the individual child. These decisions, which may involve the parent, teacher, counselor, principal, psychologist, and the child, should use the score of the measurement instrument only as one piece of information—one of many data inputs into the process.

Your efforts to understand and help your child will require that you seek from your child's teachers and other knowledgeable school personnel additional explanations and clarifications of these terms and how they are used. We provided this glossary to help inform you and to guide you in determining the information you will need, as well as the questions you might raise, to improve communication and build a collaborative relationship with the school. Alice marveled at how words might mean so many things, and although this is true in relation to testing in schools today, we hope this glossary will help you to better understand many of the terms you may encounter.

References

Carroll, L. (1974). *Alice in Wonderland and through the looking glass.* New York, NY: Grosser & Dunlop. (Original work published 1865)

PART II

Characteristics and Development

by Joan Franklin Smutny

THE stereotype of giftedness—what it looks like and how it appears in the classroom—is still so strong that even the keenest observers tend to equate giftedness with achievement. But parents see much more in their children—the exceptional ability, yes, but also their heightened sensitivities, intuitive understanding, empathy far beyond their years; also, their untraditional ways of learning. Taken together, these characteristics can present special challenges in school. Parents wonder how their gifted daughter will function in a kindergarten where no one is reading, how their creative son will turn a new page in a middle school where he can't make any friends, or how their brilliant daughter will face the disconcerting prospect of having to settle for a college that accepts her average SAT scores.

Spanning the years from preschool to college, the Characteristics and Development section provides a range of articles on how to effectively support gifted children's growth at some of the most critical junctures of their lives. The guidance offered by these articles acts as a much-needed compass for parents who often wonder when and how they should intervene in their children's school experience. The articles not only inform them about the common challenges of gifted children, but how they can become more proactive in responding to them. For example, an awareness of the fact that gifted students sometimes lack organizational and other skills due to being underchallenged in school (if they can excel without these skills, why should they bother learning them?), alerts parents to a need that they can address *before* their children get to college or struggle in a high school honors program. By reading these articles, parents will appreciate their unique role as advocates and consider more options than they might have thought of on their own.

The section is divided into four parts. The first addresses issues common to all age groups while the next three focus on specific age groups (preschool, middle school, and the transition from high school to college). Sally Reis' chapter, "Self-Regulated Learning and Academically Talented Students," begins this section by dispelling the myth about gifted and talented students as self-sufficient learners. As Reis makes clear, having exceptional ability does not guarantee self-regulated skills and without such skills, even the most able child can fall short of his potential. Reis shows how self-regulation equips gifted students to take care of their own needs as learners, adjust to different circumstances, and monitor their progress. This chapter follows with one by Rita Dunn, Karen Burke, and Janet Whitely titled, "What Do You Know About Learning Styles?" Understanding their children's unique learning styles places parents in a stronger position to communicate with teachers and other school personnel. The authors provide a useful way of looking at two distinct kinds of learners—those who think more *analytically* (in a step-by-step sequence) and those who think more *globally* (conceptualizing many issues or domains related to a topic). Included are many practical ideas on how parents can apply their knowledge of learning styles to issues their children have with homework, resources and materials for study, and classroom assignments.

The second part focuses on the preschool years with a chapter by Ken W. McCluskey called "The Importance of Being Early: A Case for Preschool Enrichment."

He advocates for greater flexibility in the schools, particularly in allowing early admission for young gifted students ready for the challenge. Provided are a variety of strategies for parents to enrich their young children's lives at home. Giving quality time to their children in these earliest years and working toward better communication and cooperation with the schools, parents can build a solid foundation for future learning. The chapter "Too Busy to Play?" by Robert D. Strom builds on this, examining play as the preferred method for learning among many preschoolers. The article suggests how imaginative play can significantly contribute to the creative growth and well-being of young gifted children with tangible gains noted in vocabulary, imagination, and higher level thinking.

The third part attends to the adolescent/middle school years, beginning with "Growing Up Too Fast—and Gifted," by Sylvia Rimm. Based on a survey of 5,400 students from grades 3 to 8 and meetings with 400 students, the author explores the social-emotional landscape of today's middle schoolers. Regardless of how gifted children *appear*, fourth, fifth, and sixth graders, even among high achievers, have marked anxieties about social acceptance and popularity. The chapter counsels parents to let their gifted children enjoy their childhood—to challenge them in ways that feed their gifts, but without pushing them into early adulthood. "Creating Successful Middle School Partnerships: A Parent's Perspective" by Rebecca Robbins reports on the unique challenges of gifted middle school students from a parent's personal experience. The chapter examines the help parents can find in high school partnerships, distance learning classrooms, online high school courses, independent study, and school programs like the Science Olympiad. Parents play a critical role in middle school success and need to be proactive and current with new developments in the middle school grades.

The last part of this section focuses on that critical rite of passage from high school into college through two chapters. The first chapter is "College Planning With Gifted Children: Start Early" by Maureen Neihart. The author notes key benefits to early college planning in the middle to junior high grades. Early exposure to educational options after high school and to professionals in different fields can inspire gifted learners about their future and give them adequate time to plan for scholarship opportunities. Parents need to support their sons and daughters in discovering their greatest passions in life and in weighing the choices they have for pursuing these interests. Parents who start this process early—in middle school—enable their children to explore the full range of options available to them.

The section closes with one other chapter, "Real Fears of Incoming First-Year College Students: What Parents Can Do" by Mary Kay Shanley and Julia Johnston, which illustrates how to support gifted students facing the pressures and adjustments of their first year at college. Echoing previous articles, Shanley and Johnston examine ways parents can be proactive—supporting the development of study skills, time management, and organization throughout high school. During the transition to college life, parents should continue to support their sons and daughters —often by sharing the wisdom and life lessons they gained from their own struggles and triumphs in college.

The chapters all stress the role of parents in bolstering the confidence of gifted students and providing an anchor when their children feel afraid or uncertain. Parents are their children's greatest advocates and a vital part of this advocacy is finding resources and helping them navigate the world when social, emotional, and academic problems overwhelm them. Becoming informed has to be a priority for parents and this means addressing their own assumptions and misconceptions about their children. A key theme emphasized in all of the articles is the importance of parents *being there* for their gifted kids—being willing to share their own experiences and to spend real time with them. Parents who share themselves are more effective in advocating for their promising children than those who are too busy to do so.

As they read these chapters, parents should think about the needs of their own gifted children. Consider some of the following questions:

- Where do I need more information on my child's challenges in order to better advocate for him or her?
- What assumptions do I have about my child's abilities, skills, and preparedness?
- What needs might my child have that I've never considered?
- What resources should I explore in my own environment and among my own acquaintances?

- What strategies can I use to communicate the needs of my child to his or her school and to work out the best arrangements for him or her?
- How do I help my gifted son or daughter to become more resilient, more able to persist in hard times, more determined when circumstances are discouraging?

This latter question leads to a point that should receive more attention in gifted education today: the need to instill inner strength and resiliency in gifted children by cultivating the creative spirit. This cultivation, however, is more about *being* than doing—how we as parents go about living our daily lives, how we express ourselves to our ever-watchful kids, how we plod along the beaten path, or, conversely, take risks and relish the experience.

Fostering the creative spirit may begin with supporting a child's artistic interest or instilling an atmosphere of openness in the home. But creativity offers a great deal more to the developing gifted child. The practice of drawing on his or her inner resources is immensely strengthening and nurtures a sense of independence and ownership of the learning process. Creative work—and the honoring of the creative force by parents—brings a sense of dignity and personal power that can endure for a lifetime. To understand as a parent that the imprisoning circumstances of school or society cannot strip you or your children of this "personal power" to be and do is one of the great and often hidden gifts of creativity in its broadest sense.

Chapter 5

Self-Regulated Learning and Academically Talented Students

by Sally M. Reis

F OR some parents of high-ability students, this scenario is familiar:

Peter is a fifth grader who seems bored and disinterested in all academics most of the time in school. He fidgets constantly, is in trouble often for being "off-task," and has been referred for assessment as having attention deficit/hyperactivity disorder (ADHD) for the last 3 years. His teacher reports that he rarely finishes his schoolwork, daydreams often, and is rarely on task. He is in danger of not learning basic information required by the district and state curriculum standards. His mother, a pediatrician, does not believe that he has ADHD, but rather, that he is not provided enough opportunities for challenge and movement in his traditional school environment. Peter and his father, who also has an extremely high energy level, frequently build intricate rockets together, and Peter can sit quietly for hours when he is engaged in work of his own selection. Peter has tested at the 99th percentile in general aptitude but his work in school is often well below average. His lack of completion of schoolwork is becoming increasingly problematic, particularly when it appears that he does finish the work he wants to pursue at home. Peter is being labeled an underachiever and his teacher believes he needs to gain some work strategies to achieve at higher levels. How can his parents or teachers help him in this process?

Peter's underachieving behaviors may be emerging for various reasons. Peter may not be challenged in school and may have to learn how to discuss these issues with his parents and teachers and arrive at a solution. Many strategies, such as curriculum compacting and differentiation, can be used to address the lack of academic challenge experienced by high-potential students. However, if Peter has problems finishing work that is appropriately challenging in school, he may need to learn and apply skills that experts refer to as "self-regulation."

According to Zimmerman (1989), self-regulation enables students to develop a set of constructive behaviors that can positively affect their learning. In less technical terms, that means learning some skills that students need to have if they are going to be responsible for decisions about their own performance. Students face different types of challenges in learning how to meet their parent's and teacher's expectations while they also learn to develop their own strengths and talents. Research suggests that they may benefit from learning to assume responsibility for their own learning. In particular, Peter may need to develop his own self-regulation to become more successful in school.

Self-Regulation Strategies Used by Successful Students

Zimmerman (1989) has demonstrated that there is a common set of self-regulation strategies and an individual set of skills that each child can develop to be successful in school and life. These include methods of organization for the time and place in which academic work is completed, the types of regular patterns of homework and test preparation one learns to use, and the way self-control emerges. Research by Zimmerman and others strongly suggests that self-regulation skills can be taught, learned, and controlled. In my experience, the absence of self-regulation in learning can be one of the most negative experiences encountered by high-potential students.

Self-regulation strategies used by successful students usually fall into three categories: personal, behavioral, and environmental. Parents can help children learn and apply these strategies, with the goal that, eventually, the children will be able to apply them independently. These strategies include:

- *Personal Strategies:* Personal strategies involve how a child organizes and interprets information and include organizing and transforming information. These strategies enable children to become much more efficient at learning, but even some of our brightest students do not always understand how to study well or efficiently. These skills include strategies such as outlining, summarizing, highlighting, using flashcards or index cards, and drawing pictures, diagrams, or charts.

- *Planning and Setting Goals:* This includes identifying goals, with strategies such as sequencing, timing, time management, pacing, and thinking about how to accomplish the best work. For example, parents can help their children learn to complete homework at night, before they watch television, or to limit the time they spend on entertainment to a certain number of hours each night.

- *Keeping Records and Monitoring:* The goal of this strategy is to help children learn to be in charge of understanding their strengths and what needs improvement and to take the time to assess why they do well on some kinds of assignments and tasks and less well on others. These skills include strategies such as note-taking, listing their own errors, keeping drafts of assignments, considering their own improvements, and maintaining a portfolio of their most special work.

- *Written and/or Verbal Rehearsing and Memorizing:* These strategies help children learn to memorize more efficiently and learn how to be better at written and verbal language. This includes using mnemonics to memorize important materials by remembering the first initials of each word, using imagery to remember diagrams or visualize concepts, teaching someone else the material, or making sample questions.

Behavioral Strategies

Behavioral strategies involve students checking their own progress or quality of work by examining the actions they take during the learning process. Children must learn to evaluate their actions and to understand the consequences of these actions. In self-evaluation, children analyze the learning task to determine what their teacher expects and whether they want to put the time and effort necessary into the task. They also learn to reflect on their self-instructions, feedback, and attentiveness. When they think about the consequences of their actions, they may ask themselves important questions (e.g., "What will happen if I do not study my 25 spelling words instead of playing this video game?"), and come to understand that if they fail to study, they may very well fail the spelling test tomorrow.

Children also can provide their own rewards to motivate themselves to meet their goals. They also can learn to delay gratification until they have achieved a goal. For example, Jonna can learn to say to herself, "I really want to watch that DVD. If I finish 25 minutes of studying for that spelling test, I will watch a half hour of the movie and then go back to studying until I know all of the words!" Zimmerman (1989) learned that the most successful students and adults often use these strategies.

Environmental Strategies

Environmental strategies for self-regulated learning involve the use of resources and the adaptation of the environment, such as:
- seeking information from the library and Internet;
- seeking social assistance from peers, teachers, and other adults;
- emulating exemplary models;
- reviewing records; and
- rereading notes, tests, and textbooks.

Structuring the study environment for optimal results also can help children to become more self-regulated. These strategies include:
- selecting or arranging the physical setting;

- isolating, eliminating, or minimizing distractions; and
- breaking up study periods and spreading them over time.

How Parents Can Help Children Develop Self-Regulation

Parents can guide children in becoming more self-regulated by helping them to acquire specific strategies that enable them to increase their control over their own behavior and environment. They also can help by modeling those behaviors at home and discussing how they learned to pay bills on time, handle responsibilities, and set goals for personal choices or work decisions.

Researchers believe that self-regulation is enhanced when someone carefully observes and considers his or her own behavior and acts upon what has been learned, enabling children to learn to decrease negative behaviors and increase positive behaviors. Self-regulated students learn to ask themselves, "Does this strategy work for me in this situation?" For example, students who struggle with reading or writing must learn to allocate much more time to complete their written work and lengthy reading assignments. In order to help their children learn better self-regulation skills, parents can encourage children to avoid comparing their performance to peers and to consider carefully their own goals and the work patterns they use to achieve their goals.

Children should learn that there are different ways to attain goals and then learn how to select the best way to complete a specific task, both at home and in school. In many classrooms, teachers assume most of the responsibility for the learning process and students may begin to depend on a teacher-directed approach. It is critical that, at home, parents encourage and support students to take control of their learning. You can accomplish this goal by modeling good learning strategies at home as well as by providing time and a supportive environment for quiet learning and homework completion.

Professor Harold Stevenson is a developmental psychologist whose current research includes several crosscultural studies of school achievement. Stevenson directed a large project investigating and comparing the achievement of American, Chinese, and Japanese children. His work focused on achievement in mathematics and reading. He has worked for many years to identify characteristics associated with the high performance of Japanese and Chinese students, who consistently exceed other students in achievement. One fascinating part of Stevenson's research explored how parents in these cultures support the high achievement of their children by having a quiet time every evening when everyone in the family works and reads together (Stevenson & Newman, 1986). During this quiet study time, parents read and do their own work while their children are in the same room with them so parents are available to help or guide them if necessary. The parental monitoring of homework and study skills that Stevenson has found in other cultures might be increasingly necessary for some students. When I speak to many parents of high-ability students who underachieve, they tell me that their children "do hours of homework each night." When I ask them where they do this homework, they respond that they do their homework in their own bedroom. When I ask whether detractors might be present in their children's bedrooms, they explain that their children have access to computers, instant messenger, telephones, music, and perhaps even television. Children who have many temptations and distractions may not learn to develop fully their own unique set of self-regulation skills.

Some academically talented students possess better self-regulated learning strategies than their peers, while other talented students may have done very well in school without using good self-regulation strategies because of a combination of their high abilities and an unchallenging curriculum. If learning is relatively easy for someone, less effort, organization, and other self-regulated activities are expended. Some social conditions or personal issues may prevent students from developing self-regulated learning strategies or from using them regularly. They may need to be helped and encouraged to do so. Some gifted and talented students display perfectionism and need to learn to strive for their personal best effort rather than perfection. Some talented students with high potential may find it difficult to learn self-regulation when it is not taught, modeled, or rewarded by the adults in their home and family. Even if students interact regularly with adults who demonstrate self-regulation, they may fail to use these skills themselves due to peer pressure, or refuse to use the strategies their parents or teachers regularly employ at home or school.

Compared with low-achieving students, high achievers set more specific learning goals, use a variety of learning strategies, self-monitor more often, and adapt their efforts more systematically. The quality and quantity of self-regulation processes is crucial. We must recognize that one self-regulation strategy will not work for all students, and that the use of only a few strategies will not work optimally for a person on every task. It is important that students learn to use multiple self-regulatory learning skills rather than single strategies. They also must learn that their goals and their choice of self-regulation strategies have to be continually adjusted. Parents should help students focus on understanding the material and on persisting when they are challenged. This is especially critical for talented students who have seldom experienced high levels of challenge, as illustrated in the following scenario:

> Jamie's an eighth-grade student who was identified in first grade as academically talented. She read at the seventh grade level by the time she finished second grade and consistently scored at the 99th percentile on all areas on standardized achievement tests. Jamie did not like math and coasted through her school district's math curriculum from first through seventh grade, doing minimal homework and getting top grades. Because of these high scores on achievement tests and previous grades, she was recommended for an advanced algebra class in eighth grade and encountered, for her first time in school, some challenge in mathematics. She struggled with a few concepts and began to tell her parents that they had erred in their assessment that she was smart. Jamie gave up almost immediately whenever she encountered a homework problem she could not solve while doing homework and told her parents she would ask the teacher the next day for help. She continued to do her homework each evening, completing only the problems that she could easily master. On the harder problems, she either sought help from her friends and teachers if she could not

quickly and correctly solve a problem. The answers to problems were in the back of the book so that after a few minutes of work, if she could not solve the problem, she often looked it up in the back of the book but failed to learn how to solve the problem. She failed a couple of tests, became convinced she was terrible at math, and considered dropping out of the algebra class. How could Jamie gain the self-regulation skills she needed to succeed in a more challenging class?

Jamie's parents worked with her to help her develop self-regulation. With patience, they encouraged her to do her math homework on the dining room table each evening. Using humor, they encouraged her to increase the time she spent trying to solve more challenging algebra problems. They also suggested she think about how she could control her temper if she could not easily solve a difficult problem. They discussed the challenges of hard work and the role of effort in their own work. They encouraged her to think about what strategies worked for her and to consider how she could modify her study strategies by thinking about her own successes. Over the course of a few months, Jamie learned to spend more time on algebra, to carefully consider how she could become more successful to discuss problems with her friends, and to try different approaches. By the end of eighth grade, she had become a very successful student in algebra and had mastered a number of the self-regulation strategies. She was much better prepared for the challenging honors and Advanced Placement classes that she would encounter the next year.

Self-regulation enables children to develop and learn constructive behaviors that affect one's learning. These behaviors are planned and adapted to support the pursuit of personal goals in changing learning environments. Learners with high levels of self-regulation have good control over how they attain their goals. Conscious self-regulation requires a student to focus on the process of how to acquire these skills. Many researchers agree with the importance of self-regulated learning for students at all academic levels and the principle that self-regulation can be taught, learned, and controlled. In fact, in Zimmerman's (1989) studies, successful students reported that the use of self-regulated learning strategies was directly tied to their success in school.

Phases of Self-Regulation

Acquiring self-regulation skills seems to proceed through three phases evolving over time.

Phase 1: Forethought

This phase precedes the actual performance, sets the stage for action, maps out the tasks to minimize the unknown, and helps to develop a positive mindset. Realistic expectations can make the task more appealing. Goals must be considered as specific outcomes, arranged in order from short term (tomorrow and this week) to long term (next month and next year). As children begin to receive more homework assignments, parents can ask them to consider the following questions:
- When will I start this work?
- Where will I do the work?
- How will I get started?

Students have to consider what conditions will help or hinder their learning activities as part of this phase. For example, Jamie's parents needed to help her to think about her algebra homework and reflect on what she could do to be more successful. They helped her to consider whether there was a better time or place to do her homework and whether it would help her to begin it in school with her friends who are successful in algebra. They helped her to try to spend at least 5 minutes on a problem before giving up and moving on and encouraged her to have a friend, either in person or on the phone, who would be available to talk about some of the steps used to solve the algebra problems.

Phase 2: Performance Control

This phase involves processes during learning and the active attempt to use specific strategies to help a student become more successful. Parents can ask their children to consider the following questions:

- Am I accomplishing what I hoped to do?
- Am I being distracted?
- Is this taking more time than I thought?
- Under what conditions am I able to accomplish the most?
- What questions can I ask myself while I am working?
- How can I encourage myself to keep working (including self-talk, such as, "Come on, get your work done, so you can watch that television show or read your magazine!")?

Jamie, for example, had to consider her performance in math as opposed to other content areas. When frustration increased, she had to consider whether she should stop and take a break. She had to think about whether she should do her math homework first in the afternoon, rather than putting it off until later in the evening. Should she have background music or work in silence? She also used and considered the success of some of the strategies she thought about in Phase 1.

Phase 3: Self-Reflection

This phase involves reflection after the performance, a self-evaluation of outcomes compared to goals. Parents can ask their children to consider the following:

- Did I accomplish what I planned to do when I studied for my math test?
- Did I become distracted and if so, how did I get back to work?
- Did I plan enough time or did I need more time than I thought?
- Under what conditions did I accomplish the most work?
- If I was successful in my homework or in tests, I might ask myself, "What did I do differently to make it work this time?"
- Did a change in time or in my work habits help me solve more algebra problems?

- Did calling a friend who was doing algebra homework at the same time make a difference?
- Did using self-talk to praise myself during this time have a positive impact ("All right, I did it! I solved that problem!")?

Summary

The development of good self-regulation usually involves self-observation or monitoring one's performance and keeping records. It involves helping children gain self-judgment or compare performance with a standard or goal that may involve re-examining answers and checking procedures. It also involves self-reaction with goal-setting, self-administered praise or criticism, rehearsing, memorizing, structuring the environment (e.g., changing the academic setting or the environment or creating a study area), and asking for help. Guiding your children in acquiring these strategies can successfully increase their self-regulation and enhance academic achievement.

Resource

Reis, S. M., & McCoach, D. B. (2000). The underachievement of gifted students: What do we know and where do we go? *Gifted Child Quarterly, 44*, 152–170.

References

Stevenson, H. W., & Newman, R. S. (1986). Long-term prediction of achievement and attitudes in mathematics and reading. *Child Development, 57*, 646–659.

Zimmerman, B. J. (1989). A social cognitive view of self-regulated academic learning. *Journal Of Educational Psychology, 81*, 329–339.

Chapter 6

What Do You Know About Learning Style? A Guide for Parents of Gifted Children

by Rita Dunn, Karen Burke, and Janet Whitely

MARK does homework curled against pillows and cushions he places on his bedroom floor. Before he opens a book, he ties a bandana around the shade of his desk lamp, turns on his wrap-around music system, and surrounds himself with snacks. Mark intermittently takes breaks to telephone a classmate or watch a sports event on television for 10–15 minutes before he returns to studying. If you were Mark's parent, would you be concerned about this homework pattern?

Most parents think that their offspring will learn as they do! That only happens half the time; our studies suggest that the first two siblings in many families learn differently, and often in diametrically opposite ways. How people learn is called their learning style. Everyone has a learning style but, in the same family, spouses often tend to learn differently from each other, and each of their children's styles differ from each other and from one of their parents' styles.

There is no good or bad learning style; each enables that person to learn. However, many parents and teachers do not understand and, therefore, do not acknowledge children's diverse learning patterns. When those adults disparage how certain children try to learn, they inadvertently encourage those youngsters to study in the wrong way (for the youngster). This scenario is particularly accurate for many talented youngsters whose learning style preferences also differ from those of other learners.

What Is Learning Style?

We define learning styles as the different ways in which an individual begins to concentrate, process, internalize, and remember new and difficult academic knowledge. Many children understand and master basic ideas and information without using their unique learning styles. But even adults do not learn new and complex knowledge without capitalizing on their styles. When people use, rather than ignore their natural styles, they learn more, more quickly, and with less frustration than they do when trying to use someone else's style. That is why using your learning style is similar to playing to your strengths.

How the Environment Affects Learning

Relatively few parents tell their children about learning styles; fewer teach them how to use their learning-style strengths. Those learning-style strengths are affected by where learning takes place. Thus, some very talented children need to learn in an environment that is very different from where other children need to learn. While concentrating, some learners require:

- Quiet, whereas others need sound (e.g., music, voices, waves crashing, or birds singing). The latter individuals may actually hum or talk to themselves to create a sound-packed environment that allows them to "think";
- Bright light, whereas others need diffused or soft illumination. Some people wear caps with visors or sunglasses inside their homes; those items allow them to "relax" while learning;
- Warmth; others literally think better in cool temperatures; and
- Formal seating, such as a desk and wooden, plastic, or steel chair; others learn better when relaxed in an easy chair or on a bed or carpeting.

How Physiology Affects Learning

Children's physical beings affect how they learn and are part of their learning style. Thus, some must:

- Concentrate in the early or late morning, whereas others do not "come alive" until afternoon; some are foggy all day and first become energized at night. See Figure 6.2 to identify when, during a 24-hour period, you, your spouse, and each of your children have energy highs, concentrate best and, therefore, should study;
- Eat or drink while they are concentrating; others only can nibble or snack after studying when they relax;
- Move about from one part of the environment (at home or in the classroom) to another or they lose a lot of their ability to focus; others do not need to move about;
- Hear information to make sense of it, whereas others must see or visualize it; and
- Some of our research also suggests that as many as 15%–20% of extremely able children engage in complex reasoning when their bodies are in motion. Such highly alert and energetic youngsters rarely sit still. Another 15%–20% seem to need to have their hands actively involved while their brains are working.

How Processing Affects Learning

One important dimension of learning style involves determining whether a child thinks more analytically or more globally. Analytic thinkers begin to process information or work in a step-by-step sequence. They keep at a task until they have learned what they need or want to, or have accomplished what they set out to do. Global thinkers, on the other hand, begin to process information by thinking of everything related to what they need or want to learn. They do take many breaks but, eventually, focus on the most salient points and get the task done.

Directions: Answer TRUE or FALSE to each of the following questions, including all of the parts of Question # 15. If your answer is, "It depends," leave the space blank.

	TRUE	FALSE
1. I usually hate to get up in the morning!	____	____
2. I usually am wide awake at night!	____	____
3. I wish I could sleep late each morning!	____	____
4. I stay awake for a long time after I go to bed.	____	____
5. I only feel wide awake after 10:00 a.m.	____	____
6. If I stay up very late at night, I get too sleepy to remember anything.	____	____
7. I usually feel "low" after lunch.	____	____
8. When I have to do a task that requires concentration, I get up early in the morning.	____	____
9. When I can, I do most concentration-requiring tasks in the afternoon.	____	____
10. I usually begin the tasks that require the most concentration after dinner.	____	____
11. I could stay up all night!	____	____
12. I wish I didn't have to go to work before noon!	____	____
13. I wish I could stay home during the day and go to work at night.	____	____
14. I like going to work in the morning!	____	____
15. I remember things best when I concentrate on them:		

    a. in the morning   b. at lunchtime   c. in the afternoon
    d. before dinner   e. after dinner   f. late at night

Figure 6.2. Questionnaire on time-of-day preferences.

Both types of processing—analytic and global—are good, but the children who have one style, as opposed to the other, learn very differently from each other (see Figure 6.3).

Figure 6.3 indicates a few ways that you can tell if anyone in your family is more analytic than global or vice versa. Anyone with three or more characteristics in one column tends to reflect that processing style.

Analytic Processors Learn Best With:	Global Processors Learn Best With:
Quiet	Sound (music or voices)
Bright illumination	Soft illumination
Formal seating	Informal seating
Snacking when relaxed	Snacking while concentrating
Persistent on-task behavior	Frequent breaks
	Working with others (when beginning a task)

Figure 6.3. Determining analytic and global processors.

Four characteristics in the same column indicate a strongly analytic or global learner, and five in the same column suggest that a person has a very strong need to learn that way—strong enough that learning in other ways is likely to be extremely difficult. Mixed characteristics (fewer than three or many in one column but a couple in both) usually describe an integrated processor—someone who learns in both ways but only when he or she is interested in what is being learned.

How Emotions Affect Learning

For many, motivation is strongly linked to how well they achieve. Many gifted children enjoy learning new and difficult material; it makes them feel accomplished. Other children strive for good grades because they want their teachers', parents', or friends' approval. That is not negative; whatever works is good!

When children are interested in what they are learning, they become increasingly motivated. Obviously, the reverse is true too. That is why motivation changes day-to-day, teacher-to-teacher, and class-to-class. The relationship between interest and motivation is crucial for talented youngsters who often spend hours, days, weeks, or years deeply involved in what absorbs them. Indeed, that sustained interest over time is an essential factor in giftedness and talent development in young people.

Persistence refers to each child's ability to stay with a task until it is accomplished, whereas responsibility is more closely related to some children's emotional need to do what others have told them they should. Some youngsters enjoy doing the opposite of what they should do and are called nonconforming. These children rarely respond well to authoritative adults. If you have a nonconforming child in your family, (a) speak collegially (as if to a respected friend), (b) explain why the action or behavior you want from the youngster is important to you, and (c) give the youngster choices for how to do what you want done.

Children also differ in their need for structure. Some want a great deal of direction and feel best when they know what is required and how to proceed. Such youngsters appreciate specific directions and models to follow.

Conversely, children who prefer less structure enjoy doing things their way. Such individuals want to know what has to be done, but want to do it their way. These children often are extremely creative; they enjoy options and like stretching their minds and using their innate abilities.

How Social Choices Affect Learning

Some children learn best when they are able to work and interact with other children. Interaction stimulates and motivates them. Working together develops some social skills. Other students—often the brightest and most analytic—learn best by themselves. Once they have mastered the content, they often can work with others but really prefer working alone. Whenever you urge your children to play or work with others, remember that most gifted and talented youngsters prefer concentrating either alone or with an authority figure.

Do Gifted or Talented Children Learn Differently From Others?

Children's learning styles differ when they are high- versus low-academic achievers. Although gifted youngsters learn differently from each other, and underachievers have differing learning-style patterns, gifted and underachieving students have significantly different learning styles and often do not perform well with the same methods.

Interestingly, when we studied gifted adolescents in nine diverse cultures, the students with talents in athletics, art, dance, leadership, literature, mathematics, or music evidenced essentially similar learning-style characteristics to other learners (in different cultures) who shared a common talent area. That is, talented dancers or talented musicians in any one culture tended to have similar learning-style strengths to those of students with similar talents in the other cultures. Students with similar talents from different cultures had greater similarity of learning-style preferences than did differently talented students from the same culture.

Our research also suggests that there are several common patterns of learning-style differences between boys and girls. Boys, more than girls, tend to be kinesthetic and tactual, needing an informal design and the freedom to move around when concentrating on academic studies. Their third modality strength, if one is evident, often is visual. As a group, boys tend to learn less by listening, and they are more nonconforming and peer motivated than girls. Girls, more than boys, learn by listening, and they often are more conforming, authority-oriented, and better able to sit passively at conventional desks and chairs. Girls also tend to need significantly more quiet while learning. Despite these facts, all girls and all boys do not behave identically. But that the two groups have different learning-style strengths is evident.

Learning styles often change as children move from elementary to middle school and between middle school and high school. They continue to change in college and during adulthood, and the styles of older adults in the 65–85-year-old range differ in many ways from those of younger people. Nevertheless, individuals change in unique ways. Some people hardly change at all, and others change more than once as they mature.

Sociological Preferences

Preferences for learning (a) alone, (b) with peers, (c) with an authoritative versus a collegial teacher, and (d) with routines and patterns, as opposed to in a variety of social groupings, develop over time, change with age and maturity, and are developmental. Young children tend to enter the primary grades highly parent-, teacher-, and/or adult-motivated. Many become peer motivated by fifth or sixth grade and remain that way until approximately ninth grade when they often become self-motivated. High-ability children tend to become self-motivated early, frequently by first or second grade, and rarely experience a peer-motivated stage. Underachievers become peer motivated earlier than average students and tend to remain that way longer—often well past adolescence.

Emotional Preferences

Motivation, responsibility (conformity versus nonconformity), and the need for internal versus external structure are perceived as developmental. Motivation fluctuates day-to-day, class-to-class, and teacher-to-teacher. Many people experience several stages of nonconformity, which correlate with high and low "responsibility" levels. The first period of nonconformity occurs for many between the second and third years of life. In the United States, that period euphemistically is called "the terrible twos" and coincides with children beginning the pattern of saying, "No!" For most children, that stage lasts for less than a year. The second period of nonconformity often begins at about 6th grade and tends to last until 9th or 10th grade for many average children. Underachievers and some gifted students often remain nonconforming until well past high school; others into adulthood.

Perceptual Preferences

Young children tend to understand best the things they can touch, play with, or handle. We call that tactual learning. By the time they enter school, tactual learners can remember three quarters of the information they write about or draw. Kinesthetic learners understand and remember best information they experience actively. Kinesthetic preschoolers learn from doing things. When they are older simulations, pantomime, performing (as in a play, chorus, or band), or interning permit these students to absorb complex information.

Data from our research indicate that less than 12% of elementary school children are auditory. Few children (or adults) are likely to remember at least 75% of the academic information they hear during a 30–40 minute period. In addition, we have found that less than 40% of students are visual learners. Few children (or adults) can remember at least 75% of what they read during a 30–40 minute interval.

The older children become, the more their auditory and visual modalities develop. However, many adult males are neither auditory nor visual learners; some remain essentially tactual or kinesthetic all their lives. Poorly achieving students in traditional schools tend to be only tactual and/or kinesthetic. However, when taught with tactual or kinesthetic approaches or resources—rather than with lectures or readings—these children perform well. When taught the way they learn, these youngsters achieve significantly higher scores on tests and enjoy school more than when they are taught traditionally. We believe, then, that perceptual preferences are very important to effective learning for students at all ability levels, and for those who are not doing well in school, as well as for helping successful students be their best.

How Parents Can Use This Learning-Style Information

High-ability children can be either analytic or global learners. If they learn analytically, they easily conform to the behaviors required by traditional teachers because they naturally learn that way. On the other hand, global children have a more difficult task conforming in conventional schools because those requirements are so at odds with the natural ways in which they learn. Global learners naturally:
- hum to themselves to provide the sound they crave while concentrating;
- seem to be hyperactive and tense in brightly lit rooms;
- can't sit in regular classroom furniture for more than 10–15 minutes without sprawling, extending their feet into the aisle, and/or moving; and

- snack, whisper, crouch, and lose interest in analytic teaching.

If children cannot remember three-quarters of what they hear, they may listen to the teacher, but not retain it. If they learn by seeing, listening does not help. If they learn through pictures and drawings (as many young global children do), reading printed matter will not entice them. If they are tactual learns, they tap their desks, touch items, play with whatever gets into their hands, and write poorly. If they learn kinesthetically, while actively engaged in doing, their teachers perceive them as being hyperactive, restless, and often unable or not ready to learn.

If children are not *morning* learners, teachers may think their parents allowed them to remain up until well past their bedtime. If they happen to be evening learners, children probably have been admonished to "go to bed" just when they are experiencing their energy high.

At School

Consider the following tips:
- Don't fall into the trap of thinking that because your children may be doing well in school, there is no need to urge their teachers to identify and respond to their learning-style strengths. Many gifted children become bored or irritated in school precisely because they are required to follow the same rules in the same way and in the same amount of time as everyone else. Teachers tend to say that it is *fair* to treat everyone in the same way! Instead of being fair, it is being arbitrary, capricious, and unfair to require that children who think creatively, faster, and more divergently than their peers must:
  - sit and wait until everyone else has finished the class assignment;
  - help slower children who take longer than everyone else; or
  - work at the academic level of the average child in the class instead of competing with their equally talented or gifted peers.

- Praise children for doing well in whatever it is they do well. Each child has unique talents and no one is talented in every area. Encourage children to excel in whatever it is that interests them.
- It is important to make your child's teacher aware of his or her learning style.
- It always is important to make children aware of their styles— and why they feel uncomfortable when they are not permitted to learn their way.
- Obtain "Homework Prescriptions" that describe how your children should study through their individual learning-style strengths. Anticipate that each child in your family will receive suggestions that differ from those given to their siblings. Guidelines based on learning-style strengths make studying easier and more enjoyable than the usual study skills suggested for everyone.
- If your child is experiencing school-related problems, learn as much as you can about learning styles before making any judgments about causes or responses.

At Home

Provide the kind of study environment in which each child functions best. They need to feel confident that you understand and appreciate their learning-style patterns. They also need to recognize that everyone needs to learn. Don't permit one person's working and learning preferences and styles to interfere with another family member's. Help them to find alternative ways of working in which their styles do not distract others.

- Don't force your gifted child either to play or work with others just because they are the same age. High-ability children very often think differently and quickly become bored or irritated by the pedantic thinking of less-able children of the same age.
- Children need to find a place in their environment—both at home and at school—in which to feel comfortable. Develop

your child's awareness of sound, light, temperature, and seating preferences and help to identify what is best in different situations.

- After taking learning-style characteristics into account, determine whether your child learns best alone, in a pair, as part of a team, with adults, or in any combination of these. Whatever the preference, adopt it for at least a short period of time to determine whether your child actually performs best that way.
- Do not be concerned with the amount of time it takes children to do homework. They may move faster in the *wrong* style, but they will remember what they study better and longer in their *right* style.
- Almost two fifths of learning style seems to develop over time and gradually changes as children age and mature. Test for learning style any youngster who may not be performing well in school to know how to help him or her. Everyone can learn; however, half the population learns differently from the other half.

Back to Mark. Now that you know a little about learning styles, you understand that he prefers informal seating, low light, music, and snacks while learning. He also takes breaks, but does finish his homework. Undoubtedly, Mark is global. If his grades are good, his parents have no need for concern. If his grades are not good, they ought to have him tested for learning style and then encourage him to follow the suggested guidelines for doing homework.

Authors' Note

Parents and teachers interested in learning more about learning styles can visit the following website: http://www.learningstyles.net. Information and downloadable brochures are available from this site.

Chapter 7

The Importance of Being Early: A Case for Preschool Enrichment

by Ken W. McCluskey

I N my past life as a school psychologist, I would now and again encounter some very young children who could do amazing things. For example, one day when assessing a 4-year-old boy for an early entrance to a kindergarten program in our district, I received a request from another clinician to use my office for a group meeting. I moved with the youngster into our audiologist's room. Imagine my surprise when the little fellow, observing and reading from a piece of equipment, asked: "Impedance audiometer. What's that?" I didn't know the answer, but I knew I had come face-to-face with something special.

A 4-year-old girl being considered for the same program produced a startling signed self-portrait, complete with detailed hair, eyebrows, fingers, and high-heeled shoes. A kindergarten boy answered all of the items on one segment of a popular IQ test—he knew that silica is the main material used to make glass, Darwin proposed the theory of evolution, and that turpentine is made from the sap of fir trees. And a 9-year-old girl I was working with on a project wrote:

> What is life? Does it end at death or begin anew for eternity? Eternal life is a tantalizing thought, but maybe an unrealistic one. Is death to be feared or welcomed? . . . My mother says I'm not to worry my pretty little head about such things . . . but these ever-intruding thoughts cannot be willed away.

Rather powerful stuff!

Now changes in my own life are causing me to revisit my interest in early years enrichment. As I write this piece, I'm about to become a grandparent for the fourth time. It's a grandparent's prerogative to think that all of his grandkids are talented, and I do. Kristjana, an early reader, is a sensitive, altruistic, highly verbal girl whose joy in life is to go on "dates" with her doting grandpa. Kail, a truly warm and cuddly baby, has learned to walk quite early and also demonstrated a superior set of lungs.

Here, however, I will focus on 2-year-old Hunter. She reached and rushed through certain developmental milestones at a rate that caused my wife and I to take notice. In a postbirth reunion of mothers from a prenatal class, nine moms reconvened with their infants for a celebration and photo opportunity of the babies. Only Hunter could sit by herself, so the shot was taken with her in the middle and all the others leaning inward. By 8 months, she was taking tentative steps; by 9 months, she was running and climbing in stable fashion; and by a year, she could—in her reckless, devil-may-care style—climb up and descend a playground slide on her own. Before turning 2, she had no hesitation in jumping into a pool and trying to swim. Language and concept development were equally rapid. At 18 months, Hunter—who had learned to hit the redial button—put in a call for help. The phone conversation went like this:

> *"Papa!" (that would be me)*
> *"Hi Hunter. How are you doing?"*
> *"Papa loves Hunter!"*
> *"Of course I do, but why are you phoning me?"*
> *"Daddy angry Hunter."*
> *"Why is Daddy mad at Hunter?"*
> *"Hunter color walls!"*

Two months later, our daughter took Hunter to the pediatrician and bragged that her offspring could now recite the ABCs and count to 20. The doctor was skeptical. Hunter demonstrated flawlessly. Taken aback, the good doctor noted that this situation was "highly unusual." At a wedding shower shortly thereafter, uninhibited Hunter grabbed the microphone and entertained guests with alphabet recitation and a unique rendition of *Twinkle, Twinkle, Little Star* (the words were right, but the tonal quality left something to be desired). At 2½, Hunter surprised us as we were driving on a bridge over our city's railway yard by commenting, "I'm on a bridge and there's no water beneath me."

As Piaget himself noted, many preschoolers have difficulty understanding that their grandmothers are their parent's mothers. Not Hunter. When my wife Andrea phoned one day, Hunter grabbed the phone and asked demandingly, "Who's this?" My wife naturally answered "Grandma." Hunter queried, "Andrea?" She laughed and said, "Don't call me Andrea!" Hunter's response: "How's Ken?" She knows the first names of all of the grandparents (and surviving great-grandparents), and knows who is "mommy's mommy," "daddy's daddy," and so forth.

There is a downside. Unlike our other grandchildren, Hunter can be downright recalcitrant and defiant. She is extremely overactive and impulsive. With sponge-like curiosity, she gets into everything, scurries tirelessly from hither to yon, and enjoys pushing the envelope to the limit. Recently, when her mother was caring for her year-old niece, Hunter became resentful about sharing attention with her cousin. Taking matters into her own hands, she slipped out to the porch, met the mailman, and asked him to take her cousin away in his bag! Right now, knowing that she's waiting at our home for her weekly "sleepover," I find myself—at the end of a long day—preferring to stay at the office writing about her rather than actually going home and having to deal with her endearing, but incredibly wearing, antics.

Naturally, faced with this talent and the concomitant challenges, my wife and I began to wonder how to respond. Would it be a mistake to "push" our granddaughter too early? Many teachers, believing that we should not destroy the joy of childhood by putting on too much pressure too early, favor the "let-the-children-be-children" approach. Adherents of this school of thought use David Elkind's work on *The Hurried Child* to illustrate that damage can result if we push little ones too soon. However, recognizing that it is generally best to base decisions upon fact rather than myth, we searched and discovered that Elkind was never opposed to moving high-ability students ahead on the basis of their achievement and skill level. Indeed, he supported early school entry and grade acceleration for certain talented children. Many others agree. For example, John Feldhusen observed that talented children are typically accelerated as quickly as possible in sports, music, and the arts. Would it have been "best practice" to insist that Tiger Woods, during his early childhood, be allowed to attempt only age-appropriate golf shots? Yet, in school, high-ability children frequently are trapped in a lockstep, grade-to-grade system.

Perhaps educators ought to be thinking seriously about designing more flexible schools. Certainly, research suggests that acceleration and early admission can be healthy for many individuals. Long-term studies of large numbers of children have found that early starters are, in general, stronger academically in the elementary grades, and that this superiority continues in high school. Many reviews of the research conclude that, in terms of both academic achievement and social adjustment, early entrants and accelerated students perform well compared to their classmates. Interestingly, in several studies, there are signs that behavior problems surface if high-ability children are not allowed to proceed at a faster pace. This observation adds an oft-neglected dimension to the debate, suggesting as it does that the social risks may actually be greater for talented students who are compelled to "march in place" than for those who are fast-tracked. Tiger Woods, for one, looks happy with his golf record to me.

What happens early in a child's life makes a tremendous difference. For one thing, during the first 2 years there is rapid growth accompanied by major changes in structure and functioning of the human brain itself. And there is compelling evidence to suggest that, in the early years, the physical development of the brain is more than simply "preprogrammed unfolding." It is, in fact, also tied to the type and quality of early experience. Early environmental enrichment can make a very real difference to learning ability throughout life. From laboratory research with animals, we know that the brains of rats allowed to climb, sniff, and explore objects are, in general, larger than those of animals denied such opportunities. Isolation and experiential impoverishment tend to retard neurological growth. Environmental stimulation has a direct effect on the physical properties of animals' brains, including the number of synaptic or physical connections between neurons.

Burton White, a proponent of the early experience view, suggested that the first 3 years are crucial in human cognitive and emotional growth in his 1995 book, *The New First Three Years of Life*. He asserted that the critical period may well come in the 8- to 18-month range. According to White, it is important to ensure that children have stimulating toys and materials in the home. Another key is the quality of environmental interaction, in particular between mother and child. The capable mother, in his view, provides encouragement, support, and stimulation, without becoming smothering or unnecessarily intrusive.

Most of us, quite rightly accepting that lifelong learning is a laudable and possible objective, continue to acquire new knowledge and skills as we age. However, a very powerful case also can be made for the importance of early years' stimulation. More and more, it looks like the earlier, the better. Learning may well come easier later in life if a solid foundation has been laid through environmental enrichment in the beginning. The U.S. federal government recognized the need for early intervention in 1964 and responded by introducing the Head Start program to help prepare disadvantaged children for school entry. Designed to provide opportunities and services to preschoolers from low-income, at-risk families, it focused on early education, physical and mental health services, nutrition awareness, child and family social services, and parental involvement. Since its inception, millions of children have been served through this initiative. More recent federal programs, such as Early Start and the Head Start Transition Project, also have been developed to provide young at-risk children, under 3 years of age, with enriching environmental experiences and opportunities.

It is true that research concerning the long-term impact of Head Start has been equivocal in many respects. For one thing, a "fade-out effect" has been found, where, after registering immediate gains on intelligence and achievement tests, children later fell back. However, part of the problem here might be the unfortunate tendency of investigators to assume that IQ scores are the primary indicator of success (a dubious assumption to say the least), or to compare Head Start children to those from more advantaged backgrounds. Thorough reviews of several programs suggest that environmental enrichment has had both immediate and long-range benefits. When "graduates" of Head Start and similar projects were followed over several years, their academic achievement in elementary school showed marked improvement. Long-term behavioral and social adjustment gains also were found. In adolescence and beyond, there are indications that early intervention programs contributed to higher high school completion rates and higher rates of employment after graduation. Reductions in delinquency, teenage pregnancy, and adult dependence on social assistance also were noted.

In light of all of this information, what are parents (and grandparents) to do? My wife and I decided it would be a serious mistake simply to "leave well enough alone." Rather, we intend to get actively involved and help "stretch" (a better word than "push") and challenge Hunter to develop her talents. For parents and educators who share our interest in enrichment in the early years, here are a few specific suggestions.

1. Look For Talent Strengths Early

As children grow, it is important, as Grover Young and others emphasize, to become "talent spotters," to be aware of developmental milestones, to be watchful of a child's progress, and to be responsive to emerging gifts. We need to appreciate a wide range of abilities, and to look for and nurture the strengths in all of our children. Sometimes, to identify talent, it is necessary to step back, change one's perspective, and reframe reality. Stubbornness in early childhood may be setting the stage for the later development of perseverance, seeking and monopolizing attention may grow into leadership, and unfocused daydreaming may evolve into creative invention.

2. Encourage Infants and Toddlers to Explore, Play, and Learn

Provide an enriching early environment through plenty of contact and cuddling, singing and music, pictures and mobiles, and age-appropriate (not necessarily expensive) toys. Talk! talk! talk!, so that children are immersed in language (and not constant "baby talk"). Celebrate successes—clap hands and create excitement about your youngster's accomplishments. However, do not overdo it and "flood" children; there also is a time and place for peace, solitude, and independent play and reflection. To use a sports analogy, a good quarterback doesn't always throw the ball to the receivers with as much speed and power as possible. Sometimes he does need to get the ball to the receiver very quickly ("firing a bullet"), but on other occasions a gentle, hanging floater might be much more effective and might even be essential. Similarly, although an abundance of stimulation is a plus, enrichment isn't unrestrained bombardment; judgment and balance are needed.

With infants, it often is a good idea to carry them facing forward, so they can view the world more easily. We go for family breakfasts with our grandkids in a local hotel. After the meal, grandpa is charged with taking each child for a walk to visit the game room, wander through boutiques, look at paintings in the hallways, ride up and down the elevator, and peer out of windows on the different floors. With the forward-facing babies, I always make a point of chattering continuously in a soothing manner. One might not think that infants would care for discussions about the wax candles in the shops, the relative merits of two paintings, the weather, or the cars in the parking lot, but they soak it up. All the while, I encourage them to look, touch (one never knows what button they'll hit in the elevator), babble, and take turns.

3. Let Young Children, For a While at Least, Be the Center of the Family Universe

Researcher Urie Bronfenbrenner observed that every child needs at least one adult who is "irrationally crazy" about her or him. For a time, it can be desirable for the child to be the main focus of our attention. In their book, *Starting Out Right*, Nancy Leffert, Peter Benson, and Jolene Roehlkepartain noted that, for healthy mental and emotional growth to take place, children require some specific developmental assets. For infants and toddlers, these include support (e.g., high levels of affection, positive family communication, and an encouraging climate), constructive use of time (e.g., exposure to creative activities at home and elsewhere), and empowerment (e.g., valuing, protecting, and involving children; placing them at the center of family life).

4. Give Young Children the Most Important Gift We Have to Give, Time!

Educators often make a mistake here. All too frequently, they come home after a frenetic day working with children, and they just don't want to see another kid. Yet their own await. In today's fast-paced world, too many adults, virtually consumed by their jobs, rationalize neglect by saying that they enjoy "quality time" with their young children. What this usually means is that they're simply not giving enough time. A great deal is lost by parents who mistakenly think they can "make it up" to their kids later. If you find you're not providing enough enrichment during your children's early years, change your priorities. Setting aside a "family night" might be one good place to start. For a decade and a half, we spent each Friday together as a family, with the children picking the evening's entertainment. (I still bitterly resent the fact that I had to sit through both of the *Care Bear* movies.) It isn't always easy finding the time, but find it nonetheless.

5. Teach Responsibility

Although it is natural to want to do almost everything for little children, preschoolers are quite capable of managing simple tasks around the home, helping out with younger siblings, and making choices. To be allowed to help others teaches valuable lessons about altruism and compassion, lessons we want talented young children to learn. During family trips, preschoolers can become cartographers, showing us where we've been, where we are, and where we're going. At weddings (we do take even young children to such events in our family), children learn the meaning of kinship, giving, celebration, and, if properly guided, acceptable behavior. Parents, of course, must set the limits. As Haim Ginott noted, it often might be a mistake to expect a 4-year-old girl to pick out her own clothes, but she can learn something about responsibility and decision making by selecting from among three outfits deemed suitable by mom and/or dad.

6. Model Appropriate Behavior

It's easy to slip into the "do-as-I-say-not-as-I-do" trap. A coworker of mine recalls when his daughter was a preschooler. She enjoyed sitting beside him in the front seat of the car, pretending to drive the vehicle. One memorable day when engaged in this activity, she looked out the window and bellowed: "Get out of the way you stupid ass!" My colleague knew it was time to make some behavioral adjustments of his own. If you want children to stay on task, model stick-to-itiveness; if you want them to read, read; if you want them to be excited about learning, show enthusiasm for your own projects. For young children, silent modeling may not be enough. State what you are doing out loud, so they notice and understand.

7. Never Say No To a Book

Even with infants and toddlers, make frequent visits to bookstores and libraries. As soon as they're able, let children (again within limits) choose their own material. There's plenty available for the young reader: waterproof books for babies in the bath, picture books, hands-on activity books, and beautifully illustrated stories. Reading to young children daily will help build in a love of books and a sense for the flow, rhythm, and beauty of printed language.

8. Infuse Learning School-Readiness Skills With Joy and Excitement

More and more educators recommend that we begin teaching the fundamentals of reading and math to capable preschoolers. Respect the pace of the child, and because risk taking is an essential ingredient for effective learning, make it safe to experiment and make mistakes. Counting, reciting the alphabet, and recognizing numbers and letters should be fun. Many television programs and videos are educational, but be selective. From an early age, drawing and writing also should be encouraged. If possible, preschoolers should have their own black or whiteboards. Artwork and writing samples should be displayed proudly—isn't that why fridge magnets were invented? My wife and I put up the children's products outside our offices at the university. After a few weeks, new masterpieces replace the old displays. In addition, in this day and age it would be negligent not to embrace technology and expose young children to it. It's amazing to see what some 2- and 3-year-olds can do on a computer.

9. Strike a Balance Between Nurturing Specific Talent Strengths and Creating Well-Rounded Individuals

Encourage and help young children to identify and run with their strengths, for it takes time, commitment, and hard work to develop talents to their fullest. On the other hand, also be mindful of the need to be well-rounded. Don't immediately force young children into one particular area, but rather let them explore and allow their talents to unfold naturally. The ancient Greeks emphasized the "golden mean," where the truly talented individual was seen as having interests and abilities in a variety of domains. Early overspecialization in a single realm can be limiting and cause other talents to be overlooked.

10. Strive For Positive Home-School Communication, Cooperation, and Collaboration

Sometimes parents may have a somewhat biased view of their children's abilities, and perhaps that's as it should be. Unfortunately, in many cases, I have seen teachers dismiss out-of-hand some logical and well-founded parental concerns about meeting the enrichment needs of children. Sensitive parents are the ones best positioned to make accurate observations about their youngsters; they shouldn't be hesitant, in a positive way, to share information, ideas, and expectations with teachers, even in nursery school and kindergarten. However, while I feel parents should make their voices heard, it's also important not to be too shrill; nonadversarial home-school interaction usually works best. When school personnel lack awareness, time, or resources, and are unable to respond sufficiently, parents and others should be willing to help out and pick up the slack. As Don Treffinger has emphasized in his work, education should not be seen as the responsibility of the school alone; it should ultimately occur within an "ecosystem of learning." Enrichment can and should take place in school, in the home, at the computer, on athletic fields, and in community clubs, churches, museums, theaters, and other potentially stimulating environments.

Incidentally, feeling guilty after writing suggestion #4, I forced myself—tired as I was—to head home for time with Hunter. The moment I opened the door, she held up a shoehorn and asked what it was. After I told her the name, she ran around trying to blow into and play it. Exhausted, my wife and I nevertheless clarified the true purpose of shoehorns, chatted with Hunter about her day, read a book, watched and discussed the ramifications of a Disney cartoon, and essentially added another page to our own little talent development project.

Resource

Berrueta-Clement, J. R., Schweinhart, L. J., Barnett, W. S., Epstein, A. S., & Weikart, D. P. (1984). *Changed lives: The effects of the Perry preschool program on youths through age 19.* Ypsilanti, MI: High/Scope Press.

References

Leffert, N., Benson, P. L., & Roehlkepartain, J. L. (1997). *Starting out right: Developmental assets for children.* Minneapolis, MN: Search Institute.
White, B. (1995). *The new first three years of life* (3rd ed.). New York, NY: Fireside.

Chapter 8

Too Busy to Play?

by Robert D. Strom

P ARENTS of preschoolers have a difficult teaching role because they have to accomplish some of their goals primarily through play. Using play as a medium for instruction may not seem demanding until we recognize that parents (the teachers) have a much shorter attention span for fantasy interaction than do their children (the learners). Then too, the children usually possess greater imaginative strength. Given these conditions, it is obvious that parents can succeed only when they regard themselves and their children as partners in play. But, how can this kind of collaboration be established in the context of family play? What assets do parents bring to the merger and how should these be combined with the strengths of children? How can families use their time together for mutual benefit? Mothers and fathers realize that complete answers for these questions are not currently available. Nevertheless, they are eager to apply what is known about play with young children.

My own motivation to study parent-child play grew from dissatisfaction. As a father of two sons, I had searched in vain for advice about how to join them in their favorite activity. Most of the literature on play ignored the human variables. Instead, play usually was described as though the players were interchangeable and had a uniform influence. Intuitively, I felt that different benefits could be obtained when children played with parents, with peers, and by themselves. In order to test these assumptions, a setting for experimentation was needed. With assistance from The Rockefeller Foundation, various toy manufacturers, and a group of creative student architects, a colorful spacious laboratory was constructed. Looking back over several decades of experimentation, I believe that we initially underestimated the possibilities of teaching and learning through play. Parents commonly report that they are able to make better decisions about the imaginative play of 3- to 6-year-olds after considering our research findings in relation to the following questions.

- How long can I remain interested while at play?
- How important is my influence during play?
- How can I support my child's self-esteem while we play?
- Should I praise my child during play?
- How can I encourage creative abilities in my children?
- Am I willing to set aside time for play?
- How worthwhile am I as a model for leisure?
- How important is it to spend time together?

How Long Can I Remain Interested While at Play?

Even a casual observer will notice that going shopping with parents does not have much appeal to young children. Usually they ask to go home well before their parent is ready. When boys and girls complain, "We've been shopping too long," parents recognize it as being "only a few minutes." However, this attention deficit is reversed in fantasy play. We involved 300 families of preschoolers in an experiment. When families entered the laboratory, they were greeted and invited to play together with toys until I could meet with them. They did not know that the duration of their playtime was being measured. Upon my arrival I said, "It looks like you've been busy while you were waiting. By the way, how long have you been playing?" Most of the parents guessed that they had played for about 20 minutes even though the actual lapsed time was 6 minutes. When someone says that another person has a short attention span, it can depend on the activity. For many parents, this means they can initially expect to play for 10 minutes or less without becoming bored or noticeably distracted. Because it is unwise to play beyond the point of interest, tell your child, "It's time for me to stop now. I cannot play for as long as you can." When you take this approach, you will soon experience satisfaction, become less inhibited, and your attention span for pretending will increase.

How Important Is My Influence During Play?

Parent-child play offers unique benefits for children. They gain a broader perspective than when they play alone or with friends. Whatever play theme children choose, parents can help them enlarge their vocabulary by introducing and defining new words in context. The more words young boys and girls understand because of play and televiewing experiences, the greater their comprehension will be when they begin reading. Plan to play at times when you are energetic and insightful rather than when you are intolerant and fatigued. Sometimes tired adults read to a child, supposing the effort will support literacy. But reading in a monotone voice offers little benefit. In contrast, when you express emotion while reading, then enthusiasm for spending time with books is a more likely result.

Much of what children learn before they attend elementary school comes through guessing, questioning, and playing. These activities fit most definitions of the creative process. Because children prefer to use their imaginations, our first concern should be to preserve this important asset. Creativity develops when family members encourage it by joining children as play partners. Youngsters often base self-esteem on the amount of family involvement in things they like to do. It is not surprising that parents who are most willing to participate in play are the ones who establish closer relationships with children.

How Can I Support My Child's Self-Esteem While We Play?

Several of our experiments offer clues about the ways in which parent-child play contributes to the sense of power on which early self-esteem can be built. We discovered that children need opportunities for sharing dominance with adults. To understand this need, think about the kinds of games you like most. Usually, adults prefer a close game, one in which the outcome remains in doubt until near the end. When a football team beats another 40–0, the spectators may be heard to say that what they witnessed was not really a game at all. By this, they mean the imbalance of power eliminated the uncertainty and consequent excitement about who would win. The draft in professional sports was established to ensure parity among the teams in the league, or else there would be no competition and the fans would not watch.

Parents experience a similar motive when they try to play games with young children. The adults are too competent for the children to win. Thus, during a game of checkers, when the child starts to complain, threatens to quit, or appears on the verge of crying, grown-ups must decide what to do. Often they cheat in favor of their young opponent, perhaps moving a checker in such a way that the child can double jump them. This is not an attempt to teach dishonesty; it is an effort to convey a temporary sense of power. But it is an inappropriate method. There is a better way to respect boys and girls: become involved with imaginative play where their strength surpasses our own.

A child's need for power and consequent self-assertion should have a place in adult-child play. Many adults can play with children for only a short period, because they can't stand being dominated for a long time. The same reason describes why some children cannot tolerate certain classes at school. The child who is continually dominated, no matter how kindly, will cease in some measure to grow because his or her power needs remain unexpressed and unsatisfied. Identity requires self-assertion. Yet when children assert themselves with playmates, the usual sequence is adult intervention, reprimand, and guilt. By contrast, when preschoolers play with parents, they do not feel guilty about assertion. Instead, the typical consequence of child assertion during parent-child play is parent concession.

When we ask 4-year-olds who they prefer to play with, friends or parents, they almost always choose parents. The reason they give is, "Then I can be the boss." The power possibility also may explain why preschoolers prefer to play alone with the parent, rather than include a sibling. Older siblings are less accepting of dominance by younger brothers and sisters because they have a narrow scope of power compared to their parents. In other words, the fact that preschoolers choose a less competent partner, like a parent, to a more competent one, like a peer or sibling, suggests that a desire for play with parents is partly to redress imbalance of interpersonal power.

Should I Praise My Child During Play?

Adults commonly rely on praise as a substitute for spending time with their children. But giving a child attention is a higher form of reward. Suppose a child comes to you with a picture that he is coloring. You are busy, so you say, "That's a wonderful job," "That's great," or, "I like it better than the one you did before dinner." He soon returns to demonstrate his next product and solicit your praise. Change the strategy by sitting down and watching him while he colors. Now he knows that what he is doing is important enough to warrant your attention so he no longer has a need to seek praise. It is not just listening to a youngster that is important. Observation also can have a great effect by reinforcing what you consider to be most important. Hopefully, that includes an expression of imagination.

Children seek recognition but it is less for praise than acceptance. Because people who are accepted can remain who they are without risking a loss of affection, they do not have to change their behavior to continue being valued. In this way, acceptance is the greatest reward we can offer children. Although praise is well-intended, it often is used to shape behavior in ways that deflect a child from normal development. It is when we want to develop initiative, creativity, and problem solving that praise fails us most. To liberate these qualities in people, we need to rely upon internal motivation, that is help people feel they are free of our control. Any serious observer will notice that children experience the intrinsic satisfaction of play so they do not praise one another. Certainly they may try to control playmates and playthings, but praise is not their tool. On the other hand, adults who rely on praise seem oblivious to play satisfaction and insist upon acting as judges whose function is to verbally reinforce selected behaviors. If parents found pleasure in play, they would not have difficulty maintaining their own attention for the activity. When someone finds play boring or disappointing, it usually shows up in terms of a short attention span and use of praise as an extraneous reward system.

Because praising adults are easily distracted from play, they often lapse into a pattern of near constant superlatives. Consider 4-year-old Darin who was playing a submarine theme with Jill, the grown-up partner. When Darin announced that they were coming close to an island where the monsters live, Jill replied, "OK, you keep watching the controls." Almost immediately Darin exclaimed, "Oh, oh, we're out of gas." Without delay Jill said, "Good, keep going." Darin, who was the only person involved in this play theme, then declared, "Good, what do you mean good?" Many children at play could ask Darin's question of their distracted parent partners who substitute praise for involvement, and use praise as an excuse for not investing attention or time.

People who become dependent upon praise must look outside themselves for confidence, so they remain incapable of judging their own behavior. The need for undue praise happens most often in families where the adults impose inappropriate expectations. If praise is used inappropriately as a substitute for engagement (or when a child isn't ready to learn a skill), the unintended result may be that the child becomes overreliant on praise to persevere. When our son, Paris, was in the second grade he asked me: "Dad, how come I was good at football right away?" I told him it was because we started to play catch when he was 6 instead of 4. He was incompetent at age 4 and would have required frequent praise to remain involved with football. To support a favorable self-concept without incurring the high cost of dependence on continual praise, it is important to emphasize the main motive and strength of preschoolers. That strength is imagination, and it is always expressed through play. Watch children play, and you will confirm they do not praise each another. Praise discourages independence in favor of constant feedback, something that cannot be attained when people become involved with long-term and difficult tasks.

How Can I Encourage Creative Abilities in My Children?

Research has shown that the single most important factor that distinguishes creative children from less creative peers is family support for imagination. Play is the method most children prefer to express their imaginations. So I urge parents to watch children play. That boys and girls want adults to observe them is clear from their near constant appeal to "see me, look at this, watch how I do it." By watching a child pretend, you are able to communicate approval of this activity and acceptance of creativity. In this environment, boys and girls realize they do not have to change what they are doing in order to get your attention. They must feel that creative play is worthwhile for you to bother watching before they can conclude that the ability to pretend is important enough to retain. More of us must learn to value the qualities we want children to keep beyond childhood.

Parents are quickly distracted when they watch a 4-year-old play. Is it because we do not know what to look for, what to find pleasing, how to identify success, what to say about a form of play that has no rules, no hits, no runs, and so cannot be scored? Why was it that my wife Shirley and I could invite friends to see our 10-year-old son Steve participate in a hockey game, but if we asked them to stop by and watch our 4-year-old play, they declined and asked, "Why? Does he have a special trick?" Whatever prevents us from becoming regular observers of little children pretending should be revised if we seek to nurture creative thinking.

It is one thing to lack the power to pretend and quite another to reject that power in someone else. This has been made clear from our many observations of 4- and 5-year-olds during play with their parents. When Greg wanted to drive his toy truck to Africa and join a safari, his father did not react with enthusiasm. Instead, he dismissed the venture by reminding Greg that Africa is across the ocean and trucks cannot travel by water except when they are put on boats.

A similar discounting of imagination is likely to occur when children identify relationships between toys that adults do not recognize. Steven did not feel that his account of what was happening had to be plausible. But his explanation that a man in a crash between two toy trucks was not hurt because he was wearing a brick coat was immediately dismissed by the parent, who insisted on using this occasion to point out the value of seat belts.

A parent's preference for realism and unwillingness to accept divergent thinking combine in Maria's case. Her mother felt compelled to remove the policeman from a group of cowboys because "He doesn't fit." Maria saw the matter quite differently and kept the officer in the group. She pointed out that because the fort was already surrounded by Native Americans, the cowboys needed all the help they could get and should not turn against this person just because he dressed differently than the rest of them by wearing a blue suit. Encourage creativity by resisting criticism of ideas and discouraging words or phrases.

Am I Willing to Set Aside Time for Play?

Some parents seem unable to schedule play. Grandparents often recognize the continual state of fatigue of their sons and daughters and are concerned about it. Parents come home tired or late and excuse themselves from play until "some other time." But a child's need for play is not a Saturday or Sunday phenomenon; it is continuous. A better plan is to amend the daily schedule so 10 minutes can be devoted to playing together. Recognize that some unscheduled play may be necessary as well. Occasionally, almost every child will make demands or provide other clues that a bit of extra attention is needed. In such cases, a few minutes of play may help avoid unnecessary frustration. Successful parents share an attitude that the members of their family always come first.

How Worthwhile Am I as a Model for Leisure?

People have greater leisure today compared with past generations: more holidays, longer vacations, and a much longer retirement. Children need to know what adults enjoy doing when they do not have to work. Yet, parents who overschedule themselves and their children indicate, "I'm sacrificing my free time to make extra money so you can have special things." They overlook the fact that sharing moments together is more valuable than the things adults can give to children. Certainly, happiness is one of our most elusive goals. When parents provide a model for how to attain satisfaction, children are the immediate beneficiaries. But, if we refuse to pursue pleasure in the presence of our children, we are unable to convey how to find satisfaction or attain happiness. It is possible to provide a good example of how to work hard while failing to present children with a model of how to enjoy life.

Being a model becomes more difficult for parents as children get older. In this connection, our studies show that early adolescents assign parents poor ratings for teaching them to cope with stress. To provide credible advice on stress reduction, parents must be able to demonstrate this capacity in their own lives. One method is to periodically withdraw from daily tasks in order to recover a sense of perspective. It is troubling that the lowest self-rating parents report is their ability to arrange leisure time for themselves. Working mothers suffer from the stress of multiple responsibilities that usually include child supervision, obligations to their husband, satisfying the employer, managing the household, and perhaps caring for aging parents. Such pressures can cause mothers to pass problems on to children by overscheduling them so they lack discretionary time.

Fathers resemble mothers in reporting that their greatest difficulty involves arranging leisure time for themselves. This lack of ability to schedule free time is bound to impact parenting. When fathers are stressed, the time they spend with children is likely to produce more arguments and less mutual satisfaction. Fathers do not accept as much responsibility as mothers do for the care and guidance of adolescents. Therefore, it is improbable that a father can educate teenagers about how to deal with multiple demands on their time when he is unable to set aside periods for self-renewal. Living with too many options, feeling hurried, and sensing a lack of control over events has become an ever-increasing complaint. Fathers and mothers who do not deal with these issues cannot teach their children essential lessons about how to manage time or how to enjoy leisure.

How Important Is It to Spend Time Together?

Successful families are characterized by common strengths, one of which is spending time together. The reason time is crucial is because it impacts all of the other traits of a healthy family. Communication, learning, and emotional support are bound to decline when a family loses control of how it spends time. This is why American parents often express the desire to be with children more than they currently experience. When asked to describe their greatest difficulties in raising children, parents commonly report being too busy and not having enough time (see Strom & Strom, 2009a; 2009b; 2010). Fathers admit to having greater difficulty than mothers. Parents believe child development requires that families spend more time together in an increasingly impersonal world. Our studies confirm that actually spending more time with children is powerful and important.

Working longer hours is usually intended to increase family affluence. But it also makes parents less available. A related consequence is that parents tend to be perpetually tired so they are unable to contribute much during the moments they are with their children. Instead of giving daughters and sons the best moments when they have the greatest energy and insight, these parents offer children the time that is second best, as shown by their admission of fatigue. Other parents rationalize that the periods when they are with children is quality time. However, quality time is any time boys and girls need parents, rather than when parents can fit them into their busy schedules. Most parents need a better sense of balance so that their investment of time is an accurate reflection of their priorities.

Researchers who study parental competence usually emphasize differences in socioeconomic status and formal education. It is assumed that advantages in bringing up children are closely related to these characteristics. In my opinion, this approach is too narrow and in need of revision. Accordingly, the collaborative studies that I conduct involving parents in the United States, China, and Japan include the effects of an additional factor, which can be directly manipulated in ways that more fixed socioeconomic traits cannot. For each of these populations, we have discovered that differences in children's access to parents' time is a much more influential factor than parents' income or education in child and adult perceptions about parent success. Mothers and fathers who invest more time with their children know them better, so they are more able to offer relevant advice than parents devoting less time. In addition, children more often seek advice from parents who make themselves available. Some adults consider an excessive work schedule as a sign of their importance and status. But, when parents are too busy for children, their influence and success are limited to the workplace, and their success as parents and family members may suffer.

In summary, play is the dominant activity of preschoolers, their favorite way of learning. Parents should make an effort to pretend with young children. Some adults regard fantasy practice as an unimportant activity only suitable for children. The fact is that imaginative play can contribute to creativity and positive mental health at every age. We are accustomed to having adult models in most sectors of life but children are the best models for learning how to play. The conclusion for parents can be stated as an admonition: Don't be embarrassed about your inability to play. Be embarrassed about your reluctance to participate and learn. Better yet, get down on your knees—and play.

Resources

Rosenfeld, A., & Wise, N. (2000). *The over-scheduled child: Avoiding the hyper-parenting trap*. New York, NY: St. Martin's Press.

Taylor, M. (2000). *Imaginary companions and the children who create them*. New York, NY: Oxford University Press.

References

Strom, R., & Strom, P. (2009a). *Adolescents in the Internet age*. Charlotte, NC: Information Age Publishing.

Strom, R., & Strom, P. (2009b). *Parent Success Indicator research manual*. Chicago, IL: Scholastic Testing Service.

Strom, R., & Strom, P. (2010). *Parenting young children: Exploring the Internet, television, play, and reading*. Charlotte, NC: Information Age Publishing.

Chapter 9

Growing Up Too Fast —and Gifted

By Sylvia Rimm

ARENTS and educators who recognize gifted children's need for challenge and acceleration too often hear, "Don't push your child" or "What's the hurry?" Schools seem anxious to set limits on academic advancement of gifted children. Parents and educators alike are hesitant about saying "no" to children's requests for social acceleration. Requests to date early, dress in sexually suggestive clothes, attend parties where alcohol is available, or join with friends of dubious reputation may be allowed by adults in the name of fitting in and social success. Ironically, the limits for academic acceleration and the push for social acceleration are rooted in the same parent/educator worry that children won't accept peers who are different.

I surveyed 5,400 students from grades 3 through 8 and met with almost 400 of the children in focus groups. Approximately half of the students were in gifted programs. My goal was to determine the issues and anxieties that were at the forefront of the thinking of middle schoolers. (Keep in mind that many schools define the grade levels for "middle school" quite differently.) Perhaps you won't be surprised to find that popularity ranked highest, tied only with terrorism, as the most frequently selected worry for both regular and gifted program students. There was no significant difference between the two groups in their anxieties related to popularity with either the same or opposite sex friends. Furthermore, students in focus groups reminded me repeatedly that they were feeling pressured to dress with particular labels, not study too hard, be thin, or abandon old friends to be included in the popular crowd. Some told of rejection by best friends or frustrations because parents wouldn't buy the clothes that would permit them to be included, while others complained that the popular students sometimes manipulated teachers. In some schools, the popular students were described as bullies, while at other schools, students viewed them as really nice kids who were very powerful, but with whom they wished to emulate or be friends. The focus groups were certain that their parents couldn't have experienced similar pressures when they were growing up.

Benchmarks for Growing Up Too Fast

Adolescence, the path from childhood to adulthood, is marked by familiar benchmarks, including physical and sexual maturity, pushing of adult limits in the name of independence, and interest in the opposite sex. In the generation of the parents of today's middle schoolers, these turning points tended to begin in seventh-, eighth-, and ninth-grade for most children, or a little earlier or later for some. For today's middle schoolers, physical maturity may begin earlier, and adolescent-like rebellion and interest in and involvement with the opposite sex often begin much earlier.

Answer the brief survey below to recall when you experienced activities that some middle schoolers are experiencing today.

- What grade were you in when you worried about being popular with the opposite sex?
- What grade were you in when you thought your parents didn't understand you?
- What grade were you in when you first started dating?
- What grade were you in when you drank alcohol at parties?
- What grade were you in when you tried drugs?
- What grade were you in when you first saw a sex scene in a magazine, movie, or on TV?
- What grade were you in when you first kissed someone sensually?
- What grade were you in when you first had oral sex?
- What grade were you in when you talked with others about homosexuality?
- What grade were you in when you first had sexual intercourse?

Psychologist Erik Erikson referred to middle childhood as the developmental stage of building competencies and confidence and as a time when children eagerly learned skills from their parents and teachers. If adolescence begins earlier than it previously did, it steals precious time from middle childhood, thus making it much more difficult for parents and teachers to teach children important foundational skills. Figure 9.1 allows you to compare your answers for the brief survey with data and quotations from the students in the study. (Note that throughout this article the data in all figures represent the results from the entire sample. Quotations from students came from the focus groups.) While you undoubtedly recognize that times have changed, the research findings and statements from middle schoolers reveal that today's middle grade students' experiences are more like those you experienced in high school, college, and sometimes not until adulthood.

Similarities and Differences for Regular and Gifted Program Students

Students were asked to check any of a list of 50 characteristics they believed described themselves best. Figure 9.2 includes characteristics that weren't significantly different for the two groups (that is, similar numbers of students from both categories checked those characteristics). Numbers represent the percent of gifted students who described themselves with those terms. Surprisingly, gifted students viewed themselves as athletic, cool, beautiful, popular, and social to the same extent as regular students did. Despite stereotypes to the contrary, the students' responses suggested that there weren't more gifted chatterboxes or more who were bossy, sensitive, or lonely.

Figure 9.3 shows the characteristics that were chosen significantly more frequently by those in gifted programming, except "mean," which was chosen significantly less. Gifted program students chose the characteristics related to ability more than regular students (e.g., smart, gifted, creative, talented), but notice that a significant number of students in gifted programs didn't describe themselves as gifted, and a significant number of students who weren't in programming did check

1. Popularity

By fourth grade, 17.5 % of the children worried a lot about being popular with the opposite sex. Slightly more boys worried more about being popular with girls than girls with boys, which is not developmentally typical.

The popular people are the classifiers. They walk around the school and put scorn on you if they see you as unfit to be talked to. They either insult you or turn up their noses and walk away. (Seventh-grade boy)

2. Parent Understanding

By fifth grade, 20% worried a lot that their parents didn't understand them.

My parents won't listen to me. My dad thinks I should be treated differently just because I'm a kid. I want the same treatment as my parents. He says, "I'm the adult here and I should be treated differently because I'm older." I don't agree. (Fifth-grade boy)

3. Dating

By fifth grade, some students reported dating.

Some girls in my grade have boyfriends. They talk to each other in school and go on dates to movies. Sometimes they go in groups, and sometimes it's one girl and one boy. Some girls had boyfriends in third grade. (Fifth-grade girl)

4. Alcohol

By fifth grade, 6.4% of kids indicated they had drunk beer in the previous year and 13% were worried about peer pressure to drink alcohol. By grades 6–8, 37% indicated they'd used alcohol during the previous year ("PRIDE questionnaire," 2003).

I have a friend who brags that she can chug a Bloody Mary in less than 10 seconds. (Seventh-grade girl)

5. Drugs

By seventh to eighth grade (middle school), 15% indicated they had used illicit drugs, and in fifth grade, 11% were worried about peer pressure to try drugs ("PRIDE questionnaire," 2003).

In my apartments, a couple of kids get high on drugs. I try and stay away from them. They try to get us good kids to buy drugs. (Fifth-grade boy)

Figure 9.1. Matching facts and quotations for *Growing Up Too Fast* survey questions. The data and quotations are from *Growing Up Too Fast* (Rimm, 2005), except where other sources are referenced.

Figure 9.1, continued

6. Sex Scenes

In 2000, the National Center for Missing and Exploited Children reported that 25% of children had unwanted exposure via the Internet to pictures of naked people or people having sex (Finkelhor, Mitchell, & Wolak, 2000).

We knew as much about sex in second grade as our parents knew in middle school. We know everything about sex now because we've seen it all on television and the Internet. (Sixth-grade girl)

7. Kissing

By sixth grade, kids reported seeing kissing around them in school.

Kids play truth or dare on the bus. The boys dare the girls to sit on their laps and play pony so boys can feel girls on their penises. Some kids dared a boy to kiss a girl on the bus, and he kissed her on her you-know-where [breasts] in front of everyone. Those kids got into big trouble. (Sixth-grade girl)

8. Oral Sex

Parents of middle schoolers indicated that by seventh and eighth grade, there were rainbow or oral sex parties. Kids say it isn't "real sex" and believe it's safer than sexual intercourse.

9. Homosexuality

"Gay" is used as the worst insult or bullying word. Homosexuality is not part of the curriculum in most middle schools today. School boards avoid the controversy.

Robert called me gay because I wouldn't tell him who I liked. So I just finally told him I liked the hottest girl in our class, and then he stopped calling me gay. (Seventh-grade boy)

10. Sexual Intercourse

Child Trends Research Group found that 16% of girls and 20% of boys reported having sexual intercourse by age 14 (8th grade; Painter, 2002).

We all like girls. We learn about everything from the movies and try out the sex we see. (Fifth-grade boy)

Characteristic	%
Kind	62
Athletic	62
Funny	62
Cool	47
Risk Taker	41
Very Social	41
Chatterbox	37
Sweet	36
Popular	32
Good Little Girl or Boy	32
Beautiful	27
Sensitive	26
Secure	22
Modest	22
Shy	20
Quiet	19
Fashion Leader	15
Troublemaker	13
Bossy	11
Lonely	6

Figure 9.2. How similar are gifted program students? Characteristics selected by gifted students to describe themselves that were not significantly different from the selections of regular program students.

these high-ability categories. Other differences between gifted program and regular students were in expected directions, but weren't nearly as different as is often assumed by parents and teachers.

Most of the gifted program students expressed worries similar to the regular students (see Figure 9.4). This should alert parents to being sensitive to the social pressures their children may be experiencing. Gifted program students aren't exempt from worries about popularity, the right clothes, or being overweight. Neither do they show differences

Characteristics	Students in the Gifted Program %	Students in the Regular Program %
Smart	77	59
Gifted	71	38
Creative	68	59
Talented	66	54
Happy	66	63
Hard Worker	60	54
Confident	52	46
Special	43	34
Independent	42	37
Leader	40	30
Different	40	33
Courageous	34	30
Strong-Willed	32	27
Brainy	29	15
Bookworm	27	18
Emotional	26	22
Adult-Like	26	22
Perfectionistic	22	16
Persistent	22	17
Tomboy	17	14
Self-Critical	15	13
Nerdy	5	2
Mean	2	3

Figure 9.3. How are gifted program students different? Characteristics listed show statistically significant differences between selections made by gifted and regular program students.

Similar Worries	Students Surveyed %
Terrorist attacks on my country	30
Popularity with girls	30
Pressure to have nice clothes	24
Popularity with boys	23
My parents don't understand me	23
I'm too fat	21
I'm not tall enough	17
I'm not social enough	15
People who bully me	14
Loneliness	13
My teachers don't understand me	13
I have acne or skin problems	12

Figure 9.4. What worries are similar for gifted and regular program students?

related to parenting or teachers not understanding them. Contrary to typical assumptions, they don't worry more about acne than regular program students. Because middle school children are often secretive, they may not confide to parents about the pressures they feel, particularly because almost one quarter of gifted and regular students indicated that they worried a lot about their parents not understanding them.

Figure 9.5 lists those concerns that were less worrisome for gifted than for regular program students. They were somewhat less worried about appearance, confidence, and intelligence. Fewer indicated concerns about peer pressures to try alcohol or drugs. Consider, however, that for those areas where fewer claimed worries, there were still sizeable numbers with concerns. You may remember some similar anxieties when you were in junior high school, but it's likely that your junior high school began in seventh grade and not in fourth or fifth grade where some middle schools and these worries begin today.

Worries	Students in the Gifted Program %	Students in the Regular Program %
I'm not pretty enough	16	19
I'm not confident enough	13	16
I'm not smart enough	12	19
Pressure to try drugs	10	12
Pressure to drink alcohol	9	12

Figure 9.5. What worries are different for gifted students? Differences between gifted and regular program students are statistically significant.

Gifted Program Students' Optimism

There's some good news in the study that shows some real advantages for gifted program students as they look toward the future. Not only were they more likely to expect their education to go beyond a 4-year-degree program (58% compared to 44%), but they also were significantly more likely to believe they would grow up to be happy (56% compared to 51%) and significantly less likely to be afraid about growing up (8% compared to 11%). Priorities for their futures also were different. Gifted program students were more likely to set priorities for happy family lives, making the world a better place, and having creative and challenging jobs and happy personal lives. Regular program students were more likely to set priorities for earning a lot of money, having a good reputation in the community, and becoming famous. These choices support the altruism that's often attributed to gifted children.

How Parents and Teachers Can Help With Students' Worries

The data suggested three factors that may decrease the anxieties that middle school students experience. First, students who viewed themselves as above average in intelligence tended to experience fewer anxieties than those who considered themselves average or below average. There also were some differences between the above-average intelligence groups. Those who described themselves as far above average were worried about being bullied, being lonely, not being pretty enough, and not having enough self-confidence. More also were worried about teachers, parents, and friends not understanding them. However, compared to students who believed they had average or below-average intelligence, fewer indicated worries. So of the five categories of intelligence students could choose, those who chose somewhat above average indicated having the fewest anxieties.

The second factor that reduced student social worries was above-average family relationships. (Students rated their family relationships on a one-to-five scale. I characterized scores of 4 or 5 as "above average," 3 as "average," and 1 or 2 as "below average.") Throughout the study, above-average family relationships seemed to improve almost all issues for middle school students. A surprising third finding was that fewer children experienced anxieties if they rated their self-confidence as average, compared to those who rated their confidence as either above or below average. That finding seems counterintuitive, but perhaps if children had a great deal of confidence in themselves, they felt more pressures to maintain their high social status, while if they believed they were above average in intelligence, they could rationalize popularity and the right clothes as not as important as their intelligence.

These findings should provide some guidance and comfort to parents of gifted students. Maintaining close family relationships through supportive and fun activities and encouraging your children to feel intelligent, but not necessarily brilliant, can go a long way in helping kids navigate middle school worries. Parents may not need to fret if their children have only reasonable self-confidence and don't consider themselves in the most popular clique, because that social confidence may be less important if feeling intelligent and parent support help them manage their anxieties.

How Parents Can Help Prevent Children's High-Risk Involvements

Children are less likely to get involved in high-risk activities like alcohol, drugs, and promiscuous sexual behaviors if they have above-average grades, above-average family relationships, and plenty of extracurricular school involvement. There are many good reasons to keep kids involved, although many parents may often wish for a little more downtime for both themselves and their children. The problem for today's middle schoolers is that when they're not involved, they're almost magnetically attracted to screens: big screens (movies), middle screens (TV and computers), or little screens (video games and cell phones).

Counting only TV, computers, and video games, the students in this study spent more than four times as much time watching screens each day as doing homework. Furthermore, when they spent more time on the screen, they were involved in fewer activities. Students who described themselves as having above-average intelligence and above-average family relationships also indicated spending less time on all screens, but particularly on TV and video games. They also were less likely to get involved in high-risk activities than those who described their intelligence as average or below average or who had average or below-average family relationships (see Figures 9.6 and 9.7). There's a great deal of evidence that supports the conventional wisdom that keeping kids busy helps keep them out of trouble.

Parenting With Foresight

Middle schoolers are self-absorbed with their daily lives and what's happening to them now. They rarely think about how their behaviors can affect their futures because the future seems very distant to them. They make decisions based on consequences that will occur in the next hours, days, or weeks, but they usually don't consider repercussions that could affect them in upcoming years. Living in a way that enhances

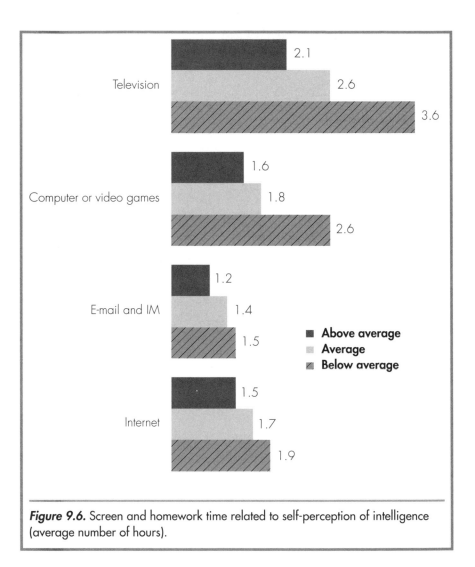

Figure 9.6. Screen and homework time related to self-perception of intelligence (average number of hours).

their long-term health, their higher education, and the preservation of our society seems irrelevant to most middle schoolers.

On the other hand, through their life experiences, parents and educators have the gift of foresight that permits them to guide children toward positive and healthy futures. Confidence in your ability to inspire children is essential for encouraging them to think intelligently, to believe in themselves, to consider others, and to be inspired

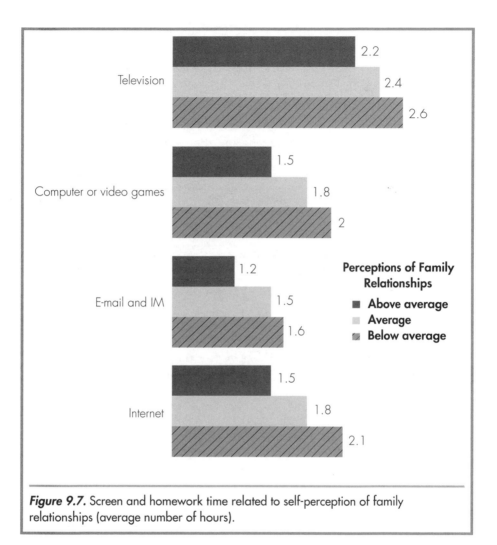

Figure 9.7. Screen and homework time related to self-perception of family relationships (average number of hours).

to make the world a better place. Your guidance will help keep them from getting sidetracked by negative peers, high-risk behaviors, or the temptations of immediate gratification. No matter how they cry out in anger at you, you will at times have to disappoint them for the sake of long-range goals. Despite how much you love them and want them to approve of you, you need to set reasonable limits and actually say no to their requests from time to time, even when they claim that you're too strict or blame you for their worries about popularity.

Although the timing of adolescent development appears to have changed, the basic principles of parenting have remained the same. Allow your gifted children to experience the joys of childhood by challenging them academically, but not pushing them socially to adulthood too soon. By parenting in a moderate and balanced way and providing your children with both love and limits, they'll internalize your wise values as they move into their teens and then adulthood.

References

Finkelhor, D., Mitchell, K. J., & Wolak, J. (2000). *Online victimization: A report on the nation's youth.* Alexandria, VA: National Center For Missing and Exploited Children.

Painter, K. (2002, March 15). The sexual revolution hits junior high. *USA Today*, p. A. 01.

PRIDE questionnaire report for grades 6 thru 12. (2003). Bowling Green, KY: PRIDE Surveys.

Rimm, S. (2005). *Growing up too fast: The Rimm report on the secret world of America's middle schoolers.* New York, NY: Rodale.

Chapter 10

Creating Successful Middle School Partnerships: A Parent's Perspective

by Rebecca Robbins

I HAVE yet to meet a parent who didn't fret a little about sending his or her child to middle school. While students look forward to more independence, more class choices, and more afterschool activities, parents worry about academic challenge, social pressures, and school safety. As a parent of a child entering middle school, I held preconceived notions and myths about large classes and cookie cutter learning at the middle school level, and I wondered whether my daughter would have opportunities to maximize her academic potential during the in-between years. I had enjoyed the nurturing environment of the gifted program at her elementary school, and I knew that our high school would be a great learning environment for her in a few years. Now, after almost 2 years as a middle school parent, I can report that the middle years can be great years. In my view, parents can play a critical role in middle school success. By availing ourselves of the resources and partnerships available during the middle years and supporting the educators and administrators who work together to form those partnerships, we become better educational advocates for our children.

The National Middle School Association (NMSA) and the National Association for Gifted Children (NAGC) issued a powerful joint position statement, "Meeting the Needs of High Ability and High

Potential Learners in the Middle Grades" (http://www.nagc.org/index.
aspx?id=400). The NMSA and the NAGC (n.d.) acknowledged that

> [b]uilding a middle school culture that supports equity and
> excellence for each learner requires sustained attention to part-
> nerships among all adults key to the student's development . . .
> [including] partnerships between home and school, specialists
> and generalists, and teachers and administrators. (para. 9)

There are many ways that middle schools can affect such partnerships as
they address the needs and strengths of children during the important
"tween" years.

Many middle schools respond to the need for academic challenge
by engaging in partnerships with the feeder high schools. For example,
joint arrangements for mathematics are quite common in order to meet
the needs of gifted students, which are often beyond typical middle
school offerings. A Virginia parent shared that the middle school allows
its geometry students to walk to the high school, conveniently located
next door. An Indiana middle school provided bus transportation during the first period of the day for advanced math classes at the high
school. At my daughter's school, a distance-learning classroom was
established for students taking second-year algebra in the eighth grade.
Distance learning works particularly well when scheduling doesn't
permit bus travel time or when parents feel their students aren't quite
ready to walk the halls of high school.

Middle schools and high schools also can work out individual
accommodations where appropriate. With appropriate planning and
coordination among principals, counselors, and subject-matter teachers,
it may be possible for gifted students to enroll in high school classes
for part of the day, while attending middle school for the portion of
the day that includes lunch, electives, and afterschool activities. I have
learned from my daughter's experience how important it is to maintain
social connections at her middle school, including being part of sports
teams and music ensembles. As the NMSA and the NAGC (n.d.) have
concluded, middle school educators "need to understand and address
the unique dynamics that high-ability and high-potential young ado-

lescents may experience as they seek to define themselves and their roles among peers" (para. 8). For middle schoolers, balancing social interaction with appropriate academic challenge is often the greatest goal of a successful educational plan.

Independent study is another way to provide academic challenges to middle school students, during the school year or during the summer. Online high school courses are now widely available and work well for self-motivated students. My daughter took Michael Thompson's "Word Within the Word" course through Northwestern University's Center for Talent Development, and she thoroughly enjoyed it. Although these options are not without cost, the offerings are numerous. Middle schools often are willing to allow students to work on independent study courses during the school day, in the library, or at a computer station within the classroom.

Websites of middle schools across the country reveal a variety of enrichment activities that employ partnerships with outside experts, parent-teacher groups, and community volunteers. Science Olympiads, geography and spelling bees, academic "super bowls," and clubs exploring specific interests such as photography, chess, drama, or foreign languages are just some of the many creative ways middle schools are helping middle school students become, in the words of the NMSA/ NAGC (n.d.) statement, "more powerful and productive" (para. 8). Equally important are the opportunities for volunteerism and community service that many middle schools provide.

Becoming active in parent-school organizations and programs is an excellent way for parents to monitor the middle school's pulse, particularly because students at this age often are more focused on their own world than they are in keeping their parents informed of everything that happens at school. Middle schools, in partnership with parent groups and community health organizations, are taking a much more proactive role in addressing sensitive topics such as drugs and teen sexuality. Many provide regular roundtable discussions for parents, as well as safe outlets for students facing the challenges of the teen years.

For parents, keeping abreast of developments nationally as well as locally is important if we are going to be effective advocates for our children. Resources such as the NMSA and NAGC websites, and workshops and conferences hosted by our state gifted education associations are excellent places to begin. Books such as *Genius Denied: How to Stop Wasting our Brightest Young Minds* and *Re-Forming Gifted Education: How Parents and Teachers can Match the Program to the Child*, provide a wealth of information on advocacy and options for innovative delivery of appropriate services for gifted students. Our school district recently performed a self-study of its gifted program, allowing parents, teachers, and administrators to brainstorm and exchange ideas about how to make our program even better.

In sum, I've learned that middle school is not a dark tunnel to be passed through while on the way to a brighter place. Middle school can be its own safe passage to the precollege world of high school, illuminated by a balance of academic challenges and social opportunities. As parents, we can help our schools by suggesting and taking advantage of partnerships among all of the adults that play a role in our students' successes. For me, taking a proactive role in my daughter's educational plan has been the most important gift I could give her during her middle school years.

Resources

Davidson, J., & Davidson, R. (2004). *Genius denied: How to stop wasting our brightest young minds.* New York, NY: Simon & Schuster.

Rogers, K. B. (2002). *Re-forming gifted education: How parents and teachers can match the program to the child.* Scottsdale, AZ: Great Potential Press.

Reference

National Middle School Association, & National Association for Gifted Children. (n.d.). *Meeting the needs of high ability and high potential learners in the middle grades.* Retrieved from http://www.nagc.org/index. aspx?id=400

Chapter 11

College Planning With Gifted Children: Start Early

by Maureen Neihart

areesha's parents worry about financing her college education. They want her to be able to go to the college that best meets her academic and social needs, but they wonder if they are being realistic about her chances for a scholarship. Should they and Mareesha resign themselves to the less expensive state universities and forego applications to more competitive schools? How can they reconcile their hopes and her dreams with the financial realities?

Tim is a gifted high school freshman and is the first in his large family to consider going to college. College planning is new ground for them all. When do they start? How do they start? The school counselors tell Tim not to worry; they'll help him figure it out when he's a junior. They don't seem to have much time for him now, but it's on Tim's mind. He wonders if he's doing the right things to get himself ready. Is there anything he should be doing now? He and his parents have so many questions!

Bobbi is talented in many different ways. She seems to excel at everything. As a seventh grader, she wonders aloud how she will ever narrow down her interests. Her parents wonder if she'll end up playing musical majors in college.

Why It's Important

No matter their interests or backgrounds, all gifted children should begin college planning early—no later than junior high school and as early as fifth grade for some children. Beginning early provides the time some gifted children need to sort out their interests and abilities, as well as the extra time required to prepare and apply for some of the most competitive and rewarding scholarships that are available to motivated students. Research suggests that an early start also helps maintain the high aspirations of gifted students, particularly those who are interested in specialized careers.

Gifted students often think about their future earlier than other students. One eighth-grade girl, eager for college information, put it this way, "No one else I know is interested in this stuff, but I think about it a lot." The best time to teach children is when they demonstrate a readiness and an interest. It is no different with college planning. Many gifted children welcome specific information about college and career planning in junior high, and some are ready for it earlier.

Unfortunately, many school counselors simply do not have the time to begin this early with students, but they can be excellent resources for information and guidance for the family that is willing to take the initiative to follow through.

For All College-Bound Students

There are many ways you can help your child begin early to plan for college. You can make occasional references to "when you're in college . . . " to plant the expectation in your child's mind that he or she will in fact be attending postsecondary school. You can visit college campuses with your kids when you are traveling. You can take a walk or play in a park on campus, take your child to see an interesting event happening on campus, or stop in at the student union to have a soda. You also might visit college-age relatives or neighbors in their dorms. If children have experiences on college campuses, it will be easier for them to imagine themselves as a college student later on. They also will gain firsthand experience that different colleges *feel* very different from one another.

Another way you can help your children prepare now for college admission is to encourage them to maintain a portfolio of activities and accomplishments. Include dates, names of people who supervised or evaluated their work, and a sample of their work when applicable. Keeping a portfolio will make it easier years later to organize and document information for scholarship and college applications.

Sometimes gifted children are keenly interested in specialized career fields for which the course of preparation is not clearly outlined. There are career fields and specialty areas that are so new that there is little printed information available on how to train for them. Extra planning time is needed to determine the steps to take to pursue such career fields.

Jason, for example, has always wanted to create special effects for movies. Special effects creation has been his passion since he was at least 10 years old. He already knows quite a bit about various effects, and inspired by science fiction movies and novels, he has already created quite a few of his own latex creatures. Now in eighth-grade, he knows that in a few months he will be asked to outline his course of study for high school. His elective hours are limited, and like so many talented youngsters, he would like to be able to take everything. But what will best prepare him for a career in film and special effects in particular? This career interest is not something he can look up in the *Dictionary of Occupational Titles*. Should he take art classes? Photography? And what colleges would do the best job of launching such a career? These are questions for which neither Jason's parents nor his teachers or counselors have ready answers.

Jason is wise to be asking these questions while he is still in junior high school. One of Jason's teachers suggests that for guidance he ask a professional in the field. There is no one in this field in his state, but Jason has been subscribing to the trade journals for several years and knows "who's who" at Industrial Light and Magic, one of the leading special effects studios in Hollywood. With some persistence, he is able to contact Craig Reardon, the creator of *E.T.*

Mr. Reardon gives generously of his time and tells Jason that the way the field is changing, he will need a degree in mechanical or electrical engineering. Mr. Reardon advises Jason to forego the art classes in high school and instead take all the math and science courses he can. Though he is surprised with what he learns from Mr. Reardon,

Jason gladly changes his high school course of study and signs up for additional math, science, and computer classes. He now has more of a focus for college. He is looking for schools with engineering programs where he also can study film. Because he started to plan for college early, Jason avoided some mistakes and prepared himself well for college.

Students With Multiple Interests

All gifted children are not like Jason, with a single passion and well-defined career goals. Many talented children have the ability and interest to do a number of different things well. This ability is known as multipotentiality. The multipotential child certainly has advantages in college planning because he or she has more options than the average child. However, multipotentiality also can cause some stresses or conflicts. It can be viewed as both a blessing and a problem because while children may feel they have lots of opportunities, they also may feel torn among their diverse interests. They may need assistance in planning to pursue and integrate more than one career path or to discriminate among several strong interests.

Kaitlyn, for example, has never failed at anything. Everything she tries is a success. First she writes science fiction stories, then she becomes an expert on mythology and begins teaching classes. She loves science, and her mother keeps talking with her about the security, prestige, and economic comforts of a career in medicine. Kaitlyn excels in foreign languages, too, and dreams of a career in the foreign service. During her junior year, she tries out for the school musical and lands the lead. To her surprise and delight, her character steals the show, and the following year she takes second place in the state drama competition. As time rolls around for her to seriously contemplate college applications, she is at a loss about where to begin. What path should she pursue? There isn't one thing she likes a lot more than the others. Her mother is concerned that Kaitlyn will jump from one major to another in college.

To assist Kaitlyn in understanding herself and her interests better, the school counselor suggests that she do some volunteer work in her areas of interest—in other words, that she get some real experience. Kaitlyn arranges to volunteer in the research lab at one of the local hospitals. Medical research is one career field she is interested in; maybe this experience will help her decide. Any experience that allows your child to work alongside professionals in the field of his or her interest will help your child clarify interests, abilities, and goals. Encourage your child to have at least one such experience a year from grades 6 to 12.

In some cases, specialized careers are so competitive that early training is required to increase chances of job entry. Or, a gifted child may have outstanding ability and passion for a specific interest that may require atypical postsecondary training (e.g., professional schools, immediate career entry, training in professional companies). The performing arts are an example.

Alicia, for instance, has been dancing since she was 3. She has won several regional competitions and at age 14 is thinking seriously about a career in dance. Should she take a traditional approach to college and major in dance, or should she audition to join a ballet company? What would be the immediate and long-term implications of each of these choices? By starting to explore her options early, Alicia and her family have time to seek answers to those questions, to weigh her options in light of her talent, desires, and maturity in order to make well-informed decisions. Talking with professional dancers and with the dance instructors at a few colleges helps her decide to audition with a company.

What Parents Can Do

There are other simple steps that parents can take now to help their gifted child begin the college planning process.

- Begin a file about private scholarship sources (i.e., those sponsored by corporations or other organizations).
- Surf the web for funding sources or check out scholarship resource books from the library. Talk positively about your own college experiences if you attended or facilitate these conversations for your child with other adults.

- Communicate that you expect your child to save money toward college. Help your child develop a college savings plan.
- Encourage your child to take high school classes that prepare him or her well for college. A strong college prep transcript will include at least 3 years each of math, science, and foreign language, and 4 years of English. Often, students are also better prepared if they take honors or advanced classes whenever possible. Support your child in taking the most challenging courses, even if it means he or she might not earn an "A." The more challenging classes will prepare your youngster better for college and for the college entrance exams.
- Be sure to include in your record keeping examples and references from you child's extracurricular activities. These outside projects and leadership opportunities reveal much to college admission counselors.

Starting early may be the most important thing for parents to remember about college planning with their gifted children.

Chapter 12

Real Fears of Incoming First-Year College Students: What Parents Can Do

by Mary Kay Shanley and Julia Johnston

COLLEGE acceptance letters in hand, deposit mailed to the final choice, graduation glee, and finally gone is the worry about your college-bound student. *Au contraire.* Your teenager's fears about getting into college are now being replaced with new fears about actually going to college. And, as you know, when teenagers have angst, parents experience angst as well.

Such college-bound fears are common fodder for graduating seniors heading off on the adventure of a lifetime. But like so many other situations in the world of gifted students, their fears may be more intense, deep-seated, and challenging. As a parent, you already know that, but what you may not know is what those new fears are and how you can be supportive.

In interviews with 175 college students throughout the United States for our book, *Survival Secrets of College Students,* young people talked, sometimes painfully, about what they wished they'd known ahead of time and what they would tell a younger sibling going into the first year of college. Their tips, stories, and common-sense directives about fears and how they dealt with them can serve as a blueprint for your child as he or she heads off to college—and as a guide for how you can support your child's transition to independence and adulthood.

Fear #1: What if I Don't Have What it Takes?

So far, your child has been at the top, or near the top, of the heap. Beginning in kindergarten, gifted students often are big fish in a little pond, receiving everything from smiley faces to A's with precious little effort. But now, facing college, they sense they're about to become little fish in a big pond. One parent recalls a presentation for incoming freshmen and their parents at Harvey Mudd College in Claremont, CA. "The students in this freshman class were in the top 4% of their high school graduating class," the speaker said. "But here, only 4% of all our freshmen students will be in that top 4%."

The reality of such math can cause gifted students to wonder about their ability to do well in college. "When I first got here, I thought they all were so much smarter, more hard working," Erin Pirruccello, University of Pennsylvania, Philadelphia, told us. "In calculus class, I thought everyone was getting it and I wasn't. I was scared, but I found out later everyone else was just as clueless."

Like Pirruccello, gifted students do successfully compete academically but first, many must develop study skills, learn to manage their time, and quite simply, get (and stay) organized. As Niki Gangruth, St. Olaf College, Northfield, MN, said, "The difference between high school and college is a big shock. In high school, maybe you'd put in a couple of hours the night before the test and do fine." Gangruth's wake-up call was a D on her first psychology test at St. Olaf.

Bryn Rouse, University of Montana, Missoula, had all five classes on her first day. Afterwards, she cried, fearing she couldn't handle college. "The next day," she said, "I wrote out a weekly calendar for each class and followed it."

So, what's a parent to do?

- Encourage the development of study skills, time management, and organizational skills throughout high school. Students can learn time management skills by joining extracurricular activities—not just any activities but those that demand energy, lots of time, and personal commitment. Encourage your child to consider classes and activities such as debate, mock trial, newspaper, music, theater, or an individual or team sport.

- Suggest taking a hands-on class like woodworking or car repair either at school or through community education or community college. Such classes teach practical problem solving and develop self-sufficiency. After all, how many students can change a car tire, check the oil, or understand the check engine light? These are all skills your child will unpack at college and release you from managing your child's life.
- Even if your child did not participate in extracurricular activities in high school, college offers a whole new world. There are literally hundreds of opportunities through campus organizations, the Greek system, and volunteering through community, college, or religious groups. Encourage trying at least three things early in the first semester.

Fear #2: What if I Can't Find Friends Like Me?

Leaving family and friends for college creates angst for many new freshmen. Going home for a decent meal or seeing old friends may not be an option until Thanksgiving. They now share a postage-stamp-sized room or suite with one or more complete strangers. Then, there are the assorted friends and study partners who form a continuous stream of people through their room. So, for somebody who values alone time to think, sort, plan, or just be, crawling into a shell seems easiest.

Now, add to that the high expectations gifted kids hold for others—another trait of gifted children—and the discouragement felt when new friends don't live up to those expectations. Is it little wonder that worries exist about finding compatible friends?

"What I missed really was that when I was in high school, I knew a lot of people," said Martha Edwards, Marquette University, Milwaukee, WI. "At college, I walked down the street and there were no faces I knew. Even with all those people, I felt lonely."

So, what's a parent to do?

- Share your own college stories—good and bad—and what you learned. We realize from personal experience that communicating with an 18-year-old seems as hopeless as herding cats. But you never know how much of what you say ends up getting serious consideration.

- Encourage participation in college orientation. (See Orientation Fills the Void).
- Send care packages with plenty of goodies to share.
- Discuss the fact that friendships may change throughout the semester. Most college students told us the people they called friends in the beginning turned out, instead, to be acquaintances. Solid friendships seem to develop second semester or even sophomore year, after the first blush of college wears off. As Angela Kinney, Saint Louis University, St. Louis, MO, succinctly noted: "Your roommate doesn't always end up being your bridesmaid."

Fear #3: Do I Have to Party Hard?

In this new environment, some incoming students eschew the party-central life entirely; some dabble; some consider it a chance to finally fit in. Gifted children are no exception. Possessing great intellectual capacity doesn't necessarily equate with any more wisdom and maturity than the youngster three doors down in the residence hall.

Gifted children experience asynchronous development, meaning that unlike other children, gifted children's intellectual, physical, and emotional development do not progress at the same rate. Instead, gifted children's intellectual development may be ahead of their physical and emotional development—and those last two components are not necessarily in sync with one another.

In layperson terms, their intelligence is advanced but social skills lag behind. Family and friends understood and accepted this difference in development. This new environment may not be so accepting or understanding.

However, peer pressure to party may be overrated. Zack Barr was afraid everyone at Brandeis University, Waltham, MA, would be partying, drinking, and staying up late and he'd be sitting alone in the dorm on Friday and Saturday nights. "But it's a lot tamer than I had anticipated," Barr said. "All of a sudden, I see other people also there,

Orientation Fills the Void

Our students described orientation from "summer camp on steroids" to "way too many people to meet at 30-second intervals." Their orientation reviews were mixed. But they did agree that orientation is a way to meet people who are equally lost or unsure, so just go.

During orientation, your child will be urged to get involved in a smorgasbord of extracurricular activities. That is, perhaps, the best way to seek out other high-ability students with complementary values and to build a niche in a smaller community. Elizabeth Joyce, Stanford University, Palo Alto, CA, says you learn which activities are right for you by trial and error: "[The activity you choose] may be related to your discipline or future career, or connected with you culturally or religiously." Allison McAndrew, Williams College, Williamstown, MA, told us she wished she would have "made a stronger attempt to join more clubs and meet more people rather than hanging out solely with the people I lived with first semester."

Jason Kaplan, Colgate University, Hamilton, NY, found his niche in sports. "After I played almost every intramural sport offered," he said, "I realized I couldn't have managed being away from all those friends." For Molly Egan, it was going Greek. She didn't know anyone at the University of Tennessee, Knoxville, and believes orientation was "a great way to meet people day one of my college experience. In a nutshell, sorority life is a family for me at college."

Students readily acknowledged that some activities they tried were not what they expected. One student was amazed that in women's rugby they actually tackled each other. She lasted 3 days before finding something else with less bruising and people with whom she had more in common.

and we hang out. Maybe I found the right group of people who also aren't into partying."

Our students advised that whenever someone feels pressure from his or her social group, it may be time to look for a different group. One student says she wandered into the social room of her church and found the room packed with other students interested in almost everything—except partying hard. She started to like college a whole lot better with this new community.

So, what's a parent to do?

- Discuss ways to be safe on campus rather than condemn parties altogether. For example, our students suggest: Never go to parties alone. Have a designated nondrinker friend keep an eagle-eye on your group.

- Encourage carrying important numbers such as campus security with you or programming them into your phone. Students are given resource numbers at orientation for help with everything.
- Talk about the Residence Assistant (RA) system. For residence hall issues—whether it's parties brought back to the dorm room or a roommate's sleepover partners that infringe on privacy and room access—there is an RA. (If that fails, go higher up the administrative chain.) RAs told us they wish students would talk to them at the beginning of the first semester, before issues have time to fester. Further, the RAs say students should know that they do not have to do anything that feels counter to their instincts.

Ideally, new students figure out that they and their lifestyle are just fine. It is not unusual for a student to grow and change during college in terms of personality and interests. Be supportive as your child tries on different clothes, literally and figuratively, in college. The students interviewed emphasized that who a student was in high school isn't who he or she must be in college. That's good news for high achievers who may well have spent grade school, middle, and high school trying to fit in.

"You get to re-invent yourself in college," says Alix Lifka-Reselman, Brandeis University, Waltham, MA. "In high school I did things I didn't want to do, and that carried over to first semester of college. I made bad choices. I decided to change. I'm trying new things, like rugby and getting back into photography. I'm finding the nerdy Alix, finding myself. I have actually reverted to an earlier me. I don't need to change to make friends, so I change to make me happy with myself."

These students' experiences about trying to fit in socially and academically in a new college environment are not necessarily universal. Still, lessons can be learned from their journey to being happy with themselves, which involves both self-analysis and courage. Parents can be supportive of their children in this journey from angst to independence while in college.

Letting Go

One of the hardest points for parents of college-bound students to acknowledge is that their child is a young adult who must now take responsibility for making major decisions about big issues. Parents who continue to be a huge part of their child's college decisions and life have earned the sobriquet of helicopter parents. They may call a professor or dean about a particular grade, stop by weekly to clean their child's room (really—we did not make this up!), or choose a child's classes and schedule. Other parents have been slowly letting go, sensing that college will be the last stop for their child to make some mistakes, recover, and learn—but with a parental safety net available.

Likewise, some students will have difficulty thinking and acting on their own, especially if they've not been given the opportunity to develop and refine those skills growing up. Other students who've increasingly made their own decisions—and sometimes had their world come crashing down as a result—may ask for an opinion. More likely, they'll want to think out loud, which is definitely not the same as asking for an opinion. Sometimes, your child will simply announce the decision after the fact.

These issues include:

- *Handling homesickness.* It's real and just because a student is gifted doesn't mean homesickness won't happen.
- *Choosing a major.* Gifted students often have multipotentialities, which can make choosing just one major tough.
- *Transferring.* It often takes gifted students longer to find their niche, so they may wonder whether they are in the right college.
- *Dropping out.* For some, college is the first time they've been challenged, and when the going gets rough, this becomes an option.

It's hard to stand by and watch. But consider what Austin Hudson, Mississippi State University, Starkville, told us: "The toughest lesson (first year) is learning to be responsible for yourself when your parents aren't there to pick you up when you fall down."

That is, truly, when independent decision making emerges.

PART III

Diversity

by Jennifer L. Jolly

G IFTEDNESS often is viewed one-dimensionally. Lack of thought past the intellectual characteristics this label provides disregards the vast array of diversity that gifted children represent, gifted children often are lumped into one homogeneous category. By acknowledging and understanding the diverse experiences and backgrounds that embody gifted children, parents and educators can provide academic and social-emotional experiences that better meet their needs. This section includes chapters that examine giftedness in terms of race and ethnicity, socioeconomic status, gender, learning disabilities, mental health issues, institutionalized youth, home backgrounds, and life experiences. These three chapters provide parents and educators with ways to address diversity of varied types by providing practical advice and strategies.

In the first chapter, Joan Franklin Smutny reinforces once again that parents provide the example for children to follow in order to respond to people and situations that are different from the norm. Smutny provides the following five guidelines: (a) be a model in word and deed, (b) share your experiences with diversity, (c) nurture acceptance of your children's difference, (d) draw on your children's interests, and (e) involve your children in outreach experiences.

In "Looking for Gifts in All the 'Wrong' Places," Ken McCluskey examines talent development in underachievers, First Nation students, disadvantaged and at-risk youth, special education students, incarcerated youth, and those suffering from mental health issues—students not typically referred or identified for gifted education services. He encourages parents and educators to "reframe our thinking" in order to not deny or delay talent development for this "vulnerable" population.

Jean Peterson's "Parents as Models: Respecting and Embracing Differences," tells the stories of 10 students who at first glance fit the profile of gifted and talented students or "this ostensibly homogenous group," but on further examination represent an array of "diversity within." Peterson challenges parents to consider whether these students would be a welcome friend for their own child and how they react to "differentness." She suggests rather than solely concentrating on what makes us different, we also should identify commonalities that draw us together. Also parents can model self-respect and respect, rather than tolerance, for differentness.

While reading these chapters, these are some questions you may want to keep in mind:

- In what ways do I respond to "differentness"?
- How is my own family/child diverse? And how does giftedness make my child different or similar to his or her peers?
- Is there advice from the authors that I already support or model in my home?
- Are there examples of persons who have overcome obstacles that can encourage my child in the face of adversity?

Chapter 13

Nurturing an Awareness and Acceptance of Diversity in Our Gifted Children

by Joan Franklin Smutny

B ECAUSE of their sensitivity and high potential, gifted children often notice differences in culture, language, religion, ability, and interest at an early age. Awareness of their own difference is probably a contributing factor here, making them more sensitive to those who feel outside the mainstream. A gifted third grader, for example, will tend to empathize with a foreign student whom other students ridicule for her accent, clothing, and manners. A fifth grader in an advanced mathematics class will notice the small percentage of girls in the class and ask if math is a boy's subject. A gifted seventh grader will understand global influences on poverty, such as the policies of the World Trade Organization that discriminate against third-world nations. Because of their awareness of diversity in all its complexity, gifted children need support in navigating ethical questions and understanding issues that their peers may not have to confront at all.

Whether your children are part of the mainstream American culture or are from a minority culture, are facing a learning disability, or struggling with issues related to their gender, you can help create a foundation of respect for and acceptance of diversity. Begin with what your children already understand, sense, and intuit from their living environment, culture, experiences, books, and cultural events. Look at their comments, projects or hobbies, conversations, and their interactions with other children. Examine what television programs they watch, the books they prefer, the music they like, and the interests that expose them to other kinds of people.

> After we moved to the suburbs, I was concerned that my child would lack the exposure that I had as a child to different kinds of people. One day, though, my child's friend made a comment about the fact that there are a lot of Chinese girls in the school, but not Chinese boys. My daughter quipped, "Well, of course, that's because in China they don't want girls as much as boys and so they put them up for adoption. At least they have a chance with their new families here." I never told her this and I was amazed that she grasped the inequity of a system that values boys over girls and was utterly accepting of these Chinese girls. But it also made me realize that I had done nothing to foster this awareness and it made me wish I had.—Mother of third grader

> What surprises me is how kids can intuit things about other people without anyone explaining anything. My son's teacher told me that during a game, my son had drawn a diagram of how the game worked for a child with a verbal learning disability. She said he somehow sensed that a drawing would help this student understand the game better. When I asked my son about it, he said that the child was artistic and could easily build things, and that's how he got an idea about making a diagram to help him.—Mother of fourth grader

> My daughter grew up with two brothers. In our house she and her brothers played with trucks, cars, dolls, and stuffed animals. She grew up loving the outdoors and proudly told me that she planned to become an environmentalist—a word she pronounced perfectly at the age of five. But by second grade, she had started staying at other girls' homes. Trucks and airplanes lost their lure. She played outside, but refrained from bending over to examine different plants or stopping to listen to the birds. I couldn't help feeling that she was picking up other people's ideas about what girls are supposed to be.—Mother of third grader

> I have a teenage boy who's an artist. He wasn't doing well socially and I made the mistake of trying to solve the problem by pushing him into a sport that I was coaching. When he met Gaurav from India, a studious child as quiet and introverted as my son, I didn't

feel great about it because I felt this friendship would only make him even more of an outsider. But since meeting this boy, my child has felt less alone and more comfortable about himself. I was shocked when he asked me if I would mind if he went to a party at Gaurav's house even though he's Indian! I asked him why he would think that and he said, "Because every time I ask you if I can go to his place you get this look that makes me think you don't like him. And since you don't know him, I figured it was because he's Indian." I had to really face up to my own desire for my son to be more like me.—Father of ninth grader

These parents all have concerns about how their children may be affected by bias and intolerance. They wonder if they should introduce the subject to their children and how they should do so. Knowing when to speak and when not to, how much to say and how, depends on your relationship with your children, their unique needs and abilities, and on the situation at hand.

This article presents five guidelines for nurturing an open-minded attitude and respect for diversity in your children.

1. Be a Model in Word and Deed

Gifted children are often highly sensitive to the attitudes of their parents—both spoken and unspoken. Consider your own assumptions about different cultures, the nature of boys and girls, people from different economic backgrounds, those with handicaps or disabilities, artistic or creative people versus science and math people, and so on. Do you anticipate certain characteristics from people based on your experience or the media stereotypes broadcast daily? Do you see ways that you might have inadvertently imparted these to your children?

As you go through your day, watch what you say to your children or in front of them. Remember that they are always listening. Even a casual aside can be interpreted incorrectly and lead to potentially damaging assumptions. If someone in your presence makes an insensitive remark, point out the invalidity of the remark to that person. Your child will see that he should not laugh along with a disparaging comment

My daughter and I were walking into the grocery store when a homeless man wanted some money for food. I said that I would buy something for him, but he just kept asking for money. At that point, I told him about the local shelter that offers free meals for people who need them and then walked into the store. I told my child, who was watching very carefully, that I wanted to help the man but that sometimes people asked for money for the wrong reasons—like buying liquor. Later that day, she asked me how you know when a person who asks for money really needs it and I liked the fact that she had continued to think about the issue.—Father of second grader

My son told me that the class was working on a project with partners and no one picked him. "Is it because I'm Korean?" he asked (he's the only Korean child in the class). I said that it's probably because he's new and no one knows him very well, but inside, I felt my heart break. We moved here from Seattle where my child knew a lot of Korean children. Since that time, I've become more involved in the school and I feel certain that the kids are pretty open-minded. My husband and I have all talked more about our Korean culture and that America is a land of many cultures. This really helped our son. Now, he has made friends with a couple of Caucasian students (science students like himself) and an East Indian student as well.—Mother of fifth grader

about another person's appearance or difficulty. Most gifted children tend to be sensitive to the feelings of others anyway, but they need the example of adults to support their understanding of fairness and justice.

Lead by example. How do you behave around a blind person who's just asked you to help him get across an intersection? What do you do when you and your child go to a Thai grocery store and a child tries to talk to your child in Thai? If you are from a minority culture, do you still embrace your cultural traditions, or do you emphasize adopting American ones? Gifted children observe their parents closely and often draw conclusions about different kinds of people based on what their parents do in different circumstances. In some situations, you will need to talk to your child about something that has just occurred.

2. Share Your Experiences With Diversity

Tell stories to your children about your experiences with other peoples—be they people from other cultures, other religions, and so on. Children—especially gifted children—love hearing life stories from their parents and often remember them into adulthood. Think about your experiences and what they have taught you. How might you impart these to your children? The following are examples I have heard from gifted students in a creative writing class:

- My grandfather is blind and he always tells about how people treat him like he can't do anything. So I never treat blind people like that. Sometimes being super nice to a person with a handicap can be like an insult.—Eighth grader
- My mom told me about how mean people were to her and her sister because they were from Appalachia. Other kids called them "white trash" and put garbage in their desks. She said that they moved to another place that year and then they made friends. No one cared about their accents or the fact that they didn't have the coolest clothes.—Sixth grader
- My dad did some work in Guatemala and his stories of what he saw there were amazing. He told me about the poverty and the culture and how the police treated the Indians. All that really made me see what we have here and also made me want to be nice to other kinds of people. He always says, "Never say we're poor. We live in an apartment, but we're much better off than most Guatemalans." I'll always remember that.—Fourth grader

In sharing with young children, help them to see that it's fine to notice differences between themselves and others. Many of us have had the experience of shrinking in horror as our child makes a loud statement about someone in earshot such as, "Mom, what's wrong with that man with the stick?" Or, "How come those people wear such funny clothes?" Instead of shushing your child and dragging her into a corner (which only confuses her or makes her feel she's done something wrong), be prepared to respond with such explanations as:

- "He has a stick because he can't see very well and the stick stops him from bumping into things." or
- "Yes, their clothes are different; aren't they beautiful? People wear many different kinds of clothes."

3. Nurture Acceptance of Your Children's Differences

An essential part of nurturing acceptance of others is helping your children accept and even enjoy their own differences. Gifted children who feel at peace with their own individuality will be open and accepting of what makes others unique. Consider ways you as a family can encourage acceptance of your children's differences. You can include such areas as:
- family interactions;
- points of view;
- different likes/dislikes;
- preferences in food, music, or clothing; or
- interests and activities.

Families can challenge stereotyped views the children have picked up from the media, school, friends, and each other about what boys or girls are supposed to be, what different races are like, what's cool or not cool, and what hobbies or interests they should pursue.

4. Draw on Your Children's Interests

Use what your children love to do as a catalyst for exploring other cultures, lands, and peoples. Gifted children quickly overcome differences in appearance, language, religion, or culture when they're focusing on their interests. It is not uncommon for high-ability students to feel more kinship with their counterparts in another culture, religion, or language group than peers in their own community. In our Project Program (under the auspices of the Center for Gifted at National-Louis University), students in grades 6 to 10 from both the suburbs and city of

> Our one really tough family rule is that we do not make negative comments about each other or other people. Criticism and intolerance are deadly to self-expression and self-esteem and I think our kids know this. "That's really stupid" or "that'll never work" or "you look weird" don't fly in our house. The home may get chaotic and messy at times with everyone busy at different things, but we at least feel that our kids will emerge as confident people who will be kind towards others and not easily sabotaged. They've also become quick to notice when a sabotage is going on in their own kid society and that's fantastic because this means they're applying what they've learned in our family to the world out there . . .—Father of three

Chicago participate in projects in the sciences, arts, and liberal arts. The race, gender, socioeconomic background, and learning style of the students shrink into the background as the children share their knowledge and experience in laboratories, theater productions, writing projects, and so on. Many of the Caucasian students from the suburbs said that they felt enriched by mixing with young people from other cultures and the urban students were surprised to discover how at home they felt in classes with their more affluent peers.

The focus on a subject or interest area can provide new ways to teach children about diversity. In the case of visual art, for example, the technique of painting can lead to new insight. An art teacher had this to share:

> When I teach my kids about portraits, I show them how to mix a range of skin tones and, in the process, they learn that all skin tones are basically varying shades of brown. I always say to the kids, "We're all just different shades of brown and brown is the combination of all the colors in the rainbow. "The kids accept this without question. As we work on portraits, there's no talk of a black or white or Asian or Mexican person; but only variations of the brown. Mixing paint can be a great way to teach kids about skin tone that breaks out of our society's polarized concept of race.

The arts also give talented children a medium for exploring other creative traditions. They could make a Chinese mask, play a game from Africa, dramatize a story from a Native American civilization, or create a dance to music from Central America. Using your local library, museum, community center, and the Internet, you can easily locate materials that will broaden your child's exposure to other peoples, practices, and worlds. A focus on your children's interests will provide an avenue for them and you to explore a wide range of traditions, ideas, and materials.

5. Involve Your Children in Outreach Experiences

Because their abilities make them more informed and more sensitive to the plight of other people, gifted children frequently have a strong commitment to making the world better. A mother once told me that her 9-year-old daughter surprised her one day when shopping for clothes and said, "Mom, have you noticed most of these clothes say 'Made in China'? We better make sure it's not sweatshops." Her daughter would not rest until her mother inquired about the clothes. When the clerk said she couldn't say for sure, the girl would not let the matter rest. She asked about it later that night and even the next day said, "Mom, I just can't wear this if it's made in a sweatshop."

It's important for gifted children to feel that they can make a difference in the world. One way to give your children more exposure to other peoples—especially those who may be in need, is to get them involved in a service project. Some examples from real families follow:

- Our church had this "family-to-family" program, whereby we could connect with a family in Mississippi in a community where many people had lost their jobs. I jumped at the opportunity because it wasn't about just sending a check. We wrote a letter to the family and they wrote back and sent pictures. My kids loved helping to find the right size shoes and clothes for the children who needed them. After we gathered all of the items we could, we packed up the box and enclosed letters from each of us. This has become a long-term relationship during which time my gifted children have learned so many life lessons and have become the voices of compassion in their own school.

- One of the things that has made a huge difference with my kids is a pen pal. I have a daughter who loves to write and she has a pen pal from India. They are now connected through the Internet and every day after school, she dashes upstairs to find out if Sarita has sent her a message. Because of her connection to Sarita, she has learned so much about India—the customs of her friend's people and political, economic, and social challenges in that country. My daughter has explored the Internet for information she would ordinarily not seek out. It's exciting to see my child becoming a global thinker.

- One of the challenges we have is keeping our children connected to their own culture. My youngest son Tekle knows little of Ethiopia, although he can speak the language. One of the things my husband and I decided that has helped a lot is to involve our family in an Ethiopian association that helps newly settled refugees and immigrants. All three of my kids have enjoyed helping people adjust to this country. We do everything from teaching them how to shop for groceries to helping them with English, organizing games for Ethiopian children, and participating in fund drives. We love seeing our children not only reconnect more with their own culture, but be such active helpers for people who have such a desperate need to be connected to a community.

A Final Note

By their nature, gifted children are open to learning about others. They quickly grasp differences between people and, at the same time, recognize that every person is an individual, unlike any other. As we nurture this understanding and respect for individuality in our children, they will become more at peace with who they are and embrace the unique qualities that make all people different. Such a foundation will go far in helping our children respect and honor what each individual has to contribute in a world shared by so many peoples.

Resources

Books

Cortes, C. E. (2000). *The children are watching: How the media teach about diversity*. New York, NY: Teachers College Press.

Eisenberg, B., Ruthsdotter, M., & National Women's History Project. (1986). *101 wonderful ways to celebrate women's history*. Santa Rosa, CA: National Women's History Project.

Kindersley, B., & Kindersley, A. (1995). *Children just like me: A unique celebration of children around the world*. New York, NY: DK Publishing.

Smutny, J. F. (2003). *Underserved gifted populations: Responding to their needs and abilities*. Cresskill, NJ: Hampton Press.

Products and Websites

Skipping Stones: An International Multicultural Magazine—http://www.skippingstones.org

WeeBee Tunes Travel Adventure Set —http://www.geomatters.com/products/details.asp?ID=235

Chapter 14

Looking for Gifts in All the "Wrong" Places

by Ken W. McCluskey

NFORTUNATELY, strengths and talents are frequently over-looked, ignored, dismissed, or marginalized among young people from several segments of society. While almost every-one today pays lip service to the idea that talent has no racial, cultural, or socioeconomic boundaries, opportunities still are not evenly distributed.

Insofar as in-school enrichment goes, the playing field often has been far from level. The late Dr. E. Paul Torrance observed that the educational system often penalizes children whose values and attitudes differ from those found in the dominant culture. Some researchers have found that African-American, Hispanic, or Navajo students were seldom nominated, yet alone selected, for gifted programs in some school settings and that high-ability Native students seldom had opportunities to hone their talents; indeed, their abilities often have been unnoticed and unappreciated. Reports in the early 1990s suggested that participation by American Indian/Alaska Native students was less than one fourth of that of other student populations.

It may not be possible to change attitudes and reform systems overnight, but by becoming sensitive "talent scouts," parents and educators can make a definite beginning in identifying emerging abilities in children. Grover Young proposed several guidelines for talent spotting, including searching constantly (every day) for special passions and interests, staying alert over an extended period of time, designing open-ended activities that allow hidden abilities to surface, behaving like a detective gathering information and keeping a note pad on hand to record observations.

However, the issue is not just, "How to look for talent effectively?" but "Where to look?" To my mind, the answer is obvious: Everywhere! As W. Somerset Maugham wrote,

> There is no more merit in having read a thousand books than in having ploughed a thousand fields. There is no more merit in being able to attach a correct description to a picture than in being able to find out what is wrong with a stalled car. The stockbroker has . . . knowledge too, and so has the artisan. It is a silly prejudice of [intellectuals . . . that theirs are] the only ones that count.

We must seek out talent among all young people in all areas of human endeavor, with breadth of vision. We would do well to consider education as taking place within an ecosystem of learning. In addition to schools and classrooms, education is influenced by what happens in homes; at computers on the Internet; in community workplaces; in churches, museums, and theaters; on athletic fields; and in correctional facilities, youth homes, and health care centers.

Not All Gifts Come Nicely Wrapped

Our experience in Manitoba has convinced my colleagues and me that talent, albeit often hidden, disguised, or dormant, will surface in unexpected places. As a consequence, we believe it is critical to extend our search well beyond the usual settings to encompass the following (frequently overlapping) populations.

1. Disconnected Underachievers

High-ability individuals don't always show their talents at school, and many end up leaving or being "pushed" from the system. A survey by Statistics Canada some years ago indicated that only 8% of school dropouts in the country mentioned academic problems as their reason for quitting; more than 30% had been maintaining A or B averages before exiting. Obviously, many left who should not have been lost. Dr. Jean Peterson has highlighted in her research how decidedly few enrichment opportunities are offered for one group of potential drop-outs—the "tough bright." In some instances, their life situations make the school curriculum virtually irrelevant.

Lost Prizes, a shared project initiated by three school districts in our province, was designed to "reclaim" at-risk, talented high school dropouts (see the McCluskey, Baker, O'Hagan, & Treffinger, 1995, listing in this chapter's References section for more information). Their talents notwithstanding, the youth in question were producing virtually nothing. At best, they were floating aimlessly; at worst, they had run far afoul of the law. Several had serious substance abuse problems. The intent was to reconnect with these individuals, awake dormant creative potential, and motivate them to do something more productive with their lives.

During the first phase of the program, a facilitator worked directly with the participants in an off-site classroom setting. The classes fea-tured information sessions (on anger management, learning styles, non-verbal communication, and the like), career exploration, and Creative Problem Solving (CPS) training. Using CPS tools, the reengaged stu-dents learned to make reasoned educational, career, and life decisions and considered how to move from their "current reality" to a "desired future state." Individual Growth Plans were mapped out to help identify and work toward goals. In the second phase, students gained experience in the world of work through on-the-job placements. More specifically, they had an opportunity to encounter and resolve some real-life prob-lems with caring, philanthropic mentors in the business community.

Ryan Gauthier has shared his "From Down-and-Out to Up-and-Coming" story in a number of presentations and publications (e.g., his 1999 publication in *Reclaiming Children and Youth: Journal of Emotional and Behavioral Problems*). As a child, he had been nothing but trouble in school. By junior high, he was involved in various criminal activity (assault, robbery, and break-and-enter offenses) to support his drug habit. After spending the greater part of his adolescence in and out of the local youth center (mostly in), Ryan decided to take a different path after his stepfather was killed in an alcohol-related car accident. It wasn't easy. However, Ryan's artistic talents were recognized and celebrated in the Lost Prizes program, and he was one of seven participants invited to present at the National Association for Gifted Children conference in Tampa in 1995. After talking about his life and displaying his art during the session, Ryan was inundated with commissions and requests for his sketches. He summed up the experience and the program by remarking: "This is a bigger high than drugs." Ryan went on to graduate from high school, to gain experience in several responsible jobs, and to produce cover art and illustrations for many books and magazines. During the journey, he "rebonded" with his mother, who provided tons of encouragement and support. Now married with three children, Ryan is currently attending college in pursuit of his new goal: working with at-risk children and youth.

There were many Lost Prizes like Ryan, who—once their talents were identified, appreciated, and nurtured—turned their lives around. To be precise, over the 3-year life of the project, 57 of the 88 participants (64%–77%) responded by returning to high school, entering postsecondary programs at a university or community college, or obtaining employment (two now own their businesses). Not bad for formerly troubled and troubling ne'er-do-wells.

2. Children and Youth Not of the Dominant Culture

As mentioned earlier, schools often find it difficult to meet the needs and develop the talents of children from minority groups. In Canada, we are struggling to address the plight of one group in particular—Native students. However, to do so effectively demands that we take into account their cultural beliefs and values. In contrast to the goals of many in today's dog-eat-dog, look-out-for-number-one world, traditional Native teachings tend to place sharing and generosity above materialistic gain. And in contrast to the oft-used linear approach to pedagogy, such teachings emphasize a holistic, circular style. It is essential that parents and teachers recognize and validate these differences.

The track record with Aboriginal students (First Nations Native, Inuit, and Métis—those of mixed ancestry) in our province has not always been strong. In an attempt to do better, the tridistrict partners embarked upon another venture, Northern Lights, targeting at-risk Aboriginal school dropouts and nonattenders. In most ways, the program mirrored Lost Prizes, with the in-class CPS training and the work placement phases. However, this time around, we found it necessary to add a substantial cultural component, to hire Aboriginal social workers and educational assistants to reach out to participants and their families, and to deal with the incursions of Native youth gang recruiters. Once these variables were addressed, the results were again powerful, with 38 of 58 (65%–52%) of the youth returning to school, being admitted into postsecondary programs, or entering the workforce on a full-time basis.

3. Disadvantaged Young People

The term *at–risk student* became popular soon after America was identified as a "nation at risk" by the National Commission on Excellence in Education. According to many sources, risk factors include being poor, transient, male, of minority group status, and coming from a separated family. However, if I were a Native single parent mother of a 10-year-old son living in poverty in the inner city, I might not think all that highly of this definition. Clearly, for those trapped in unfortunate life circumstances, this view is extremely pessimistic and, since it ignores or masks variations within groups, limiting. Some youngsters from affluent two-parent families are very much at risk. And I know several economically disadvantaged, single Native mothers who have created loving, caring, and supportive homes for their children, where school is deemed critically important, where identification and development of childhood talent is a priority, and where appropriate, socially responsible behaviors are modeled in exemplary fashion. Children from such homes may have challenges to deal with, but they are not necessarily at risk for school or other types of failure.

Dr. Richard Curwin has made the point that it is what parents and children do, not their ethnic background or where they live, that determines the degree of risk. The behavior, rather than the situation, is the key—and behavior can be changed. Perhaps it has been too easy to take a deficit rather than a strength-based approach when dealing with certain kinds of children. We might do well, particularly with hitherto marginalized populations, to consider possibilities rather than problems and talent development rather than remediation.

4. Special Education Students

Some children with special needs become known for their disabilities rather than their abilities. To counteract that tendency, learning disability associations across the continent send out considerable literature about "disabled" students who have made good. Similarly, Dr. Bonnie Cramond—in her intriguing work exploring possible links between ADHD and creativity—has referred to biographical accounts of "problem" individuals who have achieved eminence. Borrowing indiscriminately from this and a variety of other sources, here are some examples: Einstein and Churchill were, to put it politely, far from stellar students; Henry Winkler, along with many other actors, has had to cope with a serious learning disability; Edison's teacher described him as "addled" and incapable of benefiting from school; Samuel Johnson was described as being in "perpetual motion;" and Pope Leo X said that Leonardo da Vinci would "never accomplish anything" because "he thinks of the end before the beginning."

My wife and I have a firsthand illustration. Our daughter Amber, a classic ADHD person if ever there was one, caused us no end of grief during her early years. By the time she reached 9 years old, she had been diagnosed from various quarters as exhibiting "schizophrenic tendencies," "severe learning disability," "functional illiteracy," and eventually "profound ADHD." One principal described her as "the worst child in the school district." Obviously, as parents, we were incredibly worried and depressed. Then something happened that caused us to look at Amber differently.

Discouraged, we decided to drive for a family holiday in Mexico City (where we had some accommodating friends who were always willing to put us up for a couple of weeks). Our hyperactive youngster fit in without much trouble. Amber clearly relished the luxurious environment in which we found ourselves and made friends, quickly and for the first time in her life. Our host summed it up wisely: "You Canadians and Americans. You're robots. This girl is alive! She's like us!" The stay was enjoyable and invigorating. The Sunday prior to our return, all members of both families decided to head out to the market for a souvenir-hunting expedition. Amber, in an uncharacteristically subdued tone, surprised us by asking to stay back—a marked change in routine from someone who always wanted to be out and about. Because Sunday is, by tradition, the maids' day off, only one elderly cook was to remain behind.

This compassionate soul graciously volunteered to babysit, and we acquiesced. Naturally, we should have known something devilish was afoot. Somehow, our 9-year-old had acquired enough Spanish during the brief visit to search through the Mexican telephone directory in our absence, identify a beauty salon, put in an "emergency" call, and make herself understood. Upon our return, we found that Amber had ordered a bevy of beauticians to the home. They were all busily engaged in doing her hair, the works!

After that episode, we set about recognizing—and redirecting—our daughter's talents. And, with time and fine-tuning, the weaknesses have become strengths. Now a successful young adult, Amber is excelling and showing exceptional talent in her work with children. It's helpful that there's not a child born on the face of this Earth who can wear her out. And Amber brings her energy into her own parenting: She is the only mother we've known who would wake the babies up to play!

5. The Institutionalized

There are many examples of talent bursting forth from institutions. Kenneth Donaldson was committed, wrongly, for more than 15 years to a state mental hospital. Insisting all the while that he was sane, he wrote a book during his institutionalization, *Insanity Inside Out*, which helped secure protection for the rights of mental patients. And Janet Frame, the poet and novelist from New Zealand, was diagnosed as schizophrenic, placed in a mental institution, and subjected to many rounds of electroshock "therapy." A scheduled lobotomy was canceled only after her first novel won an international literary award.

Like Ryan Gauthier, many young people with talent—whose paths to legitimate goal attainment are essentially blocked—look instead in unsavory directions. And, as unpalatable as it may be, it takes considerable ability to become a successful criminal or member or leader of a youth gang. Waln K. Brown, himself a former incarcerated delinquent who went on to earn a Ph.D. from an Ivy League university, has examined the cases of several talented and resilient individuals who beat the odds. For example, Warren Rhodes has chronicled his story of dropping out of school, gang involvement, shooting a friend, near death from a drug overdose, and jail time, and then his personal and academic rebirth culminating in a doctorate. His book, *From the Jail House to the White House*, was written after Rosalyn Carter invited him to Washington to speak about his life. Along similar lines, Phil Quinn discussed his odyssey through the child welfare system and foster care in his book *Cry Out* and his life in a motorcycle gang in *Renegade Saint*. And, looking further into the past, Huddie Ledbetter, or Leadbelly, the noted blues musician, did much of his song writing (which included "Good Night Irene" and "Midnight Special") from a jail cell.

My coworkers and I also have some direct experience with Native Canadian inmates incarcerated in Manitoba jails for drug offenses, fraud, breaking and entering, assault, physical or sexual abuse, or even murder (as a juvenile). Truly, it would be difficult to find a population more at risk. In all, 31 prisoners (27 male; 4 female) took part in Second Chance, yet another project featuring Creative Problem Solving, career awareness, and work experience (as part of prerelease training). After these inmates had "done their time," completed the program, and been released into society, they were monitored for a year to see if they would "go straight" or run afoul of the law once more. Members of a matched group of Native offenders—from the same home reservations as our participants—also were monitored over the same period. Individuals in this control group, however, were simply warehoused through the correctional system in the traditional manner and left to fend for themselves upon release. That is, unlike their Second Chance counterparts, they received no prerelease support whatsoever. Recidivism during the follow-up year was 90.32% (28 of 31) for the unsupported control group, but only 38.71% (12 of 31) for our "second chancers." While the distressingly high rate of reoffending in the nontreated group is an indictment of our present judicial and penal systems, the results suggest that promising alternatives—emphasizing a talent development approach—are worthy of serious consideration. Importantly, a progress review of Second Chance participants a decade later showed that the recidivism rate held firm—the former inmates had turned their lives around and kept them turned around.

So Let's Get To It

John Seita is another reclaimed at-risk youth who has gone on to a life of academe, service, and advocacy for the disadvantaged. In their 1996 book, *In Whose Best Interest?*, Seita, Mitchell, and Tobin asserted that at-risk children and youth will be more likely to develop resilience and overcome adversity if they are provided with what he termed CCDO during their formative years. The letters refer to connectedness—children need to belong and be attached to someone or something; continuity— they must have that sense of security over the long term; dignity—for self-efficacy to grow, children need to feel they are important to others; and opportunity—they must have a chance to experience success, build confidence, and recognize and develop their abilities. Far too many disadvantaged, vulnerable young people don't get that chance. The true cost of talent delayed or denied is virtually impossible to discern. What is the cost of a symphony unwritten, a cure not discovered, a breakthrough not invented? In today's complex world, and in preparing for tomorrow's certainly more complex one, we can scarcely afford such waste of talent capital and human potential.

We must, as parents and educators, change attitudes and reframe our thinking. Talent is not the sole province of "teacher pleasers" and other compliant children. Black sheep, annoying nonconformists, the disadvantaged, and children from markedly different cultural backgrounds have much to offer. And without doubt, negatives in childhood can evolve into great positives in later life: it is a small step from stubbornness in early years to determination in adulthood, from off-the-wall behavior to creative thinking, and from unfocused daydreaming to productivity and inventiveness. Let us, therefore, expand our search and give all young people an equal opportunity to have their talents recognized and nurtured.

Resources

McCluskey, K. W., & McCluskey, A. L. A. (2001). *Understanding ADHD: Our personal journey.* Winnipeg, MB: Portage & Main Press.

McCluskey, K. W., & Treffinger, D. J. (1998). Nurturing talented but troubled children and youth. *Reclaiming Children and Youth, 6,* 215–219, 226.

References

Cramond, B. (1995). *The coincidence of attention deficit hyperactivity disorder and creativity.* Storrs: University of Connecticut, The National Research Center on the Gifted and Talented.

Gauthier, R. (1999). From down-and-out to up-and-coming. *Reclaiming Children and Youth: Journal of Emotional and Behavioral Problems, 7,* 197–199.

McCluskey, K. W., Baker, P. A., O'Hagan, S. C., & Treffinger, D. J. (Eds.). (1995). *Lost prizes: Talent development and problem solving with at-risk students.* Sarasota, FL: Center for Creative Learning.

Seita, J., Mitchell, M., & Tobin, C. L. (1996). *In whose best interest? One child's odyssey, a nation's responsibility.* Elizabethtown, PA: Continental Press.

Chapter 15

Parents as Models: Respecting and Embracing Differences

by Jean Sunde Peterson

L ET me first introduce some students I have known. As you read, try to picture them in your mind and consider whether you would welcome them as your child's friend at the grade level indicated or at any other. Consider, too, whether they would have been a good fit in the gifted program in your child's school. These are real students, but their names have been changed.

James was a bright, sensitive second-grader, a significant presence in his classroom. His engaging personality drew his classmates to him, and his teachers were amazed at his capabilities. His parents actively cheered his accomplishments.

Gabriel was a handsome, articulate sixth-grader, who had first been identified as "gifted" in third grade. He actively participated in class discussions, interacted intelligently with his teachers, and tuned in to his classmates.

Sara was elected to the student council in ninth grade, glad for an opportunity to be a leader. Her scores on standardized tests were at the 98th percentile, and she was a serious student. She was tall and attractive.

Tristan, as a sophomore, had already conducted maze-type experiments with his pet rat at home, and he dreamed of becoming a behavioral psychologist. He eagerly invested in Future Problem Solving and appreciated the camaraderie there.

Tina, also a sophomore, had had nothing but A's during her school years. She was attractive, was attentive in class, and was appreciated by her teachers. Her standardized scores on achievement and ability tests were at the 99th percentile. She had a gifted boyfriend.

Mike was a superstar in the theater department of his large high school, having played several leading roles. Not shy, he was well known among his peers, had many friends, and had long been a stalwart in the gifted program.

Tiffany sustained her straight A average as a senior, was active in band and choir, and had participated in a gifted program since her early elementary years. Her parents felt grateful that she had been easy to raise and was so successful in school.

Devon, a senior, was widely regarded as one of the brightest students to have gone through his high school in several years. A gifted musician, he was valued by his orchestra peers, and his team competed well in academic competitions.

Josh, Devon's classmate, wasn't as well known as Devon, partly because he had limited his activities to science, but his instructors were in awe of his brilliance and foresaw a great future for him.

These nine gifted individuals probably fit the stereotype of "gifted kids." Everyone except James, who had not yet experienced them, also scored well on standardized tests, the kind that are commonly used for identification for gifted programs. In addition, all had experienced success in some area of school life. If giftedness translates to good student in your school district, then these individuals appear to fit into that frame. Depending on how much you value talent, school fit, and "being a good kid," you might have no objection if your child claimed any of these individuals, as described, as a good friend. As a group, these nine appear to be quite similar to each other.

This article could now move easily toward a focus on how important it is to find mind-mates for some of these bright children. Or on common stressors in the lives of stereotypical gifted students and how gifted students deserve attention to social, emotional, and general developmental concerns at school. Or on whether ability predicts future success. Or on giftedness across cultural groups, especially as related to identification procedures, since these individuals all came from the dominant culture in the United States. These are certainly topics worth discussing. But that is not my plan here.

Diversity Within

This article will instead explore the diversity within this ostensibly homogenous group. On closer examination, the students described earlier represent considerable diversity. Stereotypes of any group unfortunately ignore important individual differences and miss idiosyncratic strengths, needs, and concerns. Here, I will simply use one familiar stereotype to make a point. Gifted education teachers need to beware of creating program curricula based on inappropriate general assumptions about students to be served. Parents, too, can be cautious as they determine what is "good," "acceptable," and even "gifted" based on faulty assumptions about individual students. Let me continue my introduction of the nine students.

James had cerebral palsy, his speech was difficult to understand, and he required a paraprofessional to assist him with all aspects of his school life and personal care. James laboriously dictated his schoolwork to his "para" (paraprofessional).

Gabriel was on medication for ADHD and carried items with him to fiddle with in classes so that he could contain his hyperactivity. He also had been kidnapped by his father as a child, starved, and kept in a closet for punishment.

Sara's parents had each experienced several marriages, and Sara and her many siblings, products of these marriages, had experienced various blended families. Sara's current family moved often, sometimes because rent was due. The last house they lived in could have been in a blighted urban environment; yet it was in a Midwestern town of less than 20,000. After student council members repeatedly ignored her comments, she dropped out of that activity, discouraged and believing that her lifelong dream of college had been unrealistic.

When a social worker made a home visit after Tristan had missed 2 weeks of school, they found him ill with untreated pneumonia, wrapped in sheets that had not been washed in months, with no food in the refrigerator, and parents unresponsive after crashing from a metham-phetamine high.

Tina had been a victim of incest, one of several victims across generations in her family. Her boyfriend was emotionally and physically abusive. Achievement was the only aspect of her life that she could control. A failed suicide attempt finally brought attention to her pain.

Mike was gay, and, unlike most gay youth, he had been unabash-edly open about his sexual orientation since ninth grade. In spite of being repeatedly bullied and traumatized over several years, he had achieved a level of confidence that allowed him finally to be himself at school. He surrounded himself with outgoing friends and enjoyed his stardom, even though a group of athletes continued to harass him.

Tiffany revealed a serious eating disorder to her gifted education teacher during her senior year and, encouraged to seek help after her discussion group for gifted students, interacted with a speaker on that topic. She said, "I've done everything everyone wanted me to do all my life. I've taken no risks, been on a narrow path that everybody laid out for me. I'm realizing I don't know who I am."

Devon was one of the most significantly underachieving students in his high school, to the consternation of teachers and parents alike. He also suffered from depression.

Josh was a classic "nerd"—painfully shy, unassertive, intense, not athletic, small, and a cartoonist's dream. He helped administrators at his high school set up a new computer system.

What Kind of Diversity Is Represented Here?

These individuals are not meant to represent any particular distribution of categories in the gifted population. Because so many non-stereotypical high-ability students are not identified for programs, and because their ability potentially helps highly capable students mask distress and even disabilities, it is difficult to know what exceptional ability looks like, collectively. In spite of appearing at first glance to be typical gifted students, the students I have introduced here are real examples of bright, highly capable individuals who do not fit usual definitions and are different—beyond the differentness inherent in high ability.

In economic terms, Mike came from an upper middle class family. James, Tiffany, Devon, and Josh were from middle class families. And the families of Gabriel, Sara, Tina, and Tristan had low socioeconomic status—coming from a different culture than the others, one could argue. James had a physical disability, and Gabriel and Tiffany each had a psychological disorder to wrestle with. Five others had experienced severe depression. Gabriel and Tina had been traumatized, and Tristan had suffered severe neglect at home. Four had experienced the divorce of their parents. Mike was gay.

Are these typical gifted kids? They certainly were all good kids. None used illegal drugs, all were respectful of adults, and they were not assigned afterschool detentions. They were thoughtful, insightful, and mature for their age. All had intense interests and were interesting to talk with. All were physically attractive.

Yet most of them also were lonely. Whatever made them *different* interfered with social ease and sometimes with social contact. Most felt uncomfortable in school fairly often. Differentness precluded independent socializing for James, made school an unsafe place for Mike during middle and high school, gave Tina and Tiffany heavy secrets to guard, meant a long period of isolation for Gabriel, kept Tristan from inviting friends to his home, fed Devon's and Sara's depression, and often isolated Josh. At some level, their extra layer of differentness was a problem. In many ways, because they were *different*, these individuals were at risk for poor emotional and educational outcomes. Healthy social and emotional development and comfort are important to thriving during the school years, and these highly able students were particularly challenged. Short- or long-term school success could not be assumed. These kinds of differentness are not usually what come to mind when educators and the media refer to diversity. Yet these differences potentially affect all aspects of a gifted child's life, certainly including social comfort and academic success at school.

Differentness

Why are differences unsettling? Do they vaguely threaten us? Is it simply that "different" children are unfamiliar? Perhaps their presence challenges our assumptions, our values, and even our identity. Then, too, we often do not move beyond first impressions based on a child's behavior or appearance. Differentness may in fact distract us, and we may automatically see it as deficit. We may even steer our children away from children who are different.

When there are differences, it is easy to miss even an individual's giftedness, because it may not be demonstrated in ways teachers are trained to identify. My own research revealed that teachers routinely identify as gifted children those who have good social skills, verbal skills and verbal assertiveness, a strong work ethic, parents with good reputations and involvement in school, and good behavior. Remember that some children, at a certain time in their lives, might not be able to demonstrate their talents and abilities in ways teachers expect to see "gifts" revealed. These might be children with low English proficiency, difficult family circumstances, or social discomfort in school, or children from cultures that do not value "standing out." Classroom teachers, who often are the gatekeepers for programs when they are asked to nominate students who have not been identified through initial screening, may then miss many who should be identified. Not only might they not see a child's abilities, but they also might not value some qualities, prized in a child's culture, that could enrich the classroom more than their presence already does.

I argue that parents also may, intentionally or unwittingly, discourage their children from enriching their lives by seeking out *different* classmates or neighbors. There is much to be learned from those who are different—in addition to learning about them.

Parental Modeling

Parents model many behaviors for their children—a strong work ethic, punctuality, trust, self-care, healthy eating habits, concern for the environment, service to community, frugality, interest in the news, and involvement in a faith community, for instance. Similarly, of course, parents can model self-abuse, isolation, poor coping with stress, poor work habits, antiauthority attitudes, distrust, and dangerous aggressiveness. What about parental modeling regarding diversity? Two parenting behaviors come to mind.

Respect for the Self

When parents see their child as a separate individual, not just as an extension of themselves, the child's process of forging an identity and moving toward a level of autonomy appropriate to a particular culture is likely to be relatively smooth. When control of a child's behavior or future is not a white-knuckle issue, rebellion and defiance are probably not so likely to occur. When adults do not use shame, intimidation, and humiliation to control a child, respect is not translated as fear. When appropriate sexual boundaries are honored, a child is not scarred for a lifetime. When parents do not throw tantrums when their child mirrors characteristics they do not like in themselves, they protect the child's sense of self. When parents remember to listen to their children, they are more likely to learn about the inner life of their unique child, who is, yes, separate from them. In other words, when parents respect the "self" of the child, they send a message that individuals differ from each other, even within families, and that it is good to respect differences including those in school peers who are quite different from them. They also communicate that the eventual goal for adulthood, regarding the family they came from, is separate, but connected—at a level appropriate for cultural norms.

Respect, Not "Tolerance," for Differentness

I have often recoiled at references to "tolerance" for differences, whether in connection with culture and ethnicity, lifestyle, sexual orientation, religious practices, or political persuasions. The implication seems to be that if we can clench our teeth and hold our tongue, we can " put up with" people we do not like. I would like to vote for using terms like respect and affirmation, instead of tolerance, when we speak of differences.

We will probably continue to live in a world where we move too easily into an us-versus-them mode, whether in our school, community, country, or world. It will be increasingly important, given our interconnectedness at each of these levels, for parents to send messages to their children about respecting and valuing differences. Gifted children and gifted families can lead, in this respect, just as they often have done in the past, and help to make the world a better place. Parents can begin to move in this direction even before their children enter elementary school. Rather than setting tight limits on who is worthy of friendship, parents can encourage their children to take a step past the differences of others and get to know peers like the nine introduced earlier, even when their stories are known. Encouraging them to become acquainted with peers who do not fit the "gifted" or "good" stereotypes at first glance, and to stand up for those who are different, also can send the message that respect for differences potentially enriches life. Purposefully exposing our children to diversity and helping them to see other perspectives will help them live and lead in the real world now and in the future. Modeling nonpatronizing respect for diversity in large and small ways, including in casual conversation about differences, can have a powerfully positive effect on a growing child.

Who Is "At Risk"?

I did not include Randall at the outset of this article. What if I had included him in the group I introduced, rounding off the group at 10? He, too, was bright, with good self-presentation and social skills. However, his behavior and his story, if known, might have given some parents pause. After his parents divorced when he was 2, he lived with his mother in another state. At 16, after becoming familiar to the juvenile court system, he was sent to live with his father, who found that trying to impose discipline on his angry son was not easy. There were behavior problems when Randall first arrived at his new school. About his father, he asked, rhetorically, "What right does he have to tell me what to do when he hasn't been in my life?"

Randall became a valued contributor in one of the discussion groups for gifted adolescents that I facilitated. Discreetly and appropriately, he articulated his sadness, anger, regrets, and insights. His gifted peers were edified about life, feelings, and transitions. I learned later that by age 22 he was doing well, by any measure. By affirming his gifts and bringing him into contact with others with similar ability, the gifted program had helped him through "a rough patch." I was grateful that his administrators, father, and teachers had not restricted him from attending the weekly group discussions that he loved during the years he received only "Ds" and "Fs." He needed to be around mind-mates who were not failing developmentally and academically. The other group members benefited in many ways from the presence of this sensitive, articulate, sad, and troubled adolescent.

His group epitomized the diversity within the stereotypes associated with giftedness. The comments of some of the underachievers were the most insightful. I sometimes wondered if some of them, with a poor fit at school, might be future agents of change in society. They thought "outside of the box" and seemed less likely than the achievers to ask for rides in order to avoid error. The verve of Randall's group lay in its diversity and the bonding that occurred because the emphasis was on growing up, not competing. Bravado quickly disappeared. These handsome, social students appreciated having a place to be complex, diverse, human, and real.

Randall was clearly an at-risk child. But we might argue that all gifted kids are somewhat at risk—not just in being different and potentially misunderstood, but also in facing normal developmental challenges and environmental stressors with somewhat unique sensitivities. Maybe all will, at some time, face circumstances that are unexpected, traumatic, or disabling in some way. No parent, no matter how conscientious, can ensure that life will always be good and that loved children will always be protected. Misfortune always reminds us that we are all vulnerable—and interconnected. Through it we join the human race, humbled.

Parents can help their gifted children understand that high ability does not preclude unusual stressors. Giftedness also does not necessarily mean precocious social or emotional development. Every child and adolescent faces developmental challenges. Parents give their children a gift when they convey, instead of deny, that commonality. My experiences with 1,300 group sessions with gifted adolescents convinced me that too many do not get that message. In fact, according to some, parental messages seemed to focus largely on performance, not development. Discovering developmental commonalities with diverse peers, especially in the social and emotional realms, seems inevitably to ease the tension inherent in the competitive school environment. Parents who celebrate those connections model both respect for differences and affirmation of shared human experiences and help their children to function effectively in the larger world in the present and in the future.

Conclusion

That is how I will conclude. The 10 students I introduced earlier, regardless of their cultural homogeneity, were quite diverse. They all needed respect, friendship, and support during their school years. They needed to feel connected to their peers and to their school. They needed to feel valued for who they were at that point in their lives. Fortunately, although at times they felt overwhelmed, they were all resilient. Some had supportive parents, and others had the ability to engage at least one adult advocate. A gifted program was an important support for many of them.

Parents and programs hold a great deal of power, in terms of encouraging or discouraging affirmation of strengths and of *differences*. When both parents and programs can affirm and embrace gifted individuals who are coping with difficult circumstances and give them support for developing their abilities and talents, the ripple effect can be amazing. Even when students do, in fact, fit common stereotypes of gifted, they can benefit when both commonalities and differences are celebrated.

PART IV

Programming Options

by Donald J. Treffinger

THE 11 chapters in this section all deal with programming options—activities or services that are essential for appropriate and challenging learning and development for high-ability students. In today's world, we look beyond a single, *one-size-fits-all* gifted program for all high-ability students. Instead, we recognize that the school, the home, and the community are all partners in nurturing students' gifts and talents. In that partnership, we all share the goals of bringing out the best in children and youth, engaging them in learning that is at once rigorous and supports their interests and passions, and challenging them to aspire to new heights and to work creatively in new directions. This section provides information and resources that will help you as parents to be informed, proactive, and supportive participants in that partnership, not only for your own children, but for others in your community as well.

This collection of chapters span a broad array of topics, from quality programming in the school setting to personalized programming at home or in the community. The topics include acceleration, differentiation, and talent development (often, but not exclusively school-based concerns), creativity (a concern at home and in school), enrichment through afterschool and summer programs, mentoring, and homeschooling.

Stephen T. Schroth analyzes afterschool programs, identifying three important factors that contribute to successful experiences. In each of these areas, he poses two questions that parents can ask when considering programs for their children. He also describes and gives examples of several types of successful programs.

Two chapters examine the nature and benefits of mentoring experiences and programs for high-ability students. Julia Roberts and Tracy Inman provide answers to several fundamental questions: what is mentoring, why do it, who needs to do it, how do you establish a mentoring relationship, and what makes for a successful mentoring relationship. Diane Nash, in "Enter the Mentor," also addresses the nature and benefits of mentoring, considers how to assess your child's chances of being mentored, and explains what mentors and mentees (students working with a mentor) do together. She also describes several successful mentoring programs with quite unique formats and approaches.

James J. Gallagher and Sandra Warren both address the nature of educational acceleration and the factors parents should consider in making an informed decision about acceleration for their children. Gallagher describes several different accelerative approaches and their benefits. He also offers four practical suggestions for parents to follow as advocates for accelerative opportunities for their children. Warren's chapter recognizes that acceleration often is misunderstood by educators and parents, gives clear guidance about its rationale and importance, and shares anecdotes from both parents and students. She identifies a number of potential issues and concerns and offers practical suggestions to guide parents in reaching a wise decision.

Two chapters on homeschooling, one by Lisa Rivero and the second by Vicki Caruana, describe the nature, benefits, and issues relating to parental provision of education for children outside the formal school setting. They describe several potential goals and benefits of homeschooling, including legal and policy concerns, curriculum and assessment challenges and opportunities, and factors to consider in making a decision. Both chapters consider the topic from both personal and professional perspectives and offer practical resources to guide parents in investigating this topic.

Differentiation of instruction and talent development programming are important concerns in many schools and school districts today, and the next three chapters help to clarify these subjects, defining some of the common professional "jargon" and offering insights into the parents' important role in effective programming. Joan Franklin Smutny describes several practical, readily observable ways that differentiation can occur in the classroom setting, focusing specifically on young children, and uses statements from a variety of parents to illustrate the value of those strategies and the ways in which parents can contribute. Joyce VanTassel-Baska describes the importance of differentiation (and the negative consequences of the school's failure to differentiate). She presents 13 features of appropriate curriculum options for high-ability children, emphasizing ways that parents can contribute in each instance. In "The Path From Potential to Productivity," Nancy A. Cook, Carol V. Wittig, and I describe four "levels of service" in an inclusive programming approach. We offer examples of behaviors (both positive and negative) for which parents can be alert and specific suggestions of ways that parents can provide valuable opportunities for children at each of the four levels.

Creativity, a common goal of gifted programming and a concern of growing importance for educators, is the focus of two chapters in this section. Courtney Crim explains the challenges of life with children expressing their creativity at home and in school, gives examples of some behaviors most and least typical of creativity, and offers several strategies and resources supporting creativity at home.

Taken together, the chapters in this section will ask parents to examine a variety of activities, experiences, programs, and resources that will challenge high-ability students to discover, develop, and apply their strengths and talents. As you are reading the chapters in this section, think about how any of them might speak in a personal way to your children's strengths and talents. Do they describe activities or services that your child is now receiving? Do they identify ways of responding to your child's unique characteristics and talents? Would mentoring, accelerative options, or greater emphasis on creativity, as examples, "light up" your child and create a platform for significant growth? These chapters encourage thinking about giftedness and talents in your children in ways that focus on engagement in learning, real-life thinking, problem solving, and productivity. They lead us to think about opportunities and goals that extend beyond doing well on high-stakes tests or building a grade point average and being the first one to know "the right answer" that the teacher wants to hear. If they are not part of the menu of services available to students in your community, how might you become a catalyst for those to emerge in your schools? Or might it be more rewarding and effective for you to consider the possibility of a homeschooling option?

These are not easy questions, and there is no universal set of responses that is appropriate for all high-ability students and their families. Because every case is so distinct, along so many different variables, the most important challenge for you is to learn more about the kinds of conversations you, your children, and the schools in your community should be having together. One of the greatest opportunities (and challenges) for education is to bring students, parents, professionals, and community members together in a dynamic effort to bring out the best in our children. It does not diminish the importance of that opportunity (but I believe it certainly enhances it) to observe that the challenge it holds up for schools, homes, and communities is to be places where we intentionally bring out the best in every learner.

Chapter 16

Selecting Afterschool Programs: A Guide for Parents

by Stephen T. Schroth

N appropriate afterschool program can create magical interactions between a child and learning. Afterschool programs focus on a wide variety of options, with some programs emphasizing academic pursuits, such as advanced mathematics or writing, while others stress development of talent in music, drama, dance, or the visual arts. Regardless of program concentration, students are able to focus upon areas of interest, study subjects that are not part of the school curriculum, or discover ways that best fit their learning profiles. Many students return to the same program year after year, with this loyalty grounded in deep satisfaction with the offerings provided and the opportunities for student growth. Such offerings frequently have been sponsored in whole or in part by public school systems that sought to provide both educational opportunities for students and a safe and controlled environment for children whose parents work.

Unfortunately, recent budgetary problems in many states have reduced funding schools receive. Federal mandates, including No Child Left Behind, have focused attention on struggling students. Increased assessment has disclosed that many struggling students lack even rudimentary literacy skills. Faced with these issues, many school districts have reduced funding for, or eliminated entirely, afterschool programs that focus on enrichment activities. Parents with a gifted child facing such a situation often attempt to augment, or, in some cases, solely provide their child's educational opportunities. Opportunities provided within the home, of course, significantly contribute to a child's progress. Popular offerings for outside-the-home enrichment also are an option. Such options include weekend classes, summer enrichment programs, and specialized instruction in areas of interest. Indeed, such opportunities have multiplied in recent years, offered by a variety of sources at an often-astounding cost. If you're a frantic parent, faced with this cornucopia of alternatives for your high-ability child or children, you may feel immobilized by the array of choices available. What, then, should you do? Enroll the child in the most readily available program? Find the program attached to the most prestigious institution? Take out a second mortgage to pay for it all? Do nothing?

Fortunately, if you are searching for an enriching opportunity for your child, you can greatly expedite the process if you ask a few important questions and look closely at a few key components of the options offered. You might consider each option in light of its rigor, appropriateness, and fascination for your child. Additionally, you will seek an environment that ensures your child's safety and speaks to his or her passions. Those programs with a track record of success, of course, can provide such an environment for a fee. Investigate less-expensive options that exist close to home, too, especially for younger students or older children just beginning to develop a new enthusiasm. Thinking about your child's needs in relation to various programs' relative merits will help clarify your decision-making process. Because each child's needs are unique, this article provides a framework through which to examine the panoply of choices available.

Components of Successful Programs

Many factors influence the development of the whole child, including family, community, friends, and relatives. A child's external activities should thus support, or augment, the programs that he or she experiences during the school day. Programs sometimes use a *one-size-fits-all* approach when generating options for children, which overlook

Table 16.1

Key Questions for Parents to Ask When Looking at Programs

	Questions for Parents
Focus of Program	• What are my child's talents and interests? • Do we want to build upon existing talents or offer exposure to new areas?
Quality of Engagement	• Is my child at a beginning, intermediate, or expert state of development in his or her area of interest or talent? • How advanced are the available courses? What level of supervision is provided? Are there other participants of the same level?
Motivation for Learning	• How much experience has my child had in his or her area of interest or talent? • How much extrinsic motivation does my child need at this time to pursue his or her interest or talent?

each student's unique strengths and needs. Far too many programs offer a slick brochure, a prestigious setting, and little else. Look for programs that pay attention to your child's learning profile (that combination of factors that influence how students learn best, including learning styles, intelligence preferences, culture, and gender). Quality programs have in common an emphasis on:

- program focus,
- quality engagement, and
- motivation for learning.

Each of these should be present in any program for the development of talent. Table 16.1 presents some key questions to consider for each of these areas.

Program Focus

The needs of the whole child are differently defined and can be met by various types of afterschool programs. Although a wide variety of offerings can be deemed afterschool programs, gifted children's parents usually seek opportunities that offer academic enrichment and appeal to special interests as divergent as opera or physics. Programs that allow children to engage in recreational activities or belong to clubs also are popular. Traditionally many afterschool programs have focused on a child's academic needs, which often included providing access to foreign languages, writing courses, poetry, or other classes not offered in school. Developing a child's recreational and cultural needs also has been a popular option. The recreational category includes all activities that are social and fun, such as athletics, but also chess clubs, scouting, dramatic undertakings, and the like. Cultural events include music, art, drama, and dance but can similarly be expanded to include woodwork, fishing, and crafts. All options have something to offer.

When faced with the plethora of options available, many parents are understandably uncertain and even confused regarding how to select an effective and appropriate program for their child. It might be best for you to focus on your reason for searching for such an option in the first place—your child's need for above grade level academic nurturance or the opportunity to explore fields not offered at school. A potential program for gifted students must thus, as part of its mission, develop students' athletic, artistic, or academic talents. Students finding the right program for their needs and talents often are very satisfied. For example, 8-year-old Jason was enrolled in the gifted program at his suburban elementary school. While this meant that he met twice a week with a gifted resource specialist, Jason's parents wanted to develop his interest in music, which was not addressed at his school. Enrolling him at a music conservatory for Saturday lessons meant a 90-mile drive each way, but the joy he showed at playing the violin was well worth it. The program Jason entered clearly stressed the development of musical talent as its mission. At a minimum, prospective programs should emphasize the goals for desired student development and growth in their mission statement, their brochures, and their communications. What to look for next depends largely on the age of the child, as needs change as the student passes from early exposure to middle learning, and finally, to perfection of skills (see Table 16.2).

Table 16.2

Developing Levels of Expertise

	Early Exposure	Middle Learning	Perfection of Skills
Time	Initiation to 2 years	2 to 6 years	6 or more years
Focus	Introduction to field	Progression to proficiency	Expertise at a high level of mastery
Location	Near home (1 to 20 miles)	Regional (20 to 100 miles)	National (anywhere in the country)
Cost	Inexpensive	Moderate	Expensive
Motivation	Extrinsic; positive reinforcement	Self-interest; increased commitment	Intrinsic; self-motivated

Quality Engagement

Any program must have quality adult supervision and leadership to be effective. At an early age, or early in the development of a particular talent, the key role of the mentor, teacher, counselor, or troop leader is to make learning fascinating and worthwhile for the child. The programs that are most useful to children in the early stages of development often are easily accessible, in that such programs are plentiful, inexpensive, and easy to find. Early stage programs often are provided by local schools, museums, or sporting facilities. These programs make learning enjoyable and provide a great deal of positive reinforcement. After several years of progress, the students, their parents, family friends, an expert, or the initial teacher, may suggest that even greater progress might be made with a more specialized program.

This new program is seldom located in the child's neighborhood. The new program frequently is some distance away, has a reputation for developing talent in the field, charges a great deal for lessons, and is selective about the students selected for tutelage. These new programs often have a significant reputation in their field, and are affiliated with orchestras, sporting facilities, or universities. Students are frequently referred by friends or colleagues met during the early stage of development. Marisol, for example, had participated in ice-skating at a local center since the age of 4. When she was 9, her parents were told about a more advanced summer program by her initial coach. The summer program led to her meeting the coach who helped her prepare to compete in the Olympics. While not all students will demonstrate this level of devotion or enjoy this type of success, those who do progress to the final stages of talent development seek a master teacher or coach, usually one recognized as being among the 10 best in the country. These master teachers and coaches have reputations for developing great talent in their chosen fields. Students expend much effort and expense in obtaining an interview or audition with the master teacher. The cost of lessons is even more expensive. When finished with the master teacher, the students themselves are recognized practitioners in the chosen field.

Motivation for Learning

Recognition from others, rewards, and acknowledgment from a larger group of people often are essential during the early stages of talent development. Motivation of this type often assists learners in the early stages to persevere and continue with learning. Status as being a "special student" or "fast learner," actual or perceived, also assists early talent development. As learners move to a more mature stage, increasing commitment to the chosen field is a symbol of this transition. Teachers assist students in setting short- and long-term goals, and initiate the student into the meaning and purpose of the field of study. Students also begin to see how they could become a part of the talent field. As more and more of the students' friends come from the field of interest, students begin to see themselves as athletes (i.e., sprinter or swimmer), artists (i.e., painter or sculptor), or academics (i.e., historian or writer).

Motivation shifts from external to intrinsic. Finally, those pursuing talent at the highest levels become responsible for their own motivation. The students participate in public forums for objective prizes, such as recitals, publication, or rewards. The students, as much as the master teacher, evaluate their own performance and ways of improving preparation and effort. For example, César, a precocious math whiz, went to math camp at age 8 mainly because he liked socializing with the other campers and enjoyed the trophy he received for participating. After several summers of this, Cesár began to identify with the counselors and instructors at the camp, many of these were former campers. Cesár ultimately pursued college-level calculus while still in middle school based upon his love for the subject. Intrinsic motivation thus typically evolves over time and follows a period in which the child is encouraged to participate. Cesár's evolution to an intrinsically motivated mathematician thus came after a period when extrinsic rewards drove his interest.

Program Options

This article focuses on those searching for outlets to develop their children's talent at an early level, which can be expressed as any point from early elementary school through the beginning of high school. The reason for this emphasis is simple; those with children further along in the process have, by virtue of their exposure to the programs, more contact to the next steps necessary. But where to begin? The focus needs to be on programs that focus on the academic, artistic, or athletic development of the student. Additionally, and especially with academic programs, there should be an emphasis on higher order thinking skills, such as application, analysis, synthesis, and evaluation. An emphasis should be placed upon both process and content, so that students develop creative thinking and problem-solving skills while also becoming familiar with subject matter through the projects and activities by which the processes are developed. Places where such development is available include Saturday programs, summer programs, academic competitions, and other local resources.

Saturday Programs

Saturday programs offer the attractive enticement of allowing gifted students the chance to interact and work with others away from the routines and pressures of the regular school setting. Usually taught in the form of seminars, discussion groups, or mini-classes, Saturday programs allow in-depth coverage of one or several topics of intense interest to the student. College professors, graduate students, master teachers, or museum or symphony orchestra members or staff teach such classes. Teachers, both those who work in the regular classroom or in-school gifted programs, often are a good source of information about such programs. Music and art teachers also may know of programs related to their specialties of which others are unaware. Such programs often are advertised in local papers and at community art centers, as well as at the host institutions themselves. Parents will want to investigate the qualifications and experience of the teachers leading the sessions, as well as talk to parents whose children have participated in previous years.

Summer Programs

Summer programs usually constitute two distinct varieties, those sponsored by universities and those that are sponsored by art museums, music conservatories, and other cultural institutions. University sponsored programs often are residential in nature and offer the students an opportunity to explore in depth a subject of interest to them. Many prominent universities, such as Stanford, Johns Hopkins, Northwestern, Purdue, and the University of Virginia offer such programs for gifted students on an annual basis. Many art and music organizations, as well as some universities, also sponsor music, art, and language camps to build individual skills. Examples of such programs include the Interlochen Center for the Arts, the Pueblo Opera Program, the Peabody Institute, and the Tanglewood Music Festival. Although many art and music programs are not specifically geared toward the gifted, the process of self-selection often ensures a high level of bright, motivated students keenly interested in a particular area.

Although ivy-laden quadrangles or sylvan settings may bedazzle students, one special area of concern to many parents will be the level of supervision a particular program offers. In these uncertain times, many parents have legitimate concerns about the safety of their children when away from home, especially if this is the first time. It is essential that parents ascertain the level of security and supervision the program demands. There is a difference between the option of adult-supervised activities and the requirement that students take part. Parents should choose a program that mirrors their own philosophy of parenting.

Academic Competitions

Many students enrich their school experience through involvement in an academic competition. Although school budget cutbacks and testing pressures have threatened many programs, parents often can sponsor such activities as an afterschool endeavor. These activities can be team-oriented or individual in nature. Some options among the many available include the Academic Decathlon, Destination ImagiNation, the Future Problem Solving Program, Mock Court, and Odyssey of the Mind. Academic Decathlon is a high school program that features competitions between teams from different schools. The teams are composed of two A, B, and C students in the 11th and 12th grades. Teams compete against schools of a similar size in areas such as mathematics, physical science, social studies, fine arts, essay writing, and conversation skills. Destination ImagiNation and Odyssey of the Mind also feature competitions between teams, but focus more on building creative thinking, problem solving, self-confidence, and self-image. Divided into three age classifications, roughly mirroring elementary, middle, and high school, Odyssey of the Mind and Destination ImagiNation teams each include seven students, only five of whom compete in formal competitions. Founded by a creativity pioneer, the late E. Paul Torrance, the Future Problem Solving Program seeks to stimulate critical and creative thinking and problem-solving skills and encourages students to develop a vision for the future. Mock Trial is designed for high school students, especially those interested in law or politics or both. Local, regional, and state competitions are held to judge students' performance in each of the four roles of a given case. Such programs build students' oral advocacy presentation and logical reasoning skills.

Conclusion

Parents concerned that their children are not receiving adequate challenge in school have an unprecedented array of choices available to them. If schools provide inadequate services for gifted learners, enrichment services can become a lifeline for certain students. When examining choices, parents should look for those programs that focus on the academic, athletic, or artistic talents of their child. Good programs have certain traits in common. All have a well-defined focus and quality teaching and motivate their students to strive for peak performance. Programs with these qualities allow gifted students to investigate an area of interest and to develop a lifelong love of a field. Gifted students enrolled in such programs have the opportunity to make new friends and expand their horizons in ways that can have a life-changing effect.

Resources

Books and Articles

Bloom, B. S. (1985). Generalizations about talent development. In B. S. Bloom (Ed.), *Developing talent in young people* (pp. 507–549). New York, NY: Ballantine Books.

Bronfenbrenner, U. (1986). Alienation and the four worlds of childhood. *Phi Delta Kappan, 67,* 430–436.

Davis, G. A., & Rimm, S. B. (2003). *Education of the gifted and talented* (5th ed.). Boston, MA: Allyn & Bacon.

Fashola, O. S. (1998). *Review of extended-day and after-school programs and their effectiveness* (Rep. No. 24). Baltimore, MD: Johns Hopkins University, The Center for Research on the Education of Students Placed at Risk.

Subotnik, R. F., Olszewski-Kubilius, P., & Arnold, K. D. (2003). Beyond Bloom: Revisiting environmental factors that enhance or impede talent development. In J. Borland (Ed.), *Rethinking gifted education* (pp. 227–238). New York, NY: Teachers College Press.

VanTassel-Baska, J. L. (Ed.). (2007). *Serving gifted learners beyond the traditional classroom: A guide to alternative programs and services.* Waco, TX: Prufrock Press.

General Websites

Afterschool Alliance —http://www.afterschoolalliance.org
The After-School Corporation—http://www.tascorp.org
Education First —http://www.ef.com
Institute for Educational Advancement—http://www.educationaladvancement.
    org
National Association for Gifted Children—http://www.nagc.org

Websites for Academic and Enrichment Competitions

Odyssey of the Mind—http://www.odysseyofthemind.com
Destination ImagiNation—http://www.idodi.org
United States Academic Decathlon—http://www.usad.org
Future Problem Solving Program International—http://www.fpspi.org
National High School Mock Trial Championship—http://www.nationalmocktrial.
    org

Websites for Arts and Music Organizations

Interlochen Center for the Arts—http://www.interlochen.org
Peabody Institute—http://www.peabody.jhu.edu
Pueblo Opera Program—http://www.santafeopera.org/communityactivities/
    youthprograms/pueblo.aspx
Tanglewood Music Festival—http://www.bso.org/sessionOverload.html

Websites for University Enrichment Programs

The College of William & Mary Center for Gifted Education—http://www.cfge.
    wm.edu
Johns Hopkins University Center for Talented Youth—http://www.cty.jhu.edu
Northwestern University Center for Talent Development—http://www.ctd.
    northwestern.edu/sep
University of Virginia Curry School of Education—http://curry.edschool.virginia.
    edu

Chapter 17

Mentoring and Your Child: Developing a Successful Relationship

by Julia Link Roberts and Tracy Ford Inman

THOUSANDS of years ago when Odysseus set off to fight the Trojans and reclaim the captured Helen, he realized that his young son, Telemachus, would lack guidance during his absence. He called on his trusted friend, Mentor, to guide his son, nurture him, and lead him in the right direction. Telemachus thrived under this mentorship— just as other mentees have done through the ages.

Where would young Luke Skywalker be without the advice of Obi-Wan Kenobi and Yoda? Without the tutelage of his father, what might have happened to baseball great Cal Ripken, Jr.? And without Cal's guidance where would Alex Rodriguez be? (Probably not one of the highest paid baseball players!) Consider Rachmaninoff's music minus the influence of Tchaikovsky or Carl Jung's work without his mentor Sigmund Freud. From T.S. Eliot's reliance upon Ezra Pound to Ralph Ellison's guidance from Richard Wright, mentorships have proved life changing.

As the caregiver of a gifted and talented child (perhaps the next Rachmaninoff or Eliot), you well know the challenges facing these young people. For many of these children, a mentor may be the ideal answer to these challenges.

Consider the results when your precocious daughter with an interest in science is teamed with a research biologist. Imagine the impact of a relationship between your aspiring young writer and a published author. What might transpire when your curious son who has a passion for languages pairs up with a linguist or a naturalized citizen who speaks several languages? The possibilities are endless.

If you feel that your child would be a strong candidate as a mentee, it isn't necessary to wait for his or her school to initiate the relationship. After all, you know your child best— you know his or her passions, needs, and talents. Although a school's involvement strengthens the endeavor, school involvement isn't necessary. However, before you establish this relationship, take the following ideas into consideration.

What Is Mentoring?

Mentoring is a one-on-one relationship between a young person and someone who is an expert in a field or has passion and knowledge in a particular area. These shared passions (such as aviation or insects), common academic interests (from geometry to French), or career interests form the basis of the relationship. This relationship differs from the typical teacher-student relationships. Mentors and mentees work as partners or cohorts as they explore their passion, interest, or career. This exploration can be accomplished face-to-face, over the phone, through mail, or via e-mail. Many combinations work.

Dr. Homer White of Georgetown College in Kentucky has mentored Thomas Johnston, a homeschooled high school student from Stamping Ground, KY, for 3 years. He views mentorships this way:

> Gifted children have this consuming interest in certain ideas, but their peers aren't ready to take a similar interest in those ideas. Many adults in their lives (parents and teachers) might be able to take such an interest, but frequently they are taken up with relating to the child as a child: that is, these adults are primarily concerned with the child's moral or social development, worrying whether he or she will be well-adjusted or will turn out all right. Gifted kids want and need contact with people who are interested in their ideas for their own sake. Without it, they experience a unique—and very acute—kind of loneliness.

Mentoring, then, is a rare relationship, one different from other relationships in the child's life.

Why Do It?

The benefits to both the mentor and mentee can be tremendous. These benefits extend beyond the cognitive realm into the emotional and social realms as well.

Benefits for the mentee include the following:
- real-world applications of passion or interest;
- self-confidence;
- expanded possibilities for learning;
- increased knowledge base;
- continuous progress;
- deepening enthusiasm for a subject;
- extension or enrichment of the curriculum;
- career direction;
- gaining a role model; and
- growth in an area of giftedness (e.g., academic, leadership, creativity, visual arts, performing arts).

Benefits for the mentor include the following:
- joy in sharing a passion or interest,
- perpetuation of interest and knowledge in passion area or career field,
- personal satisfaction of helping others and bettering lives,
- renewed enthusiasm for a subject,
- talent created or developed,
- friendship,
- sense of commitment to community and young people, and
- pleasure of knowing and working with a young person on a personal or one-to-one basis.

Dr. Karen Powell of Western Kentucky University's Community College mentored Bowling Green, KY, middle schooler Ashlee Shaw in a science experiment. Dr. Powell believes the benefits for Ashlee were numerous, "She learned how to apply the scientific method, diligence, and most of all that science is a blast—and that she possesses the capability to become a scientist if she so desires." Ashlee concurs,

> Since I've been working with Karen, I've worked harder in all my classes to keep good grades. I feel smarter, so when I walk into a class I want to try more. I didn't think it would transfer over, but it's helped me a lot in other classes—especially math.

As a mentor, Dr. Powell explains the benefits for her, "I had the privilege to be a part of the metamorphosis. I watched Ashley go from being inexperienced and unsure to confident and self-fulfilled. Plus I had a lot of fun!" The benefits are indeed many—and may be unexpected.

Who Needs to Do It?

Mentorships are appropriate for all ages but are especially effective in later elementary years, middle school, and high school. Mentees must be ready for this type of relationship. If they are independent learners, are diligent workers, and have a strong grasp of subject matter coupled with an earnest desire for mentoring, then the mentoring relationship should be successful. Mentors, too, must demonstrate readiness. Mentors must possess expertise in the area to be explored. "The thing to avoid in mentoring," cautions Dr. White, "is the urge to influence the youngster to follow all the paths that you would like to have taken but didn't or couldn't take, but be willing instead to follow along with his or her interests as they develop."

How Do You Establish a Mentoring Relationship?

There is no one right way to establish mentoring. Parents, schools, children, and even mentors themselves can initiate a mentoring relationship. In Thomas Johnston's case, Dr. White was a family friend who discovered that Thomas wanted to learn Latin. This professor of mathematics encouraged the mentoring relationship (after 2 years of Latin, they've moved on to Geometry). In Ashlee Shaw's case, her middle school science teacher, Ms. Ronnie Shuffitt, realized that Ashlee needed an outside influence. She paired the two together, quite successfully.

Before matching a mentor with your child, realize that just because someone is a skilled architect doesn't necessarily mean that he or she will be a skilled mentor. A desire to mentor and the ability to establish a nurturing relationship must be present. Becoming a mentor is a major commitment.

To find a mentor, take into account your child's gifts and talents. Then, find experts in that area. For example, if your son is a budding musician, check with your local or state arts council. If your daughter is considering becoming a neurosurgeon, talk with someone at the American Medical Association. Other places to check include your child's school, universities (don't limit yourself to your local college; with e-mail anything is possible), family, friends, professional associations, and even the web (just plug in mentoring in your search engine and you'll be amazed).

Some additional possibilities for locating a mentor include:

- a statewide chapter of a national organization that addresses a student's interest;
- local or state historical societies, museums, parks (docents and other volunteers or professionals who love their topics may be willing to mentor);
- organizations whose membership includes people with a range of professional experience, including local service organizations (e.g., Elks, Kiwanis, Rotary), religious groups, or chambers of commerce;
- the local senior center as retirees with expertise in your child's area of interest could make excellent mentors; and
- the local newspaper, which should list meeting times of local or regional "clubs" organized around an interest area (e.g., ornithology, automobile clubs, antiques clubs, aviation), providing a way to meet amateurs or professionals with those interests.

Seek out as many avenues as possible to find the best match for your child. You will want to check the credentials of a possible mentor, of course, especially when you are using the Internet. Speak with or meet the prospective mentor. If the person has been a mentor for other students, you might find it valuable to speak with them or their parents. As in any relationship outside school, safety and security can be important to consider. The person initiating the relationship must feel confident that the child will be safe in the presence of the mentor. Many school systems perform criminal checks; parents must be just as certain. Be certain to know where and when any person-to-person meetings will take place.

In order for the pairing to be successful, the mentee must have a voice in the relationship. It must be a comfortable match not only in the topic to be studied but in personality as well. Eighth grader Ashlee elaborates: "Karen actually listened to what I had to say. She talked to me. I could tell she liked me by how she treated me." The rapport established is just as critical as the work accomplished (if not more so).

What Makes the Mentoring Relationship Successful?

Once the right pairing occurs, there are certain guidelines that ensure success. Objectives and goals must be planned as a team. For Ashlee and Dr. Powell, the idea was Ashlee's. Together they structured the experiment following the scientific method and set goals that included everything from securing equipment to dissection to writing the results. For Thomas and Dr. White, the desire to learn Latin was Thomas's, but then he relied on Dr. White to guide the mentoring. Some sort of end product or final goal steers the relationship. An end product could be that the experiment is ready for the international science fair (as in Ashlee's case) or that Thomas learned Latin.

Duration of the mentoring needs to be established. Mentoring can last as long as a project lasts or last a lifetime. Plus, mentoring can occur during any time of the year.

A time structure must govern the communication. Whether contact is made bimonthly, weekly, or daily, a schedule ensures that the communication occurs. For Thomas and Dr. White, the mentoring was set up on a weekly basis. Thomas explains,

> We would meet in Dr. White's office or some other convenient location and go over my work for the week. The rest of the week was largely spent in independent study. Much of the tedious drill and practice aspects of learning a foreign language were done at home, and I could get help with specific problems during our weekly meetings. It worked very well!

The contact for Ashlee and Dr. Powell included many telephone conversations plus scheduled work visits.

The mentoring itself must be honest, respectful, and nurturing. Remember that those benefits reach far beyond the academic goal. For Ashlee, it was life changing:

> A lot of kids my age say they don't need someone to back them up or help out because they want to look 'big and bad.' But you're better off to have a mentor. She's going to be there for you. You're more comfortable and safe. If you fall, she'll catch you. Now I'm more confident in myself. None of my family went to college. I want to go to college. I want to make something of myself. I want to be a doctor—that's science. That's because of Karen.

In spite of the planning and structuring, expect the unexpected—and rejoice in it. For example, Dr. White discovered something unexpected in mentoring Thomas:

> The joy in mentoring is that it doesn't feel at all like real work. Gifted kids learn independently, usually acquire an interest in ideas for their own sake, and are nourished more by the mentor's enthusiasm than by smoothness in the mentor's teaching technique.

And Dr. Powell discovered how rewarding it is "to help someone realize she possessed the ability all along."

Once the who's, what's, when's, how's, and where's are decided, the mentoring relationship takes on a life of its own, and your high-ability child will blossom in many ways. Think of Ashlee's new life goals and self-confidence. Consider Thomas's conquest of Latin and Geometry and his acquisition of a lifelong friend at the same time. Imagine the difference a healthy pairing could make in your child's life. Research shows that mentors can have significant impact: In a 22-year study of 212 young adults, Dr. E. Paul Torrance found that those who worked with mentors completed a greater number of years of education and earned more adult creative achievements than peers who did not have mentors. Mentoring changes lives, both of the mentor and the mentee.

Would young Telemachus have possessed enough skill and cleverness to fight off Penelope's suitors upon his father's return without the years of Mentor's nurturing and guidance? Would Helen Keller have earned honorary degrees and humanitarian awards without her one-on-one lifelong relationship with Anne Sullivan? And what type of philosophical impact would Plato have made without Socrates? Ask yourself, now, how a strong mentoring relationship could affect your child—then take action.

Resources

Whitton, D., & Siegle, D. (Eds.). (1992). *What educators need to know about mentoring* (Practitioners' Guide–A9406). Storrs: University of Connecticut, The National Research Center on the Gifted and Talented.
Mentors Peer Resources. (2001). *The mentor hall of fame.* Retrieved from http://www.mentors.ca/mentorpairs.html

Reference

Torrance, E. P. (1984). *Mentor relationships: How they aid creative achievement, endure, change, and die.* Buffalo, NY: Bearly Limited.

Enter the Mentor

by Diane Nash

You see things and you say "Why?" But I dream things that never were and say "Why not?"—George Bernard Shaw

MAGINE your child . . . eager and engaged about a truly challenging project. Now think of that excited youngster receiving ideas, support, and encouragement from an expert! Consider a scenario where your child confidently and enthusiastically shares meaningful goals with the "right" people—those with power to inspire students to put forth their personal best. Wishful thinking? Not really! This academic year more than 100,000 students of all ages are being mentored by caring adults. Many of these students will enjoy a peak learning experience that can take them beyond classroom learning in many powerful ways.

What's a Mentor Anyway?

A mentor is a role model with considerable knowledge who teaches, counsels, engages, and inspires students with similar interests. Some people distinguish between career mentors (who focus on career issues) and life mentors (who may deal with a variety of issues—personal development, learning projects in advanced content areas, or academic and career issues). Mentoring experiences can be formal, arranged through a deliberate or structured planning process or program, or informal, developing naturally through a more serendipitous process. In either case, mentoring can be a powerful relationship, characterized by mutual caring, which very often results in substantial intellectual pursuits, exceptional creative production, and personal interests and hobbies and career development. Mentors and mentees (the term usually used to refer to the student in a mentoring relationship) both benefit from this unique, rich learning experience.

What's So Great About Mentors?

What's so great about having a mentor you might ask. Plenty! Obviously there is the academic advantage. Mentors frequently share their unique knowledge and talents, resources that extend beyond the confines of school libraries. They also increase dividends in the personal development and career development columns. Mentorships often foster greater student self-awareness; at times they teach practical career skills. Both the adult and the student in this special relationship mutually benefit as they collaborate in creating a shared vision with a meaningful plan of action. The bottom line here is that quality mentorships are indeed powerful.

How Do I Know If My Child Will Benefit From Having a Mentor?

Mentors can be called upon to help students in several key areas of a young life. For example:
- The development of in-depth academic projects.
- The exploration of strong personal interests and hobbies.
- The examination of career opportunities.

If your child fits any one of these categories, turning to a mentor for assistance might be very appropriate.

What Are My Child's Chances of Being Mentored?

Connecting your child with a mentor may be easier than you think. Parents have at least three promising approaches:

- Research the established mentor programs within your school district and community. An afternoon of telephoning might reveal some real jewels!
- Advocate for the establishment of a mentor program in your school district or community organizations. The National Mentoring Partnership has a wealth of specific information on that topic. This approach would be a gift to both your child and the entire community.
- Work as an independent coordinator for your child and locate a caring expert who would be willing to help your child. Traditional networking can be effective here.

Today a range of established mentor programs exist that key into a variety of student needs. Let's look briefly at two examples of programs that have produced excellent results.

YouthFriends

YouthFriends, whose central office is in Kansas City, MO, is an outstanding mentoring program that has enjoyed almost exponential growth. Its mission is "to connect young people with caring adult volunteers in schools to promote success, encourage healthy behaviors, and build stronger communities."

YouthFriends connects young people, ages 5–18, with caring adult volunteers in schools. As positive role models, YouthFriends volunteers enhance young people's ability to succeed. YouthFriends began in 1995 in six Greater Kansas City area school districts. Since then, it has expanded to more than 80 school districts in the Greater Kansas City area and the states of Kansas and Michigan. This dynamic program, which is a signature partner of the National Mentoring Partnership, is school based and can take place before, during, or after school, depending on the circumstances. Students are connected with adults who share interests, whether it be academic subjects, music, sports, computers, or a special hobby. Helping students with academic projects and offering career advice are natural outcomes. Interested in the migration patterns of monarchs? Farm pond fishing? Creating your own web page? YouthFriends helps students tackle these kinds of issues and many more.

The use of electronic volunteers has been added to the YouthFriends menu. In 2001, for example, one group of students learned about digital career opportunities. For 14 weeks, mentors—many of whom are professional web designers and owners of technology-based companies—taught 75 students how to research specific subjects on the Internet and prepare for a career in technology. As part of the Dot.com Mentors pilot, funded through a grant from the Center for Substance Abuse Prevention (CSAP), students designed and built their own websites.

A recently released outside evaluation of the YouthFriends program indicated that the volunteers reported having a very positive and meaningful impact on young people. More than 85% of the students, volunteers, teachers, and parents described the program as an important and valuable personal learning and growth experience. YouthFriends currently has more than 300 people who have volunteered for more than 5 years. Liz McClure, one of the volunteers, said:

> I'd heard about the program and thought it sounded like a good idea. I was matched with two fourth graders—Bianca and Timberlyn at a nearby elementary school—and we hit it off immediately. It's been an incredible experience watching them grow over the years . . . It's an incredible friendship that I wouldn't give up for the world.

For more information or for a complete listing of participating school districts, visit http://www.youthfriends.org.

International Telementor Program

Today's significant technology headlines are about the profound ways technology is changing our lives. The International Telementor Program (ITP) has capitalized on this point by focusing exclusively on virtual mentors (mentors who make extensive use of electronic communication; also called e-mentors or telementors). Does the ITP work? From its inception in 1995 to 2000, the ITP program matched 9,000 enthusiastic mentors with 9,000 interested students, with record numbers of mentors serving elementary through college age students electronically in the years since. The program already has served elementary, middle school, and college students successfully. Program director David Neils notes that fourth-, fifth-, and sixth-grade students, as a group, are particularly eager to begin exploring the magic of mentoring.

The ITP is based at the Keystone Center in Colorado but facilitates mentoring between adults and students worldwide. Although most students and mentors are based in the United States, more than 16 countries have already participated to date. A physics teacher, Maria Teresa Degrandi from Ivea, Italy commented,

> I heard about the International Telementor Program from a teacher at school, who has U. S. friends. I liked the idea that some students in our school could have a chance to "work" with skillful people with a great passion for science and to share their ideas and cultures. So the adventure started and we are all happy that it did.

An American sixth-grade teacher, Maureen Pajak, concluded,

> I have nothing but positive comments to make about ITP and the wonderful people who volunteer their time to make it work so successfully. My science students are now speaking and debating in scientific terms, and clarifying definitions, discussing additions sent by mentors, devising new experiments to test potential and kinetic energy, and sharing interesting facts gleaned from website information. Not only have I seen an increase in interest and motivation in science, but I have noticed increased attention to spelling, punctuation, and composition.

By e-mailing students two to three times a week, adult mentors in ITP share their experience and expertise, helping students achieve academic excellence in science, math, and communication skills; they also help youngsters think about career choices and future education. David Neils, an ardent champion of virtual mentors, sees the following advantages of ITP virtual mentoring:

- Students develop as they learn to evaluate their own success.
- Mentor enthusiasm is fueled by an electronic menu (which changes every 10 minutes) that allows mentors to select their own student in a matter of minutes after a mentor is requested.
- Matches are project based.
- Students elect to participate; it takes, on average, only 6 ½ minutes to locate a mentor electronically.
- The "24/7" nature of electronic communication increases the number of people who can participate.
- Teacher/supervisors submit project plans.

Neils sees another advantage, which he refers to as indicators of "proactive" learning (initiating one's own learning experiences, not merely waiting to react to assignments or requirements). In order to stimulate independent learning, he identifies three important questions for students to ask themselves:

1. Exactly what is my plan (i.e., To examine how frogs are used to study acid rain in California? To become a national news anchor?)?
2. Have I communicated that plan to the "right" people (i.e., top scientists, top news anchors)?
3. Have I gotten the "right" people to invest in my plan?

When students execute their own plan with confidence, they become proactive learners—and proactive people who contribute to their communities as well.

Neils also is a mentor in the program. This year he worked with a student in Columbus, MS, on a research project focused on the explosion of the snow goose population. At the beginning of the project, the student was more interested in turning in the next assignment than in basing his success on the execution of his plan. Over time, Neils noticed a shift in the student's perspective. He gained confidence that he could explore this topic with all the passion and intensity he felt deep inside and exceed his teacher's expectations simultaneously! This process is all about moving a student from a reactive learning position to a proactive learning position. Telementoring was an effective tool here.

For further information about the ITP, go to http://www. telementor.org.

So Where Does an Interested Parent Begin Looking For a Mentor?

The most comprehensive mentor resource currently is the National Mentoring Partnership (http://www.mentoring.org). Designed to be the premier one-stop destination site for mentoring, it has a database of more than 5,000 mentor programs. Although it does not provide direct mentoring services, it does provide a wide range of resources and tools for mentoring organizations, mentoring initiatives, and individuals wishing to learn more about the topic. The site includes information about how to be a mentor, how to find a mentor, and how to organize a quality program. The partnership is currently focusing on establishing standards for quality e-mentoring.

Further searches on the Internet will reveal additional mentoring paths. Talking informally with neighbors and people in various leadership positions also will uncover a number of opportunities in your own backyard.

In using any of these research approaches, one soon learns that mentor programs range widely in their focus, types and ages of students, and "curriculum." Program sponsors also will vary; for example, K–12 schools, universities, nonprofit organizations, the media, government agencies, civic and faith-based institutions may all be sponsors.

One common thread in the mentor tapestry is that of the university mentor. Formal university programs held after school, on Saturdays, and during the summer attract eager students and passionate instructors engaged in challenging and creative production. The Purdue University Gifted Education Resource Institute (GERI) Summer Program (http://

www.geri.education.purdue.edu) is one such excellent model providing accelerated learning and enriched experiences in math, science, humanities, and the arts for students in grades 3–12.

Programs with tightly focused themes also are commonplace; one such program is sponsored by the nonprofit, 35-year-old International Women's Writing Guild (http://www.iwwg.com). With an e-mentor format, girls between the ages of 10–18 who love writing connect with writing mentors. The government's NASA mentoring program (http://www.nasa.gov/offices/education/about/index.html) is one among many that promote careers in math, engineering, and science. Some of the NASA programs even target minorities; for example, the Goddard Space Flight Sister program in Greenbelt, MD, is designed for middle school girls.

Summer learning with its relaxed format often can naturally give birth to mentor relationships that develop informally. (A lengthy list of summer enrichment programs for elementary and secondary students can be accessed at http://www.nagc.org/index2.aspx?id=1103&term s=summer+programs). The summer camp for the arts at Interlochen, MI (http://www.interlochen.org), is a prime example of the power of mentor relationships that develop naturally. Elementary and secondary students, along with teachers who are passionate about their subjects, have gathered here annually for years to develop talent and celebrate the arts—creative writing, dance, music, theatre, and the visual arts. This truly is a haven for kindred spirits.

Exactly What Do Mentors and Mentees Talk About?

Of particular interest to students, parents, and program organizers is the National Mentoring Partnership's list of activity guidelines designed for students at a wide range of ages. The guidelines are, of course, intended to govern activities taking place over a period of months—not just one session. These suggestions are valuable in helping students overcome any initial shyness they might feel in the early communication stage. The focus is on sharing information. Examples of some activities to help mentors and students begin to develop their relationship, excerpted and adapted from the National Mentoring Partnership's list of activities, include:

1. Talk about your favorite movies, historical figures, or heroes, why you like them, and what you learn from them.
2. Talk about a book you are reading and why you like it, or don't like it.
3. Share your favorite uses of the Internet, and talk about the websites and online discussion groups you find most helpful or entertaining.
4. Talk about your favorite uses of computer and software applications (including games) you find the most helpful or entertaining.
5. Talk about your pets. Talk about animals that particularly intrigue you and why.
6. Share information and details of things that might be unique to your particular culture or geographic area (e.g., clothing, ceremonies, music, traditions, food).
7. Discuss your favorite and least favorite classes or teachers, and why.
8. Mentors—talk about your job, how you trained for it, what you do, and whether it is different from what you planned on doing when you were in high school.
9. Work on the mentee's resumé, and discuss questions that are commonly asked on college applications or in job interviews.
10. Talk about what you do outside of work or school (e.g., hobbies, things you collect, how you spent your weekend).
11. Talk about how to balance work and leisure.
12. Talk about hopes, dreams, goals, and aspirations.

Once mentors and their mentees have gotten to know each other a little better, they might work together on some advanced activities. Some possibilities, also adapted from the National Mentoring Partnership's suggestions, include:

1. Create a website together. It can be something related to school work or to the mentor's professional work or a guide to an issue or subject in which both mentor and mentee share an

interest (e.g., the environment, a particular sports team). It could include links to your favorite websites on this subject and artwork you create yourselves.

2. Doodle and create artwork together. Many programs can read .gif, .jpeg, or .pict files, so it doesn't matter what kind of computers you are using. (In fact, you might even consider exchanging products by mail, without relying on your computer!)

3. Keep a journal on a regular basis (perhaps weekly) in which you discuss what you've done and your feelings about what's happened. Send the journals to one another and talk about what's happened.

4. Attend a concert, class, seminar, lecture, or interview together, in person or through an online webcast or chatroom that features a special guest. Talk about the event together afterward.

5. Work collaboratively on learning something new or "digging deeper" into a topic of mutual interest to expand your knowledge of that area.

Mentoring offers opportunities for advanced or in-depth academic study that can extend the student's school experiences in many ways. In addition, in these times of rapid-fire change, we can easily see value in teaching young people to connect with caring mentors who can provide relevant career guidance. At a time of confusing cultural shifts, we can clearly see value in encouraging students to find their own personal voice. And, at a time of "constant connectivity," we can certainly see the value of a new electronic twist on an old theme—the "virtual mentor," through which technology enables personal, sustained learning connections that cut across time and distance. For many young people, now may be the ideal time to enter the mentor relationship.

Chapter 19

Education Acceleration: Why or Why Not?

by James J. Gallagher

Some children are performing in school several years ahead of their age peers. In many cases, parents have the opportunity to request that schools move their children ahead. They need additional information on acceleration options. At some time in the young lives of gifted students, many parents are faced with the issue of acceleration or moving the child through the educational system faster than the normal progression. What should we do? Where might parents go to get necessary information? How can this educational acceleration be carried out if we decide to pursue it?

The major objective of educational acceleration is to find a more suitable educational environment for students who already have demonstrated performance far beyond the normal classroom in educational attainment. An important byproduct of acceleration would be the reduction in time that the student will spend in various educational settings. Although many parents do not consider the "saving of time" issue, perhaps they should. It is hard to project a decade or more into the future for a 10- or 11-year-old, but it might be worth doing. Table 19.1 shows the expected years at which a student will normally complete each segment of education. He or she will be 18 years of age when finishing high school and 22 years old when finishing college.

Gifted students often will have a long postgraduate education facing them. If the students are going on to graduate or professional training (such as medical school), they could well be in their late twenties or early

Table 19.1

Age of Completion of Educational Benchmarks for Medical Students

School Program Completed	Expected Age at Completion
Elementary School	12
Middle School	15
Senior High School	18
College	22
Medical School	26
Internship	27
Residency	29–32

Note. From *Teaching the Gifted Child* by J. Gallagher & S. Gallagher, 1994. Copyright 1994 by Allyn & Bacon.

thirties before completing their education. They can, in fact, spend a quarter of a century in school! Their college classmates could be in a career and community life as much as 6 to 8 years before these students actually become self-sufficient. Cutting the 20+ years in the educational system by a year or two would seem to be worth doing, so that students can begin a productive life earlier than would otherwise be possible.

Most parents would agree to acceleration but ask, "Can you assure me that nothing untoward would happen to my child in the process?" They may remember a horror story of a neighbor's child who was accelerated and who later suffered grievous social problems and even threatened to drop out of school. Saving a year is not worth that outcome, certainly.

Even if a child who has been accelerated reveals later emotional disturbances, there is not necessarily a causal relationship between the two conditions. There are usually many other forces at work in a student with serious emotional problems. One of the myths circulated in some educational circles is that the gifted student might be unable to handle the increased "pressure" of the academic programs beyond his or her current grade placement. As a matter of fact, the evidence finds the exact opposite. Students who have been accelerated tend to perform better academically than gifted students who were not accelerated, perhaps due to the welcome challenge these students derive from content that more adequately extends their abilities.

There is an extensive literature base on the topic of educational acceleration and its impact on students that goes back several decades and reveals a consistent story. If the child is reasonably physically mature and emotionally well-adjusted in the first place, no harm can be expected from well-planned acceleration. Students have generally been happy that they have saved a year or more of their life and career.

One of the latest of these results comes from a 10-year follow-up of 320 youngsters by Dr. David Lubinski and his colleagues at Vanderbilt University. These students had been identified, before the age of 13, as having outstanding mathematical or verbal reasoning abilities. Ninety-five percent had been accelerated in school sometime before the age of 23 and more than 90% of them reported positive results from their acceleration. There were few reports of social problems accompanying the acceleration, the most frequently noted concern of educators and parents. This finding reproduces results reported by just about all of the major studies that have looked at large samples of gifted students who have been accelerated.

Adults who have reflected retrospectively about their own personal experiences with acceleration have supported the positive findings from research by Lubinski and others. The most common problems cited by students are some minor social dislocations such as that of a male 16-year-old who had been accelerated and was now trying to date an 18-year-old girl in college, only to have her discover that he had been accelerated and then discover his real age. The resulting snub certainly was an embarrassing situation, but when weighed against the saving of a year or two of his career and becoming personally independent at an earlier age, to be able to start a family or enter the community earlier, clearly the acceleration was deemed worthy.

Still, acceleration is not for every gifted student. Consider Jerry, a student who is doing excellent work in school. He has a particular gift for words and his creative essays and poetry are the marvel of his teachers. Yet, Jerry is physically small and immature for his age group, and he has been noted by his teachers and his parents as socially isolated from his peers. It would be wrong to think that educational acceleration would cure his social problems by mixing him in with a more mature

Table 19.2

Most Common Methods of Acceleration of Gifted Students

Grade Level	Type of Acceleration
Primary (K–3)	1. Early admittance to school 2. Ungraded primary 3 years instead of 4
Intermediate (4–5)	1. Ungraded classes 2. Grade skipping
Middle school	1. Three years in two 2. High school classes for credit
High school	1. Early entrance to college 2. Advanced placement

Note. Adapted from "The strange case of acceleration," by J. Gallagher, 1998, In C. Benbow and D. Lubinski (Eds.), *Intellectual talent,* pp. 83–92. Copyright 1998 by The Johns Hopkins University Press.

group of students. Most educators would recommend that Jerry should stay where he is with the school developing his social skills as well as his creative writing. Instead of acceleration, Jerry could participate in an Individualized Education Program with a team of educational personnel who have created, with Jerry's parents, some meaningful objectives in developing social skills along with his creative writing.

Contrast Jerry with Denise who has shown a penchant for science and math, unlike many of her friends at school. Denise is physically mature for her age, resembling girls a year or two older than she. These older girls are her closest friends, and she also is well able to cope with social situations. Because her parents already see college and postgraduate work as a part of her future, some form of educational acceleration might be considered. Such a move should be considered only after discussions about the process and its advantages and potential problems between child, parents, and educators take place. In particular, the child should be eager to move forward after the issue has been explained.

The most common methods of acceleration are noted in Table 19.2. Such actions can be taken at any point in the school career where it would seem most appropriate. It can even take place right at the beginning of the school career when the gifted child can be admitted to school early (½ to 1 year) if he or she is physically mature and obviously developmentally advanced, such as reading or doing math at a second grade level even before beginning kindergarten. There have been no negative findings reported on this early admission as long as the child's physical and social development are taken into account.

The most common public perception of acceleration is grade skipping, but it is one of the least used in actual practice. Some educators would recommend that, if skipping a grade were desirable, then skipping the last grade in elementary school might be the desired move. This would allow the qualified student to move into the middle school a year early when all of the other students would be experiencing a new and different academic and social situation in middle school anyway.

Another strategy used to provide acceleration for bright students is to cluster these gifted students together in one class that will allow them to move forward, experience greater challenge, and master the necessary content in less time. The ungraded primary program could reduce the 4 years normally needed to get from kindergarten to third grade to 3 years, reducing the likelihood of repetition and boredom.

A similar strategy can be used in the middle school where a cluster of gifted students could be brought together to master the content in 2 years as opposed to 3. These attempts to telescope the content need the enthusiastic support of educational leaders and faculty to succeed. In the current atmosphere favoring inclusion (the process of bringing all, or nearly all, exceptional children into the general classroom for their education with special education support), it might be difficult to convince educational administrators of the desirability of separating off a group of gifted students for special instruction.

If your school system has a magnet school (so named because it is designed to draw students who are interested in the program that the magnet school has to offer) that focuses on art, science, or mathematics, this could be a means of bringing bright students interested in a particular topic area together for instruction.

A very common and popular device for educational acceleration is to take Advanced Placement (http://www.collegeboard.com/ap/students/index.html) courses in secondary school for college credit or to take college courses while still in high school. Another strategy is early entrance into college, leaving off the last year of high school (which often is referred to by gifted students as boring and a waste of time). A high school student earning college credit can even save some tuition money, no small matter these days. Some colleges also provide special programs for highly gifted students. One example of such a program, focusing on high-ability female students, is the Program for the Exceptionally Gifted (PEG) at Mary Baldwin College (http://www.mbc.edu/peg).

Although student acceleration is designed to allow gifted students to move forward to encounter more complex content and subject matter, another strategy has been to bring more complex content down to the student's level. This form of moving the curriculum downward is referred to as content acceleration. Sometimes parents of a student such as Denise do not want their child to move more rapidly through the school program but do want challenge for their child. Content acceleration is designed to do just that. Content acceleration can be as simple as allowing the student to take algebra one year earlier than normal, or it can involve something as complex as the International Baccalaureate program (http://www.ibo.org) which was designed to facilitate admission to colleges around the world. When students complete this challenging secondary education program, they will have mastered two languages and have taken such courses as the Study of Man in Society, Experimental Sciences, Higher Mathematics, and Art/Design, and they also will have engaged in independent study.

Distance education (providing students with opportunities to take courses by correspondence or using the computer for Internet-based courses) is another emerging way of providing content acceleration for high-ability students. In addition to convenient access to advanced study, distance learning can provide learning opportunities that highlight the student's ability to do the work, without concern for his or her age or personal characteristics. You can find a very thorough overview of distance learning opportunities for gifted students at the following website: http://www.hoagiesgifted.org/distance_learning.htm.

One of the best-kept secrets in education is how much bright students hunger for intellectual stimulation and challenge. Their common cry is that they are bored to death with the standard curriculum. Although moving bright students more rapidly through the mathematics curriculum, for example, solves the problem of challenge in middle school years, it also runs the risk of running out of content before the gifted students complete secondary school, leaving little or nothing of interest or challenge for the last year in high school. After you have taken the last course in calculus what do you do then? It is these students who are particularly willing to seek early admission to college or take a group of Advanced Placement courses to keep their interest in education and learning alive.

A relatively new approach has been the development of special residential schools devoted to establishing a complex program of studies for gifted students in mathematics and science. Fifteen states currently support some form of residential schools for students who qualify. The advanced curriculum of such schools represents true content acceleration. Educational acceleration with such students often enables them to enter college at an advanced level, perhaps at the sophomore level.

Some attempts have been made to support fast-paced classes during the summer. In these courses, the students will study one subject in depth for 3 weeks. There have been many such experiences demonstrating that gifted students can master a year of high school physics, or even college philosophy, in these intense programs when surrounded by other talented students and a competent faculty.

There is no reason why both student acceleration and content acceleration should not be considered together if the conditions are right and the student willing. One doesn't have to choose between them.

Parents may find many educators opposed to educational acceleration, and that is something of a puzzle given the strong positive evaluation findings. It may be their unwillingness to upset the standard routine, or their unawareness of the evidence available, or their inability to take the long view of the total career of the gifted student. It may be necessary to provide information (including the recommended resources below) for the school to help educators make better and more informed decisions. Parents who are interested in pursuing the possibilities of acceleration for their child might consider the following steps:

1. A thorough review of your child's academic status and an estimate of social and personal maturity for his or her age group with current school staff.

2. Discuss acceleration with your child and the possibilities of greater challenge and reduction of time in school.
3. If your child is intrigued by the idea (few students think they have options of this type), then an exploration of the various types of accelerations might be considered.
4. Discuss with the local educational staff the means for facilitating such a move with the steps that need to be taken.

Although acceleration is not for every gifted child, it can benefit many and is worthy of parental discussion and consideration.

Resources

Benbow, C., & Lubinski, D. (Eds.). (1996). *Intellectual talent*. Baltimore, MD: The Johns Hopkins University Press.

Brody, L., Assouline, S., & Stanley, J. (1990). Five years of early entrants: Predicting achievement in college. *Gifted Child Quarterly, 34*, 138–142.

Schiever, S., & Maker, J. (2003). New directions in enrichment and acceleration. In N. Colangelo & G. Davis (Eds.), *Handbook of gifted education* (pp. 163–173). Boston, MA: Allyn & Bacon.

Southern, W., & Jones, E. (Eds.). (1991). *The academic acceleration of gifted children*. New York, NY: Teachers College Press.

VanTassel-Baska, J. (1998). *Excellence in educating gifted and talented learners* (3rd ed.). Denver, CO: Love.

References

Gallagher, J. (1998). The strange case of acceleration. In C. Benbow & D. Lubinski (Eds.), *Intellectual talent* (pp. 83–92). Baltimore, MD: The Johns Hopkins University Press.

Gallagher, J., & Gallagher, S. (1994). *Teaching the gifted child*. Boston, MA: Allyn & Bacon.

Lubinski, D., Webb, R., Morelock, M., & Benbow, C. (2001). Top 1 in 10,000: A 10-year follow-up of the profoundly gifted. *Journal of Applied Psychology, 86*, 718–729.

Chapter 20

Acceleration: Difficult Decision—Easy Solution

By Sandra Warren

WHY is it, when faced with the decision to accelerate frustrated, bored, struggling gifted children, that the opinions we listen to the most come from uninformed, yet well-meaning family, friends, and even school personnel? It's time to listen to the real experts—the volumes of research conducted over the last 50 years by the most learned in our field and the families who have done it. In a recent survey, 22 parents, representing 26 children who were offered acceleration as an option, shared their experiences. All but two of the families jumped at the chance to accelerate. Even so, none of the families made the decision without a great deal of soul-searching. Most had to initiate the discussion themselves and bring forth the volumes of literature that supports acceleration as a positive move, before administrators would even consider it. The very people who should know and understand—teachers, administrators, and school psychologists—often are the least supportive.

Rationale and Importance

Let's take a look at what the surveyed parents had to say.

There is so much concern for social development and maturity level. What educators and administrators don't seem to understand is the depth of harm done from the frustration and isolation of a starved intellect! (Karen Whipkey, mother of an 11-year-old accelerated from fifth to sixth grade)

Karen had watched as

increasing boredom drove my child from being extremely orga-nized to disorganized; self-motivated to listless and unmoti-vated; from bright intelligent eyes to blank and lifeless ones. The acceleration move transformed her back to being excited about learning, motivated, and challenged. Peer relationships also became more fulfilling.

Asked if she would do it again, she replied, "Absolutely! All negative personality changes due to being unchallenged a long time disappeared overnight! There were no negative replacements, only positive ones!" The other parents reported similar experiences. For example, Colleen Grady, whose son accelerated from first to fourth grade said,

We were not accelerating our son; we were adjusting his instruction to better match his needs. While it was not a per-fect solution, grade-skipping combined with subject accelera-tion and curriculum compacting provided the best fit. It also provided a group of intellectual peers and allowed our son to remain in a school setting and experience typical milestones of childhood: extracurricular activities, prom, etc.

"The move kept my child challenged and made him feel his perceptions were important," said Deborah Davis, whose son initiated the move from fourth to sixth grade. Wenda Sheard accelerated three children: "Acceleration brought excitement about being in a new situation and time to do exciting things, like spend a year or two abroad." Another parent whose child was accelerated from preschool to kindergarten, then to third and fourth grade math and then again to fifth and sixth grade math said, "My child is challenged so behaviors are improved. She is learning to learn and to have to find answers instead of just automatically knowing everything—she is learning to work!" Andrew Mance, whose son accelerated from third to fourth grade said,

> Acceleration presented more challenge and opened more opportunities for activities not available to elementary students. He seems to have more friends that he can talk to on an intelligent basis, and the teacher seems to take more of an interest in him.

Another parent, whose son accelerated from sixth to seventh grade, had this to say:

> His self-esteem soared. He became respected by his same age and older peers and he now has a goal worth pursuing and a reason for trying to do his best. It also showed him how much I cared (to fight more than one and a half years to accomplish the acceleration); he now feels more valued for his gifts.

Kris Sigman shared that her child, accelerated from first to third grade, "is still receiving top grades but isn't complaining about being bored." The child said, "I'm more like the other kids now. And, I still get good grades!" Stephanie Miller, who grade-skipped two children, found that

> once the initial adjustment is made, this type of adjustment is less disruptive to the student's day-to-day schedule than other types of alternatives such as pull-out programs. Students who are candidates for acceleration are often more comfortable with older students anyway so finding a peer group is sometimes easier.

Sharon Montgomery's son is a precocious math student accelerated on several occasions to accommodate his abilities. She said,

> They want you to believe that accelerated students will have social problems being in a class with older students. That not only wasn't a problem for my son, it also solved problems! Being accelerated helped him feel less like a misfit, instead of more

so as predicted, and gave him about the only opportunity to experience having his intellect valued.

Finally, Mary Collier accelerated her son from eighth grade to college classes. "My child pulled out of chronic underachievement, became a happier child and learned things, including more than 5 years credit of a foreign language not offered in his high school."

Benefits and Positive Outcomes

If acceleration has been offered to your child and you're struggling with the decision, take a look at the following words of wisdom from parents who said, "yes" to acceleration:

- "I would tell any parent who is contemplating acceleration to do so and see what happens. I believe that in the vast majority of cases, the child will do just fine and be better off for it." (Andrew Mance)
- "Do not expect that educators know any of the positive arguments for acceleration. Expect that you will have to take the lead. Get test scores privately if you can. Read *A Nation Deceived*." (Name withheld by request)
- "Become knowledgeable about the different options available to you. If grade acceleration is the best choice for your child, be persistent. Do not let the school tell you 'we do not do that here.'" (Sheila Henault)
- "We accelerated our son in the spring of the school year . . . I believe he benefited from having the last 9 weeks of the school year in his new grade to meet the new kids and form friendships before the summer." (Name withheld by request)
- "Ask your child how he or she feels. When I asked Kaylyn, she said, 'I want to go to third grade because it will be harder and I want to be like everyone else.'" (Kris Sigman)
- "Respect the fact that you know your child and do what is best for her or him. Of course that means educating yourself about the options, laws, school requirements for acceleration, and the pros and cons, but it also means standing your ground, even

if your school district, family, or friends don't agree with your decision." (Stephanie Miller)

- "Never take no for an answer. All of the people (teacher, principal, school psychologist) were against it. They felt our son's underachievement was evidence of a personality or familial deficiency. They refused to recognize that this underachievement was a direct result of unmet educational needs." (Name withheld by request)

- "Trust your own instincts even though others have their doubts or do not provide moral support. Remember you know your child best. Take the risk and enjoy the experience. Let the child take ownership in the decision. I would never have done this unless he also wanted the opportunity." (Mary Collier)

- "... if your school agrees to a skip, chances are you have a child who actually needs more than that, so be prepared to continue to provide enrichments, ask for additional subject acceleration, provide outside opportunities, etc. Do whatever it takes to give them the experience of challenge and to keep them engaged in learning as an enjoyable and exciting pursuit." (Name withheld by request.)

- "Consider the whole child. The child needs to be not only academically, but socially, emotionally, mentally, and even physically prepared to be outside the peer group." (Deborah Davis)

- "Each child is different, and it is important to listen to the child. If he or she is begging for more appropriate curriculum, and if whole-grade acceleration is too scary, try subject acceleration. Once the child does this, be prepared for whole-grade acceleration. Also, understand that acceleration is not a permanent solution. Future adjustments, including more acceleration, may be necessary." (Name withheld by request)

- "Trust your child and the process. Your child needs to want this so leave it child led and not parent led. If your administrator is not willing to think outside the box, find someone who is." (Name withheld by request)

- "Talk to your child. He or she may not want to do it. Ours was begging for it!" (Name withheld by request)

- "Trust your instincts that this is the right option for your child then make sure he gets it!" (Sharon Montgomery, whose son was subject-accelerated 2–3 years ahead of classmates through middle school and high school)
- "Accept that there will be ups and down and roll with the punches. Obtain the best information and advice, make decisions with your child's best interest in mind, ignore the idiots, get help if/when you need it and don't beat yourself up if you make a mistake. Having a sense of humor also helps." (Colleen Grady)
- "If my son had to do everything over again with our current knowledge, he would have accelerated earlier and more drastically, skipped more middle school curriculum." (Student subject-accelerated from eighth grade to the high school, spending his junior and senior years in college courses)
- "Some people asked me why I was pushing my son. My answer was that I was not pushing my son, but merely opening doors he was so desperately trying to get through." (Parent with child accelerated from first to third grade)
- "I told my son all year to 'look for the nugget' during the day, the one thing he had never heard before. It was 2 months before it occurred to me that I'd walk out of a conference on day 2 if I had to sit all day looking for one thing I didn't already know." (Parent of child accelerated from first to third grade)

Here's what accelerated children said:
- "I like to do harder stuff and have it more challenging as my grade level work is too easy!" (A fourth grader subject-accelerated to sixth grade math)
- "Acceleration made school coursework at least somewhat appropriate. While I still didn't have to work very hard to do well in school, it was definitely a better fit academically. I was able to go to a top college sooner. High schools are by nature not particularly intellectually stimulating." (A 19-year-old Ph.D. student who had been subject-accelerated from first grade to fourth grade as a child)

- "The positives are easy, there are so many. The negatives are easy too . . . I was younger than everyone else in my classes. There is still jealousy and name-calling like 'nerds,' but that exists for kids who are gifted and not accelerated too, so you might as well accelerate!" (Student accelerated two and three grade levels through middle school)
- "Well, I feel good about it. It was really rewarding to be moved up a grade. The cool thing about it is that you feel that you have succeeded and have done a really good thing." (Student accelerated from fourth to sixth grade)
- "I really like being accelerated. The hardest thing was leaving my best friend behind. Also, starting in a new classroom with a teacher and kids I didn't know was a little intimidating. It was a relief to leave my fifth grade class though. I had more friends in the sixth grade—friends that were long term. I liked having more challenging work. It felt good to learn harder things. Library resources were better also. Everything felt right!" (Student accelerated from fifth to sixth grade)
- "I'm more like the new kids now and I still get good grades! It's good because I'm learning new science stuff. It's a little more challenging but still easy." (Child accelerated from first to third grade)
- "More challenging; not being bored and screwing around! I'm happy when others are jealous that I'm smart versus them being jealous because I have cool shoes, a new item, or blue eyes." (Child accelerated from first to third grade)
- "I enjoy the challenge." (Student accelerated from fifth to seventh grade)

We wouldn't blink an eye or stop for a second to consult others if the decision was to accelerate a child gifted in sports. We all understand that in the sports arena, competition without proper challenge stunts athletic prowess. We would never hold back a gifted soccer or basketball player to the local recreation league if what he or she really needed was specialized coaching and the competitive challenge of a private traveling team, even if others on the team were a year or two older. Yet we hesitate, examine, worry, and stew over doing the same for our academically and intellectually gifted children—a decision that could affect their academic, intellectual, emotional, and social well-being for years to come.

Gifted children need differentiated education. And, as much as we'd all love for that to happen within the framework of regular classrooms with age peers, we must face the facts; for most gifted children, in many schools, it just isn't possible.

Potential Issues and Concerns

When a child is accelerated and problems occur, we're quick to blame those problems on the acceleration, forgetting that no one gets through school without a few problems along the way. Acceleration is usually not the cause for everyday school concerns. When a child is accelerated, many factors contribute to a successful experience. There are negatives, but those expressed by our 20 families are not what you'd expect. The following is a list of things the parents found problematic:

1. "Ate up time and increased car expenses driving to and from college classes."
2. Parents were made to feel guilty by school personnel and society.
3. "An accelerated child may lack the study skills to learn at higher levels. These are easily taught, however."
4. "An accelerated child may lack the stamina to study that older students have." Time spent per subject generally increases per grade, as well as length of papers and amount of homework.
5. "One grade level acceleration may not be enough so other accommodations may be needed." The ability to learn quickly allows gifted children to grasp the advanced curriculum at a rapid pace. Therefore, they may still need additional stimulation.
6. "Giving up a year with your child because he or she will enter college earlier than age peers."
7. "Sports teams are difficult because there's one year less of practice under their belts."

8. "Extracurricular activities are confusing; if grouped by age she's with last year's classmates, if by grade, she's with current peers."
9. "Sometimes he feels teachers 'dumb down' things in his class and he doesn't know why."
10. "Accelerations don't last long. My rule of thumb is that an acceleration of 1 year will last ½ year, and acceleration of 2 years will last 1 year." The rapidity at which gifted children learn allows them to quickly absorb the more challenging curriculum of the accelerated classroom. Additional acceleration may be needed. Keep a careful watch.
11. "We're constantly having to explain acceleration."
12. "Regular classroom teachers don't know how to support such a child. Parents have to do it."
13. "Coping with a more demanding workload at a younger age."
14. "Because of administrative resistance, I put my child through testing and stress that shouldn't be necessary."
15. "People were less than kind and understanding. We were shocked at the insensitivity and ignorance of adults. We worried that our son had an all too close glimpse of the 'ugliness' of people while he was so young."

Suggestions for Making a Wise Decision

The following strategies should help parents considering acceleration make the best decision for their child:
- Read the research.
- Consult local, state, and national organizations for resources.
- Consult your state or local gifted coordinator for appropriate local resources.
- Review state and local public school acceleration policy.
- Talk to others who have accelerated their children—gifted chat rooms abound.
- Talk to your child.
- Trust your instincts.
- Never give up!

Differentiated education is not an extra or a perk deemed necessary by egotistical, pushy parents. It's a research-supported strategy. The success of acceleration as a viable option also has stood the test of time. Research supports the fact that acceleration is easy, cost effective, and often the best option for gifted children. It does not hurry them out of childhood or hurt them socially. In fact, as you've just read, it can restore attitudes, motivation, and enthusiasm for learning, as well as help to solve social problems.

Acceleration is an easy solution. The decision is difficult. Before you make a decision for your child, consult the research that has served the test of time, and listen to the parents and students who are doing it.

Resources

Colangelo, N., Assouline, S. G., & Gross, M. U. M. (Eds.). (2004). *A nation deceived: How schools hold back America's brightest students* (Vols. 1–2). Iowa City: The University of Iowa, The Connie Belin & Jacqueline N. Blank International Center for Gifted Education and Talent Development.

Colangelo, N., Lupkowski-Shoplik, A., Lipscomb, J., Forstadt, L., & Assouline, S. G. (2002). *Iowa acceleration scale manual.* Scottsdale, AZ: Great Potential Press.

Rogers, K. (2002). *Re-forming gifted education: How parents and teachers can match the program to the child.* Scottsdale, AZ: Great Potential Press.

Author Note

The author extends special thanks to contributing parents: Colleen Grady, Kris Sigman, Tara Smith, Mary Kay Helba, Andrew Mance, Paige Stretton, Terry Salvers, Tami Kamin-Meyer, Wenda Sheard, Karen Whipkey, Elaine Pelz, Trish Numbers, Sheila Ilenault, Stephanie Miller, Mary Brainard-Thomas, Karen Way, Sharon Montgomery, Laurie Ogbom, Mary Collier, Deborah Davis, Jan Sladky, and Lori Hise. Quotes from parents were reprinted with permission from "Acceleration: 22 Parents Speak Out!" published in the *Illinois Association for Gifted Children Journal,* 2006.

Chapter 21

Homeschooling . . . Making It Work

by Lisa Rivero

H OMESCHOOLING is nothing short of an educational revolution. Being educated at home is a rapidly changing and growing schooling option, chosen for nearly one million school-age children, and no longer a fringe movement or only for families who homeschool for religious reasons. The most popular reason families now choose to homeschool is to provide a better education for their children. Many of these children may be gifted, talented, and otherwise creative, sensitive, intense, and rapid learners. Homeschooling can be an appropriate and attractive choice for many gifted children because of its flexibility of grade levels, pacing, and mixed-age socializing.

Parents of gifted learners cite several reasons for homeschooling. Some parents have a child for whom classroom education is not a good academic or social-emotional fit because the child learns extraordinarily quickly, or is highly creative or sensitive, or has an unusual learning style. Some parents homeschool to sustain a love of learning. Other parents homeschool as a last resort, often because the local schools do not offer or have cut gifted programming. Homeschooling is sometimes a temporary solution for years when school classroom differentiation is inadequate or nonexistent.

As a homeschool parent who is actively involved in a homeschool support group, I know that the decision to homeschool is rarely easy and that the actual day-to-day experience of homeschooling is time-consuming and often tiring, especially when the child is a voracious learner or has uneven abilities. At the same time, I know that home-schooling can be a transformative and extremely satisfying experience for many families, leading to tremendous personal and educational growth, and that a self-directed approach to learning frees up parent time and allows children to start on the path of lifelong learning.

For this growth to occur, however, families need to take the time to reflect on some important questions: Why are you homeschooling or thinking about homeschooling? What are your state's homeschool laws? What unique benefits are available through homeschooling? What are your child's unique educational needs? What are your child's strengths and passions? How will you address weak areas and gaps? How will you use the time left over—one of the benefits of homeschooling?

This article will bring these questions into focus, help parents to know if homeschooling is right for them and help families who do choose to homeschool get off to a good start. Rather than specific recommendations for curriculum resources or a list of what needs to be learned when, you will find suggestions for ways to think about what I consider the more important issues of homeschooling—parenting, use of time, and consideration of children's interests and individual needs—issues that will help you to develop a personal philosophy of education.

A Customized Mission Statement

Your reasons for homeschooling will be unique to your family. Some families homeschool to provide for learning needs not met in schools. Others homeschool because frequent family moves make school transitions difficult, such as when a parent is in the military. Some families homeschool to offer a more nurturing social-emotional environment. And some families homeschool because they believe strongly in the parents' ultimate responsibility to educate their children.

Take the time to think about exactly why you are considering homeschooling and what you expect homeschooling to accomplish. Be specific. For example, you might say that homeschooling will offer your children more challenge. What kind of challenge? In what areas? How will you provide for more challenge? Through different curriculum materials? Individual pacing? More depth and breadth? Or suppose you are homeschooling because your child is unusually sensitive. How will homeschooling address the child's social-emotional needs in ways that are different from other educational settings? Will you use bibliotherapy—growth through reading? Small social gatherings? How will you help a highly sensitive child to reach adulthood with self-understanding and confidence? The perception that there is a problem of socialization in homeschooling is a myth. Homeschooling allows children to develop social skills through cooperative learning groups, mixed-aged friendships, volunteering, and mentoring, and a greater awareness of real life outside the classroom.

After you've focused on your reasons for homeschooling and have thought about the specific questions related to those reasons, you are ready to write a mission statement for your homeschool. Include all family members in this activity. Explain that a mission statement is simply a statement of purpose and direction, that it should be positive rather than negative in tone, and that it should be written clearly, in one to several sentences. The mission statement will not go into great detail about how you will homeschool, but it should clarify why you choose to homeschool and what you expect to gain from homeschooling.

One family's homeschool mission statement reads as follows: "Our homeschool exists to provide each child with an education tailored to individual passions, goals, and needs; to strengthen our family relationships; and to help each family member to be emotionally healthy." Note that this family has three primary reasons for homeschooling: (a) to tailor education to the children's passions, goals, and needs; (b) to strengthen family relationships; and (c) to nurture emotional health. By stating their goals, the family can more easily make specific decisions about how to homeschool by asking themselves whether curriculum and other education decisions support their mission statement.

Be prepared for your reasons for homeschooling to change. Just as corporations periodically review and revise their mission statements, homeschool families should occasionally ask themselves if their mission statement still reflects their purpose and direction. For example, we began homeschooling primarily to promote a love of learning, to allow our son to get to know himself as a learner, and to have more time together as a family. After about a year, those goals had been met, and we reevaluated our reasons for homeschooling, which now included concentration on and development of passion areas. After another year, our son was ready to include more self-direction in his education. Our mission statement has changed to reflect his changing needs and interests.

Homeschool Laws

After you know why you are homeschooling, you need to know what the law says. Homeschooling is legal in all 50 states, but each state has its own laws and requirements. Some states have minimal regulations, requiring only a signed statement of intent. Other states require testing, specific curricula or courses of study, or review by a certified teacher or individual school district.

You can get a copy of your state's homeschool laws from the state department of education, found on the Internet or listed in your phone book under state government agencies. Call or write to request a copy of the state law, then read the law carefully, and be sure that you understand the requirements for record keeping, testing, hours per day or days per year of instruction, and subjects to be studied.

Relationship Comes First

Once you understand homeschooling requirements, you may be eager to leap into the world of lessons and learning at home. Wait. Before you buy curriculum materials, before you plan for assessments and schedules, focus on your relationship with your children. Is it healthy and strong? Does it need a little work? Can it be better? How will homeschooling affect the relationship?

Homeschooling often makes for better parents, because good parenting skills are easier to develop when you can be with your children during the day, rather than only during rushed mornings and tired evenings. Put your relationship with your child first by practicing the skills of active listening, special time, and acceptance of feelings. When your child is frustrated by a learning task ("I hate math!"), listen to the child's concerns and ask questions for clarification before worrying about whether the schoolwork is getting finished on time. When a day is particularly stressful, stop all educational activities and spend a few one-on-one moments with your child doing what he or she wants to do—playing a game, taking a walk, or simply having a conversation about something of interest to the child. If your child is fearful of a particular topic of study, such as spiders or wars, accept those feelings, and realize that they will affect how the topic is learned, rather than treat feelings as separate from learning.

Remember to plan for your own needs. Everyone needs alone time or down time, and parents who homeschool must work harder than other parents to find ways to take a break, to have some alone time, and to seek adult companionship. Accepting and addressing your personal concerns and needs is more effective than pretending they don't exist. When you plan for your own needs, it will be easier to meet the needs of your children without resentment or anxiety, leading to a stronger parent-child relationship and giving you more mental energy for home-school subjects and schedules. You may need to swap child-care duties occasionally with a fellow homeschool parent, or schedule time during the day when children are expected to read or play quietly. Ask your children's librarian about other homeschool families in your area and local homeschool support groups.

A Custom-Made Curriculum Plan

Many people imagine a typical homeschooling day like this: Start promptly at 9 a.m.; have about an hour each of math, science, reading, writing, and social studies with regular but less frequent times interspersed for physical education, art and music, and perhaps a foreign language; end at about 3:30 p.m.; and do homework in the evening.

This school day is based on a traditional course of study of core subjects that is generic for all students. Parents and teachers know, however, that each child learns at a different pace. What one child learns in one hour in a given subject could take another child 20 minutes. Another student will need 90 minutes, and yet another will know the material before the study begins. Similarly, not all children learn best at the same time of day. Some of us are morning people. Some of us work best later in the day. And some children seem to be ready to learn all the time!

Homeschool parents have the freedom to individualize learning for their children by scheduling learning for optimal times. Some homeschool families don't start their homeschool day until late in the morning or early afternoon, but continue strong through the evening. Other homeschool families take advantage of early morning hours and finish by lunchtime. Still others don't distinguish between homeschool time and non homeschool time. For these families, learning continues as it did in the preschool years, all of the time. A homeschool schedule can adapt to the child and the family.

Parents can tailor learning to each child by choosing curriculum materials and activities suited to children's individual learning styles and preferences. One child might learn math best with manipulatives, while another child might prefer to learn the same concepts using a computer program. Homeschool parents can get ideas for curriculum materials from teacher supply stores, libraries, publishers of gifted education materials, gifted and homeschooling conferences, and their local schools. Bookstores and libraries carry homeschool resource books, some of which list resources by age, grade level, and learning style.

Parents can individualize learning by allowing children to work at their own pace within the allotted time for a given subject. Some students will move on to the next level sooner than average; others will take a bit longer. Because homeschool students can take as much or little time as they need to learn a specific concept or skill, little time is wasted.

Time Left Over

Homeschooling is an efficient way to learn. Because of the effectiveness of individual study and one-on-one teaching, families who homeschool often find that they can accomplish in 2 to 4 hours of focused work what classroom students accomplish in a full school day.

Children who are gifted learners often begin the school year knowing up to one-half of what they are expected to learn that year. It doesn't take a math major to see how homeschooling can free up valuable time.

Time does not need to be spent waiting for others to catch up or on busy work. Instead, homeschool students can use extra time to develop higher level thinking, creative learning, and self-directed study skills. Some homeschool students broaden their knowledge with extensive leisure reading, field trips to museums and zoos, and conversations with friends and family. Other students explore areas of interest not normally included in the school day, such as computer programming, or specialize in a particular talent or passion, such as writing or math. A child's strengths and passions often are the keys to successful learning.

Strengths and Passions

Homeschooling offers a valuable opportunity to make children's strengths and passions an integral part of their learning. If you don't know quite where to start with homeschooling, and especially if you are homeschooling reluctant learners, ask your children what they would like to study. Tell them anything goes, that no subject is unimportant or off-limits. Some children will choose core subject areas, such as math, science, or reading. Others will want to delve into less traditional topics, such as car engines, bread baking, or comic books.

Veteran homeschool parents realize that nearly any subject can be expanded to include core subjects. A study of car engines can include physics and history. Successful bread baking requires math—including fractions—and being able to follow sequential instructions. A passion for comic books can lead to a deeper understanding of art and written expression. All of these topics include reading skills. If you are worried that by letting children guide their own learning, they will miss out on important areas of study, keep in mind that you have the gift of time to figure out how to fit everything in. In the beginning, nurturing a love of learning is the first priority.

Don't be surprised if your child has surpassed your own skills and knowledge in one or more subjects. Homeschool parents often use mentors, community classes, distance-learning programs, and talent search programs to allow their children to learn at appropriately high levels. In some states, homeschool children can attend public school part-time to take core or extracurricular classes as a supplement to homeschooling. This option is particularly attractive to homeschool teens that need advanced science, math, or Advanced Placement classes.

Gaps and Weak Areas

Because of the asynchronous development of gifted learners, many children with high ability and potential have gaps and areas of weakness in comparison to areas of strength. One child may be ready to work several grade levels ahead of age-peers in math, but may progress more slowly in written expression. A different child may write and read at advanced levels, but may take longer than usual to learn arithmetic. Even within a given subject area, a child may show uneven development. A child may read silently and with great comprehension books at adult levels, but not yet know correct pronunciation or basic rules of grammar. Or a child may have a firm grasp of algebraic concepts, but not have memorized multiplication facts.

We often use "weakness" to describe areas of study that do not come easily to a child, and "gaps" to describe knowledge or skills a child has not yet learned, but should have learned according to grade-based standards. Homeschool parents may be tempted to start homeschooling by aggressively addressing these weaknesses or gaps with a program of extensive drill and repetition, often at the expense of higher level thinking or more satisfying learning. A better plan is to find creative ways for children to strengthen their skills and fill in the gaps. Two particularly effective strategies are (a) to use knowledge of children's learning styles and (b) to encourage interdisciplinary study.

If parents do not know or understand their children's preferred learning styles, several resources can help them to pinpoint how their children learn best. Once you know your children's learning styles and preferences, apply this knowledge to learning tasks. If a kinesthetic learner is struggling with an addition math workbook, for example, allow the child to learn addition facts using a hopscotch grid or with manipulatives such as dice or beads. A child who learns best visually can make a poster of addition facts, using different colors to distinguish fact groups. An auditory learner can listen to and recite addition facts in the car or while playing with clay. Some highly gifted children have more than one preferred learning style. Such children will learn best with a combination of approaches and activities.

Interdisciplinary study can help a child to approach a difficult subject or skill in a new way. A child who has difficulty with spelling may be more motivated if spelling words are tied to reading choices about a topic of interest, such as horses. At the same time, the child can write stories about horses, including the spelling words. If a child resists science but loves history, parents can look for books that combine the two subjects, such as children's biographies of famous scientists or those about the history of scientific inventions.

Another strategy for helping children to learn information and skills they would otherwise avoid is to practice what one parent calls "stealth homeschooling." This nonintrusive approach to learning includes watching entertaining but educational television and videos, listening to audiotapes, and playing board and card games that include incidental learning. One 13-year-old student who has homeschooled for 8 years suggests that parents place interesting activities and reading at various places in the house, such as the kitchen table or living room sofa, so that children's interests will be piqued without coercion or pressure.

One Day, One Year at a Time

Don't try to do everything at once. If you are interested in homeschooling, but don't want to commit yourself to several years of teaching your children at home, treat the first year as a trial year. Remember, the decision to homeschool is not irrevocable. After one year, you can always decide that homeschooling is not the best option for your family after all. Meanwhile, your family will have had the valuable experience of getting to know one another better, and you will understand your children as learners in a new way. Families also can "practice" home-schooling during holiday breaks, the summer, or on a weekend.

Homeschooling often is misunderstood, and you will occasionally need to explain or even defend your choices. Many homeschool parents cite a lack of understanding from family and society as their biggest challenge. One homeschool parent explains,

> The biggest problem is my mother. She does not believe in homeschooling, and she puts herself in opposition to every-thing we do. I still do what I think is right for our child, but the lack of moral support and the negative attitude of close relatives is a big challenge.

Another parent is frustrated by society's constraints on children:

> My biggest challenge has been dealing with society. The chil-dren can't go out during the day, because our community has a daytime curfew. They can't volunteer until they're 16. In many people's eyes, children are a nuisance rather than fellow human beings who want to learn to become adults.

Time spent at the beginning of homeschooling focusing on your per-sonal reasons for homeschooling and developing a homeschool philoso-phy and mission statement will help you stand up to potential criticism. The best defense is a purpose and a plan in which you believe.

Conclusion: The Decision to Homeschool

Homeschooling is not the right fit for every family. Families who are successful at homeschooling enjoy being with their children most of the time, are flexible in their attitude and approach, put their child's needs ahead of generic guidelines and timetables, and are willing to rethink many of the accepted beliefs about learning and education. But even families who find that homeschooling is not the right choice for their children can learn from homeschoolers, just as homeschoolers have learned from what does and doesn't work in the classroom. Homeschooling has the potential to revolutionize how we view life and learning, but only if we open our minds to new possibilities.

For our family, homeschooling has allowed our son to rediscover his passion for learning and to get to know himself as a learner, to soar in areas of strength and interest, and to learn joyfully in areas that come less easily. Homeschooling has allowed me to view learning in a new and exciting way, to learn or relearn aspects of history and math and science that I either never learned or had forgotten, and to challenge myself to set high personal goals as an adult learner. For this positive growth to occur for our family, however, we as parents first had to focus on why we were homeschooling in the first place, what we expected from homeschooling, and how to adapt homeschooling to our child, rather than vice versa.

If you decide that homeschooling is a good fit for your children and family, you are in for an exciting journey! Hang on, let go of expectations, remove all barriers and ceilings, and enjoy the ride.

Resources

Books About Homeschooling

Albert, D. (1999). *And the skylark sings with me: Adventures in homeschooling and community based education.* Gabriola Island, BC: New Society Publishers.

Colfax, D., & Colfax, M. (1998). *Homeschooling for excellence.* New York, NY: Warner.

Dobson, L. (2000). *Homeschoolers' success stories: 15 adults and 12 young people share the impact that homeschooling has made on their lives.* Roseville, CA: Prima Publishing.

Guterson, D. (1993). *Family matters: Why homeschooling makes sense.* New York, NY: Harcourt Brace.

Leistico, A. (1997). *I learn better by teaching myself. Still teaching ourselves* (Combined ed.). Cambridge, MA: Holt Associates.

Llewellyn, G. (1996). *Freedom challenge: African–American homeschoolers.* Eugene, OR: Lowry House.

Rivero, L. (2002). *Creative homeschooling for gifted children: A resource guide.* Scottsdale, AZ: Great Potential Press.

Rowland, H. S. (1975). *No more school: An American family's experiment in education.* New York, NY: Dutton.

Sheffer, S. (1992). *Writing because we love to: Homeschoolers at work.* Portsmouth, NH: Boynton/Cook Heinemann.

Books About Learning and Parenting

Amabile, T. (1989). *Growing up creative: Nurturing a lifetime of creativity.* New York, NY: Crown Publishers.

Barbe, W. (1985). *Growing up learning: The key to your child's potential.* Washington, DC: Acropolis Books.

Barron-Tieger, B., & Tieger, P. (1997). *Nurture by nature: Understanding your child's personality type—and become a better parent.* New York, NY: Little, Brown.

Covey, S. (1997). *The 7 habits of highly effective families: Building a beautiful family culture in a turbulent world.* New York, NY: Golden Books.

Dunn, R., Dunn, K., & Perrin, J. (1994). *Teaching young children through their individual learning styles: Practical approaches for grades K–12.* Boston, MA: Allyn & Bacon.

Llewellyn, G., & Silver, A. (2001). *Guerrilla learning: How to give your kids a real education with or without school.* New York, NY: Wiley.

Vitale, B. M. (1982). *Unicorns are real: A right-brained approach to learning.* Rolling Hills Estates, CA: Jalmar Press.

Williams, L. V. (1983). *Teaching for the two-sided mind: A guide to right brain/ left brain education.* New York, NY: Simon & Schuster.

Websites

A to Z Home's Cool—http://www.gomilpitas.com/homeschooling
Home Education *Magazine*—http://www.homeedmag.com
Homeschooling the Highly Gifted—http://www.hollingworth.org/homesc.html
Jon's Homeschool Resource Page—http://www.midnightbeach.com/hs
Smart Kid at Home—http://www.smartkidathome.com
Families of the Talented and Gifted—http://www.tagfam.org

Chapter 22

Is Homeschooling Right for Your Child?

by Vicki Caruana

Y our son is in the first grade and enrolled in a part–time gifted program at school. However, his regular classroom teacher is not interested in or willing to enrich the everyday curriculum. You realize that your child might be incredibly bored for the remainder of his elementary years! This seems like cruel and unusual punishment, especially since he already is starting to shut down due to apathy. You are willing to accelerate him to the next grade level, even though you don't prefer it. Unfortunately, skipping grades is not even an option because it is not the district's policy to move students ahead. You feel you have nowhere else to turn. What do you do?

Homeschooling is something you have entertained only briefly in the past. Now, however, the idea intrigues you. You may be wondering if homeschooling is right for your child. But could you really do it? What would people say? What would your son say? What about socialization? The questions are endless. Take a deep breath and read on. Parents who school their children at home believe it is right for their family and the best educational opportunity for their children. When asked why they have chosen such an undertaking, parents respond with a variety of reasons, including, "Because I wanted that special bond." One parent stated that "I am and have always been my children's first and best teacher. I know them better and love them more than any other teacher possibly could."

Myths About Homeschooling

Many people wonder if homeschoolers are isolated to such a degree that they don't interact well with others, especially now that cooperative learning by working in groups is popular in public schools. Homeschooled children seem to be as well-adjusted socially as children who attend school. Many homeschoolers have the advantage of learning with their siblings in multiaged groups. Others also belong to coops in which groups of families get together to teach around a preselected theme such as the Old West or medieval times. Many homeschoolers also belong to scouting groups, organizations like 4H, church youth groups, athletic teams, and other interactive groups in their communities. Still others participate in public school activities like band, art, or clubs. Many states have ruled that homeschoolers have the right to participate in public school programs such as special education, band, and sports. Not only is this a good opportunity to maintain social interactions with their peers, but it also keeps the parent in touch with what is going on in the schools. Additionally, if you decide to put your child back into school, he or she will already have friends, and you will already have contacts yourself.

Many critics mistakenly believe that all homeschoolers are truant. On the contrary, homeschooling regulations are strong incentives for parents to ensure that their children receive instruction as least as rigorous as their public or private school peers. Homeschool parents are registered with their local school board through the state's Parent Educators Association (PEA) or under the umbrella of a private school. They are accountable for the time spent on schoolwork. Homeschoolers must have explicit lesson plans ready to be reviewed by a county or state official at a moment's notice. And just like publicly or privately schooled children, homeschoolers are tested at the end of each school year to gauge their progress.

Distrust of the parent's qualifications leads some people to assume that homeschooled children couldn't possibly be learning all they need to know. Standardized test scores tell a different story. Homeschoolers, on average, score higher than either publicly or privately schooled children. Some major universities hunt for homeschooled students, because they often are more focused academically and seem to adjust to high standards readily.

Is Homeschooling for Every Family?

There are a number of reasons that homeschooling might not be right for your family. Remember, this commitment affects the entire family. For example, if both parents must work, homeschooling full time may not be possible. Other parents choose not to homeschool if their child has a learning problem they feel inadequate to address. Another reason not to homeschool might be that you already have incredible demands on your time that you do not desire to change. Also, if your spouse is completely against the idea, homeschooling may not work for you because it takes the support of both parents to be effective. Likewise, you might not be entirely convinced yourself that homeschooling is right for your family. Or, you may be comfortable with your previous decision of either private or public school. On the other hand, do homeschool if you wholeheartedly believe that it is the best decision for you and your family. Do homeschool if you are not satisfied with the educational system available to your child. Do homeschool if both parents are committed, keeping in mind that this may turn out to be a long-term commitment and is a great undertaking, one that requires careful planning and a special kind of courage. A teaching certificate is not required, but homeschooling does require an attitude that expresses "I am my child's best teacher!" This attitude and confidence seem to be enough for a parent to do whatever it takes to make sure this choice is a successful one.

What Are the Advantages of Homeschooling a Gifted Child?

Gifted children love to explore topics in depth. Unfortunately, such explorations are not always possible at school. If you homeschool your child, you can teach your child important learning and thinking skills while focusing on a particular theme. This approach is called the Unit Study Approach. Gifted education teachers have taught this way since gifted programming began. For example, take a topic such as "Ocean Life" and build reading, spelling, writing, math, science, and history lessons around it. Students can read books on ocean life, pull spelling words from those books, write stories, practice handwriting, and learn grammar using this topic. Students can calculate the different populations of ocean life and graph the results, they can learn about the different species that live in the world's oceans, and they can look at how the oceans have historically affected our lives.

How Long to Homeschool?

Once a parent decides to homeschool, the question of how long naturally follows. Many choose from the following options:

- *Kindergarten through third grade*: Many want to homeschool during the primary grades because they believe they haven't finished laying that all important foundation that allows their child to thrive academically and socially.
- *Short term*: If a child was pulled from school for remedial reasons, a short-term situation can place him or her back in school when ready.
- *Until college*: Some choose to homeschool for the duration of their child's schooling until college.

There is a prescriptive time frame for homeschooling. Some parents decide to take it one year at a time. Unfortunately, taking homeschooling a year at a time may be distracting as you may fear that your child will lag behind his or her public or private school peers. Making a decision to stick with homeschooling for several years is more advisable. A longer time frame offers you more flexibility in what and how you teach. You won't be as concerned with following the school's curriculum as you would be if you were anticipating putting your child back in school the next year.

What if I Can't Homeschool Full-Time?

There are many situations that might lead parents to believe they could not homeschool even though they desperately want to. What if you are a single parent? What if you strongly believe that homeschooling is what is best for your child, yet your spouse is dead set against it? What if both parents work full-time just to make ends meet? What if you have a physical or health limitation that makes homeschooling too intimidating to undertake? Or what if you are curious about homeschooling, but you aren't ready to do it full-time? These are all valid concerns. The first step to homeschooling part-time is to identify the area of greatest need for your child. Obviously, you will not be able to teach a comprehensive curriculum on a limited basis, nor should you as it would only frustrate your child. You need to proceed with caution so that your child doesn't come home from school just in time to face more school at home. Is your child experiencing gaps in his or her learning at school? Is it difficult for him or her to keep up? You could start by providing remediation. Or if your child is not being properly challenged, you can enrich the curriculum with additional investigations into the school's current topic of study. These are all ways to infuse homeschooling into the school year.

The summer is a great time to try out homeschooling. If you are a stay-at-home parent, you could homeschool full-time during the summer as it is a great time to do a unit study as described above. Let your child choose the summer's topic. My sons chose insect life this past summer. (It was definitely not my first choice. I wanted to do inventors and inventions, but I was outvoted.) Topics such as the ocean, space, and dinosaurs are great for theme teaching and easily provide activities for a variety of levels.

Even if you work full-time, the summer also is a good time to homeschool. Keep young minds working year-round. Don't just let one of the many summer camps have all the influence. Again, choose a theme and build in time to explore it, possibly with trips to museums and other attractions. Follow up any trip with some kind of writing assignment or creative expression.

Depending on the age of your child, he or she may be apprehensive about your teaching. Try not to make it a big deal; treat it as a natural occurrence. The summer would be a good time to get to know full-time homeschooling families through a coop or on a field trip. Spending time with other homeschoolers will help you build a support system that will be in place should you decide to homeschool full-time.

Full-time homeschoolers who are currently at a crossroads may benefit from knowing that if they choose to put their child back into a traditional school setting, it doesn't preclude them from homeschooling on a part-time basis. The way we meet our child's needs may vary as much as the needs themselves. That's the beauty of homeschooling.

Many parents thinking about homeschooling their children ask the following questions: How do I start? What do I need? Where do I get in touch with others? How do I secure teaching materials? How do I homeschool legally? There are many books on this subject. In addition, there are homeschooling associations in every state, as well as support groups, teaching coops, annual conventions, and websites. Another good way to draw strength, ideas, and valuable insights for teaching your own child is by attending local and state homeschooling conferences. They are relatively inexpensive to attend and offer a wealth of information and fellowship. There also are local support groups that meet monthly and would be happy to offer encouragement. You can find listings of area conferences and support groups by either contacting your local school board or looking for your state's homeschooling website. Below is a list of basic steps to take should you decide to pursue homeschooling. Each state's guidelines may be more or less stringent.

- Contact your local school board and ask them to send you the homeschooling regulations for your state.
- Contact your area homeschool support group and find out when they next meet. Attend that next meeting.
- Generally, you need to fill out a letter of intent to send to your state department of education telling them of your intention to homeschool your child.
- Determine your child's academic needs.
- Secure the necessary curriculum. First-year homeschoolers usually purchase a complete curriculum that is already laid out

for them step by step. You can buy new or find out about used curriculum sales from your area support group.

- Obtain a lesson plan book or something comparable.
- Determine, according to guidelines from the state, how many hours per day you will conduct school. Make a plan for each day.
- Start teaching!

Depending on your state guidelines, you may be required to have your child evaluated at the end of each school year. Your child most likely will be able to sit in with the public school children to be tested, or you can hire a certified teacher to administer the test. Which test you give is determined by the state. Check your requirements carefully.

Resources

American Homeschool Association—http://americanhomeschoolassociation.org
Homeschool World—http://www.home-school.com
National Home Education Research Institute—http://www.nheri.org

Differentiated Instruction for Young Gifted Children: How Parents Can Help

by Joan Franklin Smutny

I look at my twins and wonder if differentiating will work at this young age. Yes, they're gifted. But there are a lot of traits that make them typical young kids. They scramble around in the yard creating elaborate games; they have to touch everything, get into every closed box and forbidden object they can. Frankly, I don't think the twins are concerned about the fact that things come easily to them. When they lose interest, it's mostly because the process isn't imaginative or active enough for them.—Father of twin first graders

PARENTS of young gifted children voice common concerns about what often is presented to them as "differentiated instruction." What benefits will my gifted child receive through this approach? How effective is it for young children generally? How responsive is it to differences between and within cultural groups? Does it provide for the creative as well as academic needs of my gifted child? What can I do at home or at school to support this approach?

During the primary years, children manifest a wider range of differences than older learners. As a general rule, the younger the age group, the more dramatic variations within the group and the more likely that the differences you see in school performance reflect deeper differences in developmental level. Add to this the influence of culture,

> When my child started school, I found that the school had an arrangement for students at different levels of literacy. My child and several others were put in a cluster group for advanced readers. At our school, differentiating is a way of making lessons more or less difficult, or allowing kids to work faster or slower. I guess what I wonder is, "How is this different from the old reading groups we had as kids?"—Mother of a kindergartener
>
> Last year, we had a couple of college professors work with our elementary school on differentiating. We have a lot of bilingual and immigrant kids. I liked that they focused on the bilingual and cultural issue, and I felt that they helped a lot of teachers figure out ways to serve more students in this multicultural setting. But my child is bilingual and gifted, and I didn't feel they were tuned into the differences within our population.—Mother of a bilingual second grader

special ability, and language, and you have a classroom where the range of knowledge and understanding in any given subject can span at least several years. The need for differentiated instruction in the primary grades is therefore very great.

Fundamentally, differentiating is about honoring the individuality of the child and letting that guide what and how he or she learns. Understanding the learners, therefore, becomes the foundation stone upon which every decision about the child's education rests. Despite their inexperience in school, primary grade children bring worlds of knowledge, skill, experiences, traditions, impressions, tastes, values, and ideas to the classroom. They already have learned more in the years before school than they are likely to learn again in a span of 4 or 5 years. Once they enter the classroom, questions immediately arise:

- What special abilities and skills do these children have?
- What life experiences and knowledge have they gained outside of school (this could include exposure to a wide range of areas—animals, farming, auto mechanics, architecture, storytelling, music, etc.)?
- What special interests do they have? To what materials and activities are they continually drawn?
- What are their learning styles? How do they best absorb new information? Apply concepts?

- What cultural heritage do they have? What languages do they speak?

You will find that primary classrooms today are colorful and vibrant learning places, especially compared to those of former years, when children sat crammed into rows of straight-backed chairs silently doing pencil and paper tasks. In those days, few primary schools concerned themselves with the needs of individual children, especially gifted children. But as the quotes at the beginning of this article illustrate, today you are more likely to find teachers who differentiate for young gifted children. The most commonly used strategies are compacting, learning stations, tiered activities, and clustering. For readers who have not encountered these strategies in their child's classroom, here are examples of what you might see:

- *Compacting.* A girl comes to second grade already knowing most of the math for the first half of the year. Her teacher uses compacting to enable her to skip content she already knows and move on to more advanced work. This involves: (a) deciding what concepts, knowledge, and skills in the unit are essential for all students to master; (b) determining, on the basis of some form of preassessment, what areas the child can skip; and (c) exploring with the child what alternative project she can do. This could be a more accelerated and more complex version of the assignment, another assignment in the same subject but in the child's area of interest, or an independent project on a topic of her choosing. The teacher usually creates a learning contract that specifies the project or task the child will do and the materials she will use, as well as the criteria, learning goals, and timeline for completing the assignment.
- *Learning Stations.* A multicultural first grade class has children at all different levels of ability and skill. The teacher uses learning stations to accommodate these differences. Learning stations are designated areas of the classroom where students can work on different tasks within a unit. These areas often are sequential, with each one representing a higher level of complexity than the one before it. Students can move freely

from one task to the next as they master the material (they are not identified and locked into any particular "level").

- *Tiered Activities.* A third-grade boy attends a class where tiered activities are the norm. Like learning stations, tiered assignments demand different levels of mastery and provide different degrees of complexity. The idea behind tiered activities is that all students—regardless of differences in ability, skill, and experience—can focus on the same learning goal if this goal is broad enough to accommodate them. For example, a language arts class might focus on having students understand "point of view." At one table, the kids write descriptions of themselves as though they are a character in a popular fairytale and what they think about the other characters in the story. At another table, the kids take this a step further and write an essay on how they, as this character, feel about the whole story. Whose story is it? Do they agree with it? At another location, kids choose a character and write a fractured fairytale based on this character's point of view.
- *Clustering.* Several students in a kindergarten class are significantly ahead of their classmates in reading and math. The teacher decides to cluster these students in order to give them more advanced content. After giving the class a new assignment, the teacher spends some time instructing the cluster group and then gives them assignments or projects related to what the rest of the class is doing, but on a level that demands a greater mastery of skills and concepts, a higher level of thinking, and creative reasoning or imagining. As a rule, gifted students don't get enough time to work with other gifted students, and, for this reason, cluster groups are urgently needed in the primary grades. They significantly increase the quality of learning that happens when high-ability students pool their talents and experiences. Sometimes two teachers in the same grade will combine their cluster groups and take turns working with them. A knowledgeable parent also can perform this role.

Differentiating focuses on three areas—the content (subject, concepts, information, skills); the process (hands-on activities, applications of learning in new situations); and products (the work your child does—writing, drawings, math problems, science experiments, etc.). The question that parents of young gifted children often raise is, "To what extent does differentiating go beyond adjusting the pace and level of difficulty in a lesson or unit?" Compacting, learning stations, tiered activities, and clustering may ensure that children don't repeat content they already know, but these options in practice don't always address alternative learning styles or the need young gifted students have to do more creative work. To be carried out well, differentiation involves a variety of factors for the teacher to consider. Let's consider several suggestions about ways you can contribute to making differentiation powerful and positive for your child.

Supporting Differentiated Instruction in the Home

In many ways, differentiated instruction, especially for young children, begins in the home. Parents know their child more intimately than anyone else. They've observed her strengths and weaknesses, her passions and interests, and they understand what situations frustrate or stimulate her. Over the years, they've gained a wealth of knowledge and insight into how, when, and why their child learns best and into the situations or experiences that tend to induce confidence or disappointment, apprehension or determination, fear or exhilaration. For these reasons, they are in a unique position to respond in an immediate and spontaneous way to their child's learning needs. Here are two examples:

My son is a naturalist. From his earliest years, he quickly picked up the names of different plants and animals that people would mention. When he started reading at age 4, we bought him some nature books. He would pore over these books. At one point, though, I realized that just rattling off the names of different species was mostly an exercise in memory. It didn't really apply to anything or demand much thought. So, I took him off to the woods and fields one day and wondered out loud what this or that bird or plant was. We brought our field guides and debated the possibilities. He was thrilled! This has evolved into he and I taking a few naturalist workshops together and doing art and science projects.—Mother of second grader

My daughter loves to read. Towards the end of the day, she skulks off to a corner and reads for a couple of hours before dinner. My wife and I had this idea one day of having a family book club. We both enjoy children's books anyway and as my daughter reads pretty advanced stuff, we thought: Why don't we all read at least some of the same books and then have discussions? This has been wonderful for our family, but it's helped my daughter the most. She used to struggle expressing herself out loud. Our discussions have gotten her to come out of herself more and think more deeply about what she's reading.—Father of third grader

These parents are doing, in a natural way, what teachers do in a differentiated classroom—creating projects that inspire creative thinking and reasoning, and providing resources that pique the child's curiosity and stimulate a hunger to learn more. Experiences like this in the home are vital for a young child's emerging sense of himself as a learner and instill, in his earliest years, an anticipation and excitement for discovery. In her book, *The Sense of Wonder,* Rachel Carson illustrated the importance of these early experiences best when she wrote:

When Roger has visited me in Maine and we have walked in these woods I have made no conscious effort to name plants or animals nor to explain to him, but have just expressed my own pleasure in what we see, calling his attention to this or that but only as I would share discoveries with an older person. Later I have been amazed at the way names stick in his mind, for when I show color slides of my woods plants it is Roger who can identify them. "Oh, that's what Rachel likes—that's bunchberry!" Or, "That's Jumer (juniper) but you can't eat those green berries—they are for the squirrels." I am sure no amount of drill would have implanted the names so firmly as just going through the woods in the spirit of two friends on an expedition of exciting discovery. (p. 23)

Like Roger, young gifted children build on their knowledge by exploring their environment. They finger, touch, taste, and shape whatever they can get their hands on. They carry a "sense of wonder" everywhere they go. The world bombards their eyes, ears, nose, and tastebuds with multiple and complex sensations. The beauty of Canadian geese flying south at dusk awes them; the pounding beat of the bass from a passing car radio shakes them to their bones; the gentle breeze that sends the fallen leaves into a halfhearted spin makes them want to leap into the air; the pelting rain against their skin feels like a whipping from the sky.

Young gifted children crave artistic and creative ways to express these keenly felt impressions. But as practiced in the schools, differentiated instruction does not always address the sensibility and artistry of the young gifted child. Yet, because of the focus on observation, hearing, feeling, moving, touching, intuiting, and imagining, creativity should always be a cornerstone of differentiated instruction. As parents, you can foster this at home. You can use the arts not only to support your child's talents, but also to expand on the assignments or projects she does for school. The following descriptions provide some examples.

Juliette enjoyed her class on geometric shapes. One day after school, she showed her mother what she was working on and her mother showed her some prints from the Cubists and asked if she would like to create a geometric painting. Juliette spent a week designing her geometric painting and learned a lot about how the different shapes related to each other. (Visual Art)

Joseph loved what he was learning about the rainforest. He talked about all the creatures that live there and asked his parents if he could go there one day. His father took the family to the aquarium where there was an exhibit of lizards from the South American rainforest. Later, Joseph sketched a portrait of one of the lizards and wrote a "Day in the Life" story about himself as the lizard. He particularly enjoyed describing how each of his eyes moved independently and how his tongue lashes out at insects. (Visual Art)

Kara was studying the solar system in her science class. After a trip to the planetarium, Kara and her friends began arguing about which way certain planets moved. Kara's mother suggested that they look at the material they got from the planetarium and recreate the solar system using their own bodies. The children became excited about performing the solar system for their class. For hours, she could hear the children discussing orbits, directions, and distances. (Dance)

Jimmy did very well in math, but could never go far with it when people just explained how it worked. He had to do it. His father understood this and so together they would often dramatize the word problems (acting out the people, actions, or events presented in the problem). Jimmy always figured out the solution right away and sometimes they would continue the problem like a story and create even more complicated problems. From these experiences, Jimmy began to see math as a kind of theater. (Drama)

Simon didn't like social studies and groaned when he had to do a report on Henry David Thoreau. His mother suggested that he assume the role of the author and naturalist, rather than just report on him. She got a video about Thoreau from the library and she helped him with costumes while he did some research on the man. They went to a nearby pond so that he could practice reading a few passages by Thoreau while dressed like him. Simon discovered that he had to do so much research to impersonate Thoreau that writing the report was easy. (Drama)

Laura had to create a visual display and some text describing where her family came from and how they came to the United States. As her mother and grandmother told her about how her people came from Canada, they asked Laura if she would like to create a dance/mime about their emigration. Her parents helped her select important events in the journey. They looked at old photographs and told stories. They found costumes and props and when she finally performed it, her mother videotaped it to share with other family members. (Dance)

Young gifted students with agile, hungry minds always need a rich and varied medium for learning within different disciplines. Creativity facilitates this. It enables them to discover that the shapes and patterns they see in math also occur in art, movement, architecture, and countless natural phenomena. Without this creative dimension, differentiating cannot accommodate their unique sensibilities and talents.

Support Differentiated Instruction in the Classroom

Primary teachers may have limited time to acquaint themselves with each young child in a class that is diverse in ability, background, and learning style. Many of them know that parents are a rich and often untapped source of information and insight. There are many points in a unit or lesson when the feedback of parents could aid the teacher and child in significant ways. Parents can do this by sharing an example of the child's work before a new unit begins. Or, they might be able to shed light on a misjudgment about their child's ability or learning style that will guide the teacher to other options. Some examples follow.

When I got this note from the first grade teacher about Brandon's need for extra help in math, I laughed. Brandon was already multiplying and dividing! I went to the teacher and showed her the sheets of paper with his math scribbles. I said that my son loved math so much that he had learned how to multiply and divide from his older brother. From then on, she worked out a way to accelerate Brandon through first-grade math and then put him in a cluster of kids from first and second grade who worked with the third-grade teacher on more challenging and, to Brandon, much more interesting material.—Mother of a first grader

I was nervous about asking the teacher to help my child at the beginning of the year. We are from South America and it just isn't our way to make demands on teachers. I told her that I caught my son doing the homework of a much older kid in our neighborhood—for money! I told her I was concerned because he acted like school was just nothing to take seriously. He didn't work that hard in class and probably didn't look like much of a student. Anyway, the teacher was kind to me and said that she would take what I said and look at him more closely. She had another student who was doing more difficult work in the class and she would have them partner with each other.—Father of a second grader

To gauge how your gifted child is doing in a differentiated classroom, discuss class activities in different subjects. Let him explain the papers, projects, tests, and assignments he brings home. If he says he's bored or unhappy about something, try to discover why. Is it that he's not interested in the topic or skill, that he finds the activity predictable, difficult, or confusing, or that he has to repeat content he's already mastered? Avoid quick judgments based on one or two comments the child makes or on a project he brings home. Try to find out as much as you can about your child's complaint before going to the teacher. Is the problem what the child says or could it be something that he's not saying? For example, does he think his language arts class is boring because the content isn't challenging or is it because he has to do an oral report that he dreads? Is this complaint part of a pattern?

Many parents find that primary teachers are open to feedback and suggestions, provided the parents approach them diplomatically. Here is the story of a mother whose child was not thriving in an arrangement meant to help her:

My daughter's second grade teacher has a cluster group of gifted students and she had Marianna join them. After a couple of weeks, I sensed that something was wrong and Marianna finally admitted that she didn't feel comfortable in the group. When I pressed her for details, she said that the other kids were all friends with each other, but not her. I tried telling her that she was still a new kid in school, but she kept saying that she didn't like doing any of the things they had to do in the group. I finally met with the teacher and explained the problem. The teacher said that she would try grouping Marianna with some of her friends and give her more challenging assignments within that group. She knew Marianna was a voracious reader and loved challenge, but understood that, for now, she needed to feel like she fit in somewhere.—Mother of a second grader

Because differentiating rests on who your child is as a learner and what she brings to the learning table (i.e., strengths, interests), you as a parent are indispensable to ensuring that your child benefits from the strategies a teacher uses. As the school year progresses, you will get a better handle on how this system is working for your child and whether or not the teacher really understands her abilities and learning needs.

Getting Involved in the Classroom

Some parents have had a significant impact by participating in the classroom itself. As districts continue to experience budget cuts, they are turning more than ever before to parent volunteers to help them provide enrichment and guide groups of children in different activities. Parents of young gifted children have helped instruct and support cluster groups, acted as aids at learning centers, and provided one-on-one support and guidance for children doing independent studies. Differentiated instruction is a daunting task for any teacher and it practically cries out for helpers. Because of this, classrooms today are more open than ever before to the contributions of parents, particularly if those parents understand how the system works and have specific skills or areas of expertise to share.

Here are several examples from parents:

I come from a family of journalists. I did some journalism in my twenties and then in my thirties went into business. But I had the chance to reignite my love for journalism by working with a group of gifted kids in my daughter's class who wanted to start a school newspaper. It's been an incredible experience. We study a variety of newspapers, we explore interview techniques, writing styles, photojournalism, and discuss what departments we want to include. We've worked out who should handle what. We have movie and book reviewers, reporters and feature writers. All the kids in the class now want to get involved and write for the paper. It has become a catalyst for writing, discussing, and debating all sorts of issues.—Father of a third grader

I've always loved art, and I do a lot of art activities with my kids at home. One of the parents who volunteers at the school told my child's teacher about me, and she asked if I'd like to share some of my techniques with the class. That was 2 years ago and now I'm doing these "sessions" in different grades. I meet with the teacher, we talk over how I can relate my session to specific topics, and then plan to meet different needs. I love it because it encourages divergent thinking and the gifted children go wild over it. I also enjoy working with other gifted children besides my own. It's taught me a lot and given me a larger sense of the needs of gifted kids.—Mother of a first grader

Participating in a classroom may not happen right away. Often, you need to build a relationship with the teacher first. It helps to present yourself as someone who understands the enormous responsibilities of a differentiated classroom, but as someone who also is committed to the ideal of giving children (including the gifted) the kind of education they need. As the teacher comes to know you as a supporter, learns what you can do and how you can help, opportunities will open up for you to become more involved in your child's classroom. And each time you assist with a cluster group or tutor a couple of students about to embark on a new project, you will be helping to make differentiation a system that really serves young gifted students.

Resources

Belgrad, S. (1998). Creating the most enabling environment for young gifted children. In J. F. Smutny (Ed.), *The young gifted child: Potential and promise: An anthology* (pp. 369–379). Cresskill, NJ: Hampton Press.

Moll, L. C. (1992). Funds of knowledge for teaching: Using a qualitative approach to connect homes and classrooms. *Theory Into Practice, 31,* 132–141.

Morrison, G. S. (1997). *Fundamentals of early childhood education.* Upper Saddle River, NJ: Prentice Hall.

Smutny, J. F., Walker, S. Y., & Meckstroth, E. A. (1997). *Teaching young gifted children in the regular classroom: Identifying, nurturing, and challenging ages 4–9.* Minneapolis, MN: Free Spirit Publishing.

Smutny, J. F., & von Fremd, S. E. (2004). *Differentiating for the young child: Teaching strategies across the content areas (K–3).* Thousand Oaks, CA: Corwin Press.

Reference

Carson, R. (1998). *The sense of wonder.* New York, NY: HarperCollins.

Chapter 24

Differentiated Curriculum Experiences for the Gifted and Talented: A Parent's Guide to Best Practice in School and at Home

by Joyce VanTassel-Baska

L ILA was an intellectually active child whose interests far outstripped what was available to her at home. Her parents thought she would be deeply challenged when she began her school experience in the neighborhood school. To their dismay, she began to withdraw from her classmates, complain of stomachaches, and cry to stay home. Upon examination, they found that she was doing work well below her ability and achievement level and working on repetitive tasks that upset her. When they confronted her teacher, they were told that the school did not modify its curriculum for gifted learners.

This story is not an uncommon one among parents of gifted children at various ages. It tells a sad tale of parental expectations for schools that are frequently not met because of lack of flexibility in the curriculum. The key variable in children's attitudes toward school often is the appropriateness of the level, pace, and the delivery of the curriculum. This article describes several important ingredients of a rich curriculum for high-ability students.

In a world full of expanding choices, developing carefully planned courses of study for gifted students has become increasingly necessary. As parents, you share with the school the responsibility for ensuring that your child's learning experiences are well-planned and challenging. In order to search out alternative ways of providing the best curriculum experience that matches your child's needs, you will need some knowledge about the criteria for good and appropriate curricula. In addition, to be an effective parental advocate for your child, it will be helpful for you to consider active engagement with the design, development, and implementation of curriculum. I often meet with parents in my office to discuss what curriculum experiences have worked well and which ones have not and to work with them on how to build optimal experiences into their child's learning. In order to do this as parents, you must first understand what you are looking for. A key to understanding appropriate curriculum is knowing your child's strengths and areas of relative weakness as well her interests and passions. It would be even more helpful to know how your child is advanced in relevant strength areas and be able to document it. For example, one of the students in our Saturday program at The College of William and Mary was able to recite all license plate numbers and addresses for his neighborhood by the age of 3, while a 9-year-old student came up with 483 homonyms on her own over one weekend because she was fascinated with that type of word relationship. What both children did illustrates aptitude and passion working together. You are in the best position to observe advanced behavior and record it; you may wish to keep a chart of such behaviors with the date, age, and frequency of occurrence. Such indicators attest to your child's strong predispositions toward diverse types of phenomena in the world and point the way toward the most appropriate areas for differentiating curriculum for her or him.

How might you as a parent think through curriculum options for your child? The following guidelines may help you gauge the appropriateness of your child's school experience and plan engaging and fun activities at home for her. Appropriate curriculum options for gifted children should have the following features.

1. *Use materials and activities aimed above the child's tested level of performance in order to promote growth in learning.* The use of

advanced problem sets in math, open-ended experiments in science, more difficult reading material, and greater rigorous thinking about historical events are hallmarks of a strong curriculum for gifted children. As a parent, you may wish to purchase educational toys and games recommended (or "pitched") for children two age levels above your child's to see how she will respond. Take trips to the library and select more advanced books to see how your child reacts. Gifted children many times become highly motivated to become engaged with materials that they find sufficiently challenging.

2. *Provide children with experiences that move them from concrete experiences to abstract conceptual experiences.* In reading, for example, gifted students at all ages should be routinely encouraged to move from a discussion of plot, a concrete literary element, to a discussion of themes. This constitutes a more abstract element of reading because it is implied but rarely stated. Working at a more abstract level requires greater use of thinking processes. Ask your child questions about the book she is reading. Even if you have not read the book, you can engage your child in questions such as, "Why do you suppose the author decided to tell the story this way?" "What was the point of it?" "Why was the book written? or "What did the author really want us to understand?" Such questions will spur your child to more abstract reasoning.

3. *Provide opportunities for relevant applications and creative responses.* Although abstract thinking is a highly valued skill, it is meaningless if the child does not have the ability to apply it to real-world problems. Gifted students need opportunities to hone their thinking skills in the service of their society. Service learning projects that test their ingenuity, problem-finding, and problem-solving skills in an action arena can contribute to their growth in the cognitive, social, and affective dimensions. As a parent, you can involve your child in "cleanup" days in the community and help her to link her understanding of personal responsibility to community and global environmental issues. You also can encourage your child to get to know a rest home resident by interviewing,

performing needed tasks, and helping with problems encountered. Such work also helps build commitment through seeing the results of one's efforts having an impact on people's lives. Through such interaction with the community, your child can begin to appreciate others and be more sensitive to her circumstances.

4. *Work on developing depth of understanding of a particular topic or concept.* One of the best ways to ensure depth in a curriculum is through focused study on a topic of interest to the child or one that the child has selected. Teach your child to examine a topic or issue from multiple perspectives using several types of resources to enhance depth of understanding. Create opportunities for your child to hold conversations with others knowledgeable about the topic. If your child's interest persists, encourage her to conduct original research. A simple family outing or annual summer vacation could easily be converted into a research project. Involve your children in planning these events, and ask them to create holiday plans that would be economical and yet meet the family's needs. Insist that they conduct research as a backdrop to the planning, discussing where they can obtain the necessary information, what form it should take, and when it should be available for discussion with the family. Your children will begin to see that research allows for deeper learning necessary to many life tasks.

5. *Move steadily toward greater complexity and challenge.* When you go through schoolwork with your child, pay attention to the challenge level of the materials, reading assignments, and projects to be completed, and see if they contain advanced work. At home, you might wish to scan the editorial pages of local newspapers for relevant issues for family discussion, highlighting for your children multiple perspectives on real-world issues and the assumptions that account for various points of view. For this purpose, you might find it easy to use the editorial debate format used by *USA Today*.

6. *Help children experience curriculum that reflects a world view.* Effective curriculum experiences deal with global interdependence and examine multiple perspectives of cultures and

religions, based on their history and geography. Analyzing the history of world regions gives students an appreciation for how current world conflicts have a long history of development and no easy solutions. As a parent, you can promote this understanding through travel to other cultures, having friends from other cultures, and exposing your children to different religious and local cultural activities. Attendance at important rituals of other cultures not only helps to ease the sense of differentness but also enhance children's appreciation of diversity.

7. *Emphasize the importance of using critical and creative thinking in tandem.* Projects should involve children in both creative and critical thinking. Using predetermined criteria to choose the best option after a brainstorming session is one example of this combined process at work; another is synthesizing multiple points of view in a written or oral presentation. Share your own passions and expertise with your child, and then discuss the processes involved in pursuing an interest area successfully. For example, if you are an avid photographer, you might share the skills, both artistic and technical, for photographing a particular scene or subject. Then, ask your child to critique the photo on both artistic and technical criteria. Next, have your child apply these skills to her own picture-taking and suggest creating an album of "best shots." You also might appoint your child the official photographer for your family vacation, and encourage him or her to consider the best ways to capture shots on traditional, digital, and video cameras.

8. *Emphasize the key ideas, themes, processes, and skills that underlay all areas of study to give students an integrated framework for understanding.* Concepts like change, systems, and models have come to be seen as central to understanding more than a single domain. Guided by specific questions of interest, children can understand skills like research within and across areas of study. As parents, you can be helpful tutors to your children in many fields that you understand very well. Try teaching your child the foundations of your own vocation. What skills, activities, and attitudes are essential in your work? If your child wanted

to know more about your specialization area, how could they inquire about it? What are key questions and resources they might explore? Organizing the "big picture" for a topic can contribute to your child's capacity to look for the basic patterns in any area of study.

9. *Provide both required and optional opportunities.* A combination approach of optional and required work ensures the element of choice, as well as a sequenced learning pattern in core areas that is sufficiently rigorous. You also can provide opportunities for learning that contain just such a balance. When attending a science museum, for example, decisions for everyone to visit and explore key exhibits will allow for common understanding, while some exhibits in a given room could be open for your child's selection, especially given limited time. Then you might ask your child to share with the rest of the family what he discovered and learned at an optional exhibit.

10. *Involve children in collaborative and individual work.* Group or collaborative learning has become a staple of our educational systems. However, even within collaborative projects, the integrity of individual work must still be maintained to ensure a good balance between collaborative efforts and individual ones. You can define family projects according to individual responsibility and collaborative effort. Responsibility for preparing dinner, raking the yard, and cleaning the house are all viable avenues to use in making these important distinctions. Not everyone has to be working together on each of these activities. Dad might prefer to make dinner alone; mom might prefer to do the yard work with the children. These are real-world choices made based on individual preferences. Letting your child voice such preferences and act on them provides a healthy balance between independence and interdependence in getting work done.

11. *Be clear about the expected results and how to assess them.* You and your child have a right to know upfront what desired learning will result from school experiences and how teachers will assess those results and outcomes. If the school organizes an

orientation session devoted to curriculum, make it your priority to attend. Many schools also now post their instructional objectives, outcomes, and assessment criteria on their websites. These sites are a wealth of information. At home, you can practice this same behavior with your children by answering the question, "Why do I need to know that?" before the child asks, providing ways for your children to demonstrate their learning. You can help your children define a new learning outcome to be mastered during the year, such as swimming, piano playing, or learning French. Set up a special context and time for them to demonstrate how they have learned the material. In sports and the arts, it is typical to set up matches and recitals. You can use this model in academics as well. Your child, even though high in ability in some areas, may need to improve in others (e.g., she may be very good in reading, but need to improve in math skills). Defining the specific areas for improvement, specifying a time frame, and providing a platform for displaying their progress can help children view academic learning as a personal challenge that is worthwhile.

12. *Recognize that your child's teachers should have qualification in the areas of study and/or have education in working with gifted learners.* A central feature of effective learning is the quality of instruction delivered by knowledgeable and caring educators. It is important that educators who work with high-ability learners have the expertise necessary to help their students grow. Knowledge of content-relevant teaching strategies (as well as content understanding) is an essential qualification. In relation to your teaching role as parents, it is important for you to consider your special gifts. One parent once apologized to me for teaching her child French, thinking she had provided a disservice. I suggested that she had done a quite wonderful thing—she had given a gift of herself and her own learning to her child and in the process created a special bond between them. All parents have knowledge in key areas to consider passing on. Working out a time and place to engage in such learning with regularity may be difficult, but it is potentially

highly rewarding for both you and your child. You will learn more about your child's learning habits and quality of thinking than through any other process you might undertake. The development of eminent individuals in many domains often has included family sharing of learned skills.

13. *Gifted students at all levels should be engaged in work "beyond the standards" both in level and scope.* Although it is true that new state standards often are rigorous, they might still be accelerated and extended for gifted students at all levels and in all subject areas. Minimum standards are insufficiently complex and advanced to be used as the sole curriculum base for gifted learners. You should try to be familiar with the standards of learning your child is expected to meet and exceed at school. Such knowledge can provide a basis for discussions at home, special math applications, or home projects, science experiments, or demonstrations. Beyond the minimum content standards, you also want to know if your child is learning the intellectual tools of inquiring and problem-solving and the ability to transfer or apply those skills in the real world.

Application of the Curriculum Guidelines

There are many ways you can directly apply guidelines for effective curriculum experiences in the home setting to stimulate the development of your gifted child. Quality time spent discussing ideas, viewing television and movies, and playing games and doing puzzles with your children are all important. A recent study by the University of Chicago suggested that parents taking children to science museums contributed more to science achievement at age 10 than any other intervention. Your power as educators of your children is truly profound.

You also may apply these guidelines in conversations with teachers and principals about your child's learning on a regular basis. They could be used to make judgments about effective extracurricular academic work as well. When choosing summer and Saturday programs or even schools for your child to attend, use these guidelines to evaluate their offerings.

Conclusion

In an age of consumerism where a free enterprise mentality rules, marketing is the key skill employed to attract customers. Education is not exempt from these pressures, and many programs for gifted learners are offered with an eye to the market. The burden of judicious decision making therefore rests with you and your children in deciding the quality of the program they receive. Hopefully, you will find this set of guidelines timely and useful to judge programs by their curriculum features, as well as apply key principles to your child's learning in the home.

Resources

Burke, J. (1995). *Connections* (Revised ed.). Boston, MA: Little, Brown.

Cothron, J. H., Giese, R. N., & Rezba, R. J. (2007). *Students and research: Practical strategies for science classrooms and competitions* (4th ed.). Dubuque, IA: Kendall/Hunt.

Kaplan, S., & Cannon, M. W. (2002). *Curriculum starter cards: Developing differentiated lessons for gifted children.* Waco, TX: Prufrock Press.

Renzulli, J. S., Leppien, J. H., & Hays, T. S. (2000). *The Multiple Menu Model: A practical guide for developing differentiated curriculum.* Mansfield Center, CT: Creative Learning Press.

Saul, W., & Newman, A. (1986). *Science fare: An illustrated guide and catalog of toys, books, and activities for kids.* New York, NY: Harper & Row.

Tomlinson, C., Kaplan, S. N., Renzulli, J. S., Purcell, J., Leppien, J., & Burns, D. (2002). *The Parallel Curriculum: A design to develop high potential and challenge high ability learners.* Thousand Oaks, CA: Corwin Press.

VanTassel-Baska, J., Johnson, D., & Boyce, L. (1996). *Developing verbal talent.* Boston, MA: Allyn & Bacon.

VanTassel-Baska, J., & Little, C. A. (Eds.). (2010). *Content-based curriculum for gifted learners* (2nd ed.). Waco, TX: Prufrock Press.

The Path From Potential to Productivity: The Parent's Role in the Levels of Service Approach to Talent Development

by Nancy A. Cook, Carol V. Wittig, and Donald J. Treffinger

YOUR child spends about a third of his or her weekday in school and a third sleeping. But what about the other third? What about weekends and school holidays? And what about summer vacation? During this time are you using your parenting skills to develop your child's high potential?

We propose that your major goal in parenting for high potential is to help your child develop into a healthy (in many ways) and effective person who is an independent learner and a creatively productive person. Keep this three-part goal in mind whenever you're making decisions about what you might do to help your child continue to grow in his or her strengths and talents.

To help your children reach this complex goal, you need to manage and monitor your children's activities and behavior and to communicate with your children and their school about their strengths, interests, and needs. It also is very important for you to play an active role in guiding the development of qualities and skills your children will need to reach this goal. Finally, although we often think about instruction as

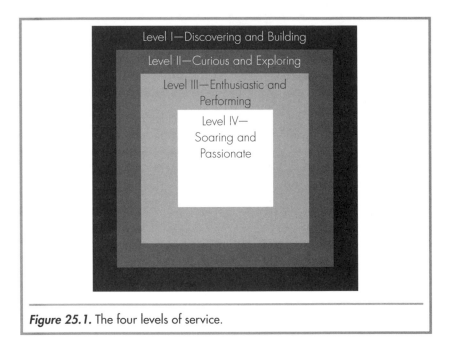

Figure 25.1. The four levels of service.

the school's job, you can play an important role as an educator for your child, too. Creating an effective partnership among school, home, and community can be an essential part of discovering and nurturing any child's strengths and talents.

In our school district, and in a number of other schools in several states, we have been working to implement an approach to programming for talent development called the "Levels of Service" (LOS) approach, which involves four levels or stages. ("Services" refers to any planned, deliberate experiences or activities that contribute to talent development. See Figure 25.1 for an illustration of the four levels.) In the LOS approach, we emphasize the school-home-community relationship for recognizing and developing talents and meeting the goal we stated at the beginning of this article. This article focuses specifically on the important role of the home in the LOS partnership, presenting examples of experiences and activities you can provide at each of the four levels in developing your child's potential.

At Level I, you will help your child discover and build interests and potential strengths. At Level II, your child's natural curiosity will lead to exploratory activities that may verify those interests and potential strengths, and at Level III, your child's enthusiasm may lead to more in-depth activities that will help to develop those unique potential strengths further. At Level IV, your child may pursue a passion as he or she combines knowledge, skill, and sustained interests to act as a creative, productive, and independent learner.

As we discuss each level in more depth, we'll look at three main themes within each of the four levels: Provide Opportunities, Watch For, and Build Thinking Skills and Dispositions. In Provide Opportunities, we give suggestions for activities and where to find them. Under Watch For, we discuss positive behaviors that should be evident, as well as negative behaviors you might observe. You might make notes or record your observations about these behaviors, use them to identify new activities to do at home, or discuss them with your child's teachers. In Build Thinking Skills and Dispositions, we present information on nurturing your child's creative thinking, critical thinking, problem-solving, and decision-making skills, as well as the attitudes and dispositions that children need to become independent learners and good citizens.

Level I: Discovering and Building

At this level, your role is to provide your children with exposure to talent or interest possibilities and to build thinking skills by:

- Offering a rich and varied array of opportunities that provide exposure to many topics, themes, or talent areas. (A "talent area" is any field, domain, or performance area in which a person might engage such as writing, acting, chemistry, local history, sculpture, or soccer.)
- Exploring areas of possible interest to build a foundation for talent recognition and development.
- Looking for your child's unique strengths and preferences as a learner (all children differ in their style, rate, pace, and preferred styles of learning).
- Engaging your children in learning and practicing tools and strategies for thinking creatively and critically.

Provide Opportunities

Level I activities are generally brief in duration and readily accomplished. You can find opportunities in the daily newspaper, a school newsletter, the local library, and on the Internet. Talk with your child's teachers or guidance counselors to find out the opportunities available at school. Listed below are some suggestions and examples that will help you discover and build strengths in your children.

- Playing games with your child can develop many different strength and interest areas. Strategy games such as tic-tac-toe, chess, checkers, Clue™, Master Mind™, and many card games help to develop logical thinking, while word games such as SCRABBLE™, Boggle™, charades, and crossword puzzles develop linguistic thinking.
- Taking your children on mini field trips to museums, the zoo, art galleries, and the library can help you identify their interests in a wide variety of talent areas.
- Attending live concert and theatre performances may stimulate interest in music or the performing arts.
- A special interest in nature may arise when children are exposed to hiking, camping, and nature walks.
- Volunteer with your child by collecting money, organizing a food or clothing drive, or helping out at the local animal shelter. Your teenager might find it rewarding to volunteer at an assisted living facility or a nursing home. These experiences will lead to developing personal and social responsibility.
- You may find that your child is a young philosopher if you provide opportunities for pondering and discussing. Some parents we know organized a parent/child book club. Everyone read the same book and met at someone's house to discuss the ideas from the book. Your local library or bookstore also might have story hours or book clubs for young children and teens.
- Provide opportunities for sports and physical activities as part of an active, well-balanced lifestyle. Be sure to try a variety of different individual sports that can be long-time sources of enjoyment, such as horseback riding, biking, or rollerblading.

Opportunities for Level I activities can arise in many ways and can involve a variety of places and resources. One father, for example, read in the newspaper that the local zoo planned to build a new habitat for prairie dogs. Because he knew that his son was interested in animals and their habitats, they went together on a visit to the zoo. They saw the sign and the plan for the new habitat. The child wanted to find out more so he located several books, went online for more information, and found a video in the school media center.

Watch For

While your child is engaged in activities, watch for signs of sustained interest and potential strengths. Is your child enjoying the activity? Look for smiles or intense concentration. Does your child request the activity be repeated? Is it difficult to tear your child away from the activity? Does your child show signs of craving more of a challenge?

Everyone has different learning styles, rates and paces of learning, and interest areas. Keep in mind that your child may be different from you and different from other children in the family. Ask questions such as: Does your child learn best alone or with others? Does your child need to move around when learning? What is your child's attention span and frustration tolerance level? Does your child prefer following directions or doing things his or her own way?

Build Thinking Skills and Dispositions

As a parent, you can help your child develop his or her creative and critical thinking abilities in a number of enjoyable ways. Creative thinking involves generating many ideas, looking at ideas from many points of view or in different ways, or producing novel and unusual ideas. Begin by encouraging an attitude of deferred judgment (not criticizing ideas when you're thinking of many possibilities), searching for as many ideas as possible, accepting all ideas (even those that might seem silly), and making connections among ideas. You can ask open-ended, creative questions to apply these guidelines in everyday situations, including at the meal table ("What are all the things we might use a fork to do?"), when brushing teeth ("How might we improve the toothbrush or the toothpaste container?"), or in the car ("What are many things we might see that are round and red?").

Critical thinking involves focusing your thinking by developing, improving, analyzing, selecting, or evaluating ideas. The guidelines for focusing one's thinking include looking at ideas constructively (building ideas up, rather than putting them down), being deliberate when making decisions, remembering to look for novelty (not disregarding unusual ideas), and keeping your eye on your goal.

You can apply these guidelines at home by using several tools or strategies. For example, one helpful tool is called ALOU (advantages, limitations, overcome, and unique). When you are considering an idea or a decision, begin by identifying its advantages (what's attractive about it or why you like it). Then, think about its limitations (areas of concern or weaknesses). Be constructive about the limitations by asking "How might we . . ." (e.g., rather than saying, "It will take too much time," ask, "How might we find or make the time to do it?"). Then, think about ways to overcome the limitations. Finally, ask yourself what's unique about the idea, or what makes it stand out and appeal to you.

Many everyday situations offer excellent opportunities to practice using some tools for creative and critical thinking. For example, a mom, a dad, and their two daughters were discussing an aunt's upcoming birthday and what gift to buy for her. They wanted to give her something really special and decided to use creative thinking to generate options. Within a few minutes, they had listed 20 ideas. They switched to critical thinking, and as they reviewed the ideas, three really stood out as promising. They used the ALOU tool to focus their thinking, and chose an idea that would be novel, reasonable in cost, and a present that they were confident the aunt would really enjoy.

Level II: Curious and Exploring

At this level, enable your child to explore and verify interests or possible talent strengths through organized activities. To stimulate curiosity and heighten anticipation, it's important to seek opportunities that appeal to your children and that they play an active role in selecting. Many activities are available that stimulate children's interests, engage them in active learning, and provide excellent learning opportunities that extend beyond the classroom and provide practice with thinking skills and tools.

Provide Opportunities

Your school district's community education program often is a good source of activities and information about program opportunities. Also look to your local museums, art galleries, zoos, and colleges for opportunities for students in the elementary, middle, or secondary grades. Some specific examples of Level II opportunities include:

- In many communities, universities, galleries, museums, and science centers offer afterschool, weekend, or summer experiences for students to pursue areas of interest and enjoyment. National programs, such as Camp Invention (http://www.campinvention.org), provide engaging programs for students to learn about science, creative thinking, and inventing.
- At this level, many children become involved in team sports. There are organizations that teach the sports and give children opportunities to participate at a beginning level. Seek programs that emphasize learning and enjoyment of the game, not just the competitive nature of the sport.
- There are clubs and organizations that may focus on your child's areas of interest or potential strength such as 4H clubs or scouting organizations.
- Individual lessons for particular interests such as music, computers, horseback riding, writing, or dancing also are appropriate Level II activities to verify and explore potential strengths and interests.
- The National PTA Reflections Program encourages children to create works in literature, musical composition, photography, and the visual arts (see http://www.pta.org/topic_parent_involvement.asp).
- Consider participating in structured creativity or problem-solving programs. There are a number of program possibilities,

but two excellent programs with which we have worked are Destination ImagiNation (http://www.idodi.org) and the Future Problem Solving Program (http://www.fpspi.org).

- The Great Books Foundation (http://www.greatbooks.org) helps readers develop their thinking skills through discussion of literary classics. This program may be available in your schools or can be run by parents who have undergone the training on how to facilitate a discussion group.

Watch For

Again, watch for the same signs of developing strengths and budding interests as you did with Level I activities. There may be times when a level of frustration might surface in more formalized activities and programs. Working through frustrations and finding success with challenging opportunities develops a positive self-concept and personal confidence. Be certain that activities and experiences are:

- appropriate (consistent with your child's needs and characteristics),
- challenging (invitingly provocative), and
- developmental (enabling progress or advancement to new or higher levels).

Keep in mind the main goals of programming that we presented at the beginning of this article when deciding whether to "push" your child to stay with an activity or to allow her or him to have a change of mind about participating. Encourage high but reasonable expectations. Also, don't overlook the importance of appreciating and celebrating growth and accomplishments; these encourage children to persevere.

Build Thinking Skills and Dispositions

In order to develop a strength to full potential, one must raise the difficulty level and often invest a substantial amount of time practicing or learning new skills. How do you persevere when something is tough? What if a task is particularly tedious but necessary? How do you get it done? Your child needs to deal with these issues. Make a list of things to do when faced with a challenge such as breaking the task into smaller steps and tackling them one at a time, walking away for a short break and returning to the task with fresh eyes, talking out the task with someone else, and if necessary, asking for help. It can be important for him or her to see you deal with similar challenges, too.

To deal with tedious but necessary tasks, your children might try listening to their favorite music, just "doing it" and getting it over with, rewarding themselves for getting it done, breaking it up into manageable pieces, getting someone to do it with them, making it into a game or adventure, or timing themselves. You and your children can benefit from practicing these responses and discussing them together.

Level III: Enthusiastic and Performing

Level I provided a foundation and basic tools, and Level II provided for exploration and trying additional challenging activities. The purpose of Level III activities is to strengthen the child's competence, confidence, and commitment in a talent area as his or her engagement and involvement grows in that area. The opportunities you connect to your child at this level should respond to his or her individual strengths, talents, and sustained interests. Level III experiences and activities build on Levels I and II, but they expand and increase the level of involvement and challenge. Appropriate Level III activities will be opportunities in which your child exhibits a great deal of enthusiasm and energy and begins to perform with emerging expertise.

Provide Opportunities

Opportunities at Level III are more advanced and may include competitions, performances, team sports, or other activities designed for children with an identified strength in a specific talent area. The activities we list below are examples for several talent areas.

- For a budding young actor, look for a youth theatre group that auditions children for local performances.

- The NAGC website (http://www.nagc.org) has an array of summer opportunities listed by region to challenge your child's specific strengths, interests, and needs. What about a summer invention program, space camp, or a computer camp?

- Find out what academic competitions your school participates in such as the National Geographic Bee (http://www.nationalgeographic.com/geographybee), Scripps National Spelling Bee (http://www.spellingbee.com), Science Olympiad (http://www.soinc.org), or Math Olympiads (http://www.moems.org). Also look for locally sponsored competitions such as writing and art contests or math and debate competitions.

- You can help your young writer learn the process that professional writers go through, which includes continually writing, revising, and submitting work for possible publication. Check the Internet for sources that publish children's work such as *Creative Kids* magazine (http://www.prufrock.com/client/client_pages/prufrock_jm_createkids.cfm).

- Drexel University offers an interactive math problem-solving website (http://www.mathforum.com) that provides children with four problems every week at different levels from upper elementary through high school. Children solve these nontraditional and often realistic problems and write an explanation of their thinking processes. Mentors provide individual feedback for the children, and exemplary solutions are chosen to be published on the website for other children to view.

- For your young computer expert, look for a user group in your area or online. You may organize your own group of children with similar abilities and interests. Often providing the proper software and like minds to collaborate with is enough to spur independent exploration and intellectual growth.

- Young computer experts often need only some basic guidance before soaring through designing their own software or web pages. If given the time and access to a computer, software, and instruction manuals, these children are able to produce amazing results. Find a mentor in the community to answer your child's questions or to discuss design ideas.

- For children with leadership potential and a strong concern for others, encourage them to use those abilities within organized groups to design and implement their own projects that will benefit others.
- Talented athletes often join travel teams or other competitive teams at this level.

Watch For

At Level III, you will watch for the same signs of reaching the goals that we stated at the beginning of the article as you did with Levels I and II. You will begin to see more independence as your child pursues areas of sustained interests and strengths, but be aware that you also will find that supporting your children as their talents emerge and develop will involve significant commitments of time and effort on your part as well as theirs! Creative productivity also may emerge here in the form of a performance or other product that demonstrates an expression or accomplishment in the talent area.

Build Thinking Skills and Dispositions

Several important life skills to nurture include collaboration, teamwork, group problem solving, and healthy competitions (directed toward the attainment of important goals, not just to winning or losing). Teaching children how to handle disappointment with dignity and to exhibit pride with prudence can be important goals for parents of competitors. We all experience disappointments in life. Your child will learn from you firsthand how to deal with these situations. Teach your child to hold his head up high after losing and congratulate the winner; that is dignity. If your child is the winner, teach him how to handle that pride in such a way as to refrain from hurting others who are trying to deal with their disappointment and how to recognize the efforts of his competitors and compliment them. Focus on the goal of learning, growth in your child's skills and expertise, and affirming the importance and value of striving for excellence and improvement.

Level IV: Soaring and Passionate

The purpose of Level IV is to respond to your child's "blossoming expertise" in a talent area. The need for Level IV opportunities arises from internal (or "intrinsic") passion within the child to pursue an area of interest or talent with intense fervor and to become engaged in that area at a very high level of involvement and productivity. Level IV represents the child's sustained investment of time and energy in a topic or talent area that matters very much to him or her and is not something that has been assigned or required. When young people are involved in Level IV activities and experiences, they are not simply "doing schoolwork;" they are talented professionals at work in an area that is special to them, even though they may yet be at early stages of accomplishment. Level IV experiences may help your children focus on an emphasis or major area for postsecondary studies, create a foundation for lifelong vocational directions, or provide personal hobbies and activities that will bring years of satisfaction and enjoyment.

Provide Opportunities

Because this level responds to your child's intrinsic motivation, your role is to provide the time, space, materials, and supervision to enable your child to pursue his or her passion. Seek real-life (or "authentic") opportunities that enable your child to reach new levels of creative products or performances. Provide an environment that supports and encourages your child to initiate and direct his or her own inquiry into ideas and topics and personal interests.

- Connect your child to a mentor who is a professional in your child's interest area. The International Telementoring Program (http://www.telementor.org) is a virtual mentoring experience for upper elementary or older children. Consider these examples of mentoring (all true stories from our work):
  - A seventh-grade child was interested in pursuing the question, "What makes us human?" Her parent introduced her to a college philosophy professor who gave her some readings and led her in dialogues. Meanwhile, the child's

English teacher allowed her to pursue an independent study project on this topic, and the child worked during her English periods with the school's gifted programming specialist to develop her theory and write a paper on it. She presented her theory to other students and has continued to pursue this topic with her mentor.

- Another child wrote a play over the summer between fifth and sixth grade. All she needed was an adult to supervise and to help her solve problems as she directed and produced her play. She dealt with problems such as choosing the actors for her play—a difficult task for a sixth grader, as she had to deal with the politics of who to choose from among her friends and classmates. Dealing with her peers who often chose to waste time and fool around was another problem she solved successfully. The play turned out to be charming, and the child is now continuing to pursue creative endeavors in performing and writing in high school.
- A sixth grader was interested in learning about quantum physics. He had read the sixth-grade science textbook for fun over the summer, so his teacher allowed him to pursue independent study and connected him with a physics professor at a local university. His mother provided transportation for meetings during which he worked on basic physics activities given to him by the professor and was able to engage in conversations with an expert.

- Provide opportunities to investigate real problems and to conduct firsthand investigations that lead to original products. A parent observed her young daughter Sarah's fascination with her family's memorabilia from the early 20th century and her great-grandfather's memories of that time. Sarah's mother took her to visit the local history museum and enrolled her in a weeklong camp at another local historical site. Over a period of 2 years, Sarah developed a slide presentation and created activities about Victorian life that she shared with her classmates. She also wrote an article for the local newspaper detailing her amazing experiences.

- Communicate and celebrate products and accomplishments through appropriate outlets. A parent noticed that the local newspaper ran a feature once a week that recognized accomplishments of an outstanding young person in the community. He nominated his son for this honor, and an article about him appeared 2 months later.
- Provide experiences that invite children to discover, explore, or construct career possibilities or opportunities. Consider initiating job shadowing or internships for your teenager that match her or his field of interest and talent.

Watch For

Your child should be setting goals, independently carrying out projects, and evaluating his or her work. Self-discipline, persistence, sustained involvement, and a desire to gain expertise should be evident. Your child should become confident, courageous, and exhibit a positive regard for learning, thinking, and inquiry.

Build Thinking Skills and Dispositions

At this level, your child should be effectively applying creative and critical thinking skills, creative problem-solving skills, and research skills when working on a problem or opportunity. Through working on real-world problems or experiencing real-world career opportunities, he or she should be learning and practicing the specific skills of experts in a particular talent domain. It also is important to help your children to translate their potential for independence into effective skills by giving them opportunities to manage and direct their own projects.

Summary

Programming for your child's high potential has many facets. Working with your child's school and with the community around you is necessary to match your child with the activities, programs, and personal challenges that are most appropriate for developing his or her talents and interests. Start with the school and then branch out into the community. Parenting groups such as the PTA or a local advocacy group for parents of gifted children are rich sources of information.

As you research the possibilities, you may find that there is much to do but so little time in which to do it. Through your efforts as supportive, proactive parents, children and adolescents will be able to think for themselves, make good choices, solve problems, deal with disappointment and frustration, and persevere in the face of challenges and tedious tasks while they are on the road to reaching their potential. They will be ready to pursue their passions and reach self-actualization as healthy, effective young citizens who can learn independently. The results of their creative, productive efforts may lead to the next groundbreaking scientific discovery, an innovative new product, a novel that affects many lives positively, or even a roadmap to world peace!

Resources

Noller, R. B. (1997). *Mentoring: A voiced scarf.* Sarasota, FL: The Snedley Group.

Treffinger, D. J., Young, G. C., Nassab, C. A., & Wittig, C. V. (2004). *Enhancing and expanding gifted programs: The levels of service approach.* Waco, TX: Prufrock Press.

Chapter 26

Raising the Creative Child

by Courtney Crim

L ET me introduce you to a child you may recognize. This child lives at my house and I am often guilty of looking at her in wonder, questioning where this little person came from, and what on Earth I am going to do with her. Our daily issues seem small when compared to the larger challenge of teaching this small individual—the one that she is so quickly striving to become—how to function in a world that many times values behaviors that are different from her own. Ironically, this same world that often values conformity will need individuals who look at the world through a different lens and who will find new solutions to the ever-changing questions that arise.

The Challenge

Like many young children, Payton exhibits unlimited energy, little need for sleep (so valued by her parents), and a spirit far beyond her 4 years. From infancy, she has demonstrated a curious mind and a determination always to be involved with events around her. Her presence is one that cannot be ignored. This presence, however, can be due to her pleasing charm or her difficult behavior—depending on her mood. Does this sound familiar? The world is a game that unfolds and develops as children grow; they are constantly acquiring more information and schema to work with. The rules are constantly shifting. The challenge as a parent is to develop guiding rules by which we all can live, without threatening the zest for life and the ability to meet new obstacles head on. We need to seek out and create partnerships with other adults who share our goals and can help facilitate positive creative development in our children.

A Different World

Many times, children who demonstrate their creativity early in life first realize their differences as they interact with their peers. One interesting experience Payton shared involved her early school activities. When taking turns picking songs to sing, she happily sang with those choosing *ABC's*, *Itsy Bitsy Spider*, and *B-I-N-G-O*. Then her turn came and the other children looked at her as if she were crazy as she belted out "American Pie" by Don McLean. Her conversation on the way home included that she had a very bad day, she did not want to go back to school, she felt different from the other kids, she didn't like this feeling, and how come the other kids didn't know her song anyway? After much discussion at home and working with a very understanding teacher, we remedied this situation by sending the CD to school so "the other kids would know it was a real song." She realized that she sometimes thought of things differently than the other children. At some point in their young lives, individuals who demonstrate higher levels of creativity early on realize that they may see the world from a different perspective than many of their peers.

Just as we can share the experience and excitement of a new "ah-ha" moment, parents also can experience sadness when their child feels hurt or disappointment at any scale. You and I may say, "it's just a song" but, to her, it was a realization that maybe she sometimes thinks differently than her friends. This realization is the beginning of creative consciousness originally discussed by Abraham Maslow. The realization that their thought processes may not be the norm and that every individual experiences the world differently is a common experience shared by children who exhibit many of the characteristics associated with creativity. Although this experience is typical for children who exhibit gifted or creative characteristics, parents are not always prepared when it is their own child. It is possible to miss or overlook the signs of what is actually going on. The challenge, as these youngsters begin to realize differences, is to identify the nonconformity and praise the differences while helping to build a supportive and safe environment in which children can grow and continue to develop their creative consciousness.

In School

It is amazing to watch a person function who has no concept of his or her own limits. As parents, we often wonder when this acknowledgement of limitations may develop; they are children after all. It is interesting to find yourself sometimes wishing the very behaviors that at times make your child unique would disappear in favor of a calmer family environment. As the world gets more hectic and many of our schools ask for conformity, the behaviors that often are associated with creativity can hinder acceptance. This is the situation we found ourselves in as our daughter approached 4 ½. She isn't a genius who can read at 3, do long division, or compose symphonies, but she is part of a large group of children who are above their peers in analytical/intellectual abilities, relate better to adults than children, and early on show a well-developed understanding of creative thought. Unfortunately, many school districts provide gifted programs based on academically gifted characteristics alone. School programs that only identify and support high academic achievement potentially miss or can even hinder creative development. Additionally, many schools give little focus to enhancing creative potential in all children. As the children who develop their own creative consciousness at a younger age begin to see their differences, they often conform to their peers in order to minimize these differences and gain acceptance.

It is important, as a parent, not to underestimate our child's contributions but to open our eyes to how our child is expressing her creativity. For several reasons, some of which may include the structure of a classroom and the pressure of peer socialization, many children tend to experience a slight dip in creative expression and open curiosity as they initially enter school and again around 4th grade. Westby and Dawson's 1995 research explored creativity in children and offered a list describing creative behaviors most typically associated with creativity

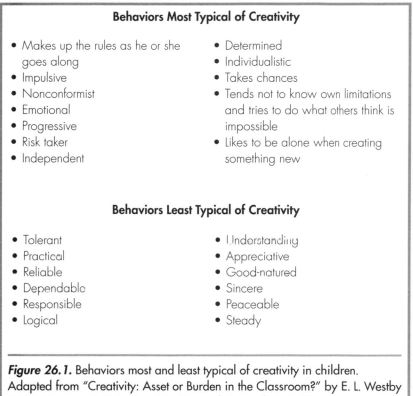

Behaviors Most Typical of Creativity

- Makes up the rules as he or she goes along
- Impulsive
- Nonconformist
- Emotional
- Progressive
- Risk taker
- Independent

- Determined
- Individualistic
- Takes chances
- Tends not to know own limitations and tries to do what others think is impossible
- Likes to be alone when creating something new

Behaviors Least Typical of Creativity

- Tolerant
- Practical
- Reliable
- Dependable
- Responsible
- Logical

- Understanding
- Appreciative
- Good-natured
- Sincere
- Peaceable
- Steady

Figure 26.1. Behaviors most and least typical of creativity in children. Adapted from "Creativity: Asset or Burden in the Classroom?" by E. L. Westby & V. L. Dawson, 1995, *Creativity Research Journal, 8,* 1–10.

as well as those behaviors least associated with creativity as derived from experts in the field (see Figure 26.1).

The traits most and least often identified as being associated with creativity are found, to some extent, in every individual. However, the combination and intensity of these traits is where creativity begins to develop and grow. It is interesting to identify the traits so evident in your own child and be gratefully reminded from whence some of her "difficult" behaviors may stem. Many children who display characteristics of creativity demonstrate a variety of these traits on a daily basis. However, some of these traits are often not conducive to the public school classroom. It is our responsibility, as parents, educators, and advocates, to help build partnerships with our schools so that the environments children experience support and foster these creative tendencies. Approaches such as differentiated instruction, interest-based study, and project-based curriculum allow these behaviors a place to exist without compromising the responsibility of the teacher to educate a classroom full of individual learners.

Support at Home

The resistance to many creative behaviors that may be expressed by some schools can create frustration at home. Have you found yourself wishing for more of the "least typical" behaviors as your child brings home behavior reports and teacher notes? As a parent, it is easy to voice frustration about many of the research-based "creative" behaviors demonstrated by your child. Parents often share this frustration when they receive the message that their child would do better to conform. The bottom line is: When the challenging behaviors are so close to home, it is easy to lose sight of the big picture. Is my child a behavior problem or does she have ADHD? Is my child a daydreamer or is she involved in creative thinking? Rather, we need to realize that all of these options can be manifested in various degrees and kinds of creative expression. The daily challenge of guiding and living with an individual who naturally exhibits creative thinking, a very young one at that, can evoke reactions from the parent that unknowingly diminish the creative aspects of a child's personality. Yet, developing an understanding of what the characteristics associated with creativity may look like can help parents and teachers see children through a different lens.

Valuing Differences

To remind me that many of our daily interactions are indeed valuable, I took a step back and formed a new perspective. The opportunity to raise a spirited child who strongly exhibits her creativity is an experience to be valued. As parents, our responsibility is to reinforce the value of a child's personality in a world that may or may not always appreciate the same traits. We need to guide her development in an environment that may push for conformity. I am sure many parents agree that, at times, it is difficult not to lose focus. As parents of young children, we need to remind ourselves to be their advocates and continue to read and learn about them. Payton will be in kindergarten in the fall, and I now recognize that the behaviors she exhibits in connection with her creative thinking may, although unintentionally in most cases, face changes. Advocating that she be included in a classroom where the teacher's style and instruction supports her creative development is important. Teachers who are supportive of the behaviors associated with creativity and who recognize and value these creative characteristics can do wonders with a child who exhibits such traits in their classrooms.

Westby and Dawson also investigated the behaviors that classroom teachers valued. Teachers' perceptions of characteristics associated with creativity agreed with the experts in the field of creativity only 40% of the time, according to Westby and Dawson's 1995 work. Teachers reported behaviors they considered to be reflective of creativity that disagreed with previous research. Behavior traits such as sincere, responsible, good-natured, reliable, and logical appeared at the top of the teachers' creative behaviors list. Additionally, many of the characteristics the researchers identified as least typical still manifest themselves in various degrees in individuals who demonstrate creative thinking. However, adjectives associated by researchers as most typical of a creative child (including the top four characteristics): making up own rules as he or she goes along, impulsive, nonconformist, and emotional, were identified by teachers as being least associated with creativity. Many of the traits linked with creativity that are embodied in young children are not always valued or encouraged by teachers as these youngsters enter school. We need to partner with teachers in our children's schools and share knowledge of these creative characteristics. We need to be the first to volunteer to organize and support programs that allow our children outlets for their creative behaviors as well as channels for development of their creative growth. Working with teachers, helping facilitate creatively based programs (see resources), and supporting the schools can all help develop the partnerships that will be necessary to promote creativity.

Going against popularly accepted behaviors or accepting a "C" on a report card because your child decided the project made more sense his way is sometimes difficult. This does not mean that I advocate promoting defiant or disruptive behaviors (indeed the behaviors listed by researchers as most typical of a creative child are difficult to manage in a classroom); all children certainly need limits and a classroom should maintain these limits. However, teachers who themselves think creatively are more apt to value these behaviors in their classrooms. Locating and supporting these wonderful teachers who support children and their growth as creative individuals is imperative. Our job as parents is to recognize traits that embody the creative nature of our children and honor them. We need to guide them gently and not be one of the many factors that extinguish their creativity. We need to find teachers who will join us on this quest while we do all we can to support this partnership. Just as children learn through modeling behaviors, teachers and schools can learn to accept and support creative behaviors in children as parents and educators model such acceptance and understanding.

Raising a child is never an easy task, but it is an eventful and challenging journey—a journey all parents share as our children embody so many different combinations and intensities of creative traits. The creative behaviors demonstrated by children can seem obnoxious, but at the same time, useful. Regardless, they also are reflective of creative thinking. These behaviors can be guided without being suppressed as we protect the traits that make our children unique individuals and offer them opportunity for expression. When the frustration level rises, as it will, gaining a better understanding of creativity as a construct will help you deal with your child in a positive way. Know that their behaviors are indicative of their talents, and as you guide them through the 120th question of the day, remember to be grateful that your child thinks to ask so many great questions. As you read about the behaviors associated with your child, smile and remember what an amazing opportunity it is to know such a unique little person and advocate for her creative development. As you meet and work with those wonderful teachers who value the creative development in children, validate their work, and promote these educators to others. The partnerships between you and your child, between you and the teachers, and between you and the schools, are multifaceted and need a creative approach, just like the development of creative traits in every individual.

Resources

Davis, G. A. (2004). *Creativity is forever* (5th ed.). Dubuque, IA: Kendall/Hunt.

Davis, G. A., & Rimm, S. B. (1998). *Education of the gifted and talented* (4th ed.). Boston, MA: Allyn & Bacon.

Cramond, B. (1994). Attention-deficit hyperactivity disorder and creativity: What is the connection? *Journal of Creative Behavior, 28,* 193–205.

Strom, R. D., & Strom, P. S. (2002). Changing the rules: Education for creative thinking. *Journal of Creative Behavior, 36,* 183–200.

Torrance, E. P. (1965). *Rewarding creative behavior.* Englewood Cliffs, NJ: Prentice-Hall.

Programs to Develop Creative Behaviors

Camp Invention—http://www.invent.org/camp/default.aspx
A weeklong summer program, Camp Invention lets children use their imagination through teamwork, creative problem solving, and inventive thinking.

Destination ImagiNation—http://www.idodi.org
This is an international program that inspires participants to practice and learn the process, art, and skill associated with Creative Problem Solving.

Future Problem Solving Program—http://www.fpspi.org
This program stimulates critical and creative thinking. It encourages students worldwide to develop a vision for the future through competitive and non-competitive participation.

Odyssey of the Mind— http://www.odysseyofthemind.com
This an international program that provides opportunities for students to apply creative problem solving.

References

Westby, E. L., & Dawson, V L. (1995). Creativity: Asset or burden in the classroom? *Creativity Research Journal, 8,* 1–10.

PART V

Family Dynamics

by Arlene R. DeVries

FAMILY dynamics is a theme clearly essential to the development of gifted children and youth. This section provides practical suggestions for parents and others who intcract with these students in the home, at school, and at the physician's office. The importance of relationships and communication is a common theme throughout each of the selected chapters.

The Tomlinson chapter stresses that just as differentiation is important at school, so must parents differentiate at home. Her example of a mother with three sons—one an academic scholar, one a technical creative inventor, and the third, a comedian with social charm—illustrates that what is best for one is not necessarily the best for the others. Different opportunities must be provided for each child's differing needs. She indicates that both school and home must provide a safe place where unique needs can be nurtured. "How does it feel here for the people who must live in this place?" After reading this chapter, the reader might ask, "In what ways can I differentiate experiences and support to meet the unique needs of each child in my family?"

The Smutny chapter begins with examples of young gifted children who exhibit exceptional talent. She indicates that parents are in a unique position to observe these behaviors. She also notes that for some children it takes time for skills to catch up with talent. A helpful list of common characteristics that can be observed at home is included along with activities that parents and children can do together. She encourages parents to extend their creative interactions with their children by using community resources. The experiences and lessons learned from these home activities can sustain children throughout their schooling. This chapter suggests a number of creative activities in which parents and their young children can engage.

In her chapter, "I'm a Kid, Mom, Not a Robot," Carolyn Cooper indicates that high-ability kids may be smart, but they wish parents would also respect their sensitivity. There are times they use one type of intelligence to solve problems and other times when they simply act silly with their friends. These children want parents to know they are not programmed like robots. Parents gain insight as to how their children learn and what they care deeply about by observing and having conversations involving current societal issues. Many gifted children are concerned about inequities in society and then act upon those convictions. If one could hear them talking to their friends, parents could gain insight on another side of their child. Parents should ask, "As a parent, am I sensitive and in tune with the feelings of my gifted child?"

Sherry Bragg introduces the concept that solo parenting provides opportunities to foster greater independence and a model for hard work and high achievement in the face of adversity. Families must bond as a "household team" to address the unique social and emotional needs of each member. The single parent who pursues her own interest is a role model for her children. She suggests that you give up the "super parent syndrome" and take care of yourself so that you can be there to take care of your children. When it becomes difficult to cope with all the demands, consider a family therapist to whom you can go for regular appointments. After reading this chapter, the reader might ask, "In what ways have I been a role model for my children?"

Amend and Clouse advocate for a proactive relationship with the child's physician. The parent is in the best position to communicate information about giftedness, a small dose at a time, perhaps from a peer-reviewed journal. Gifted children often are able to verbalize feelings and situations at an early age. If physicians are informed of physical symptoms or complaints related to school problems, the professional might assist you in advocating for appropriate gifted services. A thoughtful reading of this chapter might lead one to consider, "How might I develop a more positive relationship with my physician and share honest communication regarding my child's giftedness and behaviors?"

Effective communication with the school is crucial to your child's positive development as indicated in the DeVries chapter, "Parent Teacher Conferences." Although teachers are experts in curriculum and classroom management, parents have unique insights about their child's needs and abilities. An informed parent can have appropriate and realistic expectations for the child's education. Positive communication presents a willingness to help solve problems and avoids negative or blaming words. A suggested list of questions to ask the teacher is included. The reader might ask, "How can I prepare myself for a successful school conference?"

Each chapter suggests that positive communication can be effective in enhancing relationships with all persons interacting with gifted children. Parents play an essential role in the child's development. Parents of gifted children, however, often struggle to find information and support for their gifted child. Many professionals have received little or no training in meeting the needs of these students. A continuing challenge will be to educate communities about the importance of gifted education. The strategies suggested in these chapters provide a springboard for successful parent interventions with those who educate and serve gifted children.

Differentiation at Home as a Way of Understanding Differentiation at School

by Carol Ann Tomlinson

A N early teaching colleague of mine became a close friend. Over the past couple of decades, I've loved watching her three sons grow into young men. I've also enjoyed watching her pleasure in their differences and sometimes her bafflement in the face of those differences. She's a teacher, so she's read the textbooks on human variance and has observed it in every class she taught. Nonetheless, Christopher, David, and Jay seem in so many ways to challenge the notion of "family traits." Thinking about how this parent has responded to the differences in her children has been helpful to me on two levels. Certainly it has made me more aware of the ways in which effective parents *differentiate* their parenting in response to varying needs of their children. Thinking about the natural kind of differentiation that occurs at home also has helped me make important comparisons of the need for and nature of effectively differentiated classrooms.

Different Children, Different Needs

Christopher is the oldest of the brothers. His prodigious attention span as a 2-year-old was a precursor of things to come. He came programmed to read, compute, and see the elegance of the scientific method. There has not yet been an academic challenge that has called his hand. Academics simply are and always have been his arena.

David is the middle brother. He does well in school, but has never been drawn to it. What has always claimed his attention is creating and fixing things. Not simple things—although he fixes those too—but complex machines and technology. He built a remote controlled airplane alone at 6. And David also has a passion for work—just plain old "helping out." He is intuitive and effortless with it and raises it to the level of giftedness.

Jay, the last of the trio, also does well in school, but experiences it largely as a social event. Jay is a leader. He was a comedian even as a baby and has learned that humor is a magnet. He uses the magnet and his general charm with the aplomb of someone well beyond his early adolescent years. Jay came programmed to lead. Carol is the mother of Christopher, David, and Jay. She would be the first to say that while parenting skills are somewhat cumulative, much of what she did with and for Christopher was of little use with or for David, and much of what she did with or for David was irrelevant for Jay. In other words, this teacher-mom of three learned quickly, if not always easily, that she had to *differentiate* her parenting if she wanted to be an effective catalyst for helping each of her sons become what it seems he was meant to be.

Reflecting on what Carol learned as she effectively parented three very different children is helpful in thinking about what effective teachers do when they *differentiate instruction* in their classrooms. In fact, her experiences closely parallel those in what we call a differentiated classroom. Examining her experiences at home can help parents understand why differentiation should happen at school, what differentiation means at school, and even how it might look at school. In today's academically diverse schools, it is important for parents to understand the concept of *differentiated instruction* so that they can affirm teachers' positive efforts to address learner variance and encourage continued efforts in that direction.

Making it Safe for the Child to Be Who He or She Is

Much of Carol's success—and ultimately her boys' success—can be linked to the environment she helped create for her sons. While she consistently presented the boys with clear standards for behavior, responsibility, and interactions with others, she also provided a place where each of the boys felt safe as he was. There was never a sense that one of the boys' proclivities or strengths was preferable to the others'. From their earliest days, the boys saw her celebrate the uniqueness of each of them.

In such environments it is safe to be oneself. It is safe to fully explore one's possibilities. In such environments, young people know they are valued for who they are and will be supported as they discover and develop their unique potential. In such places, expectations are high enough to be personally challenging, but also there is support for the journey ahead.

Environments are abstract and intangible. They are constructed day by day and act by act. In the business of daily existence, there is little time set aside to ask the question, "How does it feel here for the people who must live in this space?" Nonetheless, the quality of the environment shapes everything that takes place for the young people in it.

Reading Signals About Children's Differences

It was evident from the earliest days of the three boys that their differences would be significant. In addition to their predictably different interests, they matured at different rates in different areas. They were not ready to play in the yard unattended, stay home alone, or get summer jobs at the same ages. They required very different sorts of parental support for homework, from conversational interest to dogged vigilance. They seemed preprogrammed to learn in different ways. Christopher learned through books and reasoning, David through practical and creative approaches, and Jay in the company of peers.

The boys did not require the same amount or same kind of discipline from their parents in their early years. Christopher seemed almost not to need rules and guidelines. David, who ultimately became the most sensitive of the three boys, was a pistol as a toddler. His parents took parenting classes to figure out how to provide the kind of guidance he needed. Jay was neither Christopher nor David in his need for early parenting.

Adolescence also was completely different for each of the three. They experienced it at widely different ages. If one boy experienced it gently, another was more explosive. If one was mouthy, another was withdrawn. One of the boys was an early girl magnet. One showed only peripheral interest in girls until very late adolescence, because so many other things were so much more interesting to him.

In their readiness to take on various aspects of life, in their interests, and in their approaches to learning, Christopher, David, and Jay might as well have been born to different parents. Those differences necessarily shaped the opportunities their parents needed to provide for them if the goal was to help each of the young men become what he wanted to be and seemed meant to be.

Opportunities Follow Need

If it ever occurred to the parents of these three young men to provide identical opportunities for each of them as they developed, the boys quickly showed them the folly of those thoughts. Their particular readiness to learn, personal interests, and approaches to learning made it necessary to carve out different paths for three very different human beings.

Sometimes, of course, parental inclinations resulted in common directions. Their father plays several instruments. Thus, the boys wanted to play a musical instrument as well, but not the same instrument, and not with the same duration or degree of enthusiasm. All of the boys participated in athletics, but their choice of sports reflected their inclination for the solitary versus the group. Passions for sports waned in proportion to their various capacities to tolerate failure or waxed in proportion to their various needs for perpetual motion or to be part of a team.

Even the choice of schools for the boys was not a matter of course. At various points in his public schooling, Christopher needed far more challenge than even a very good neighborhood school could offer. David needed a school that ensured that his considerable talent did not recede in the noisy crowd. Jay was fine anywhere there were peers.

The camp Christopher thought was fine for one summer, David found marginally acceptable for the same span, and Jay couldn't wait to return year after year. David sought out part-time jobs as a youngster. Christopher acquired them at a much later age and only with considerable impetus from his parents.

Two things have always been evident to me in watching my friend and her three boys. First, she and her husband want the *best* for their children. Second, what they found *best* for one would not necessarily be *best* for the others. They have worked as good parents do to make sure each boy has the opportunities he needed to be as secure, happy, and productive as possible. None of the boys has had better opportunities than his brothers. But because these parents accepted the responsibility to maximize the possibilities of three distinctly different young lives, each boy has had different opportunities based on need.

Parallels Between Home and Classroom

There's a story called "The Three Ralphs" that tells of parents who determined that the best parenting would result in treating all of their children precisely alike. Naming the first one Ralph, they decided it was only fair to name each subsequent child Ralph also—even the girl. Because the baby needed to sleep in a crib, the older Ralphs did so as well. When one Ralph was hungry, all of them had to eat. The problem becomes clear pretty quickly—except to the parents who found their child rearing plan both fair and sensible. Ultimately, the children saw the flaws in the plan and counseled their parents to continue to treat all the kids just alike—except when it didn't make sense to do so.

Christopher, David, and Jay are fortunate to have parents who always recognized, took pleasure in, and nurtured their uniqueness. In the context of an environment that balances high expectations, love, and support, the three boys have consistently been nurtured in accordance with their varied developmental patterns, inclinations, and learning strengths. What these parents did is much like what excellent teachers do. Connecting *differentiation* at home with *differentiation* at school clarifies the purpose and nature of what needs to take place in a classroom where 20 to 30 students are anything but duplicates of one another. Note the similarities between responsive teaching and responsive parenting.

Carol and Dick accepted responsibility for helping each of their sons become the best that particular child could be. Essential to that goal was establishing a healthy and positive learning environment in which everyone valued individuality. Likewise, teachers who accept responsibility for maximizing growth in each of their learners begin by investing heavily in a learning environment that values the individuality of each student—a place where it feels safe to be oneself, where expectations are high, and where there is consistent support for the journey.

While they might not have thought about themselves as "studying" their three children, Carol and Dick did, in fact, invest heavily in trying to understand what made each of their children "tick"—what worked and didn't work in helping each of the boys develop physically, emotionally, intellectually, and socially. Similarly, the teacher who regards the distinctness of each student as valuable will inevitably become a student of his or her students. In doing so, the teacher becomes increasingly aware of the student's likes and dislikes, preferred ways of learning, and points of readiness for the various tasks at hand. In much the same way as an attentive parent, the teacher uses what he or she learns to craft ways to tap the student's strengths and deal productively with weaknesses.

Whether at home or at school, what logic is there, after all, in consistently demanding far more from a child than he is ready to give, or asking far less? What is the merit in disregarding what interests a child when it is evident that interest summons motivation? And why would we habitually ask young people to explore or express important ideas in ways that are ineffective for them?

Dick and Carol didn't favor one of their children by providing superior opportunities for growth and development. Their goal was to provide what was best for each of the boys. Responsive teachers likewise do not provide better opportunities for some students than for others. What they work diligently to do is to provide evolving opportunities for each learner that respond best to that learner's evolving needs.

Home Complexities Multiply in the Classroom

The parents of three boys will readily admit that it's difficult to address the diverse and changing needs of all three. Some days work better than others. Sometimes they are better able to balance the competing needs of all three young lives. Sometimes they read the signals right, and sometimes they don't. But they keep at it because they see themselves as stewards of success for their children.

If it is difficult for two parents to "get it right" all of the time with a small number of young people, the challenge for a teacher is immense. The degree of student variance in a typical classroom is magnified by gender, number, race, culture, language, opportunity, economics, and myriad other factors. Further, whereas attentive parents have the capacity to study their children over a period of many years, the time of the teacher with a given student is inevitably constricted.

Nonetheless, a teacher determined to make school work for her students becomes a persistent hunter and gatherer of information on each child. By watching, listening, asking, and examining student work, that teacher develops an ever clearer image of what aids and impedes learning for each child. Drawing both on professional knowledge of students and on the day's image, the teacher designs learning options that seem most likely to benefit a particular student or group of students. Each day informs the next—and so on. To these teachers, teaching in a "Three Ralphs" fashion makes no more sense than parenting in that way.

From Analogy to Partnership

It's helpful for parents in thinking about the role of the teacher in an effectively differentiated classroom to again draw on the parenting analogy. Just as the parents of Christopher, David, and Jay found themselves having to differentiate opportunities and support based on the readiness, interest, and learning preference needs of the boys, so it is with teachers and their students.

Some students need additional time to master a skill and some need to move more rapidly through a skills sequence. Some students work with considerable independence and others require considerable monitoring. Some learn best in analytical ways, while others learn best in more practical or creative ways. Some students will learn math better if they can attach it to sports and some by attaching it to science. The most skillful teachers—like the most skilled parents—study the clues and respond accordingly. On any day, the results may be imperfect. In the long haul, however, it is highly likely that students benefit from the attention of adults who persist in trying to "get it right" for each of them.

Understanding the importance of *differentiating* for learners, the nature of the task, and its complexity is important for parents who seek to be informed about their children's educational experiences. It's also important for parents and teachers to understand the role that each can play in making school work for individual learners. Teachers have a greater breadth of knowledge about students of a given age than most parents can hope to develop. A teacher who has taught sixth grade for 10 years, for instance, has worked with hundreds of students of that age. On the other hand, parents will inevitably have greater depth of knowledge about their own children than a teacher could begin to have.

Students are fortunate when parents and teachers understand the complex responsibility of helping young people build strong, happy, and productive lives, and when parents and teachers work in tandem to bring their best insights to bear on the success of children whose interests they share. Parents can use their own experiences in parenting young people who inevitably differ in their needs to help them understand and support the world of the teacher who teaches in ways that also support very different young people in finding their own unique paths to success.

Parenting Young Gifted Children: How to Discover and Develop Their Talents at Home

by Joan Franklin Smutny

"My son has been studying acting (mostly Shakespeare) since he was 4 years old. Once when he was 5 or 6, he memorized an entire script (90 pages)—everyone's parts—by the second time he heard it. He has been acting and auditioning for films and commercials regularly and has done national commercials for McDonald's."

PARENTS are usually the first to notice the unusual qualities of their gifted young children. Sometimes, though, they may doubt themselves because they lack exposure to other children or because a relative, teacher, counselor, or school psychologist discounts their observations. Once their young children begin attending school, parents frequently find themselves caught between the unhappiness of their bored or frustrated children and a school system that may not recognize the needs of gifted students, or one that lacks the funds and personnel to sustain an educational alternative for them.

Despite the disbelief or incredulity they may encounter, parents need to trust their observations and instincts. They are their child's most accurate judge and are in a unique position to observe and document their son or daughter's special talents. The close relationship between

> We first noticed Elizabeth was unusual at age 2 when, upon hearing Copland's "Rodeo" in an ad on TV, she identified the title and composer. The ad was the second time she had heard the piece. Elizabeth (age 6) does fifth-grade reading. She writes great poetry and creates her own experiments and math problems.
>
> My daughter is in first grade, but goes to a second-grade class for math. The teacher was discussing the commutative property of addition with the class—that 3 + 5 is the same as 5 + 3. She then asked about subtraction: Was 5 − 3 the same as 3 − 5? They decided that it was not. The other students all said 3 − 5 was impossible, but Emily said it was possible and that it was "under zero." She said the answer was "2 under zero." She had invented negative numbers all by herself.

parents and children can provide some unique insight into the strengths and abilities of their young ones.

Identifying Young Gifted Children

One way for parents to begin identifying their young gifted children (ages 4–8) is to become aware of common characteristics they can observe at home. Below is a list that many parents find useful:

- expresses curiosity about many things;
- asks thoughtful questions;
- has an extensive vocabulary and uses complex sentence structure;
- is able to express him- or herself well;
- solves problems in unique ways;
- has a good memory;
- exhibits unusual talent in art, music, or drama;
- exhibits an especially original imagination;
- uses previously learned data in new contexts;
- is well able to order things in logical sequences;
- discusses and elaborates on ideas;
- is a fast learner;

- works independently and uses initiative;
- exhibits wit and humor;
- has a sustained attention span or is willing to persist on challenging tasks;
- is very observant;
- shows talent in making up and telling stories; and
- is interested in reading.

This list is only an outline of what might emerge in parents' daily interactions with their children. The expression of talent depends a great deal on the home environment—what the family does, the cultural and economic background, and the resources available to the family. Therefore, it is best to focus on behaviors rather than specific skills or products.

Even in populations that are relatively homogeneous, giftedness still expresses itself uniquely in each individual child. Some may begin speaking and reading early; others may not. Einstein is an example of a highly gifted child who did not begin speaking until age 4 and did not begin reading until age 7. I recently met a parent who claimed that her young son was not gifted because he lacked the ability to read or write, yet he possessed an extraordinary artistic talent. One day, he surprised her by meticulously labeling a series of dinosaurs he had drawn. Focusing on reading and writing, this mother initially failed to see her son's gifts or recognize that, in some children, it takes time for skills to catch up with talent.

Parents, therefore, need not apply rigid academic criteria to their young children, but can begin observing their strengths and abilities in the little comments they make, their observations about something they saw on television or overheard in a conversation between adults, the questions they pose, and their responses to the thoughts and feelings of others. I have always encouraged parents to look for talent in a wide range of contexts, including the most casual comment or question. Even a simple gesture in a very young person can speak volumes.

Some parents have benefited from documenting their young child's behavior. Documentation is particularly useful when children attend a school where the curriculum does not challenge or stimulate their growth and development. A portfolio of a child's work, as well as anecdotes written by parents who observed some unusual flash of insight or knowledge in their child in the course of a day, can become a useful source of information for teachers who may not realize what the child can do. In addition, a portfolio can be fortifying for a child who has lost interest in school and is beginning to doubt his or her worth. A number of gifted children stop applying themselves when the challenge is insufficient to inspire them. Then, when they experience penalties for what appears as laziness or indifference, they begin to doubt their abilities and retreat from the keen interest they once felt for learning. A record of young children's accomplishments can go far in resurrecting their self-esteem, particularly when parents bring the portfolio to school as evidence of their child's talents and abilities.

Become a Resource for Young Gifted Children at Home

Children need to know that regardless of their school experience they will be able to learn and grow in a home environment that is nurturing and stimulating. This environment is vital for students who find themselves with few opportunities in school to explore their interests and talents. Few adults really understand how imprisoning the regular curriculum feels to young gifted children.

Constraining them within certain parameters of a subject or topic is really no different than forcing babies who are ready to walk to keep crawling until they reach a certain age. When parents actively support the special talents that make their children such hungry and innovative learners, they bring fresh air and inspiration to their stifled spirits and give them the freedom they need to grow and develop naturally.

Parents can integrate critical and creative thinking into all sorts of situations and activities in the course of the day once they become more aware of the *process* and how to apply it to different contexts. The emphasis should be less on what resources parents can find in the home and more on *how* they use what they have. Parenting is a creative art. It involves improvising with materials at hand, using opportunities that arise unexpectedly, and encouraging young children to participate in problem solving and to develop their own interests and creative projects.

Parents can do much to develop the creative potential of their young gifted children and keep their love of learning alive and free. I know many talented children who, despite their frustration and/or boredom in school, still manage to preserve their inner creative resources because their parents support them unconditionally. Parents can inspire their children's creative imagination by freely exploring ideas with them, posing questions, valuing their individuality in all its expressions, and making them feel safe about taking risks. Below are examples of some creative thinking processes that provide a useful guide for activities and conversations. They come from the work of pioneer researcher E. Paul Torrance.

- *Fluency:* The child produces many ideas (through brainstorming or free association).
- *Flexibility:* The child thinks of alternatives to the conventional way of looking at things.
- *Originality:* The child innovates and invents within a specific context.
- *Elaboration:* The child extends his or her creative ideas in order to apply them (which involves testing, experimenting, analyzing, and synthesizing).

These processes do not occur in isolation, of course, and parents need not concern themselves with these definitions other than as a basic guide. These processes open up a whole range of creative possibilities that can occur at the spur of the moment. When a mother notices her young gifted girl thumbing through a book of paintings, for example, she could:

- ask her to write about what she sees from the point of view of a tree, an animal, or whatever else might be in the picture;
- ask her to describe what has just happened in the painting or what will happen after it;
- put a piece of paper next to the picture and have her draw an extension from where the painting finishes;

- discuss the strokes used in the painting (e.g., are they large, sweeping ones or many tiny ones as in Impressionism?) and use similar strokes in a painting of her own.

Visual images are excellent catalysts for either storytelling, creative writing, or other related art projects. Children enjoy looking at photographs or magazines and talking about what they see. Some gifted children will automatically begin inventing stories. Parents can buy scrapbooks or notebooks and make a book with their children by cutting out photos and creating a story to accompany them. This project can be especially fun when the focus is a book about the *children*. Old pictures of their babyhood and earlier years, places they have traveled to or things they have done, magazine pictures, and sketches, as well as imaginary storylines, will delight young gifted children. If they are too young to write or write only haltingly, parents can have the children dictate to them. Integrating media (visual images with storytelling and/ or writing) stimulates creative ideas in both parents and children and does not require expensive supplies.

Book Activities With Gifted Children

Here are a few examples of activities parents and children can do together with books:
- A mother reads her daughter two books about animals in a tropical forest. After reading them, the child is asked to draw the characters in both books and the two begin discussing what they learned from the two different stories. The mother keeps posing questions: How might the characters from both books get along with each other? Where in the forest will they live? What other things might happen to them in their homes? What adventures might they have?
  There are all sorts of variations to combining books. For example, children could discuss, draw, or write about characters in two books. Suppose the characters from these two books

got together. What might happen? How might the stories in each book change? How might the characters change?

- Parents also can combine fiction and nonfiction. Once they become aware of their children's interests, they can use books on a particular subject from a variety of disciplines. For example, a girl who wants to learn about whales might enjoy combining a science book about their natural life, another one about a fictional whale, and then perhaps watch a video about them. She may like to write a series of poems, dictate stories of her own, or possibly create a map charting the migration routes of whales.

- An important dimension to creative thinking is the ability to think of alternatives. Books offer a ready resource for this. For example, parents can talk to their gifted young children about point of view. What if you were another character in the story? How would you tell the story? What would you change in the story? Children can dramatize their own alternate endings, discuss, paint, and/or write them.

- Other activities children enjoy include changing endings to books, adding episodes of their own, creating sequels to particular books they love, and/or changing settings (e.g., place *Little Red Riding Hood* in the city).

These are only a few possibilities. Parents will find themselves using a variety of resources—from books to art to costumes to backyard imaginary games to walks in the park to common chores like baking or shopping—and will find in them many ways to involve their children in critical and creative thinking.

Using Community Resources

Parents can easily extend this creative work with their young gifted children by incorporating resources in their community. Museums, aquariums, plays, musicals, dance companies, concerts, library events, and community centers that hold classes for children can expand their exposure to and involvement in subjects that interest them. Wherever possible, parents should try to prepare their children for these outings by reading books with them and/or discussing what they will see. These experiences can then become catalysts for projects children do on their own (e.g., drawings, paintings, creative writing).

When parents take their children outside for further enrichment, they need to help them think about what they are seeing, hearing, or feeling. I know a number of parents who make it a habit to ask their children what they are noticing—what baffles, inspires, intrigues, confuses them—and to discuss any new knowledge they gain in the course of their adventure together. Experiences outside of the home should extend from the activities and/or discussions parents and children engage in at home. A young gifted daughter, for example, may suddenly discover an interest in astronomy. Her parents could share books with her on the neighboring planets, take her on a visit to a local observatory, watch a video on space travel, and perhaps encourage her to write and illustrate some science fiction stories. A young boy who enjoys nature would benefit from nature walks, a summer ecology program, trips to aquariums, zoos, natural history museums, books, and nature videos.

A Haven At Home

I know a mother who made every walk in the woods with her young daughter something to cherish and think about. She often identified favorite wildflowers, the names of plants, birds, and other creatures. The young girl developed a vivid perception of the natural world around her and an understanding of the life cycles and living habits of plants and animals in the woods. She often would pretend she was a woodland creature and wrote and illustrated stories about her experiences. Later on when she found herself in a classroom where her creative energy and ideas had no place, she relied on the inner resources she developed through the time spent with her mother to sustain her throughout the school year.

Chapter 29

I'm a Kid, Mom, Not a Robot: What High-Ability Children Want Their Parents to Know About Them

by Carolyn R. Cooper

W HAT does your high-ability child want you to know about whom he or she really is? How sure are you?

Books about bright children frequently include lists of characteristics to describe these youngsters' intellectual, social, emotional, and academic behaviors. Often missing from these lists, however, is this key disclaimer: "SOME bright children demonstrate SOME, but not all, of these characteristics."

Lists of characteristic behaviors should be used as a guide but never as a prescription for raising a high-ability child. Why? Terms used are relative, not absolute. "Highly creative," "rapid learner," or "long attention span," for example, mean one thing to Parent A, but Parent B may interpret them quite differently. Each parent bases his or her understanding of these terms on experience. Additionally, some characteristics may not apply to your bright youngster at all.

To understand such terms a parent needs the appropriate context. What do I mean? An illustration may be helpful. One child may display the "highly creative" characteristic through his ability to solve problems. By making new connections, such as using ordinary household items in innovative ways, a child is demonstrating creative thinking. Let's say the pull-tab on the zipper around the rear window of the family convertible is broken, so the window cannot be opened. Replacing the broken part with a small wooden toggle from an old chain saw is an example of the "highly creative" characteristic.

A second child's "highly creative" ability plays out another way. A first-grader may be a strikingly proficient sketch artist. Birds in flight, facial profiles, and pastoral scenes—she sketches them all, demonstrating artistic skill well beyond her years.

What might we learn about our children that they would actually like us to know? Many bright children and youth won't tell us directly; they don't want to hurt us. If we could only hear them talking with their friends . . .

Imagine for a moment that we've brought together a group of eight high-ability youngsters—ages 6 to 17—to discuss what they want their parents to know about them: who they really are. Although these young people of different ages and experiences weren't actually all in the same room together at the same time—allow me a little "artistic license"—they are all real youngsters with whom I've discussed this topic personally over the years, individually and in small groups.

Let's listen in from an imaginary observation booth. Through its one-way window we can see all eight young people. They appear to be discussing several characteristics they know well from their own experiences. Their statements are frank and straightforward and, in every instance, convey the attitudes of most, if not all, of the group. Listen carefully. What we learn may truly surprise us!

Kids First

"We're kids!" states 9-year-old Connor emphatically. "We're kids first, last, and always. And because we're kids, we like kid things. I want my parents to know that I really like to act goofy sometimes. Kids do that, and parents need to be OK with it when we do." Connor adds, "We act smart when we need to, but being smart doesn't mean you're not a kid first."

Lakeesha, age 16, explains, "We don't like stupid stuff—like being treated like a little kid. I'm a normal teenager who likes my iPod, teen magazines, music that's probably too loud, and talking on the phone with my friends. Oh, and I just love instant messaging!"

As the comments of these two bright, capable, and highly advanced students imply, there is a fine line parents must tread between accepting their children's admittedly silly behavior upon occasion and realizing they're growing up with others their age who may embrace or, just as easily, revile age mates with abilities obviously different from theirs.

Wired Differently

Often included in a list of characteristics of high-ability children is "concerned with fairness and justice" or "cares deeply about others' welfare." Every parent knows how young children tend to like animals—be them family pets or residents of a zoo. In bright children, however, beyond the natural bond between children and animals resides a deep conviction that animals must be treated with the love and respect living things deserve. Therefore, when these children learn of manatees harmed by careless boaters, mink being trapped, or land developers driving native animals from their habitats, they are angry about such practices and seek ways to take action to prevent their further use.

"I really don't like all the new houses going up in my neighborhood," says Meghan, age 7. "When my family moved there a few years ago, we loved watching all the animals that lived in the woods. It was like a forest. Now," she explains, "the trees have been cut down, and more houses are being built, but the animals are gone. It's sad that they lost their homes just for more houses. It isn't fair!"

"But Meghan, don't you think trees used to stand on the land where your house is, too?" challenges Julia, the 10-year-old in the group. "The animals in those trees lost their homes, right?" Meghan shakes her head slowly as she ponders Julia's point.

"Maybe," suggests Donnell, 17, "it's a question of which matters more—animals that live in the woods or people who live in houses. My grandma was forced to move from her house in the city so a parking lot for the zoo could be built in its place. In this case, the zoo animals won in a way, but my grandma lost her home."

Meghan is visibly perplexed by this dilemma of whether human beings or animals are more important. As she considers the scenario Donnell has related about his grandmother, we see others begin to chat quietly among themselves about this puzzling issue. After the group's brief discussion of pros and cons, Meghan states her conclusion: "I think animals and people are both important," she says, "so we probably can't say one is more important than the other. I guess nature wins sometimes, and people win other times, and that makes it kind of fair, anyway." The group nods in approval. Meghan learned firsthand the difficult process of resolving a moral dilemma centered on her concern for others' welfare.

"Last year in kindergarten I tried to protect the bald eagle," recalls David, age 6. "I sent a letter to every U.S. senator and representative and asked them what they were doing to protect our national symbol. The ones who answered my letter got a plaque I made especially for them. My dad helped me burn their name into it, too." To his surprise, David's deep sense of purpose earns a round of applause from everyone else in the group. They understand.

Youngsters with an especially strong moral sense for what they perceive as right and wrong want the glitches in the world to be addressed and corrected. As these children grow, they broaden their sphere of concern to include their genuine compassion for the welfare of other human beings and find themselves caring deeply about the indignities many suffer. Julia puts her disbelief this way, "How, in America, the richest country in the world, can so many people be homeless? Why is that allowed to go on year after year?"

"Because too many people care only about themselves and don't even see the homeless after a while," answers Donnell. "Our society seems to be about me, me, me and nobody else. That attitude makes me sick! I want to do something about it."

"Me, too!" and a few more "Me, too!" endorsements echo Donnell's desire to right the wrong that concerns both him and the others in the group deeply as well. In short, these young people are wired differently from many their age. They not only know about conviction; they also feel it genuinely, and what proves their sincerity is their decision to act upon that conviction. They embody the adage, "Actions speak louder than words."

Smart Sometimes

Inconsistencies in how your child applies his or her intelligence may baffle you at times. "How can she be so smart in science but get such low grades in math?" you ask. Or, "For a kid who comes up with brilliant solutions to problems around the house, why isn't he a better reader? We know he's smart."

The short answer is this: More than innate intelligence is at play in problem solving, reading, understanding math, succeeding in science, and every other type of learning. Different tasks require different types of thinking. For example, reading well requires one type of thinking whereas creating solutions to problems around the house or inventing new ways to use odds and ends accumulating in the basement or garage call for thinking that is quite different. These thought processes aren't interchangeable, but your youngster may well apply both types to separate situations. The human mind is extremely complex, which accounts for the variation of strengths and talents between and among individuals—sometimes, in the same family. A person's use of various types of thinking also helps explain why demonstrating high ability in one area doesn't necessarily carry over to others. This is perfectly normal for high-ability youngsters as well as for other children. Let's listen to what Tiffany wants her parents to know about this particular issue.

"I'd like my parents to accept the fact that I'm smart in some subjects but not in others. That's just the way it is," asserts Tiffany, 13, who says her parents pressure her to do as well in math as she does in drama. Asked to elaborate a bit, Tiffany notes that she's interested in and, in fact, passionate about drama; from her earliest recollections, she played school, church, and weddings and, when her playmates weren't around, she played every role herself. "The time I was in my first school play, our director told me I was a natural," she comments with a broad smile. "But I'm no natural in math! I'd really like my parents to understand that even bright kids aren't good at everything. We're not robots!"

"I know what you mean, Tiffany. My parents want me to be smart in everything, too." Cole, a 12-year-old who has been following this conversation silently, offers insight that reflects his exceptional ability to reason logically. "Math requires abstract thinking, but drama is a concrete activity that you act out with your emotions. You need to memorize certain things for both, but learning math facts is different from learning your lines or movements on stage. Besides, you sound like you're much more interested in drama than in math, anyway, right? Interest has a lot to do with how we learn."

Cole then proceeds to explain that he's "smarter" in reading and social studies than in science. He loves to read, do research, and "dig up facts and stories most people don't know. My dad would like me to be as smart in science as he is," he says matter-of-factly. "He's a science genius; we call him a 'guru' 'cuz he knows SOOOO MUCH!" After pausing for a few seconds, Cole then concludes with a statement revealing the sense of guilt some high-ability children harbor as a result of parent pressure to be equally smart in everything they do. "I think my dad's embarrassed because I'm just not good in science at all. I wish he could understand how I learn and accept it."

Sensitive All of the Time

High-ability children tend to be more sensitive than parents may expect. Also, parents often do not realize they themselves may be partly responsible for this sensitivity. "Do any of your parents," Meghan asks, "make you show off how smart you are to your grandparents? I—"

A resounding chorus of groans and "oh, yeah's" interrupts her. A few seconds later, Meghan continues. "I HATE that!" she says emphatically. "I feel like I'm on display—like some kind of trophy. Why do they do that? It sure makes me feel terrible. I wish they would understand that kids who are smart also have feelings."

"When I was little, my mom used to make me sing in front of EVERYBODY—my grandparents, the neighbors, and anybody else who would listen to me," Lakeesha recounts in obvious disgust. "I must have been like a wind-up toy! Then, in elementary school, I had to show off how smart I was in math, too. I half expected my audiences to throw pennies! It was humiliating." For this 16-year-old, the pain is still real.

"Does your mom still make you show off like that?" David inquires of Lakeesha. Our 6-year-old sounds more than a little apprehensive. He's relieved when the teenager assures him that her mother "has passed that stage," for which she is truly grateful.

The "stage" Lakeesha mentions is more likely a parent's genuine appreciation of his or her child(ren)'s strengths, talents, interests, and activities—what makes these kids tick, so to speak. And, predictably, grandparents, too, want to know their grandchildren as individuals. How better to understand them than through the youngsters' achievements or hobbies?

When I was a child, in lieu of parading out my two brothers and me to perform solo for our grandparents, my mom and dad capitalized on our family's love of singing. During our grandparents' occasional visits, my mother asked the three of us to play our musical instruments—piano, trumpet, and E flat alto saxophone—as accompaniment to the family sing-a-long she'd initiate, and, after four or five songs, the activity was over.

This approach was successful primarily because none of us was spotlighted; we were just the instrumental component of the sing-a-long. As the pianist, I selected songs I knew my younger brothers could both play, and our parents, grandparents, and anyone else who happened to be visiting at the moment enjoyed both singing and seeing us play our instruments at the same time.

That this event, our extended family's singing a few familiar songs together, was very low key made it enjoyable for all. More important for us was everyone being included in the activity, which minimized significantly the "talent show" aspect that we three would have found embarrassing. As a result, my brothers and I never felt exploited and actually were pleased that our grandparents could celebrate with us the family's love of music.

"I don't understand why my parents think being smart is anything to brag about," says Connor. "Some of us are smarter than other kids our age, but so what? Some of them are probably smarter than we are in ways we don't even know. I think being smart looks different from person to person."

The nine-year-old then describes overhearing his parents at a party held recently in the family home. "Unfortunate timing," he notes with a sense of humor that belies his age; report cards had just come out. Imitating their remarks in a disapproving tone, he mimics his parents' hyperbole. "Our Connor is so intelligent! At home he acts like a regular kid most of the time—although he does read 10 or 11 books every week, you know—but in school, well, we think he's probably the smartest boy in his class!" As Connor rolls his eyes, the group groans again, only louder. These youngsters have all been there, too.

As the conversation winds down, Julia, closest to Connor in age, asks him an interesting question. "Connor, what subject are you smartest in?"

Connor's reply is most insightful. "I like anything that has puzzles, problems to figure out. It's not the subject so much; it's what we do in class that I really like or don't like."

Connor then explains that rote memorization of isolated facts, reading out loud in a group, and doing worksheet after worksheet is "dull and boring." He much prefers hands-on involvement with his learning; using the microscope himself, for instance, is far more stimulating than listening to a teacher talk about the instrument. Connor notes, too, that he enjoys simulations in which students use role-play scenarios to apply key concepts they are learning. "I remember what I learn this way a lot more than by sitting and listening."

So, What Should Parents Know?

The comments of these eight youngsters convey strong messages about what they want their parents to know about them. So what can parents learn about their children that the youngsters sincerely want them to know?

First, they want parents to understand that they're kids first, so when they act silly, try to remember that "kids act goofy sometimes," as Connor pointed out. What's more, high-ability youngsters want parents "to be OK with it" when they do act silly. Acting like a child releases the stress many experience from being different from age-mates, perhaps from being chided or ridiculed, and, often, from their parents' unrealistic expectations for their children to apply their exceptional abilities all the time. By accepting some silliness, parents show that they understand their kids' need to act this way occasionally and are "OK with it," as we heard in our imaginary observation booth.

Second, many high-ability children are wired differently. With a keen moral sense, they care deeply about what they regard as glitches in society, but, unlike others who merely talk about their concern for others less fortunate, these youngsters act upon their conviction.

Why not watch a newscast with your child once a week? News reports often contain stories about the homeless, about mentally ill patients being displaced from group homes, or about elderly citizens unable to pay the escalating costs of prescription medicines they need. These issues are just some of the societal glitches that concern high-ability youngsters, so you might ask your child—in a casual manner—what he or she thinks could be done to address one of the issues reported in the newscast.

Be sure to make no value judgments about your child's suggestion. You're asking what he or she thinks, so honor earnest responses. Keeping the conversation informal is key to engaging the youngster in the discussion. Then, if the ideas are flowing easily, ask how your family might help someone in need. Perhaps neighbors or school friends could be enlisted to help with specific tasks.

Third, you might learn more about your high-ability child by observing how he or she solves real-life problems. Caution: While observing, again be low key; you may alienate your child if he suspects he's on display for some reason! People solve problems differently; how you approach problem solving may be completely unlike how your son does it. In fact, if your child's methods appear to be way off base, keep in mind what I've said about an individual's multiple thought processes. Then, for reassurance, remind yourself of Einstein's profound statement about problem solving: "A problem cannot be solved at the same level at which it was created." Your child's method may be as good as, or even better than yours!

Does your youngster create a solution by first writing notes or making an outline? Or, does she doodle, scribble, or sketch "chunks" of ideas? Perhaps she plays with objects on the kitchen counter or in her room while thinking about a solution. It may appear that she's paying no attention whatsoever to the task at hand, and this may be so. But parents need to know that what they perceive as idle fidgeting with nearby objects or stalling for time may well be productive thinking—perhaps, combining properties of these objects in new ways, for instance.

Another message your child wants you to hear regards the inconsistencies in how and when high-ability youngsters apply their abilities. So, when your bright child's next report card comes out, remember, high ability in one area of endeavor doesn't necessarily translate to high ability in another. The thinking skills required for success in each may vary considerably.

As Tiffany says in the group's conversation, smart kids are "not robots." And they're not "good at everything," either. Unless your child's grades are substantially lower than they were previously and you know of no cause for the difference, be accepting of the report card but ask what she wants you to know about these lower grades. If she doesn't want to discuss the report card, so be it. First, reassure her of your love for her, and your interest in her performance, too, by saying something like, "I realize that just because you're outstanding in some subjects you may not rank as highly in every class." Speaking to your youngster about grades in an honest, invitational tone may work wonders in her classroom performance, and her next report card may be even better.

Finally, what your high-ability children want you to know is that they are not only smart but also sensitive. Bright kids feel different from their age-mates because they are different. Exploitation of them by their proud, well-meaning parents can lead them to rebel, to hide their talents, and, sadly, to associate with "troublemakers" in and out of school as retribution for their parents' attempts to make them perfect children.

Because their remarkable abilities separate them from others their age, many bright youngsters are embarrassed easily. They often fear their moms and dads will brag to friends and colleagues about their achievements, something they implore their parents not to do. Parents need to appreciate this sensitivity and treat their children as normal kids with normal kids' needs.

In summary, then, remember that high-ability children are smart in different ways, a critically important fact they would like their parents to know, understand, and respect. Let your child know that you honestly want to know him or her as an individual as well as a son or daughter. On this level of openness, an effective relationship can be built between parent and child—a bond that mutual understanding, trust, integrity, and genuine appreciation will only strengthen through the years.

Chapter 30

The Tao of Solo Parenting Gifted Children

by Sherry S. Bragg

PARENTING gifted children comes with all of the typical responsibilities: chauffeuring them to lessons and enrichment classes, seeking out mentors and tutors, finding time for more frequent interaction with schools, meeting their unique social and emotional needs, and advocating for their exceptional educational needs. Such an undertaking can exhaust and overwhelm even the most competent, stable, and experienced coparenting team, but solo parents shoulder these overwhelming burdens alone and have to work even harder to raise exceptional children. Parenting a gifted child is a blessing, a sacred gift that shapes the soul. Solo parenting a gifted child tests your ability to survive the blessing! So, how can solo parents expect to raise exceptional kids with little or no support? The daunting task of solo parenting gifted children requires a detailed, multifaceted management plan that addresses many issues.

Family and Domicile

Take heart in the fact that even though a single-parent household may not be the ideal family, you are still a family in which, as a parent, you have much to offer your children in the way of empathy, as well as understanding the nuances of what it means to think and feel differently.

Thinking of yourselves as members of the same household team and conducting family meetings provides a strategy to help alleviate some of the stress associated with being a part of a solo-parent household, possibly composed of several gifted individuals. Holding regular family meetings is a practice that encourages negotiation skills as well as shared responsibility, both critically important for solo parents.

Take time to plan and dream together. Limit television and computer time in favor of imaginative discussions and reading with your kids. Even after they are old enough to read to themselves, reading the same books together or watching the same movies affords rich opportunities for deeper communication. Incorporate learning into everything you do together, even the most mundane. Plan nutritious meals, shop and cook together, and most importantly, make time to share at least one meal a day together because mealtime facilitates discussion of daily events in a relaxing and nurturing environment.

All parents of gifted children need opportunities to share the frustrations and joys of their parenting experiences with each other, but if you are a solo parent with no one with whom to share the joy and pride of your gifted child's accomplishments, this need becomes an even higher priority. Maintaining a support system of extended family and friends fills this need, as well as provides a means of practical assistance in the way of help with major homework projects or cooking a meal on those occasions when solo parents come home from work too exhausted to think.

You may wish to dialogue with other solo parents online or through support groups sponsored by your community or religious organization. Find other solo parent families to do things with, especially during the holidays when the pain and loneliness of solo parenting can feel most overwhelming. Seeking out opportunities for community service that you can share together as a family also models character qualities of compassionate service to the larger community while providing solo parents with much needed socialization with other adults.

From what we know about the role of family influences on the development of gifted children, research suggests that children who grow up in "complex" families (those that are a combination of both stimulation and nurturance), are happier, more alert, more engaged, and more goal directed than those who grow up with only one or neither of these traits. In addition, parents who (a) grant their children more than the usual amount of independence, (b) offer enriched environments with a high level of intellectual or artistic stimulation, and (c) model hard work and high achievement have the best outcomes for developing and maintaining their children's gifted characteristics. Instead of thinking solo parents are at a disadvantage in this regard, it is possible to reframe our perspective of solo parent families as a unique opportunity to become a constructive milieu for nurturing giftedness. This is because the most salient qualities of the Tao of solo parenting are its potential to exemplify a child-centered environment, foster greater independence, and model hard work and high achievement in the face of adversity.

Academic Issues

Even the best home environment may be undermined by negative learning experiences at school. Partnering with educators can provide children with quality educational experiences that nurture their gifts and talents. Offer to help locate supplemental materials or make your child's teacher aware of conference speakers or workshops for the sake of your child's optimal educational growth and development. Because it is vital to avoid any mismatch between your child's educational environment and her abilities, parents must make it a priority to observe their child's classroom, actively communicate with teachers, and advocate for learning environments where students with gifts and talents can thrive.

The challenges may be even greater if you are parenting a twice-exceptional gifted child, for whom doubly special academic needs require attendance at additional conferences for planning, monitoring progress, and evaluating results for strengths, limitations, and their interactions. These needs may contribute to the overextension of limited parental resources, causing further stress and hardship for solo parents. The extra time required for this level of interaction with teachers and administrators may prove exceptionally challenging for many solo parents, who habitually tend to feel that they are "a day late and a dollar short" in everything. But engaging school officials in compassionate and sensitive communication is not an unrealistic expectation. By being candid with teachers and letting them know your limitations as well as your needs and goals for your child, you may be pleasantly surprised to discover they can become caring and supportive members of your team.

Money Matters

Solo parents have to work harder to respond to their gifted child's demands for an enriched environment. How can this be done on a one-income, shoestring budget? Many solo parent households also receive public assistance and struggle just to provide the basics. My goal has been to provide each of my children the opportunity to receive lessons or enrichment in at least one of their areas of interest, but for years our economic circumstances could be described as "situational poverty." Little money existed for decent transportation, food, clothing, and shelter, let alone expensive lessons and extracurricular activities, such as the $35 an hour horseback riding lessons for which my daughter had begged. What's a solo parent to do? Initially, I asked my 10-year-old daughter to write a persuasive essay containing at least five reasons why horseback riding could further her learning, increase her self-esteem, and enhance her leadership skills. She responded with a detailed presentation of how learning to communicate with a horse through body language with hands, fingertips, scat, and emotion was practice for communicating with people. She explained that as the youngest of seven children, she feels like nobody ever really listens to her. Having authority over a horse that obeys her slightest command gives her a sense of empowerment. "You have to believe in yourself and you cannot lose your cool if you are going to be in control of a 1,200 pound horse." I was amazed by the many reasons she articulated to convince me of the worthiness of equestrian education. I contacted the closest stable offering riding lessons, swallowed my pride, and asked if there was any way we could barter services for lessons. As a result of this conversation, we now clean house for the stable owner in exchange for my daughter's horseback riding lessons. Exhausting in addition to all of my other responsibilities? Absolutely! But it's worth it for my daughter to know that I'm willing to do whatever it takes in order to invest in her dreams.

Discover Personal Interests

Solo parents need not feel guilty for continuing to pursue their own intellectual interests and creative pursuits. A solo parent with passion of her own inspires her children, providing them with a role model for service and industry, along with opportunities to develop greater self-reliance.

It is important to find activities with other children who share some of the same interests as your gifted child because it often can be difficult for nonconforming, highly driven, divergent thinkers to find like-minded peers in the typical classroom environment. Sports, drama, art, chess club, foreign language, swim team, music, orchestra, scouting, 4H clubs, YMCA, summer camps, religious education, community service, enrichment classes, afterschool clubs, distance learning, and computer technology all present opportunities for gifted kids to socialize and explore their abilities in a nonthreatening environment. Many of these programs also offer scholarships or financial assistance to defray expenses. Solo parents on the lookout for free extracurricular enrichment opportunities should not underestimate the value of tuition-free musical education offered by the public school as a means of encouraging exploration of a subject area, as well as nurturing undeveloped talent. In a German research study using MRI scans, Gottfried Schlaug discovered that intense exposure to music actually expands brain mass. Schlaug found that musicians who started playing music as young children were found to have a larger mass of nerve fibers connecting the brain's two hemispheres, providing a rationale for the development and stimulation of intellectual growth. Studies on the effect of classical music instruction on children's academic performance indicate that the process of learning to read music, as well as the diligent practice required to master a musical instrument, transfer to higher achievement in the classroom.

The Power of Creativity

Many solo parents struggle with not having an intact family. Their sense of guilt may be acute, particularly if they are single as a result of divorce and their children were traumatized by frequent parental discord and family turmoil. Studies done by Goertzel and Goertzel in 2004 found that "homes which cradle eminence, creativity, and contentment are not congenial." Only 58 of the 400 famous men and women whose biographies they studied had homes they classified as comfortable, content, warm, and untroubled. Solo parents can take comfort in the fact that exceptionally talented and creative individuals need not come only from harmonious and untroubled homes.

Deliberately work to nurture your child's creativity. Let children take their creativity as far as they can and don't worry that they won't be well-rounded. Set limits but actively nurture creativity by providing a place for creativity to happen. When my son showed genuine artistic promise, a professional in the field offered some sage advice. He recommended that I provide an ample space at home (well-stocked with art supplies), brace myself for the inevitable disorder, and then leave him to his own devices. When my son was a toddler, I fastened newsprint to the walls all over our house and he drew on the walls to his heart's content. As a grownup, he now receives monetary reward for painting murals on the walls of other people's homes!

Be prepared to tolerate messy projects in various stages of completion in your home. Bear in mind that the process is every bit as important as the product. Allow your children to work through the process and value it by demonstrating enthusiasm for the ongoing process, not just the final product. Remember that the process is in the journey and not only the final destination; this will help you not only in the fine art of parenting but also in the fine art of living life, as well as in the pursuit of creativity, no matter what area of creativity needs to be expressed. From the personal experience of having parented a writer, an artist, a musician, and a twice-exceptional, creatively gifted vocal performer with bipolar disorder, I can attest that adolescence often is the most difficult phase in creative growth and expression. Take heart, though, for as gifted children emerge from their teen years, their emotional stability and coping skills seem to improve.

Profoundly academically gifted individuals experience twice the rate of social and emotional difficulties found among their nongifted peers, and in general, highly creative gifted children experience more emotional difficulties than academically gifted children. Because of this, parents of all gifted children may need more support than other parents in dealing with the tensions between cognitive, emotional, and physical development.

Social-Emotional Needs

When high-ability students' social and emotional needs aren't being met at school, the family is more likely to be a source of strong support. How do solo parents help their children reduce stress, focus on positive behavior, enhance emotional security, and strengthen relationships, thus liberating our children to develop their highest potential? We must examine our own communication styles, coping strategies, and stress management skills. We cannot expect to pass on healthy communication styles to our children if we have not first learned them ourselves. The greatest service we can offer our gifted children may be to develop the kind of positive social coping strategies that maximize their energy for learning opportunities. Making time in your schedule to include your children in your quest for inner peace and serenity, although it sounds corny, really works. Letting them participate in your yoga, aerobics classes, or an at-home workout is healthy for both mind and body.

Gifted children have unique social, emotional, and psychological characteristics. They often struggle with the conflict of wanting to fit in socially and their atypical predisposition to nonconformity. They may be introverted, intense, hypersensitive, perfectionistic, and driven. Solo parents can take comfort in the fact that intellectually gifted kids appear to have better adjustment due to their emotional resilience and superior problem-solving abilities. This is good news for children of solo parents who must navigate the phases of grief due to the absence of a parent as a result of separation, death, disability, or court decree. Although high intelligence is considered a protective factor for children in the resilience literature, it must not be taken for granted. If a problem, such as anxiety, sadness, depression, or poor interpersonal relations, continues for longer than a few weeks, it would be worthwhile to consider professional consultation.

Many solo parents are dealing with difficult emotional adjustment issues unique to rearing children without the benefit of a partner or coparent or, in many cases, without the assistance of extended family. Parenting gifted children is a challenge even under the most ideal circumstances but solo parenting a gifted child without a partner presents a very real temptation to treat one's gifted child as a confidante. As the movie, *Little Man Tate* accurately portrays, gifted children, especially those with high emotional intelligence who appear older and wiser than their years, may exhibit characteristics of pseudomaturity. Gifted children sometimes appear so mature, poised, sensitive, and empathetic that we mistakenly assume that they can handle serious adult issues when they really cannot.

There are times in a solo parent's life when he or she may find it incredibly difficult to cope with all the demands of a household composed of gifted people. Solo parents may consider solving this problem by having a family psychologist, or therapist, in the same way that they have a family physician—someone they can go to for regular checkups or assistance if things seem not to be going well. This often is recommended particularly for parents of highly gifted children, not only because their intensity and sensitivity are so much greater than even that of other gifted children, but also because these children tend to be more uneven or varied in their development, and therefore even more of a puzzle to those around them.

Although an initial comprehensive psychological assessment may be expensive, solo parents may benefit not only from the specific recommendations they receive, but also because the assessment results provide a baseline with which to gauge the severity of a problem. If cost is a prohibitive factor, contact the psychology department of your local university and ask if they offer a clinic in counseling psychology or school psychology. Graduate students under the supervision of an APA-licensed psychologist run these clinics that offer a complete psychological assessment at greatly reduced rates. Many communities offer mental health counseling services for free or on a sliding payment scale. School guidance counselors also are a wonderful (and often underutilized) source of help to single-parent families and may provide individual counseling sessions and group counseling for your children.

Many schools offer counseling and support groups for children of single parents such as Banana Splits, a peer support-group program for children of separated, divorcing, or divorced parents. The Banana Splits program has been widely used in public elementary schools across the United States for more than 14 years. The meetings are confidential and use nationally recognized strategies with individual or group counseling available under the guidance of school counselors who are specially trained to help solo parent families work through this difficult time. Children meet in small, age-appropriate groups for support to learn that they are not the only students going through separation. The Banana Splits meetings provide a safe place where it is acceptable for children to share their feelings honestly and talk about things that scare them. Children read stories, do crafts, focus on positive healthy lifestyles, and make new friends as they learn how to encourage and support each other. Support and understanding for parents and students has been shown to help the child maintain grades and lessen stress. Contact your child's school to see if they offer a Banana Splits program. If not, inquire of your local church, synagogue, youth group, YWCA, extension service agency, or other organizations. Solo parenting strategies useful after separation and divorce also are available from the local library, bookstores, the Internet, and from your child's school counselor.

Our children need us now but they won't be under our wing forever. The best advice I can offer is to give up the "Super Parent Syndrome" and take care of yourself so that you can be there to take care of your gifted children. Develop an attitude of gratitude by realizing adversity can be a blessing in disguise. Difficult situations bring out the best in all of us. Look at your solo parent status as an opportunity to become a better parent by discovering ways to transform and reinvent new strengths and abilities you never knew you had. Don't underestimate your gifted child's capacity for strength, resilience, and compassion. Celebrate your children's gifts, talents, and leadership abilities. Give them a chance to show how understanding, resourceful, and responsible they can be. Cherish them, respect their uniqueness, and respect their dreams. This is the Tao of all parenting, solo or otherwise.

Resources

Books and Articles

Csikszentmihalyi, M., Rathunde, K., & Whalen, S. (1997). *Talented teenagers: The roots of success and failure.* New York, NY: Cambridge University Press.

DeFrain, J., & Eirick, R. (1981). Coping as divorced single parents: A comparative study of fathers and mothers. *Family Relations, 30,* 265–274.

Marston, S. (1994). *The divorced parent: Success strategies for raising your children after separation.* New York, NY: William Morrow & Company.

Neihart, M. (2002). Risk and resilience in gifted children: A conceptual framework. In M. Neihart, S. Reis, N. M. Robinson, & S. M. Moon (Eds.), *The social and emotional development of gifted children* (pp. 113–124). Waco, TX: Prufrock Press.

Tolan, S. S. (1982). An open letter to parents, teachers and others: From parents of an exceptionally gifted child. In J. T. Webb, E. A. Meckstroth, & S. S. Tolan (Eds.). *Guiding the gifted child* (pp. 221–241). Scottsdale, AZ: Great Potential Press.

Websites

Davidson Institute for Talent Development—http://www.davidsongifted.org
Gifted Children Monthly—http://www.gifted-children.com
GT World—http://www.gtworld.org
The Hollingworth Center for Highly Gifted Children—http://www.hollingworth.org
TAG Families of Talented & Gifted—http://www.tagfam.org
Shelia Ellison's Complete Mom—http://www.CompleteMom.com
Supporting Emotional Needs of the Gifted (SENG)—http://www.sengifted.org

Reference

Goertzel, V., & Goertzel, M. G. (2004). *Cradles of eminence* (2nd ed.). Scottsdale, AZ: Great Potential Press.

Chapter 31

The Role of Physicians in the Lives of Gifted Children

by Edward R. Amend and Richard M. Clouse

F our-year-old Joey enters the pediatrician's office. His eyes dart from the toys to the interesting people shuffling papers behind glass windows. He surveys the scene with great intent. Once inside the exam room, he immediately begins climbing on the exam table to get a better look at the items on a nearby shelf. He is fascinated by the instruments, which look somewhat like those from his toy doctor's kit at home. Much to his mother's chagrin, he is reaching for something when the physician enters. Joey is active and verbal during the exam, with questions about many different topics. The mother describes concerns about Joey's activity level in preschool. She explains how concerned the teachers are and how tiring all of Joey's questions can be.

How will Joey's pediatrician respond? Will she relate the behavior to the curiosity of a gifted child, to normal development, or to some type of pathology such as Attention Deficit/Hyperactivity Disorder (ADHD)? These are interesting questions, with answers determined by a number of factors—such as the comfort of the parent in describing behaviors, the physician's knowledge of giftedness, and her willingness to accept its implications.

This vignette highlights the important role a child's primary care physician can play early in the life of a gifted child and how this differs from what medical healthcare professionals may provide for other families. In today's healthcare arena, medical professionals are the first line of treatment and the gatekeepers for more specialized services. A child's primary care physician, typically a pediatrician or family practitioner, serves in that capacity. Creating a positive, proactive relationship with your child's physician can increase the chances that he or she will listen to your concerns about precocious development. Clear communication is needed to foster a relationship that involves prevention with a focus on overall health and well-being—not just visits when illnesses arise. Additionally, a physician's awareness of giftedness and its implications is needed so that more physicians can recognize the need for specialized services for gifted children.

For simplicity and clarity, we use the term physician in this article to indicate your child's primary care physician, regardless of whether that is a pediatrician or family practice physician. We discuss several issues related to the role of physicians, including what information a physician might need to know, why it is important for them to understand both your child and giftedness, how to discuss these issues, and finally what roles physicians can play outside of the typical medical domain.

Relationships Start Early

Typically, physicians begin relationships with you and your child very early in your child's life, years before he or she enters school and long before giftedness is even discussed as a possibility. As a result, your child's physician is in a good position to recognize early behaviors associated with giftedness and to recommend appropriate positive interventions.

An informed physician can be a source of reassurance, a positive support for gifted children, and an ally for par-

The Family Practitioner

It is important to note that most physicians follow the medical model, a problem-centered process that is geared toward prevention, recognition, and treatment of disease. The family practitioner's philosophy differs slightly from other physicians because family practitioners are trained to see the whole family from grandfather to baby sister and to be both the patient's advocate and the parent's advocate. Many family practitioners see their job as involving several facets: seeking the cause of the complaint rather than simply treating the symptom, working to keep people off unnecessary medications, ensuring accurate diagnosis by qualified practitioners, and not perpetuating a condition by simply continuing treatment. Family practitioners are trained to explore the impact of the problem on the family and relationships.

ents. He or she is in a unique position of seeing whether your child is developing appropriately, lagging behind, or exceeding typical developmental expectations from an early age. The physician's objective, though limited, view of your child is based on observations and developmental norms, allowing him or her to recognize the possibility of giftedness in a child. Although giftedness does not define a child, it directly impacts social, educational, and emotional aspects throughout one's life, and early recognition of the signs of giftedness by a physician can validate a parent's view.

Of course, physicians will have limited time with you and your child, and you should not expect them to recognize giftedness *per se*. But, you can expect them to spend extra time when you bring up advanced development. Alert him or her to developmental milestones that your child seems to be reaching earlier than same-age peers so that an informed physician can recognize the possibility that giftedness exists and play a role providing support and guidance. Your questions and clearly communicated information are crucial to the physician's understanding of your child throughout the formative years. This is useful because, with giftedness, like many conditions, early recognition and intervention can be particularly helpful to later adjustment. This cannot happen without knowledge about giftedness and its implications.

The Importance of Understanding

Unfortunately, physicians receive little, if any, training on the needs of gifted children and may need direction and assistance in order to understand the complexity of the situation. They may need information about the manifestations and needs of gifted children, and you—the parent of a gifted child—are often in the best position to provide that information. Physicians often fall prey to the same myths about gifted children that others do because they receive virtually no training about the needs of gifted and talented children and adolescents. Prevalent myths include: gifted children are well-organized, become gifted because their parents push them, show advanced emotional maturity, and seldom have emotional or interpersonal issues. Inaccurate information about gifted children may lead physicians to overlook potential or ongoing problems in a gifted child. They may believe that gifted children don't have any problems, or perhaps think that "everybody's gifted," so gifted children have no special needs.

The prevalence of myths can cause further damage by preventing parents from seeking necessary resources or even discussing potential problems with the physician. Many parents start to get "gun shy" because of the negative reactions they have received from other parents or physicians in the past. They may censor what they say to whom, including physicians. When you talk about your gifted child to people who believe the prevalent myths, they may think you are exaggerating or bragging. But, if you don't share information because you are unsure how a physician will react or fear a negative reaction, the physician will not have the opportunity even to recognize that giftedness is a possible factor affecting your child. Misinformation, myths, and subsequent censoring by parents are the first barriers to understanding and perhaps also barriers to appropriate resources or services.

Sharing Information About Giftedness With Physicians

Before physicians can assume the pivotal roles of supporting and advocating for your gifted child (and others), they must have a basic understanding of giftedness and its implications. But, how are they to get this information?

You must first avoid the tendency to censor information and then recognize that physicians are busy professionals. Handing them a book and saying, "Why don't you take a look at this?" is probably not the best strategy. Perhaps you can open the door to gifted issues by asking your physician for permission to include brochures for gifted associations among the pamphlets in the waiting room. Next, provide small bits of information, perhaps one or two pages with some sections highlighted, to the physician. Highlight the important pieces and supplement written information with comments during the brief office visit. Sending information in advance of the office visit is another good strategy. A small dose of information is the best way to start to educate your physician because office visit time will always be at a premium.

Also, be aware that physicians are likely to view information from peer-reviewed journals as more valid and appropriate than something printed off the Internet. It is not that Internet information may not be accurate—it may be both quite accurate and very appropriate—but physicians understandably trust peer-reviewed information without having to check its origin as they might information from other sources. A good starting point is "Discovering Gifted Children in Pediatric Practice" in the *Journal of Developmental and Behavioral Pediatrics* (see the Resources section of this chapter). Concise fact sheets from well-known organizations, such as the National Association for Gifted Children (NAGC) or Supporting Emotional Needs of the Gifted (SENG), might be useful supplements to journal articles.

Your physician's openness to the topics of giftedness and advanced development will allow you to be more comfortable in describing the behaviors of your child. You also need to do your homework when selecting a physician and do some research about area physicians to find someone with whom you are comfortable so that you can talk about intense and personal matters. While you can certainly give information to physicians, your child can provide perspective as well. Too often, parents and professionals alike discount the valuable perspective of the child. Gifted children often are able to verbalize feelings and situations at an early age when offered a compassionate ear.

Raising Related Concerns With Physicians

Frequently, physicians hear complaints from parents or teachers about behavioral problems. The physician's first responsibility is to determine whether there are medical causes for these behavioral problems, and later to explore behavioral or school causes. The pervasiveness of the problem can shed light on possible causes, and it is important to let your child's physician know about frequency, intensity, and duration of the problems. For example, if the problem happens only in one area during the day, the problem is less likely a medical issue.

Always inform physicians of physical symptoms or complaints that could be linked to school problems related to a child's giftedness. If your physician is aware of gifted issues, he or she will be better able to avoid misdiagnosis (or missed diagnosis) and take the next step toward advocacy once medical reasons are ruled out. A wide variety of physical complaints, including depressed mood, irritability, attention or behavioral problems, social isolation or withdrawal, sleep disturbances, changes in appetite, and headaches, all can have organic origins; however, these same symptoms also are seen with gifted students placed in a misaligned or unsupportive school environment.

Inform the physician of issues with school avoidance or behavior problems in the school setting, which can be indicators of larger problems. Frequent physical complaints or complaints about school can lead the physician to explore the nature of the problem. In some cases, after the initial assessment, your child's physician may refer your child to a child psychologist or psychiatrist for in-depth testing and diagnosis that may be outside of the scope of the physician's expertise. If medication is indicated, you and your child may return to the physician for management as well as regular care.

Any of these problems—school avoidance, behavioral issues, and complaints about school—can indicate bigger problems. Raising the physician's awareness when you as a parent first begin to see those physical complaints in your child can be helpful. For example, when the physician is aware that Susie has had stomachaches every morning going to school for the past few weeks, he or she can take a look beyond simply treating the symptoms with medication. When giftedness is contributing to the school problems, appropriate intervention cannot happen without knowledge about giftedness and its implications.

Roles for Physicians

With good parent-physician communication, your physician will begin to understand giftedness, and the developing doctor-patient relationship will ultimately allow the physician to play several different roles in the life of your gifted child. The physician can not only help you maintain your child's good physical health and mental health and diagnose and treat ailments, but also help advocate for appropriate gifted services in the school setting. The physician can provide support and guidance to you and other parents, who also may have limited understanding of the implications of giftedness in one's life. Practitioners need not be experts in gifted education to be effective, as long as they can provide appropriate referrals to resources. Physicians with general knowledge of the characteristics of gifted children can lead parents to books and Internet resources regarding gifted children. With beginning knowledge and a starting point, parents can then explore whether formal testing and identification, counseling, or other services are needed. Obviously, if you are reading this, you have already located some appropriate resources, and educating your child's physician about those resources will allow him or her to help other parents.

Let's return to the opening vignette for a moment; several variations of it may occur. A parent may say, "The teacher says my son or daughter has ADHD because she acts up in English class every day." Or, a new patient enters saying, "Fred's been on Ritalin and we are here for a refill." The physician responds, "How do you know he has ADHD?" The mother replies, "Well, he was on medication before and the teacher still thinks he needs it." What will the response be? Will the physician inquire about the child's behavior in other classes and try to differentiate the true nature of the problem or simply pull out the prescription pad?

These exchanges are not uncommon, and all require further inquiry into the nature of the problem because there are problems with both misdiagnosis and missed diagnosis of gifted children. These situations require a physician to look at the disease state, the problem, and not just the overt symptoms of the problem, which can represent a number of things or mask other problems. Accurate diagnosis is needed because, for example, many of the medications for ADHD will increase performance even if a child does not have ADHD. Unfortunately, busy physicians unfamiliar with gifted issues have a tendency to go the quick and easy route of treating the overt behaviors. Because thorough investigation often is needed, which is something most physicians are not trained to do and do not have the time to do, providing appropriate referrals is another important role for the physician.

Acting in an advocacy role, your child's physician can interact with educators and other health professionals, which may be necessary to obtain appropriate educational or professional services. Educators and school administrators respect the physician's voice, and it is not unusual for a physician to advocate for school modifications for children with medical issues—such as ADHD, asthma, or diabetes—that may affect schoolwork. But, the situation often is quite different for the gifted child because the physicians often are not aware that giftedness has implications and may create problems. They may not see advocacy for gifted services as part of their role. Awareness and recognition of gifted behaviors and needs is necessary so that physicians may assist you in advocating for appropriate gifted services.

Supportive physicians can help you feel more secure in your interaction with the teachers and administrators on your child's behalf. Part of the physician's role as patient advocate involves developing a rapport with the family so that you feel comfortable enough to challenge the school's interpretation when necessary. The physician can help you negotiate appropriate gifted services for your child within the school setting, addressing the school's concerns in a nonthreatening way while advocating for the child's needs to obtain appropriate resources.

Expanding Understanding in the Medical and Counseling Communities

Supporting Emotional Needs of the Gifted (SENG; http://www.sengifted.org), a nonprofit organization, is working toward increasing the understanding of giftedness among physicians and psychologists. SENG has become an American Psychological Association-approved provider of continuing education courses for psychologists, has created a Professional Advisory Committee of nationally recognized physicians and psychologists to educate different medical and mental health professionals, and has partnered with the National Association for Gifted Children to develop a basic "fact sheet" about high-ability children to be used in physicians' waiting rooms.

SENG recognizes that it must connect with physicians in the field and must reach out to do so. Because of the demands of their practice and the myths about gifted children—physicians simply are unaware of the implications of giftedness. The SENG Professional Advisory Committee is now working on ways to reach the American Medical Association and American Association of Family Physicians to share information. They are searching for ways to get younger doctors and residents educated at the very beginning of their training. Just as we seek to educate teachers when they are in training, we must also seek to educate physicians early in their training. Parents can assist in the education process by supporting SENG and educating their child's physician a little bit at a time.

Gifted children are not immune to medical or psychological disorders; they can suffer from difficulties at about the same rate as the general population. However, that doesn't mean their giftedness should be ignored in the process of evaluation or treatment. Medications clearly have their benefits and can help many people, but they are not the only answer. Sometimes medications are needed, and incorporating giftedness into your child's treatment may prove useful. For example, gifted people may react differently to some medications than the typical population, and some conditions, such as allergies, are more prevalent among the gifted. These factors can have implications for treatment.

With gifted children, as with all children, it is important to be accurate in both diagnosis and treatment. In the process of evaluation, especially in adolescents and younger children, it is possible to unmask other issues such as depression. For example, many ADHD patients also are treated for depression, and many gifted individuals also have issues with depression, perfectionism, and/or anxiety. Gifted children do not have more psychological issues than other children, but they may have more issues in expressing their giftedness and face risks because of their giftedness. When your child's physician is open to giftedness and issues related to alternate diagnoses, he or she may be more likely to identify the underlying problem(s), revealing alternate interventions.

Resources

Lui, Y. H., Lien, J., Kafka, T., & Stein, M. T. (2005). Discovering gifted children in pediatric practice. *Journal of Developmental and Behavioral Pediatrics, 26*, 366–369.

Neihart, M., Reis, S. M., Robinson, N. M., & Moon, S. M. (Eds.). (2002). *The social and emotional development of gifted children: What do we know?* Waco, TX: Prufrock Press.

Webb, J. T., Amend, E. R., Webb, N. E., Goerss, J., Beljan, P., & Olenchak, F. R. (2005). *Misdiagnosis and dual diagnoses of gifted children and adults: ADHD, bipolar, OCD, Asperger's, depression, and other disorders.* Scottsdale, AZ: Great Potential Press.

Webb, J. T., Gore, J. L., Amend, E. R., & DeVries, A. R. (2007). *A parent's guide to gifted children.* Scottsdale, AZ: Great Potential Press.

Chapter 32

Productive Parent Teacher Conferences

by Arlene R. DeVries

FALL is in the air. Students are established at school and the memo comes home regarding parent-teacher conferences. Of course we will attend to support our children in their education. What a disappointment when during our brief conference the teacher, with great enthusiasm may tell us only, "Your child is doing fine." Or, after checking the grade book to determine which one is your child, he proudly recites the letter grades the student is receiving. But . . . what I want to know is, "What about the 'well-being' of my child? I know what letter grades he or she brings home!"

In reality, school and home share common goals for the child's social and academic growth but from different vantage points. No teacher or parent wakes up in the morning saying to himself, "How can I make that child as miserable as possible today?" Teachers bring expertise in content areas, curriculum planning, classroom organization, and student motivation. Parents have unique insights into the child's needs, aspirations, interests, and aptitudes. The challenge is discovering the best way to communicate and cooperatively implement appropriate interactions with the child.

Educators say what they want from parents is:
- to be appreciated,
- to be respected,
- to be trusted,
- to be given consideration,

- to be understood, and
- to hear positives.

This list mirrors what parents say they expect from educators! Wise teachers and savvy parents will remember these guidelines when meeting in conferences to share ideas and concerns about the gifted child. The first step for parents is to be prepared when they come to parent-teacher conferences.

Be Informed

1. Know School Policies

Begin by gathering information about the district's mission statement and the board of education's priorities for school improvement by attending local school board meetings, parent advisory committees, and advocacy groups for parents of gifted and talented students. Does the mission statement mention educating students to the full extent of their abilities, aptitudes, capabilities, and interests? Does it include meeting the needs of each student? Are there provisions for parent and community involvement? Discover which staff persons in your district and in your school are responsible for gifted education. Become familiar with educational vocabulary in order to talk professionally with school personnel.

2. Know State and Local Guidelines for Gifted Programs

How does a parent acquire this information? One person in each state department of education has been given the responsibility for gifted and talented education. Contact that individual for information regarding state guidelines, local GT personnel, and notices about upcoming conferences. Discover in which areas of giftedness (e.g., academic aptitude, visual arts, performing arts, leadership, creativity) students are identified and served. Research the program components in your district. Are there compacted or modified assignments, grade or subject acceleration, classroom enrichment, community experiences,

Advanced Placement or honors classes, early graduation, postsecondary enrollment, independent study, or mentorships? Read books and professional magazines, attend conferences, and talk to parents in your district and in neighboring districts. Those parents who have children several grades ahead of yours can share a wealth of information regarding what worked and what didn't work for them in the educational system.

3. Know Your Child

Most importantly, you must know yourself and your child. What personality traits do you share with your child? Perhaps it's intensity, perseverance, motivation, emotional involvement, acute sensitivity, a high energy level, creativity and imagination, perfectionism, keen powers of observation, or being highly verbal. Don't be surprised if a teacher points out one of these traits in your child. Though all can be highly desirable as adults, often they are seen as negatives in a classroom. Could any of them be a negative for you at a parent-teacher conference? Make them work for you in a meeting with school personnel, or take someone with you who can balance your emotional involvement or verbosity.

It is important to be comfortable with your child's giftedness and with the label "gifted." Seek to understand the strengths and weaknesses, both academically and socially, that your child displays at school. Prior to the conference, talk to your child about his or her concerns and frustrations with school, as well as the tasks he or she especially enjoys or completes with ease. Be prepared to share any special situations or needs at home such as illness, death, divorce, remarriage, or job change that may have an impact on the child's school performance. It is helpful to share some of your child's interests and talents displayed outside the classroom. For example:

- the child's reading interests,
- hobbies and collections,
- special talents or skills,
- the family and child's recreation choices,
- participation in clubs or groups,
- private lessons taken by the child,

- trips the child has taken, and
- the child's home responsibilities.

Identifying specific examples of the child's work, feelings, and behaviors enhances the possibility of a productive conference.

Use Positive Communication Techniques

Because a teacher's time is limited, arrive and depart promptly at your scheduled time. Enter confidently and positively, shaking hands with the teacher and giving your name and your child's name. The conference is enhanced when both parents are able to attend. Single parents might ask a relative, friend, or someone who shares responsibility for the child to accompany them. When possible, arrange to sit in an "adult" chair at eye level with the teacher.

As the teacher begins the conference, listen actively. Be calm, diplomatic, and tactful. Show with your body language that you are interested in what the teacher has to say. If you feel you are leaving conferences with only "surface" information such as test scores and attendance records, you might consider asking some of the following questions used by other parents of gifted students.

1. Does my child seem happy at school? What are his or her special interests and strengths?
2. How does my child interact with others: age-level peers, older children, younger children, adults? Is he or she perceived as a "know-it-all" and made fun of, or do other students seek him or her out?
3. Does the academic work seem challenging or does he or she complete it with little effort?
4. What provisions are made for students to learn at their own pace? Are assignments being altered to accommodate their abilities and interests?
5. If my child participates in special gifted and talented experiences, is he or she expected to make up the regular classroom work?

6. How does he or she feel about trying new things or making mistakes?
7. What opportunities does my child have for critical and creative thinking and for problem solving? How does he or she respond?
8. In what ways does my child show the ability to work independently, accept leadership roles, assume responsibility, and exhibit intellectual curiosity?
9. What can I do to help my child develop his or her talents?
10. What appropriate afterschool or summer enrichment opportunities are available for my child?

Find ways to show appreciation for the positives that happen in the classroom. Avoid words that might negatively impact the teacher, such as "bored" and "brilliant." Instead, use language such as, "My child seems to learn differently," or "my child needs less time and fewer repetitions to master the content." Generalizations such as "always" and "never" can be replaced with specific examples of behavioral or academic concerns. Express a willingness to help solve problems. The emphasis is on what *we* can do together, not "What are *you* going to do?"

If you do not understand or agree with the teacher's suggestions, reflect on the possibilities and follow up later. Perhaps after giving some thought to the idea or trying it at home, it may have value. On other occasions, you might honestly respond, based on the knowledge of your child's abilities and temperament, that there might be a better way to proceed.

When making curriculum suggestions for your gifted child, be specific about a strategy that fits your child's needs and one that has been recognized in quality gifted programs. Show how it reflects the district's goals or policies and how you could help at home to make it successful. It is important that these suggestions be made first with the child's classroom teacher. Only when you have been unable to reach a mutual decision after several honest, professional attempts, should you take the issue to the principal or gifted education supervisor. Educators appreciate parents respecting the chain of command. A parent who takes the issue first to the superintendent or the school board will find difficulty later in gaining cooperation from the classroom teacher.

Successful conferences are based on:
- honesty,
- compliments,
- fact finding,
- compromise,
- expressions of confidence, and
- shared information that makes the other person's job easier!

Unsuccessful tactics include:
- blaming,
- defensiveness,
- unsubstantiated claims,
- demands,
- threats,
- yelling, and
- telling professionals what they *should* do!

Teachers appreciate follow-up notes thanking them for their time and interest in your student. School communication is an ongoing process. It might be accomplished by e-mail, phone, written notes, formal letters, or face-to-face conversations. The more insights you and the teacher have about each other and your child, the greater the chances for educational growth. Children feel secure knowing the most important people in their lives are cooperating and consistent in supporting their educational experiences.

Be prepared! Know the possibilities and policies in your school district. Know yourself and your child. Your interest and involvement in your children's education send a powerful message that you care about them. Parent-teacher conferences can be a new and exciting growth opportunity for you and your child.

PART VI

Advocacy

by Tracy Ford Inman

C HANCES are that if you're reading this book, you're already an advocate—whether you realize it or not. You're trying to find out as much information as possible in order to help your child. Passionate about your child's learning, you want to ensure that needs are met and that challenge is provided. You speak out on behalf of your child, understanding that the more information you have, the stronger your message will be—and the greater that message impacts the classroom, the school, the district, and beyond. You are an advocate.

The chapters in this section should help you become a better advocate. Filled with practical strategies, robust resources, and rich insight, each explores a different aspect of advocacy. You've come to this section with varying stages of advocacy background from the novice to the experienced. You've also come from different advocacy arenas, whether that be your child's classroom or your state capitol. Therefore, the chapters address advocacy on multiple levels: self, school, district, state, and national. They each encourage you to make a lasting difference in the lives of children who are gifted and talented—and they guide you in doing just that.

Part of our "Effective Advocates" column in *Parenting for High Potential*, the piece by Julia Roberts and me emphasizes the critical importance of being a lifelong advocate. Too often parents begin their advocacy journey when their children first experience difficulty in grade school. These advocates mature and grow as their child travels through school; by the time they're wise and seasoned, their child graduates— and their advocacy is packed away with the cap and gown. This chapter explores the whys and hows of lifelong advocacy, encouraging you to continue to speak out on behalf of gifted children your entire life.

What happens when our individual advocacy efforts meet a dead end? According to Rich Weinfeld, Michelle Davis, Jeanne Paynter, and Sue Jeweler, perhaps it's time to hire a professional advocate, someone who can assess the problem accurately and then generate myriad possible solutions working with both parents and school personnel. The authors provide great insight into deciding when a professional is needed, the characteristics to look for when hiring a professional, and strategies in working with professional advocates.

Through a creative and appropriate metaphor of dance, Diana Reeves leads you through all the steps of learning to be an advocate at the district level. Finding partners, learning the steps, experimenting with new formations—these all help readers realize that "advocating, like square dancing, is not a spectator sport" (p. 340). Filled with real-life vignettes to illustrate major points, Joan Smutny gives practical suggestions and how-to lists designed to maximize parent advocacy efforts in "Taking a Larger Stand for Gifted Education." Including questions to ask potential parent groups and tips for talking with legislators, the information encourages you to move beyond your child's individual classroom by joining other parents to impact gifted education on the district, state, and national levels.

The last two chapters span a wide range of ideas—from teaching teens to advocate for themselves to teaching others to advocate through examples. Deborah Douglas describes steps gifted adolescents can take to become their own advocates so that they "recognize and address the needs specific to their own learning abilities, without compromising their dignity or that of others" (p. 360). A powerful message in independence and responsibility, "Four Simple Steps to Self-Advocacy" illustrates each step and also includes ideas for what parents can do to help. In order to share lessons learned from others, Ann Robinson and Sidney Moon asked advocacy groups across the nation to send in success stories. An examination of the 61 responses and 6 follow-up case studies yielded important lessons for the parent advocate. These lessons focus on Policies (successful advocacy depends on knowledgeable people), Champions and Leaders (knowledgeable, motivated people make a difference), and Advocacy Tools and Strategies (planning, collaboration, and communication are key).

As you think about the chapters, use Rolfe, Freshwater, and Jasper's Framework for Reflection (2001) that consists of three basic questions. The first is "What?" What are the main messages of each chapter? What important points are made? Reflect on these ideas. The second question is "So what?" How does this message apply to you? Your child? Your child's school or district? Your state? Make connections. The last question is "Now what?" Here you need to consider your next step: What can you implement or what tangible impact will the chapters have on your advocacy efforts? Plan and strategize. Be specific in your goal setting and include timelines for meeting those goals.

You can fight the same battles each new school year with your child's teacher, winning some and losing some. Or you can be proactive by approaching advocacy on a larger scale, helping the school be more responsive to the needs of all children including those who are gifted and talented. Better yet, work at the district level so that far-reaching policies and procedures are gifted-friendly and not barriers to high-level learning. Better still, advocate on the state level by supporting laws, regulations, and statutes that take the ceiling off of learning and that mandate identification of and appropriate servicing of children who are gifted and talented. And, of course, your advocacy efforts are desperately needed on the national level as we strive to incorporate rigor and challenge in order to remain globally competitive. These chapters provide you with tools, strategies, ideas, and perspectives that should guide you in these endeavors. How you use them is up to you.

Realize that your child is one of the lucky ones. She has someone looking out for her best interests. He has someone willing to intervene, willing to question policy, and willing to expedite change. But realize, too, that for every child like yours, there are 20 other children who have the same needs but no advocate. Your responsibility actually goes far beyond your own child.

Before you dive into the reading, take a moment to reflect on this message created by a powerful education advocacy group:

> 1 parent = A fruitcake
> 2 parents = A fruitcake and a friend
> 3 parents = Troublemakers
> 5 parents = "Let's have a meeting"
> 10 parents = "We'd better listen"
> 25 parents = "Our dear friends"
> 50 parents = A powerful organization

(Henderson, Jacob, Kernan-Schloss, & Raimondo, 2004, p. 38)

None of us wants to be a fruitcake. We all want to make lasting differences for these children, and numbers are indeed important in advocacy. Hopefully this section will inform, inspire, and motivate. So read, reflect, join others, and act.

Reference

Henderson, A., Jacob, B., Kernan-Schloss, A., & Raimondo, B. (2004). *The case for parent leadership.* Lexington, KY: Pritchard Committee for Academic Excellence and KSA Communications. Retrieved from http://www.prichardcommittee.org/Portals/1059/CPL/Case_Final.pdf

Rolfe, G., Freshwater, D., & Jasper, M. (2001). *Critical reflection in nursing and the helping professions: A user's guide.* Basingstoke, England: Palgrave Macmillan.

Chapter 33

Effective Advocates, Lifelong Advocacy: If Not You, Then Who?

by Julia Link Roberts and Tracy Ford Inman

AN effective advocate doesn't just materialize out of nowhere. Rather, becoming an advocate is more of an evolution; you begin with concerns about your own child's learning. From there, you find kindred spirits who share those concerns. Together you craft a message that is communicated in a consistent, rational manner to decision makers. This process takes months (and often times years!) before change is effected. Unfortunately, though, too many advocates see their child's high school graduation as their graduation as well. Advocacy stops when college starts. The experienced, effective advocate retires—and children suffer because of it. Young people who are gifted and talented desperately need lifelong advocates willing to speak out for their educational opportunities!

Retiring from advocacy hurts untold numbers of gifted children. Being interested in gifted children for a year or two makes no sense, yet that is the pattern that many advocates follow. They demonstrate interest when their child is first identified for gifted services in elementary school and then fade in their advocacy. Consider the following: If it is important to have excellence in education today for your children, don't you want appropriate services to be in place for your grandchildren? Thinking beyond the here and now stretches us; but, when we stretch our thinking, we realize that what is important for our children is important to our neighbors' children and to children in our community, as well as in our state and country. Looking beyond our own needs to the greater good will serve us well today and in the future, especially in the flattened world in which we live.

Numbers count in advocacy! Gifted children need as many spokespersons as possible. Because the percentage of children who are gifted and talented is fairly small, it is important to retain advocates—especially experienced ones who have developed strong relationships with decision makers. Gifted children need to have parents, grandparents, educators, and interested citizens to speak out on their behalf. They need adults to realize that the needs of gifted children are created by their strengths, which often makes them look the opposite of "needy." However, their needs make them just as different from the average child as the needs of children with severe disabilities. Both groups need accommodations and services if they will have opportunities to develop their full potentials. A single message relayed in many voices has a much greater impact.

You will still be living and working in your community long after your child has graduated. Having the most challenging educational opportunities available for young people who are ready for advanced learning is important for the economy of your community, state, and nation. Lifelong advocates can ensure that those opportunities are available. In a knowledge-based economy, it is the creative mind that will fuel the economy through innovation and entrepreneurship. Gifted children offer the possibility of becoming the entrepreneurs if provided opportunities to gain the knowledge and skills to do so. Young people who have laboratories and educational environments positively impact their communities and their nation. With the emphasis in schools today on reaching proficiency, the learning ceiling is far too low for many gifted children. Certainly advocates recognize the need for young people to have proficiency in literacy and mathematics; however, that focus provides barriers to learning for children who are already at grade level or above in these important content areas. Advocates must speak out on behalf of continuous progress. Continuous progress for gifted children parallels the continuous progress of our nation's economy.

Becoming or staying internationally competitive means focusing on appropriately challenging educational opportunities for America's youth. If being internationally competitive is important today, it will remain so tomorrow, so being an advocate remains a high priority. The U. S. Commission on National Security for the 21st Century says in its report, *Road Map for National Security: Imperative for Change* (February 15, 2001):

> Second only to a weapon of mass destruction detonating in an American city, we can think of nothing more dangerous than a failure to manage properly science, technology, and education for the common good over the next quarter century . . . The capacity of America's educational system to create a 21st century workforce second to none in the world is a national security issue of the first order. As things stand, this country is forfeiting that capacity.

The United States faces one of its greatest challenges as Asia (specifically, China and India) soars to economic and scientific heights. Both Fishman's *China, Inc.: How the Rise of the Next Superpower Challenges America and the World* and Friedman's *The World is Flat* point out numerous ways that the United States is slipping academically, economically, and technologically. In *Rising Above the Gathering Storm: Energizing and Employing America for a Brighter Economic Future,* the National Academies of Science argues:

> This nation must prepare with great urgency to preserve its strategic and economic security . . . the United States must compete by optimizing its knowledge-based resources, particularly in science and technology, and by sustaining the most fertile environment for new and revitalized industries and the well-paying jobs they bring.

In a world that has been flattened by technology, remaining competitive in science, technology, engineering, and mathematics (STEM) is critical. We can only be competitive when our gifted children have no ceiling to their learning. Lifelong advocates can make that possible.

Still the most important reason to be a lifelong advocate for gifted education is that children who are gifted and talented are happier, more productive children when they are with intellectual peers and when they have challenging academic tasks to do. What could be more important than that?

The reasons for becoming a lifelong advocate are indeed numerous—as are the ways to become one:

- Belong to local, state, and national advocacy groups.
- Question elected officials: What is your role in gifted education? What does gifted education look like to you? What information do you need to help you make an informed decision about gifted education?
- Get to know legislators and their support staff.
- Show appreciation for legislators' support.
- Tell the truth: Say you don't know the answer when you don't (but find it out).
- Stay in the loop: Keep updated on the subject; know what other schools, districts, and states are doing; have copies of the law and regulations.
- Use real people to illustrate your points (cute kids make an impression!).
- Persevere, persevere, persevere.

Reconsider advocacy when your last child graduates from high school. Don't retire. Share your expertise in advocacy with those just beginning their journey. The world will be a better place because of it.

Resources

Books

Fishman, T. C. (2005). *China, Inc.: How the rise of the next superpower challenges America and the world.* New York, NY: Scribner.

Friedman, T. L. (2005). *The world is flat: A brief history of the twenty-first century.* New York, NY: Farrar, Strauss, & Giroux.

Website

Institute for Sustainable Communities, Advocacy and Leadership Center—http://www.advocacy.org

References

Committee on Prospering in the Global Economy of the 21st Century. (2005). *Rising above the gathering storm: Energizing and employing America for a brighter economic future.* Washington, DC: National Academies Press. Retrieved from http://www.nap.edu/catalog.php?record_id=11463

U. S. Commission on National Security for the 21st Century. (2001). *Road map for national security: Imperative for change.* Wilkes-Barre, PA: Kallisti Publishing.

Chapter 34

A Break in Communication: When an Advocate Is Needed

by Rich Weinfeld, Michelle Davis, Jeanne L. Paynter, and Sue Jeweler

EACH and every child is born with potential. The adults in that child's world must work to make certain that there are educational opportunities in place to ensure that potential is reached. Every time an adult acts to support a child's potential or speak on his or her behalf, we are striving to act as an advocate. In some instances, parents will use traditional venues, such as parent conferences, team meetings, or other official school processes, to advocate for their child.

If, however, there is a breakdown in the process, parents may find that they need to hone their own advocacy skills or hire a professional advocate to help ensure that their child receives the necessary opportunities and services. Hiring a professional advocate who brings special expertise to the process may allow parents the opportunity to better participate as an equal partner in decision making for their children. Advocates are more common in the field of special education where federal laws exist protecting children who receive special education services. However, there are advocates that specialize in gifted education or work with twice-exceptional children. These advocates can be particularly successful where there is state or district policy mandating gifted services.

As children progress in school, they give clues that indicate how they are doing. They may let us know that the work is too hard, that paying attention is difficult, that they can't remember their math facts, or that they have no friends. They also may let us know that school is boring and that they are not being appropriately challenged. When parents or teachers become aware of a child's obstacles to learning, then together they can plan the appropriate interventions necessary in order for a child to receive appropriately challenging instruction.

The Advantages of Having an Advocate

There are times when parents and school staff are not able, for a variety of reasons, to effectively plan to meet the needs of an individual child. Involving an advocate often can make the difference in ensuring that the child gets appropriate instruction and services. An advocate can provide an understanding of the language and processes between parents and the school. An advocate's expertise can include:

- knowing and understanding children's rights and school system responsibilities under the laws and policies governing educating children;
- making sure that the student has access to appropriately rigorous instruction;
- participating with teams to determine whether giftedness and/ or a learning disability exists, and creating a school plan;
- recommending and monitoring the implementation of educational strategies based on the student's strengths and need areas;
- navigating the school system procedures to secure school services and placement for children with exceptional needs;
- linking parents and teachers with a variety of community resources such as mentorships for students who are gifted in specific areas such as the arts or sciences; and
- monitoring legal issues and providing intervention when rights are violated to ensure that the child will receive the finest educational experience possible.

Based upon their training and experience, advocates bring a high degree of skill and knowledge to the entire process of helping students reach their potential. An advocate also can help a school team to plan proactively to ensure an individual student's success before serious problems arise.

Advocates Help Remove Barriers

Advocacy, when done appropriately, can be beneficial for any student. It may be especially crucial in cases where the parents don't feel that they are an equal part of the process because of their own cultural, language, or socioeconomic differences. In these cases, the advocate can help the parents to understand the process and effectively express their opinions, as well as ensure that parental input is treated with the same importance afforded any other parent.

Advocates also can listen for other potential biases. Is the young girl in question being excluded from opportunities just because of assumptions made about her based on gender? Are a young man's educational needs being met by research-supported practices? Many school personnel welcome the presence of an advocate at a school meeting. An advocate can communicate the issues in ways that both the parents and the school personnel are not able to do. For example, the advocate may suggest solutions that school staff may not bring up due to budgetary constraints or directives from supervisors. However, once the advocate's ideas are out on the table, school staff may feel free to support what they believe is truly in the student's best interest. The advocate also may have a mediating effect on the parents.

Although an advocate attends the meeting at the parents' request, the advocate's focus should be on the needs of the student. He or she can get the meeting past difficult sticking points by being unbiased and objective in order to move the team toward decisions that are in the individual student's best interests.

The Value of an Expert

Advocates must know how to work with school-aged children and their families as they interact with the school system. Due to their special expertise related to a wide variety of gifted education and/or special education issues, the advocate may become a valued expert who provides information to school staff members and to parents. In order to do all of this, the advocate must understand school law and district policies, interpersonal dynamics, and one's own self.

An effective advocate will perform a wide variety of tasks. These tasks may be broadly categorized as gathering information about the child, determining what action steps are necessary for achieving outcomes that are in the child's best interests, and participating in meetings in varied settings to ensure that these action steps are accepted and implemented.

In order to determine appropriate services, the advocate can:
- assess the current classroom where the child is receiving instruction and/or the classroom(s) that may be a future option for the child's placement;
- observe classrooms to determine if they are a good match for the strengths and needs of the child in question; and
- analyze the current situation to see if it is a good match and if not, if it could be a good match if some achievable changes were made.

All the while, the advocate will be looking at any environment through the lens of the individual child.

What Advocates Need to Know

Advocates must know the state law and/or district policies in order to effectively represent the children they serve. Depending on the issues that face the individual child, the advocate will refer to and use general education laws and those specific to gifted and talented and/or special education. These will vary from state to state and district to district as there are no federal laws mandating and governing gifted and talented education. Parents and educators who are able to understand the law and regulations related to the education of children will be better able to make requests, file complaints, or express concerns in a way that is directly related to state law and school district policies. Advocates also have a better understanding of the terminology used by school personnel and how to assess gifted education classes and programs.

Preparing for the School Meeting

An important part of the advocate's role is preparing for the school meeting. He or she must know the child, the child's family, school program, and current concerns of the school staff and family, and have a plan in mind for the types of requests to be made.

When an advocate helps a family to obtain appropriate services for a child, he or she forms a special relationship with one or more of the child's parents. Although there are situations where it is the school staff or a related service provider that first identifies the need for new or different services, more often it is the child's parents who bring this issue to the attention of the school. Parents' approach to advocating for their child will depend on their view of the child's strengths and needs, the structure of the family system itself, the child's educational history, knowledge from experts outside of the school, and their own personal schooling experiences. All of these issues will impact the parents' point of view and participation in the process of advocating for their child.

The advocate must understand the scope of services available for the student in the local public school classroom, including special classrooms or programs. He or she also must have knowledge of special programming found in the local community and those resources beyond the locale. A thorough and realistic understanding of what is and isn't possible for the child gives the advocate the knowledge that is crucial in working toward achievable goals. For a successful meeting experience, the advocate must:

- understand and interpret group dynamics;
- use effective techniques such as caucusing, successfully navigate individual personalities, gauge alliances, and invite additional members to the process when necessary; and
- integrate others' perspectives about the child in relation to how they work with the child.

An effective advocate acknowledges others' accomplishments; uses techniques before, during, and after meetings to accomplish predetermined goals; and adjusts his or her presentation to impact the dynamics of school meetings.

Creating a Student Plan

Depending on the school district, some students may have an Individual Education Plan (IEP), a 504 plan, a less formal type of instructional plan, or no plan at all. These plans typically include data documenting student strengths, which are matched with appropriate programs or services offered in the school (e.g., subject acceleration or participation in enrichment activities such as Junior Great Books). Parents and advocates are encouraged to find out the type of plans used for gifted and talented students in their school districts and the state regulations and/or district policies governing gifted and talented education.

In all cases, however, the plan for the individual student needs to be crafted in a way that the program effect can be monitored. Effective implementation of the plan must include knowledge of the present levels of performance, which are specific and detail the child's current academic strengths and weaknesses. This information will be used as the starting point for goal setting. The goals in the individual child's plan are written using specific condition statements that are measurable and observable, along with criteria to establish that the plan has been successful.

The advocate must monitor the implementation of the instructional plan. He or she will make sure that the decisions of the school team are documented and that there is a plan for coming back to check for progress and, if needed, to adjust the plan.

What If I Decide Not to Hire an Advocate?

Parents who choose to hire a professional advocate will want to ensure that the advocate possesses all of the skills necessary to effectively represent their child. Parents who will act as an advocate for their own child must strive to find ways to develop their own skills or bring other experts, like a psychiatrist, speech therapist, or lawyer, who can help them in specific areas where they are less knowledgeable or are unable to perform the required task.

Parents also can organize into groups to effectively advocate for their children. Public advocacy groups take a systemic and organized approach to raising public awareness about the special needs of exceptional children and work to enact policies and laws that affect the quality and range of programs and services available for these children. Public advocacy groups for children with exceptional gifts and talents and disabilities operate at national, state, and local levels. Advocacy groups include professional organizations and their state affiliates, as well as local school system parent advocacy groups.

There are other opportunities outside of organized groups to be involved in public advocacy. These include serving on educational task forces, commissions, and even the local school PTA. A venue that

Selecting an Advocate: Five Things to Look For

1. **Experience**. Is the advocate an expert in educational issues and law? How many school meetings has the advocate attended? How often has she achieved the desired outcome for the student? How is her relationship with the school system, including gifted education personnel, special education personnel, the compliance office, and attorneys? Is she experienced with the specific issue that you are currently facing?

2. **Personality**. Is the advocate's personality and personal style a match with you (and your spouse)?

3. **Cost and Charges**. Can you afford it? (Think of the investment and whether to spend money on tuition and additional programming rather than advocacy services.) Does the advocate work on any type of reduced fee arrangement when there is a financial need?

4. **Style for Dispute**. Does the advocate approach the school system staff as adversarial or as potentially cooperative? What is his thinking behind the pros and cons for dispute options? Does the advocate shy away from disputes or persist even in the face of challenging situations?

5. **Resources**. Does the advocate have knowledge of a network of experts in different fields? Does she have resources related to the various areas of your concern, including how to address your child's strengths and needs?

provides a public forum to discuss education is an opportunity to raise awareness about the needs of exceptional children.

In conclusion, it is crucial that we advocate for what each and every child needs in order to reach his or her own unique potential. An effective advocate helps parents and school staff to accurately see the problem and all of the possible solutions that may solve the problem that the individual child is experiencing. Parents and school system personnel have an opportunity to advocate for the children we serve and to tap one another's expertise as we work together. Knowledge is power. When the partners in education are armed with accurate information, positive outcomes will happen for children.

Resources

Weinfeld, R., & Davis, M. (2008). *Special needs advocacy resource book: What you can do now to advocate for your exceptional child's education.* Waco, TX: Prufrock Press.

Chapter 35

Dancing Toward District Advocacy

by Diana Reeves

ADVOCATING for change within your school district is much like square dancing. People move in predictable ways, responding to directions given by a caller with calls being many and varied. Reacting quickly to calls keeps dancers on their toes. As people connect through square dancing, they, too, can connect through advocacy. Whether challenging or easy, advocacy and square dancing are interactive, working to reduce differences.

Square dancing is useful to illustrate a few basic concepts about working to promote change within a local education association. For nearly 30 years, I have served as an information resource for the Massachusetts affiliate association of NAGC working to promote awareness and support for the needs of gifted and talented students. As a parent, educator, department of education specialist, affiliate leader, and now as a parent member on the NAGC board, I have witnessed, as well as participated in, many advocacy dances.

Advocating, like square dancing, is not a spectator sport. Success depends upon people cooperating with each other. Square dances begin with a partner, use a repertoire of common steps, often result in new formations, require frequent changes in direction, and always end where they began. District-level advocacy is very similar, but, hopefully, participants find themselves with a new understanding of the issues at hand.

Deciding to Dance

The question I receive most frequently, from both parents and teachers is, "What can I do for my gifted child (student)?" I try to assist them in identifying at least one workable local strategy and recommend that people at this stage acquaint themselves with the National Association for Gifted Children (NAGC) Pre-K–Grade 12 Gifted Program Standards (http://www.nagc.org). The standards should be examined to identify ways in which their district's services (there may not yet be any specific gifted program) align with the suggested standards. When parents and teachers begin to understand local educational options, they begin to grasp the difference between what is and what could be. Just one teacher working with one set of parents can begin the advocacy dance at the district level. At this point, the dancers or advocates assemble. They are not always together, and sometimes without a caller, but ready to move.

Finding Partners

Square dancing alone, advocating by yourself, is very difficult. As teachers and parents, we strive to promote self-efficacy, yet political realities dictate that those who might benefit from district change may not be the only ones seeking change based on the same set of needs. The power of one is important, but strength in numbers trumps. Any district advocacy effort should begin with the formation of a group. Often parents find each other through the shared needs or interests of their children. Teachers can sometimes facilitate these matches, but rarely participate openly in any group outside the school seeking to change district policy. Other community groups, once informed of the need, often are willing to help support options for high-ability students. For them, it is important to make the connection between capable students of today and participating citizens of tomorrow.

In response to multiple requests, the Massachusetts Association for Gifted Education (MAGE) has sponsored Guided Discussion Groups for Parents (built upon the SENG model) in selected regions throughout the state. When parents share concerns about their gifted children, this is the first step to discovering their common needs and the potential benefits of advocating together. Play dates also can be another venue where organization members and their children can meet face-to-face and begin to exchange ideas.

Those seeking change already may be participants in existing groups such as school improvement councils, parent/teacher organizations, or advisory committees. Teachers can join colleagues to explore curricular strategies for their capable learners as they seek to work with administrators to examine realistic educational options. Community efforts also can begin with invitations to an open awareness meeting. Invitees include parents, educators, administrators, and legislators. The bottom line is, at this stage of the dance, all partners are welcome.

Learning the Steps

Once a core group of advocate partners has been identified, they need to begin preparations for the dance. Just like square dancers, advocates need to consult resources and work with experts to acquire needed information. State-affiliate gifted organizations can play a leadership role at this juncture. They are eager and willing to discuss strategies as well as to pinpoint useful resources such as state and federal funds available to districts for program planning and implementation.

Advocates need to agree on a focus, pool their shared knowledge, gather data, and try to influence public opinion. District-level change happens when people within the school system can agree that a need exists. Getting to that place requires intricate footwork; your plan must be both artful and efficient. Here is where it helps to have someone calling the next steps.

Identifying and Listening to the Caller

When a square dancer and his or her partner join three other couples in dance, they are directed by the caller to move through a particular series of steps. The order and complexity of the steps is determined by the caller in response to the music and the dancers' ability. Your advocacy group caller will change over time as the tasks change and as the music of your district situation dictates. The person putting the group together calls the first agendas. This caller could be the director of an already existing program, a school administrator, an outside consultant, a parent, or a legislator. Advocacy group members usually begin by sharing their objectives, until a consensus can be reached concerning the goals of the group. Advocacy group callers facilitate group cohesion and direction, by serving as liaisons to the school system, planning meeting spaces and times, delegating tasks, bringing in speakers, publishing the minutes of meetings, and creating a paper trail necessary to document outcomes of conversations, expectations for actions, follow-up assessments, and timelines to evaluate progress.

An assessment of local needs is usually the opening requirement. If your group is able to work with an administrator within the system, it will be easier to devise a systematic process for gathering information and build upon the diagnosed needs of the students in the district. Often, an outside expert can be hired to assist in creating surveys, conducting interviews, and compiling evidence. The end result of a needs assessment is the creation of a planning committee. When this step is reached, the caller and calls may change. As each group member prepares to swing his or her partner and move on to new dancers, the dance becomes more intricate.

Experimenting With New Formations

During the programming planning phase, it is frequently useful to alter or enhance the music and create new connections. The planning team should include representatives from all stakeholder groups. The mission of the team is developing policies for identifying students, creating or selecting curriculum and instruction options, delivering professional development, and providing for program administration and evaluation. As tempting as it may be to move forward quickly to provide direct delivery of services to students, it is essential to spend time to craft policies that will last long after the departure of those who created them. The aim is to develop, implement, and support policies based on research and best practices. The goal of advocating, as in square dancing, is to foster the creation of something satisfying with few unnecessary steps.

As your advocacy group seeks to disseminate information about the planning process, it can be very helpful to spotlight needs by hosting or helping to sponsor professional development opportunities for teachers and counselors, outreach programs for parents, or enrichment sessions for students. This part of the dance allows the advocates to experience small successes, accomplish a tangible goal, and see that their efforts can effect change. Here again, the idea is to move people to the point where they are all aware of the same compelling tune.

This may be the moment to expand the dance. Other districts in your state may be involved in parallel dance steps, with your state department of education or state organizations calling the required formations. What your district alone may not be able to sponsor or attend might become possible when shared by other districts. MAGE has partnered, with many districts, as well as higher education institutions, to present conferences for both parents and teachers.

From the district advocacy standpoint, contributing to collaborative events demonstrates a willingness to be part of the solution, rather than just highlighting problems. Advocacy dancers can volunteer to help. There are always envelopes to stuff, tables to man, and speakers to introduce. Joining with your state organization will not only put your district on the map but also will allow you to network with the movers and shakers at the state level.

The information and ideas gained from state organizations can be shared with your district and serve as an information conduit to key decision makers. Advocates cannot mandate district change. Change only can be encouraged and supported. Square dancing has little to do with ability level but is dependent upon teamwork. In square dancing, as in advocacy, it is important to dance with your partner and allow others to dance alongside or with you.

Changing Direction

When the district plan for implementation or modification is finally completed, advocates need to work to foster acceptance of the proposed changes. Just as in dancing, directional changes need to be made smoothly. It is important for all of the dancers to understand that a change is coming and to be prepared for the next call.

If a pilot program is proposed, or if only a few schools in the district will be involved in an initial phase-in of services, careful thought should be given to making the process as transparent and equitable as possible. As the program begins to accomplish its goals, advocates can celebrate successes and highlight innovations by contacting local media sources, and by inviting local legislators to observe the program in action. Advocacy dancers also may be able to financially support professional development critical to teacher readiness for implementing proposed changes.

Coming Back to the Starting Place

If you think back to your elementary gym class, you will probably recall that all square dances end with the dancers returning to their home positions. For example, on the final step in a Virginia reel, couples are lined up facing each other. The head couple joins both hands across and raises them to form an arch at the foot of the set. The second couple joins inside hands and leads the other couples under the arch and through the set to become the new head couple. This process is repeated until all have had a turn at leadership, and everyone has returned to their original positions. At that point the dance can begin anew.

Dancing toward district-level advocacy is much the same. Advocates progress through carefully planned and executed steps to encourage change. People take turns as leaders. As policies are developed, implemented, monitored, and evaluated, needs will be redefined and adjustments to existing programs will be sought. Advocacy needs to be ongoing. No one can learn the dance in a day, and dancing faster in response to a crisis rarely works. Building support for gifted programs and services, just like square dancing, can be rewarding, sometimes frustrating, but always stimulating. And when you get the choice to sit it out or dance, I hope you dance!

Resources

Books/Articles

American Association for School Administrators. (2007, February). Gifted education left behind [Special issue]. *The School Administrator, 64.* Retrieved from http://www.assa.org/publications/saissuedetail.cfm?ItemNumber=8202&snItemNumber=950&tnItemNumber=

Bruce Mitchell, P. (Ed.). (1981). *An advocate's guide to building support for gifted and talented education.* Alexandria, VA: National Association of State Boards of Education. (ERIC Document Reproduction Service No. ED233526)

Callahan, C. M. (Ed.). (2004). *Program evaluation in gifted education: Essential readings in gifted education.* Thousand Oaks, CA: Corwin Press.

Clinkenbeard, P. R., Kolloff, P. B., & Lord, W. E. (2007). *A guide to state policies in gifted education* [CD]. Washington, DC: NAGC.

Colangelo, N., Assouline, S. G., & Gross, M. U. M. (2004). *A nation deceived: How schools hold back America's brightest students* (Vol. 1). Iowa City: The University of Iowa, The Connie Belin & Jacqueline N. Blank International Center for Gifted Education and Talent Development.

DeVries, A., & Webb, J. (2007). *Gifted parent groups: The SENG model* (2nd ed.). Scottsdale, AZ: Great Potential Press.

Gonzales, J. (2000). *Excellence through partnership: A handbook for parents of gifted and talented children.* Cherry Creek, CO: Cherry Creek Schools.

Jones, K. (2003, March). Home and school report: Be practical—effective advocacy in small town America. *Parenting for High Potential,* 6–7, 23.

Purcell, J. H., & Eckert, R. D. (Eds.). (2006). *Designing services and programs for high-ability learners.* Thousand Oaks, CA: Corwin Press.

Roberts, J. L., & Inman, T. F. (2003, March). Building advocacy with a public relations campaign. *Parenting for High Potential,* 24–27.

Roberts, J. L., & Inman, T. F. (2006, June). Effective advocates: Craft your message. *Parenting for High Potential,* 24–25.

Robinson, A., Shore, B. M., & Enersen, D. L. (Eds.). (2007). *Best practices in gifted education: An evidence-based guide*. Waco, TX: Prufrock Press.

Rogers, K. (2002). *Re-forming gifted education: How parents and teachers can match the program to the child*. Scottsdale, AZ: Great Potential Press.

Smutny, J. F. (2003, March) Taking a larger stand for gifted education: Your district, your state, and beyond! *Parenting for High Potential*, 18–22.

Websites

Advocacy Toolkit—http://www.nagc.org/index2.aspx?id=36

Description of Beyond Proficiency Summit—http://cfge.wm.edu/assets/systems_newsletter/Syst-FALL05.pdf

Glossary of Square Dancing Terms—http://www.highmountainsquares.org/Glossary.htm

Pre-K–Grade 12 Standards Introduction—http://www.nagc.org/index.aspx?id=546

Take Five! Advocating for Gifted Programs in Local Schools—http: //www.nagc.org/index2.aspx?id=697

Chapter 36

Taking a Larger Stand for Gifted Education: Your District, Your State . . . and Beyond!

by Joan Franklin Smutny

ANY influential scholars and educators in the field of gifted education today began their journey as parents confronted with the reality and responsibility of raising a gifted child. Other parents who have not entered the field professionally have nevertheless had a profound influence on services for the gifted through tireless advocacy and a commitment to communicate their message to whoever will listen. It is fair to say that without the advocacy of parents, gifted education would simply not be where it is today. Many of the services and programs that exist in schools throughout the United States owe their genesis to a small band of parents who campaigned for gifted education.

This article takes the subject of parent advocacy beyond the question, "What can I do for my gifted child?" to, "What can I do for the cause of gifted education in my district or state now and in the future?" You may be a frustrated parent who has explored every avenue you can think of to get better educational services for your gifted child. Or, you may be a parent who finally found a satisfactory solution for your gifted child, but you object to the idea that parents have to campaign to get any services for their gifted children. In either case, your concern about your own child or about gifted children generally has led you to a larger view of advocacy at the district, state, or even national levels.

Work With Other Parents, Not in Isolation

If you don't already belong to a parent group for families with gifted children, consider finding or starting one. Even contact with one other parent is better than working alone, as this mother discovered:

> My fourth-grade son and I live in the city and, except for a few gifted magnet schools, there is nothing. To get into these schools, you have to do well on standardized tests and Javier's just never scored well enough. But he's an "A" student and can write like a poet. When I started talking to his teacher, he was sympathetic to a point but said that there's nothing he could do. He said he didn't know anything about gifted education, and that the teachers in our district have a hard enough time dealing with overcrowded classes and hardly any resources. I kind of despaired for a while, but then I met another mother who was at the school waiting for her son Jerry, a friend of Javier and also gifted. We got together and contacted our state gifted association who put us in touch with a professor who specializes in gifted education. We've met with her once and she gave us a whole packet of information—books we could read, procedures for starting a parent group of our own, and ideas about how we could present our case to the principal, superintendent, etc. We have a long way to go but we feel at least we have an advocate to help us and we don't have to wait until that magical day when we move to another district. We can start working for changes right now.

Working together enables parents to pool ideas and resources, identify concerns, establish common goals, develop plans and strategies for action, and share responsibilities.

Parent groups come in all forms. Some may have only a few parents who unite to achieve specific goals (e.g., getting professional development in gifted education for the teachers at their school; hiring a gifted education coordinator; lowering the age for the school's gifted program). On the other side of the spectrum are larger, more permanent groups who hold regular meetings for a variety of purposes including social events, sponsored lectures, long-term campaigns at the district and state level, and networking sessions to organize their own summer gifted programs.

Shopping for a Parent Group

If you wish to join an already established parent group, contact your principal, your district office, or state gifted association to find out what groups exist in your area. The National Association for Gifted Children (NAGC) website (http://www.nagc.org) can help you locate an organization in your state. Once you locate one, arrange to attend a meeting. Ask in advance what activities the group is currently engaged in and what the meeting will focus on. Not all parent groups are alike. You may find some more effective and useful than others. When you visit a group or groups, consider the following questions:

- Does the group have a clear purpose or mission and goals?
- Do members have bylaws that establish the election of officers and their responsibilities?
- How does a new parent join? Are the dues reasonable for parents from different economic backgrounds and are newcomers welcomed?
- When does the group hold meetings and does it have agendas for its meetings?
- Does the group ever have events that include other family members?
- Do parents have opportunities to share information, resources, and ideas?
- Does the group ever sponsor speakers or special workshops on topics of interest to the members?
- How well does the group stay in touch with its members and keep them informed about the activities of the group?

Effective parent groups don't have to include all of these elements. Pay particular attention to the dynamics of the group and the content of the meetings. Try to avoid groups where one or two parents dominate discussion or other activities, and where there seem to be no by-laws or procedures for the group's meetings. Also, be aware that sometimes group meetings may devolve into gripe sessions. While it's normal for parents to express their concerns or frustrations, a group that spends most of its time on this will probably not accomplish much in the long run. Look for groups that respond sensitively to the needs of individual members, but also stay on course with their primary goals and commitments as an advocacy group for gifted students in their district and state.

Starting a Parent Group

If no groups exist in your area, you can start one by talking to the gifted education coordinator about getting contact information for other parents of gifted students. You can post notices on the school bulletin board, at the local library or community center, or advertise in a PTA newsletter or local newspaper. Here's how one family started a parent group:

> We were concerned about our twins even before kindergarten. They were both reading second- and third-grade books at age 4 and we thought, "How will they manage in a class where most kids are still learning their letters?" We started out attending other parent groups (some of them were pretty far away, but it was worth the ride for all the information we got). One group had parents who lived close to us and so our group started with these parents and us meeting in our living room. At this point, we all just wanted one thing—gifted education for younger kids. Theirs were in primary school and our twins hadn't even started school yet! Our first step was to do research and we divided up the topics: one person researched parent group organizations; another read up on parent advocacy strategies in schools—another investigated state policies and so on. We're still in process, but I have to say that working with these parents has inspired me to no end. I feel much less discouraged about my two kids and there's something about banding together with like-minded people to make you feel hopeful about the future.

Once you have even a few parents, you can hold an organization meeting where you establish your philosophy and mission as a parent advocacy group and your goals and objectives—both short- and long-term. If possible, consider having a consultant (e.g., gifted education coordinator, local expert in gifted education) attend the first meeting in an advisory capacity. Like the group just described, you may find that at first you prefer to focus on resolving a problem that affects your child right now, such as the lack of services for primary gifted students.

During the first few meetings, create a list of topics that interest members, as well as areas where they need more information. Here are some examples:

- learning needs and characteristics of gifted children;
- social and emotional needs;
- underserved populations (e.g., bilingual, multicultural, underprivileged, and female students) identification and intervention;
- supporting children's abilities at home and in the community;
- communicating effectively with teachers;
- school and district policy issues; and
- state legislative issues.

These topics will change as the group evolves over time, and they also should relate to immediate interests of parents (e.g., the need to improve identification methods for the school's gifted program, allocation of district funds for gifted education). Whatever other activities the group does, a central goal should always be to gain more expertise in gifted education. Parent groups need to be informed and equipped with up-to-date research in order to communicate knowledgeably to teachers, administrators, and policy makers.

Going to the Superintendent

The value of a parent group becomes evident when you go to the superintendent. First, though, be sure that you have talked to the child's teacher (or teachers), gifted education coordinator (if there is one), and principal before taking this step. If you go straight to the superintendent, he or she may send you back to the teacher and principal; you might risk losing their support when they find out you went over their heads. Also, it's a good idea to keep detailed records of all of your communications, meetings, and telephone conversations, as well as observations of your child's challenges, gifts, and experiences.

Plan Your Presentation

Before meeting with the teacher, principal, or superintendent, gather your notes, research, and any other information together and plan what you're going to say. This is the time to review your records on all of the steps you took at the school up to this point. Records combined with what you know about the needs of gifted students should practically speak for themselves. As a group, you can identify the most important points and use your records and research to support your requests. In some cases, the issue may be that no services for the gifted exist at all; in other cases, it may be that the services provided present certain problems—perhaps an overdependence on standardized tests for identifying gifted students or too few resources for the gifted education coordinator, or no coordination between the gifted education teacher and the regular classroom teachers.

Meet as a Group

Whenever possible, go to the superintendent as a group; even a few members of the group will be preferable to going alone. Superintendents usually understand that parents are a powerful constituency and that it is important to listen to even a relatively small group. A group of parents with a clear, well-conceived presentation and evidence to back their claims can be highly persuasive. A couple of parents who wanted to discuss problems with their school's gifted program came up with a unique strategy for preparing their presentations:

> We were really nervous about this superintendent because he has a reputation for being kind of hard-nosed. So, we decided who would say what and we practiced it a few times! I know

that sounds like a weird thing to do, but it really paid off. We instantly felt calmer and the superintendent actually helped us plan our presentation for the school board.

The influence superintendents have to create change depends on the relationship between them and their school board. The school board hires the superintendent and the latter's sphere of influence depends on this board's interests, priorities, and governing style. A school board who micromanages a district may limit the authority of the superintendent. But superintendents can initiate action on some issues, such as changing the criteria for admission to the gifted program or scheduling professional development in teaching gifted students in the regular classroom.

Going to the School Board

If you are seeking fundamental changes in your district, you will have to present your case to the school board. They usually make decisions about the allocation of state funding and establish educational priorities for the district. The school board, together with the superintendent, may decide the fate of a gifted program, select identification criteria, the grades to be served, and the form that services will take.

Do Your Homework

Before presenting before the school board, you will need to do some preliminary research. Here are some questions to explore:

- What are your state laws on gifted education?
- How is your district funded (specifically, how much is allocated from the state to your district for gifted education)?
- What are other districts in your state doing for gifted students?
- What is the school board's yearly schedule (e.g., when are decisions made concerning funding for gifted education and when do they schedule presentations)?
- What can you learn about individual board members that might help you with your presentation? Are there any that might be

sympathetic to your cause? (Talk to the superintendent about this and attend a couple of board meetings to get a feel for the biases and interests of individual members.)

- What is the board currently working on and how can you time your presentation to make the strongest impact?

Present Your Case

What follows are general guidelines for making presentations to a school board. You will need to adapt and adjust according to your unique situation.

1. *Start out by giving the school board the big picture:* What kind of an issue is it (e.g., curriculum issue? funding issue?); How many families or students will it affect? Bear in mind that most boards will not be that interested in issues that relate only to a few children in the district.

2. *Have plenty of evidence to substantiate your claims.* This would include information (from the most current studies and research) on whatever aspect of gifted education most relates to your issue, as well as data you have gathered from students and parents in your district. You can contact your state association to identify sources that deal with your subject.

3. *Get straight to the point.* Clearly state the reason for your presentation and what sorts of changes or adjustments you, as a parent group, feel should take place. Provide a short history of what has led your group to this point—the steps taken prior and the personal experiences of one or two members of your group that illustrate the problem under discussion.

4. *Be prepared to explain why services for the gifted are necessary.* Without overwhelming the school board with too many details, provide persuasive arguments and evidence that: (a) gifted children exist in the district and (b) gifted children cannot thrive without appropriate services.

5. *Have evidence at your fingertips that supports whatever claims you make.* If you already have a gifted program and it falls short of its goals, be ready to demonstrate this to the board.

6. *Give each board member a summary of the problem, the evidence substantiating it, and possible recommendations or solutions in writing.* (Don't overlook commendations for their efforts and past support!)
7. *Take a strong stand for what you feel is right,* but be diplomatic and patient with board members, even if they seem unsympathetic or uninformed about gifted children.

Even one school board member can become a powerful advocate for your cause. It is not unusual for one or two board members to help a parent group and advise them on the best procedures for approaching the full board. Bear in mind that change takes time and may need to occur in smaller steps than you envisioned when you first started working on your presentation.

Presenting Your Case to the State

Sometimes, parents decide to take their advocacy to the state level. Given that districts can only do so much with the funding they receive from the state, you may discover that the problem really lies at the state level: too little funding to provide adequate services for gifted students. Meeting with a legislator can be intimidating, but again, if you go as a group (or with representatives from different groups) and pool your research and expertise to present a strong case, you will probably get results. Whenever possible, try to attend your legislator's community meetings and scheduled appearances, and take notes on his or her interests, concerns, and any insights you may get that will help you in your own communications. Sometimes legislators have aides who meet with their constituents. Contrary to what parents may think, aides have considerable authority and influence in the development of policy and it is not a bad sign if a legislator sends his or her aide to meet with a parent group. Use the opportunity to find out all you can about procedure—when you should write letters or make phone calls about bills under consideration, what methods work best to ensure your message gets across to the legislator. In this regard, if you don't already belong to your state gifted education association, join! State associations (or committees within them) often publish newsletters that tell you when bills on gifted education are up for discussion and provide data on how current policies and regulations affect gifted students. Some associations even provide letter samples that address specific issues and/or outline all of the points you need to include to argue for or against a particular policy. Many state associations for gifted children provide useful pointers, such as the ones in the sidebar, from the California Association for the Gifted's *Advocacy in Action* handbook (n.d., p. 33).

The more information you can provide for the legislators about gifted students, the greater impact you will make. People unfamiliar with gifted education tend to think of gifted students as somewhat privileged—a small group of predominantly white, upper middle class kids who already have a lot going for them. For this reason, include examples of gifted students from culturally different, bilingual, underprivileged, and other communities—communities who often have the least services and need them the most. Legislators want to see the broad spectrum of a student population, not just a few parents concerned about a few children.

> ## How Can You Make the Most of a Meeting With a Legislator?
>
> Here are some useful steps to consider when planning meetings with your state legislator:
>
> 1. Call or write a letter requesting a meeting with your elected decision maker stating the topic for discussion and asking when he or she would be available. If other advocates plan to attend with you, include their names. If there is no response within a reasonable time, place a follow-up call.
> 2. Prepare in advance so that you can clearly make your points in less than half an hour. Review information supporting your request for action.
> 3. At the meeting, introduce yourself and other advocates with you. (Three to four advocates should be an easily accommodated number for an office conference).
> 4. Tell your legislator why you are there.
> 5. If possible, leave printed information for later review.
> 6. Always write a thank-you note expressing appreciation for your elected decision maker's time and for his or her consideration of your request. Also, include any information the person requested.

As you become more outspoken about gifted education, other advocacy organizations may take note. An opportunity could arise for you and a few other parents to present testimony at special hearings that affect the future of gifted education in the state. Legislators respond well to parent testimony because it provides immediate evidence of how the programs they fund are working on the ground. Your personal experience will illustrate—more powerfully than any other source—why the state should consider changes in its policy or in the allocation of funds.

Once you get to the state level in your advocacy, you have clearly stepped into an arena beyond your own child and family. Whenever you speak at a hearing or give a speech in front of a larger audience or talk privately to legislators or even journalists, you will find yourself addressing the needs of the state's gifted children, not just those in your school or district. As you gain practice, you will become more adept at developing persuasive arguments about how current legislation does not provide for them and what needs to occur to prevent the widespread loss of talent in all of the state's communities—from the inner city to rural farm areas.

Many parents who have become advocates for gifted education never thought they would go this far. What kept them going was the responsibility of caring for a gifted child and a heart-felt conviction that they were only demanding what any decent parent would ask: a chance for their child to learn. But in the process, they became advocates for all gifted children and this is a much longer journey than they originally intended it to be. As one father put it:

> It all started with me taking off from work early on Friday and going to meet Justine's teacher. One thing led to the next thing. The school couldn't do much so we formed a parent group that's still growing and we went to the school board. Now we're involved with our state gifted association and all kinds of other things. Sure, it turned Justine's life around, but in the process, it helped a lot of other families and put us on a journey I never imagined. It's like we started out doing the 50-yard dash and now we're long-distance runners!

Resources

Books

Clark, B. (2001). *Growing up gifted: Developing the potential of children at home and at school* (6th ed.). Upper Saddle River, NJ: Prentice Hall.

Knopper, D. (1997). *Parent education: Parents as partners.* Boulder, CO: Open Space Communications.

Rimm, S. (1994). *Keys to parenting the gifted child.* Hauppauge, NY: Barron's Educational Series.

Smutny, J. F. (2001). *Stand up for your gifted child: How to make the most of kids' strengths at school and at home.* Minneapolis, MN: Free Spirit.

Websites

Gifted Children Monthly—http://www.gifted-children.com
GT World—http://gtworld.org
Hoagies' Gifted Education—http://www.hoagiesgifted.org
National Association for Gifted Children—http://www.nagc.org
National Research Center on the Gifted and Talented—http://www.gifted.uconn.edu

Reference

California Association for the Gifted. (n.d.). *Advocacy in action: An advocacy handbook for gifted and talented education.* Mountain View, CA: Author.

Chapter 37

Four Simple Steps to Self-Advocacy

by Deborah Douglas

" **I** CAN'T read your mind," I told my son when he was a teenager, "so give me a little help here. What would make school better for you?" His shrug and blank stare told me that he didn't really know how to describe what he needed. So he slogged on through grades 7 to 12, sometimes challenged and interested, frequently not. Fifteen years later as a gifted education coordinator, I still get that blank stare from many of the young people with whom I work—who don't know how to ask, don't know what to ask for, don't even know that they can ask. Now, however, I have a plan to help them create a more successful, satisfying school experience. They learn to self-advocate, or to recognize and address the needs specific to their own learning abilities, without compromising their dignity or that of others. By definition, self-advocacy has to be the work of the individual. But as parents and educators, we have the role of teaching our high-ability children how to effectively communicate, negotiate, or assert their own interests, desires, needs, and rights.

The typical adolescent urge for less dependence on parents makes it particularly important for students in the middle grades to begin advocating for themselves. Each year I poll gifted middle schoolers on their comfort level in self-advocating. Not surprisingly, most are uncomfortable asking a teacher to modify something for them, and even less comfortable with their parents asking for them. Advice and assistance from parents is often shunned as teens transition into the greater independence of secondary school. But their naive attempts at self-advocacy frequently get them into trouble. Teachers react negatively to a whining "This is boring!" sometimes piling on more rather than different work. Less gifted peers often deride the student who is interested in more challenging work. Most students must be taught how to speak up appropriately on their own behalf. Parents can help to guide or lead their children through the four simple steps of self-advocacy.

Step One: Understand Your Rights and Responsibilities

Students need to believe that asking for an appropriately challenging curriculum is not asking for more than they deserve. It helps to know that state statutes, school district mission statements, and general educational philosophies convey the ideal that all students have the right to an appropriate education; everyone has the right to work hard to learn something new each day. A gifted young woman named Wendy is a good example of successful self-advocacy. When she saw that her school's mission statement included the phrase "a rigorous education for all students," she approached her algebra teacher about moving ahead at her own pace. Two years later she also asked for, and received, permission to study precalculus independently, ultimately earning eight credits of college calculus before graduation and finding the rigor she craved and deserved.

In addition to their rights, gifted students must be aware of their responsibilities, including developing the attributes of good character toward which all students should strive. Being gifted doesn't preclude turning in work on time, treating others with respect, getting organized, or working hard.

What Parents Can Do To Help

- Talk to your children about self-advocacy. Let them know that if they want to, they can make school more interesting and more challenging.

- Give them *The Gifted Kids' Survival Guide: A Teen Handbook* by Judy Galbraith and Jim Delisle, which provides much of the information they need to understand their rights and responsibilities. If you bookmark passages that relate to their current concerns, they'll be drawn quickly into the kid-friendly format.
- Ask the school for copies of your district's mission statement, goals, gifted education plan, and state mandates or guidelines for gifted education. Chances are you'll find evidence that their intention is to challenge all children. Share that with your child.
- Remind your children that while you are working together to change things, they are still responsible for demonstrating those attributes of good character. Being bored is not an excuse for doing poor work.

Step Two: Assess Your Learner Profile

In order to self-advocate, students must understand as much as possible about themselves as learners, becoming more keenly aware of their specific abilities and interests, strengths or weaknesses, and learning styles or habits. There are many fascinating ways for gifted students to examine their own tendencies and to understand better how they are different from others.

Educational Data

Reviewing their school cumulative file with a counselor or gifted education coordinator can give students important insights on test scores, grades, and teacher perceptions. While some schools may be initially reluctant to share this information, parents do have a legal right to it and should be allowed access that can include sharing this information with their child.

Student Interest

Most school guidance offices have computerized interest and career inventories for student use. The supplementary materials in Karen Rogers' *Re-Forming Gifted Education: How Parents and Teachers Can Match the Program to the Child* also will help them assess their interest and attitudes about specific subjects and school in general. More simply, students can rank their school subjects by interest and describe the best learning experience they ever had, listing the things that made it so enjoyable.

Personality

Introvert or extrovert? Morning person or night? Leader or team member? Understanding these ways in which each person is unique can shed light on student needs. School guidance offices frequently provide such assessments as career inventories and personality-type indicators. Less formally, Jonni Kincher's *Psychology for Kids: 40 Fun Tests That Help You Learn About Yourself* includes fun tests and good descriptions of many characteristics.

Learning Styles

There are several ways of categorizing learning styles: visual, spatial, kinesthetic, concrete, abstract, random, or sequential. Solomon and Felder of North Carolina State University have posted an interactive learning style assessment at their website (http://www4.ncsu.edu/unity/lockers/users/f/felder/public/ILSdir/styles.htm) and give students hints for adjusting class work to address their styles. Detailed information on learning styles research also is available in the parent section of the Hoagies Gifted Education Page (http://www. hoagiesgifted.org).

Just For Fun

For more informal self-assessments an Internet search yields many free personality-type tests. As always, parents should help students evaluate sites for credibility. Nonprofit educational organizations often are the most reliable sources. Published resources (such as the *Mental Measurements Yearbook*) are available in the reference section of many libraries; these often are technical, but they can help in evaluating instruments.

Taken together, this information constitutes an individual's "learner profile," which can help students self-reflect on their personal learning goals. Through this type of analysis, for instance, Wendy discovered that she was a "morning person;" a well-organized, abstract, sequential thinker; a passionate mathematician; and an introvert who enjoyed working alone. With this knowledge, she was able to identify the aspects of her daily schedule and regular coursework that needed to be modified—most difficult classes in the morning, faster pace in math, and more independent study.

What Parents Can Do To Help

- Set up an appointment with the guidance counselor so that you and your child can view and discuss his or her permanent record.
- Find out which learner profile assessments are available in your district.
- When possible, also do the assessments yourself. Compare and discuss the results with your child. Then celebrate your differences as well as your similarities.

Step Three: Consider Available Options

Students must be aware of the opportunities that exist within the school district as well as the community at large. Many will be listed in the high school course-of-study bulletin or gifted education plan. Districts may offer Advanced Placement courses, classroom enrichment, acceleration, independent study, mentorships, summer programs, cocurricular clubs and teams, and dual enrollment. There also are distance learning courses, virtual schools, and online college classes. Together with their counselor or gifted coordinator, students should match the available options with their personal learning profile and educational goals. Sometimes it's as easy as changing a class schedule or finding a teacher whose teaching style aligns with the student's learning style. Other times it may be necessary to work within the system to create a new option. Frequently what begins as an alternative for one student evolves into an accepted route for other similarly gifted students. It's important to remember that while the typical path to graduation is right for the majority of kids, there are many alternatives that more appropriately address the individual needs of gifted students.

In Wendy's school, all advanced eighth-grade math students studied algebra with ninth graders, but there were no other options. Because the content was new but the pace was still too slow for her, she requested curriculum compacting. In high school, she realized she could move more quickly than the precalculus class would allow. She contemplated curriculum compacting again, as well as independent study and online courses, but finally chose to work her way through the textbook during the summer and be ready for calculus in the fall. During her senior year, she studied at a community college, paid for by the school district under state law.

What Parents Can Do To Help

- Understand the graduation requirements in your district and state. What parts of the traditional route are optional?
- Look at your secondary school prospectus. Are there mentorships, independent study, or work experience programs already in place?
- Familiarize yourself with online, community, and postsecondary options. Will your district pay for college or technical school courses?
- One word of caution: Focus on your child's individual wants and needs. Not all options are right for all children. The Latin correspondence course that thrills the 15-year-old next door may not be your child's cup of tea.

Step Four: Connect With Advocates

Although self-advocacy is key, teens should remember that they are not in this alone. There are many adults who can help. Parents still play a substantial though less visible role. Supportive teachers and guidance counselors will go to bat for students, and consultants in gifted education can help schools understand and accept their role. Start by considering which options your teacher or the school might be willing to provide if asked. Galbraith and Delisle's "Ten Tips for Talking to Teachers" is a good place for students to begin, especially if a teacher is provided a copy of the tips (see p. 367). Students who are guided through self-advocacy by caring adults are more apt to find success the first time around, generating greater independence and self-confidence.

Wendy's alternative path didn't just fall into place. She needed help coping with the frustrations of red tape, scheduling conflicts, inflexible administrators and teachers, and uninformed peers. But she was encouraged by her parents, some sympathetic teachers, her guidance counselor, the math department coordinator, the gifted education staff, and other gifted students. Aware of her ability and motivation, they supported her efforts in navigating the system and creating the academic path that was right for her. One indelible image they all share is of upperclassmen hoisting Wendy into the air as they accepted the first place trophy at the regional math championship.

What Parents Can Do To Help

- Think of your advocacy as a partnership: parents, teachers, and counselors working together to support the student's decisions. Get to know the school personnel who can help make a difference.
- Get involved. Join a parent support group or volunteer for your district's gifted advisory committee. If neither exists, offer to organize one.
- Share this article with your child's teacher, counselor, or principal if the school seems resistant. Let them know you want to be partners with them and your child.

Ten Tips for Talking to Teachers

1. Make an appointment. This shows your teacher that you're serious and you have some understanding of how busy he or she is. Plan how much time you'll need, be flexible, and don't be late.

2. If you know other students who feel the way you do, consider approaching the teacher as a group. If a teacher hears the same thing from four or five people, he or she is more likely to do something about it.

3. Think about what to say before you meet with your teacher. Write down your questions or concerns. Make a list. You may even want to copy your list for the teacher so both of you can consult it during your meeting.

4. Choose your words carefully. For example, instead of saying, "I hate doing reports; they're boring and a waste of time," try, "Is there some other way I could satisfy this requirement? Could I do a video instead?" The word "boring" doesn't help teachers very much.

5. Don't expect the teacher to do all of the work or propose all of the answers. Make suggestions and offer solutions.

6. Be diplomatic, tactful, and respectful. Teachers have feelings, too. And they're more likely to be responsive if you remember that the purpose of your meeting is conversation, not confrontation.

7. Focus on what you need, not on what you think the teacher is doing wrong. The more the teacher learns about you, the more he or she will be able to help. The more defensive the teacher feels, the less he or she will want to help.

8. Listen. Many students need practice in this essential skill. The purpose of your meeting isn't just to hear yourself talk, but to have a conversation.

9. Bring your sense of humor that lets you laugh at yourself and your own misunderstandings and mistakes.

10. If your meeting isn't successful, get help from another adult, like the guidance counselor, gifted program coordinator, or another teacher that supports you. "Successful" doesn't necessarily mean that you emerged victorious. Even if the teacher denies your request, your meeting can still be judged successful. If you communicated openly, listened carefully, and respected each other's point of view—then congratulate yourself on a great meeting. If the air crackled with tension, the meeting fell apart, and you felt disrespected (or acted disrespectful), then it's time to bring in another adult.

Note. Adapted from *The Gifted Kid's Survival Guide: A Teen Handbook* by J. Galbraith and J. Delisle, 1996, Minneapolis, MN: Free Spirit Publishing. Copyright Free Spirit Publishing.

- Allow your child to make his or her own choices. Perhaps one of the toughest things for parents is knowing that wonderful academic options exist but that their child is not interested in any of them. Be patient. There is an ebb and flow of needs in every teen's life. Simply assure your child that she will have your support when the time is right.

It's never too soon to teach teenagers about self-advocacy. When students know they have the right to ask, they are empowered and will be able to use the four simple steps in this article whenever they need them throughout their lives.

Resources

Greene, R. (2000). *The teenagers' guide to school outside the box*. Minneapolis, MN: Free Spirit.
Kincher, J. (1995). *Psychology for kids: 40 fun tests that help you learn about yourself*. Minneapolis, MN: Free Spirit.
Rogers, K. B. (2002). *Re-forming gifted education: How parents and teachers can match the program to the child*. Scottsdale, AZ: Great Potential Press.

Reference

Galbraith, J., & Delisle, J. (1996). *The gifted kids survival guide: A teen handbook*. Minneapolis, MN: Free Spirit.

Chapter 38

Advocating for Talented Youth: Lessons Learned From the National Study of Local and State Advocacy in Gifted Education

by Ann Robinson and Sidney M. Moon

I N Iowa, a parent-led advocacy group elected a school board member by endorsing a supportive candidate in a tight race. They activated a phone tree to inform parents of gifted students in the district of the endorsement. The ballot box did the rest!

In New York, a parent advocacy group succeeded in getting its district to adopt a policy to specify services for gifted learners, broke down barriers to grade acceleration, started a Saturday enrichment program, and organized a regularly published newsletter. It has become a major player in district planning.

In North Carolina, the state association spearheaded an effort to pass state legislation mandating local gifted education program plans. They used a strategy called "Bag It." Participants were given two paper bags and asked to take someone at their local level to lunch. They targeted a principal, a school board member, a lead teacher, a superintendent, the PTA president, or a newspaper reporter. They also provided advocates with suggestions for beginning the conversation and with stamped postcards to return to the state association with a short summary of their lunchtime gains. Through this strategy, they built coalitions and new supporters.

In Colorado, advocates learned that a state mandate for gifted education services was not possible in the current political climate. Rather than give up or alienate their legislative supporters, they regrouped and worked with sympathetic legislators to craft an amendment that gave them increased funding and identified gifted learners. By identifying gifted students in the legislation, advocates successfully gained official recognition for this special population of learners.

Reports of successful advocacy come from every corner of the country, and parents often are key players in securing educational opportunities for their gifted children. A national study of advocacy in local school districts and of statewide efforts provides us with a fascinating picture of dedicated people at work on behalf of gifted and talented youth. The stories differ, but there are common lessons that can inform the plans and day-to-day actions of advocates.

Advocates give support to a cause or take a public position on an issue. Sometimes they work to maintain the status quo, but often they work to encourage change. This may include securing more resources to serve gifted and talented children or starting programs where none exist or making changes to those that do exist. The ways in which people took on these tasks and made things happen for gifted children interested us. In this article, we share our observations and conclusions regarding lessons learned from the national study of local and state advocacy in gifted education.

Who Was in the Sample?

Sixty-one examples of advocacy from 34 states were summarized through surveys sent to state directors of gifted education, state affiliates of the National Association for Gifted Children, and to collaborative school districts from the National Research Center on the Gifted and Talented. The people who responded to the survey came from all constituencies in a gifted child's life: parents, teachers, gifted and talented administrators, state department of education leaders, community leaders, and university researchers. Six of these 61 survey responses were selected for more in-depth investigation by case study researchers who visited the sites, talked with stakeholders (individuals affected by a program such as parents, teachers, administrators, community members, or students) and advocates and examined documents relevant to the advocates' work. Finally, the surveys and the case studies were examined once again to identify general principles and practical lessons that other advocates might use. Here's what we found.

What Happened?

Most advocates targeted one of two things: either demands for increased funding or general policy changes. Sometimes they would advocate for both at the same time; sometimes they advocated for one or the other. Most advocates, about 70%, reported that they "wanted something new." About 18% reported that they wanted to change something that already existed with which they were not pleased or felt needed improvement. Even when they focused on the new, very few of the advocates in the national study reported clean slate advocacy—advocacy in which nothing at all existed before they began their efforts.

Why so few reports of clean slate advocacy? It is probably due to the kinds of research questions we asked in the study and the kinds of advocates who responded to our survey. We asked people to tell us about successful advocacy. By that definition, something positive must have happened! We also sent our inquiries to the network of state departments and school districts that were already part of the nationwide gifted education community. These were places where some service, even if minimal, was already in place.

What Defined Success?

Looking carefully at the six sites that were developed into case studies we were able to see common threads that invited success. Although there were several factors that we organized into the categories of *influ-*

ences, leadership, and *advocacy strategies,* we concentrate here on the three factors that are most likely to be useful to parent advocates: policies, champions and leaders, and communication strategies for raising awareness. Each one of the factors led us to a take-away lesson that advocates can use, with the understanding that they are all overlapping, that not all lessons would apply in all situations, and that not *all* are necessary for success in a specific situation.

Policies

Policies are courses of action established or set by elected or appointed decision makers. In relation to gifted education, some examples of policies include: "This district does not endorse grade acceleration," or "School districts must identify and serve gifted learners in grades K through 12." In the case of the first example, advocates might work to have the policy preventing acceleration removed; in the second, advocates might work to increase funding to support the law that mandates services. In either example, advocates need to be very knowledgeable about the current policies in their local and state context. In fact, our case studies demonstrated that successful advocacy often depended on knowledgeable advocates who made thorough examinations of gifted education, local policies, state policies, and the political processes necessary to create or modify them.

The lesson for advocates found in all of these cases was that time spent studying the current policies and the political and administrative avenues for affecting them or developing new policy is time well spent.

Advocates who are well informed about current policies are also equipped to respond in a crisis (e.g., where policy makers attempt to change policy without sufficient discussion with the public). In terms of long-range efforts, advocates with a thorough knowledge of policies will be able to engage in ongoing advocacy in many and varied situations. These might include social situations where advocates come into contact with policy makers outside of the usual forums (memberships in clubs, churches, social groups, or sports organizations), where ongoing contact helps to develop a deep well of support and knowledge between advocates and decision makers like school board members and state legislators.

Champions and Leaders

Leadership that existed in two different, but related ways, influenced successful advocacy. There were individual leaders we termed champions and there were organized gifted education associations in which groups of advocates carried out the leadership function. In our study, individual champions were parents, university educators, teachers, or leaders of advocacy organizations. The gifted education advocacy organizations were either local parent groups or state gifted education associations. In one case, a teacher-champion first created a gifted education program in her local school and then worked with other teachers and parents to found a statewide advocacy association. In other words, one type of leader (a champion) could create the second type (an advocacy organization) over time. It doesn't have to be lonely out there on the advocacy front lines. A committed individual champion can create a structure of support on many different levels.

The individual champions who appeared in the case studies were motivated, knowledgeable, and possessed the leadership skills of problem solving and communication, which included knowledge of public relations. They often persisted long beyond the time their own children were involved in gifted education services and through both exciting and difficult times. For example, the two champions in one of the case studies were parents of children attending the same district. They did not necessarily agree on all of their goals or have a common approach. They did have staying power beyond the bumps and disagreements within the parent advocacy group they were part of, and through their lengthy dealings with the school district. In another of the case studies, the champion was a school employee who used a court-ordered desegregation plan to increase the participation of minority students in gifted education programming. Her strategies were varied. She designed more equitable identification procedures, improved the infrastructure in predominately minority schools, increased the numbers of minority staff involved in gifted education, and built an understanding of the benefits of gifted education in minority communities.

In addition to high levels of motivation, both individual champions and association leadership advocates needed a broad base of knowledge to help them achieve their goals. Three kinds of knowledge seemed to be important to them: knowledge of best practices in gifted education (e.g., What kinds of curricula have research support?), political savvy or knowledge and understanding of the political process in which the advocates work (e.g., Who makes what decisions in our district or in the state legislature? Who are other influential people or groups in our district or state? How do you make a positive contact with them?), and practical know-how about advocacy strategies (e.g., What is a postcard blizzard or what is a phone tree? How do we use them in our district or state?). One of the parent champions learned to use the Freedom of Information Act to request information from the school district, which was relevant to his advocacy efforts. Association leaders in another state devoted a full year of concentrated self-study of the legislative processes as part of their effort to pass a mandate for gifted education. Both individual champions and advocacy organizations used various strategies in their efforts to raise awareness and secure resources or change policies. The strategies varied to suit the context, but again we found common threads.

The lesson for advocates is that an individual champion or a small group of association leaders with an appropriate knowledge base can provide the momentum for successful advocacy campaigns. It does not take a cast of thousands to make progress.

Advocacy Tools and Strategies

Advocates used a variety of strategies to achieve their goals. They planned. They collaborated. They communicated. In some cases, they even developed gifted education programs. The national study reinforced the importance of planning in effective advocacy. Each of the successful sites we studied in depth involved powerhouse planners. And, just as advocacy model builders suggest, successful advocates have learned to collaborate with other groups of parents, educators, and decision makers. For example, members of the advocacy association in one of the state-level case studies worked hard at building positive, supportive relationships with key decision makers and other education groups in the state. One of their strategies was to make appointments to meet newly elected or appointed officials and then to maintain contact with those officials on a regular basis. This strategy led to a positive relationship with their new state Secretary of Education, which in turn, led to collaborative goal setting. Eventually, the collaboration that was forged with the Secretary of Education led to many positive outcomes for gifted and talented education. One was a series of state-level awareness initiatives, the establishment of a State Advisory Council on Gifted Education, and a modest amount of new state funding for competitive grants for school districts.

Communication is part of an advocacy strategy that lends itself to concrete examples and actions for parents who want to become successful advocates. Communication as part of a strategy seems obvious, but we found advocates engaged in a broad range of innovative communication activities, which other advocacy groups could import into their own contexts. We focused on communication activities for raising awareness and offer them as possibilities for parents and parent advocacy groups to consider.

These are the kinds of activities that form the backbone of what we call "advocacy for acceptance"—advocacy intended to increase understanding of the nature and nurture of gifted and talented children and create a positive climate for increased resources for gifted education. Advocates focused on three kinds of awareness-raising activities to communicate acceptance for the needs of gifted children: informational products for general and specific audiences, staff development activities to assist general education teachers in understanding the needs of gifted and talented students, and public relations events. Our survey respondents and the six case study sites provided several examples.

Tips for State-Level Advocacy

Build an Effective State Advocacy Organization

- Align your state organization with NAGC.
- Educate your members about gifted education and particularly the history of gifted education in your state.
- Educate your members about the legislative and administrative processes in your state and about advocacy in general.
- Build local affiliate groups of parents and teachers.
- Design ongoing and fast response systems (e.g., adopt a legislator programs and phone trees).
- Keep a database of members with particular attention to those who have personal or professional connections with decision makers.

Build Collaborative Relationships With Decision Makers and Other Education Organizations

- Build relationships and collaborations with your State Superintendent of Education, State Board of Education, State Gifted and Talented Office, university administrators, etc.
- Build relationships with other education groups such as teacher unions, administrator organizations, and other advocacy groups that may be promoting an appropriate education for children with disabilities or those with English as a second language.
- Work with your State Department of Education to establish a state-level advisory board for gifted education.
- Write position papers or adapt those developed by the NAGC
- Visit with officials before they are elected (during campaigns) and again when they take office to provide information on your organization and goals. Do the same with appointed officials and staff.
- Keep in touch with key legislative committee members and their staffs on a regular basis.
- Get to know the staff in legislative offices and offer to organize education advisory committees for them or offer to serve on an existing one.
- Be truthful, professional, and positive. Know the arguments against your issue as well as your own and always be willing to compromise to achieve your goals on an incremental basis.

Communicate a Clear and Consistent Message

- Conduct creative awareness campaigns to create a positive climate for your advocacy goals.
- Compile and disseminate factual information about gifted education in your state on a regular basis to your members, policy makers, and the media.
- Develop specific, clear advocacy goals and review them on a regular basis to see if they need to be changed or updated.
- Publicize your message in concise, clever, and consistent ways.
- To overcome the issue of elitism in gifted education, always present scenarios of GT children from all socioeconomic and ethnic backgrounds in all areas of your state.
- Be visible (e.g., attend hearings and committee meetings; make statements to the press, but only after careful consideration, develop a newsletter; write op-ed pieces for the local papers; wear buttons with your organization's message/logo).
- Before lobbying understand the limits of your association to do so under the law and then teach organization members how to lobby effectively including writing letters to legislators (e.g., include bill, recommendation for related funding, explanation of association's position on the bill, and why the bill is important to you and your child).
- Engage a lobbyist only after careful review and interviews to ensure that the lobbyist you hire doesn't have conflicts of interest in the groups he or she represents.

Say "Thank You"

- Express appreciation frequently and creatively to all who assist you.

Note. See Delcourt (2003) and Enersen (2003).

Informational Products

State and local parent associations developed tangible products such as parent handbooks, informational flyers, and position papers for use with the media, state and local decision makers, and the general public, and to use to recruit advocates. In at least one case, an advocacy handbook was published and reached a national audience.

Staff Development Activities

While staff development activities are more likely to be carried out by educators for educators, there also are examples of staff development activities by local and state advocacy organizations. In our study, state and local advocacy associations organized conferences for parents, teachers, and administrators, both to raise awareness and provide detailed information on the nature and nurture of gifted students. Some of these conferences were funded with advocacy grants from the National Association for Gifted Children, which were awarded to state advocacy organizations.

Tips for Local Advocacy

Be Knowledgeable

- Be informed about your child and your district and school, its policies, and practices.
- Learn the principles behind gifted education.
- Read books and articles on how to advocate effectively.
- Understand federal laws, state laws, court decisions, and school policies that affect your efforts.
- Gather specific data and statistics about local programming.
- Understand all stakeholders, their conceptions of giftedness, and their views of gifted education.
- Be aware of other issues and pressures facing schools and administrators and teachers.

Build Awareness and Support

- Be positive, trustworthy, and professional.
- Create and disseminate informational materials that are customized for your community (e.g., flyers, handbooks, reprints).
- Educate teachers, administrators, and school board members about gifted education and expose them to both sides of controversial issues.
- Create task forces, groups, or committees with broad stakeholder representation to make recommendations on controversial issues and draft local policy statements so that policy makers will understand what you

are asking for. These groups could include parents, representatives of the business and faith communities, and others with an interest in education in your community.

- Use varied techniques designed to meet specific situations to ensure that all perspectives on gifted education issues are heard, discussed, and addressed.

Find Champions in the School System

- Identify administrators and board members who support gifted education and work with them to create change.
- Expend most of your efforts on decision makers who are supportive or neutral but don't underestimate your ability to change peoples' views.

Set Clear Goals

- Be clear about what you want to accomplish, yet ready to compromise and accept incremental gains.
- Keep policy goals separate from implementation goals (e.g., getting the policy in place for gifted education and funding that initiative).
- Be ready to respond quickly to policy or funding changes that might affect local gifted education programs and do this by being at the table for all education discussions even if they aren't directly relevant to gifted education.

Assist in Developing Written Polices to Guide Local Gifted Education Efforts

- Address controversial local issues with clear policy statements that all stakeholders can support.
- Draft policy statements and circulate them for comments from all stakeholders.

Address Issues of Equity as Well as Issues of Excellence

- Advocate for services for all students and for gifted students from all socioeconomic levels and ethnic and cultural backgrounds. Advocate for identification practices that are effective with underrepresented populations in gifted programs.

- Work to increase minority student participation in local gifted education programs. Strengthen the understanding and commitment of minority communities to gifted education.
- Improve the infrastructure in schools with large minority and lower socioeconomic populations so that it allows for appropriate programs to be developed.
- Work to increase the involvement of minority educators in gifted education.

Note. See Grantham (2003), Hertzog (2003), and Kennedy (2003).

Public Relations Activities

Advocates used public relations at both the local and state levels to build support. For example, one district organizes an ice cream social each year to share the successes of its gifted students and its program. Parents, students, and community members are invited to a showcase of student projects and accomplishments. One of the state-level advocacy case studies reported that a statewide Gifted Education Month was established by the governor to raise awareness of the needs of gifted children and youth. Other public relations examples include a blanket of thank-you letters to legislators who voted to pass a state-level mandate and radio public service announcements read by children in a local gifted program.

The lesson is that successful advocates plan, collaborate with others, and communicate through speaking, writing, and organizing public events.

Lessons Learned

The advocates we studied provided several useful lessons for other parents, educators, and policy makers who work on behalf of gifted and talented students. First, advocacy is a continual process, a campaign in many ways, not an event around which boundaries are easily drawn. Successful advocates are vigilant and advocate all of the time for the issues and causes they believe in. Successful advocates build up a deep well of goodwill and contacts on which to draw when focusing on a particular policy or when a funding crisis arises.

Second, successful advocacy often takes the form of advocacy to improve understanding of the needs of high-ability learners, or what we term advocacy for acceptance. Successful advocates for gifted education are willing to devote time to gaining recognition for the needs of talented learners in order to create a context ripe for other more tangible advocacy goals such as increased services in the schools or extracurricular opportunities for gifted and talented children.

Third, successful advocacy can be initiated and sustained by a small group of people even at the state level. Often a single individual who serves as a champion can inspire other advocates to stay the course over time.

Fourth, chance favors the prepared advocate. Opportunities can arise quickly, and advocates with a clear message and an effective messenger make the most of them. Being a knowledgeable messenger who can speak effectively and quickly with policy makers can be extremely important.

Fifth, successful advocates use nonadversarial strategies, and believe that strategies that focus on collaboration and consensus building are most likely to be effective. School personnel, including teachers and administrators, school board members, and legislators respond more positively to parent advocates who are knowledgeable about the range of issues facing them and are willing to negotiate to reach their goals.

Sixth, successful advocacy campaigns create intermediate goals to measure progress and maintain the enthusiasm of the participants. Although many advocates view the final goal as mandated services to gifted and talented students, successful advocates use recognition, public relations campaigns, incremental policy making and implementation, and the establishment of ongoing advocacy groups as intermediate outcomes and indicators of their progress.

In the end, the keys to effective advocacy for parents are planning, becoming informed, communicating with one another, and making positive contacts with individuals and groups who can support the interests of gifted children through good decisions, enlightened policies, and increased resources. Our research found parents across the country using a variety of advocacy strategies effectively and enthusiastically. They collaborated with schools. They built networks and coalitions. They persuaded policy makers. In all of these contexts, parents were impressive advocates with interesting and inspiring stories to share.

Resources

Arkansas Association of Gifted Education Administrators. (n.d.). *Legislative handbook: How to communicate with state and national policymakers.* Little Rock, AR: Author.

Bootel, J. A. (1995). *CEC special education advocacy handbook.* Reston, VA: Council for Exceptional Children.

California Association for the Gifted. (n.d.). *Advocacy in action: An advocacy handbook for gifted and talented education.* Mountain View, CA: Author.

National Association for Gifted Children. (n.d.). *Online advocacy toolkit.* Retrieved from http://www.nagc.org/index.aspx?id=36

References

Delcourt, M. A. B. (2003). Five ingredients for success: Two case studies of advocacy at the state level. *Gifted Child Quarterly, 47,* 26–37.

Enersen, D. (2003). The art of bridge building: Providing for gifted children. *Gifted Child Quarterly, 47,* 38–45.

Grantham, T. C. (2003). Increasing Black student enrollment in gifted programs: An exploration of Pulaski county special school district's advocacy efforts. *Gifted Child Quarterly, 47,* 46–65.

Hertzog, N. (2003). Advocacy: On the cutting edge. *Gifted Child Quarterly, 47,* 66–81.

Kennedy, D. (2003). Custer, South Dakota: Gifted's last stand. *Gifted Child Quarterly, 47,* 82–93.

PART VII

Twice-Exceptional Students

by James T. Webb

FOR decades, professionals and parents have assumed that gifted children were not very likely to have social, emotional, or learning problems. After all, Terman's classic studies showed that gifted children were, in general, healthier, more resilient, and more emotionally stable than other children. Even recently, research found relatively few such problems in gifted children, although other professionals in the field pointed out that the research was primarily conducted on children who had been identified by schools as gifted and therefore were already functioning pretty well academically, and probably socially and emotionally.

More recently, many leaders in the field have pointed out that a substantial number of gifted children are not being identified as such, and that these gifted children may have disorders that, unless they are diagnosed and treated, actually interfere with a child's ability to use his or her abilities. Such children all too often are not even recognized as gifted. Because, by definition, gifted children are exceptional, if they have a coexisting disorder they are twice-exceptional, often referred to as 2E. Gifted children may have Attention Deficit/Hyperactivity Disorder (ADHD), Asperger's syndrome, learning disabilities, vision or hearing problems, or other impairments. As Robinson noted in 2006, the only condition gifted students are immune to is intellectual disability, formerly known as mental retardation.

This section provides selected chapters that focus on a few of the more widespread disorders that gifted children may have. The authors' chapters in this section provide a fundamental look at some of the most frequent twice-exceptionalities, and provide advice and direction for parents and professionals who are trying to help gifted children who have a coexisting disorder.

As author Beverly Trail notes, "Parenting would be so much easier if children came with a book of instructions" (p. 387). This is particularly true with gifted children who are 2E, and the title of Trail's chapter sums it up well: "Parenting Twice-Exceptional Children Through Frustration to Success." A wide range of disabilities—often ones that are not apparent—can prevent a child from demonstrating his or her abilities, and parents and educators must be particularly alert to this possibility. Gifted children who do have disabilities typically underestimate their abilities and have self-esteem issues; they focus on what they cannot do well, rather than on what they can do well. This chapter reminds parents to create a safe home environment, to focus on a child's strengths, to help the child develop compensatory strategies and skills, to cultivate realistic goal setting and resiliency, and to actively advocate for their children.

The twice-exceptional gifted child most often discussed is one who has ADHD. A fundamental problem is simply one of making a correct diagnosis. As Sylvia Rimm points out in her chapter, there can be many other causes of ADHD-like symptoms in a child who does not have ADHD. These problems range from traumatic to toxic family situations to families inconsistently applying family rules. Some of the special characteristics of gifted children, such as their unusual intensity, may lead them to show behaviors that are misinterpreted as ADHD.

Some gifted children, however, do truly have ADHD. Sidney Moon, a noted researcher in gifted education, knows this personally because one of her sons is twice-exceptional in this way. From her research and experience, Moon notes that children who have ADHD and also are gifted tend to have more severe social and emotional problems than do children who only have giftedness alone or ADHD alone. Their intellectual giftedness did not protect them from the problems associated with ADHD, and may have actually made them more pronounced. Moon offers some suggestions that may help parents and educators.

As you read these chapters, it is important to keep in mind some of the following questions:

- Could my child be underachieving due to a coexisting problem that has not heretofore been recognized?
- How likely is it that my child has significant asynchronous development?
- Are the teachers and parents expecting too much in some areas and not enough in others?
- Have I become informed enough to be an effective advocate for my child?
- Am I being sufficiently persistent in my efforts to advocate for my child?

Parents of gifted children, like most other parents, generally trust the advice provided by educational, health care, and counseling professionals. Regrettably, though, these professionals often receive little training and are not sufficiently informed about gifted children (Webb et al., 2005). As a result, gifted children, particularly if they are educationally misplaced or not understood at home, are misdiagnosed and dual diagnoses are missed. Pediatricians, family practice specialists, and psychologists may well overlook your child's coexisting disorder. One study (Alsop, 1997) found that a full 20% of the information and advice given by professionals about gifted children was not only inaccurate, but also "hurtful."

The implications are clear. Parents need to educate themselves about 2E gifted children so that they can educate the professionals with whom they interact. And parents need to persistently advocate for their gifted children's education, as well as to undertake remedial activities at home. There is substantial evidence that specific activities can help rewire the brain, particularly in children under the age of 12 (Eide & Eide, 2006).

The gifted education field is continuing to explore areas within twice-exceptionality, so parents should take efforts to stay informed of new developments. This can be done via researching the Internet, attending conferences, reading relevant books, and subscribing to publications such as *Parenting for High Potential*, published by the National Association for Gifted Children, or the 2E Newsletter (http://2enewsletter.com).

References

Alsop, G. (1997). Coping or counseling: Families of intellectually gifted students. *Roeper Review, 20,* 26–34.

Eide, B. L., & Eide, F. F. (2006). *The mislabeled child: How understanding your child's unique learning style can open the door to success.* New York, NY: Hyperion.

Robinson, N. M. (2006). Counseling issues for gifted students. *Gifted Education Communicator, 37*(1), 9–10.

Webb, J. T., Amend, E. R., Webb, N. E., Goerss, J., Beljan, P., & Olenchak, F. R. (2005). *Misdiagnosis and dual diagnoses of gifted children and adults: ADHD, bipolar, OCD, Asperger's, depression, and other disorders.* Scottsdale, AZ: Great Potential Press.

Chapter 39

Parenting Twice-Exceptional Children Through Frustration to Success

by Beverly A. Trail

P ARENTING would be so much easier if children came with a book of instructions. Paul's parents thought he would excel in school because in kindergarten, he was performing at the second-grade level in reading and math. He understood complex concepts well beyond his years (like "plate tectonics") and was identified as gifted. Paul continually complained that school was boring and he begged to stay home to learn. It became evident during the intermediate elementary years that he was not progressing as he should. Even though he understood the concept of multiplication in first grade, Paul was not able to pass the timed math facts tests and he could not do long division problems. He would write the correct answer where it belonged, but could not do the step-by-step process of long division. Paul's writing was a mixture of print and cursive writing that was illegible. His fourth-grade teacher gave him two desks and still papers (usually incomplete assignments that should have been handed in) were hanging out of the desks and spilling onto the floor. Paul participated in all classroom discussions, sharing knowledge and demonstrating understanding of concepts beyond his peers. However, his writing was below grade level. Written papers consisted of short sentences, low-level vocabulary, many spelling mistakes, and no elaboration of ideas. Certainly, his written work was not consistent with his verbal ability.

Paul's parents began to really worry as his grades dropped and teachers began to comment on behavior issues. Why was this bright child not doing his work? More alarming, he was very frustrated with school and his love of learning was diminishing along with their hopes and dreams for college. What should parents do when their gifted child's lack of achievement results in failing grades?

Sally's parents were equally concerned with her progress in school. During her preschool years she was not as verbal as her brothers and sisters. It was difficult to understand her speech because she mispronounced words. Testing with the Child Find project in the local school district at age 4 showed there were sizable discrepancies among her skills in various areas. She was more than 2 years ahead in some, and more than 2 years behind in others. In elementary school, she appeared to her teachers to be an average student. Sally's parents were concerned because they knew how hard she was working to get average grades. Learning basic skills seemed to be so difficult for Sally! She couldn't remember letter sounds and consequently had difficulty sounding out words. Sally could solve really difficult puzzles and demonstrated exceptional skills in problem solving and critical thinking; in those areas, she was superior to her brothers and sisters who had been identified as gifted. Some people suspected a learning disability, but teachers were not concerned because she was doing average work and her composite scores on assessments were average, so she did not qualify for special education services. Sally's attitude alarmed her parents. She used to be very outgoing and now was an unhappy loner. At school she was quiet and compliant, but at home she exhibited severe anxiety and had almost daily emotional "meltdowns." She even mentioned a couple of times that she "wanted to go to heaven." Sally's parents became really concerned about their daughter, but they didn't know what to do.

Both of these children demonstrate characteristics of gifted students with disabilities. Their school experience will be challenging because hidden disabilities can make aspects of academic achievement difficult for these gifted learners. Inconsistent performance, incomplete assignments, disorganization, and behavior problems can be indicators of learning problems. Not only does the disability influence their academic performance in school, but it can intensify social-emotional risk factors. In my role as a twice-exceptional consultant, I have become increasingly aware of the interrelationship between academic achievement and social-emotional factors. Behavior problems can result from the frustration of trying to deal with two exceptionalities. Twice-exceptional children can become very depressed when they set unrealistic goals for themselves or feel they are not meeting the expectations of their parents and teachers. Because they have both the characteristics of gifted children and also those of children with disabilities, they can have a difficult time relating to peers in either group. Parenting these children can be a challenge!

What Does It Mean to Be Twice-Exceptional?

The term *twice-exceptional* signifies the presence of a disability and gifted potential. Twice-exceptional learners have the characteristics of gifted students with potential for high performance, along with the characteristics of students with disabilities who struggle with many aspects of learning. Typically, these students have superior vocabulary, advanced ideas, a wide range of interests and opinions, and are highly creative with a sophisticated sense of humor. At the same time, their academic performance can be inconsistent and they lack organizational skills. Twice-exceptional children often can appear stubborn, opinionated, and argumentative, yet they also can be highly sensitive to criticism. Combine this with the extreme frustration gifted learners feel when they cannot meet their own and others' expectations, the frustrations of teachers who cannot understand why bright children do not achieve, and the frustrations of parents who are trying to deal with unhappy, angry, often depressed children, and the stage is set for conflict, misunderstandings, and failure in school.

A wide range of hidden disabilities can influence the school performance of twice-exceptional learners. Auditory processing deficits can cause difficulty in decoding words, spelling, and sentence structure. These learners have a hard time following oral direction and learning from lectures. Visual processing problems can affect reading comprehension and students' ability to copy information from the board. Deficits in visual/motor coordination and sequential processing can cause problems with handwriting. Sequential processing weakness influences reading speed and fluency along with ability to sound out words or remember formulas and steps. Executive functioning involves the learner's ability to plan, organize, and prioritize; learners with difficulties in this area struggle to coordinate multiple tasks simultaneously. Slower processing speed results in short-term memory and long-term memory retrieval problems when time pressures are in place. Cognitive disabilities diminish the brain's ability to process information. These hidden disabilities can cause children to struggle when learning to read, write, or memorize math facts, and can limit their ability to sustain attention or remember verbal instructions.

Twice-exceptional students are difficult to identify for a number of reasons. The student's strengths can mask weaknesses and the weaknesses can mask the strengths, creating a unique learner profile that is atypical of either a gifted student or a student with disabilities. Twice-exceptional students do not want anyone to know they have problems with some aspect of learning, and they use their gifted characteristics to hide their learning problems. It is not uncommon for the disability and the potential to both go unnoticed. Gifted students can underachieve for years before their performance falls below grade-level expectations and their disability is recognized. Some students are never identified for either gifted or special education programming. Stereotypical notions about learning disabilities and giftedness can impede identification and programming for both their disability and their giftedness. Parents and teachers need to be alert to hidden disabilities and the influence it can have on learning.

What Do We Need to Understand?

When gifted students' achievement falls below expectations, teachers and parents often attribute it to lack of effort. Expectations that gifted learners have similar abilities in all content areas can result in the assumption that these students are not putting forward a reasonable amount of effort. Twice-exceptional learners can appear unmotivated and lazy, or even defiant and oppositional, as they make minimal progress on assignments. Reactions toward students perceived as lazy are quite different from the more empathetic approach students with disabilities usually receive. What twice-exceptional students need most is encouragement. These high-potential students have a strong desire to be successful, but they lack the skills they need to achieve that success. Telling twice-exceptional learners they could get good grades, if only they would try harder, often heightens their anxiety level and only makes the situation worse.

Social or emotional issues resulting from dealing with the two exceptionalities can have a greater influence on achievement than the disability. Twice-exceptional students can be caught in a cycle of perfectionism, avoidance, and procrastination. Perfectionism can be a positive trait when it challenges the children to achieve higher goals. Dysfunctional perfectionism can result in paralyzing anxiety, self-criticism, and fear of failure; in that situation, students do not see mistakes as part of the learning process. An example of this is Paula who received an "A-" on her report card in writing. For 2 weeks she did not hand in a writing assignment; she worked for hours trying to write sentences for her spelling words, but none of her sentences were good enough. She cried every morning on her way to school and complained that her teacher hated her. It was not until her teacher told her that she had given her an "A-" to leave room for growth that Paula was able to write with confidence again. John received a failing grade on a homework assignment for not following directions. For months he completed all of the required homework but never handed in a single assignment. He was afraid of getting another failing grade for not following directions. In his mind, it was better to not hand it in than to risk getting a low grade.

How Parents Can Empower Their Children

As parents, you can empower your twice-exceptional children to overcome their disability or through your own actions foster learned helplessness. Twice-exceptional children have high potential, but that potential will not be realized unless you support their social and emotional development and help them learn to cope with their mixed abilities. It is difficult to watch your children struggle and some parents will rush in to rescue their children from failure. However, rescuing children decreases their self-esteem because it supports their feelings that they are incapable of meeting the challenges of school without their parents' help. Conversely, self-esteem increases when children learn to deal with their disability and frustrations. If twice-exceptional children realize they can successfully overcome their challenges, they will grow up to become successful adults. Avoid the temptation to focus on your child's challenge areas. Instead, use the following strategies to promote positive social and emotional development.

Create a Safe Home Environment

Twice-exceptional children need a safe, nurturing home environment because school can be such a frustrating experience. Home must be a place where children can regroup and recharge. A friendly greeting at the door, a favorite snack, or a note in a lunch box telling children how special they are can reassure children. Spending time together working on a favorite project can make children feel loved and valued. Some twice-exceptional students are able to control their frustration at school, but their frustration becomes very apparent when they arrive home. Participating in a sport after school like swimming or going on a bike ride can give these children an opportunity to release built-up anger and frustrations. Children learn more from their parent's example than their words.

If you value the unique characteristics of family members, your children will learn to value their own individual characteristics and those of others. Children need to share in family responsibilities and be included in family planning and decision making. Each family member must feel that he or she contributes to the family and his or her contribution is valued.

Nurture Strengths and Interests

Nurturing children's strengths and interests increases their confidence and resilience. As children experience success in their strength area, they become more confident in their abilities. Encouraging children to explore their interests will excite their inner passions and motivate them to become lifelong learners. Children are more likely to persist through difficult times in school if they have acknowledged strengths to counterbalance the challenges. You can nurture your children's strengths and interest in four ways. First, support your children's exploration by planning trips to the library, museum, planetarium, etc. Second, provide the material and resources the children need for their exploration. Third, search out groups, organizations, or other children with whom your children can share their interests. Finally, nurture your own passions and share your interests with your children; be a model of lifelong learning.

Foster a "Yes, I Can" Attitude

Helping children to understand that success is achieved as a result of effort and that failure is likely to result from lack of effort, can promote the development of a "Yes, I can" attitude. Children who learn that they can be successful if they put forth a reasonable amount of effort will learn to persist through the difficult times. Children who learn to equate success with effort will become achievers. Those who attribute success to luck and failure to lack of ability will become underachievers. Help your children make the connection between hard work and success by praising their efforts, not their ability. When children engage in negative self-talk, ask them to stop, to take three deep breaths, and to visualize a specific time when they were successful. Children must understand that making mistakes is part of the learning process. You can become positive role models for your children in dealing with perfectionism. Help your children understand that you, too, sometimes fail when learning a new skill.

Support the Development of Compensatory Strategies

Successful twice-exceptional students develop strategies to compensate for their areas of challenge. Use graphic organizers to help children organize their thoughts, homework assignments, and projects. Many graphic organizers are available in books, or to download free from the Internet. Encourage the use of technology to increase productivity. Word processing programs make it easier for students to edit their work and produce an impressive finished product. Software programs like Inspiration can help students create their own graphic organizers to plan for projects and written assignments. The graphic organizers can be converted to a linear outline with the click of a button. Spell checkers and grammar checkers are useful tools when editing papers. PDA/handheld devices and computer programs like Microsoft's Outlook can help students organize their time and projects.

Help your children learn to organize homework by showing them how to create a "to-do list" and helping them prioritize what needs to be done. Show children how to break the work into shorter segments. Having children estimate how long each segment will take, and then using a timer to document how long it actually took, will help them learn time management. Crossing off each task as it is completed helps children develop a sense of accomplishment. At the end of a homework session, be certain that the child puts the completed homework in a folder in his or her backpack and places the backpack in a convenient location for the morning departure. Allowing your children to do an activity of their choice for fun when their homework is finished also can motivate them to be more focused in their work.

Promote Positive Coping Strategies

Twice-exceptional children can become very adept at manipulating situations to avoid failure. They can take on the persona of a rebel who is "too smart" to complete the assignment that is "too boring" or "too stupid." Others may become the class clown because it is better to be asked to leave the class for clowning around than to fail in front of peers. Avoidance, distancing, and learned helplessness are negative coping strategies. You can empower your children by encouraging the development of positive coping strategies such as accepting responsibility for their actions instead of blaming others. Through conversations with your children, you can help them reappraise a situation and deal with unrealistic expectations. Encourage children to seek the support they need and help them to become self-advocates.

Cultivate Resiliency

Risk and resiliency factors are variables that can affect outcomes in a positive or negative way. A learning disability and social-emotional issues are risk factors, while strong family ties, friendships with peers, and relationships with a caring adult help children become more resilient. The home can be a protective setting, helping to reduce the impact of other risk factors. On the other hand, unsupportive home environments can compound the risk factors for students. A home environment that provides opportunities for children to develop their strengths and independence cultivates resilience. Seek opportunities for your children to connect with peers of similar ability and interests. Use humor to help children realize that defeat sometimes provides opportunities to cultivate resilience.

Coach Realistic Goal Setting

To sustain motivation, children must believe their efforts will result in success. Learning to set realistic goals can influence achievement positively and reduce frustration. You can be instrumental in coaching your child to select realistic short- and long-term goals.

- Start with a goal the child will be able to achieve in a short period of time. Together plan the steps necessary to attain the goal and map those steps on a flow chart. When the goal is achieved, celebrate success and appraise the steps used to accomplish the results.
- As your child becomes comfortable with short-term goals, help him or her take a long-term goal and divide it into several

short-term goals. Likewise, learning to break down long-term projects into shorter segments will increase the chances the projects will be completed on time and will decrease the probability children will become overwhelmed. When children integrate academic goals into their life goals, this will increase their intrinsic motivation.

- Begin career exploration during late elementary and early middle school. Encourage your high schooler to investigate educational requirements for his or her main career interests and visit university websites to determine entrance requirements. Teenagers who have a defined career goal and know the requirement to get into the college of their choice will be more likely to persist through difficult assignments and courses.

Encourage Children to Become Independent Learners

Preparing children for the future is an important part of your role as a parent. Make efforts to foster a love for learning and cultivate independence in your children so they will develop the skills needed to become successful adults. Instead of trying to protect your children from negative experiences, help them develop confidence in their abilities by learning how to handle difficult situations. Do not overprotect children or accept responsibility for their problems. Allow children to learn from natural consequences early in their life so they develop the skills they need to make decisions in later years. As children mature, step back and give them more control. Support your children actively during their struggles and celebrate their successes.

How Can Parents Advocate for Their Children?

Twice-exceptional children need parents to advocate for them, but you must do it with great care. It is so much easier to advocate for your children if you have a good working relationship with teachers before there is a problem. Teachers appreciate the help of parents to improve educational opportunities for all students. Become actively involved in the school by participating in PTA and school committees. Volunteer your time to assist with activities or help in the computer lab, classroom, or media center. Work with other parents to support the efforts of teachers and school staff with thank-you notes, flowers, or teacher appreciation luncheons or breakfasts. It is easier for you to advocate for your children when you have a good relationship with teachers and staff.

When you become aware of a developing problem, follow these simple steps:

- Always approach problems as an opportunity to learn and model for your children positive ways of dealing with difficult situations. Clarify the issues and try to get a sense of the real problem by discussing it thoroughly with your child. This is easier said than done because children sometimes do not understand their feelings. It is best to be nonjudgmental, rephrasing and repeating back what your child is telling you. Both you and your child will gain a clearer understanding of the problem (and your feelings) through this process.

- When you are convinced that you have all of the facts, approach the teacher with care and sensitivity to schedule a meeting at a time that is convenient for both of you. Do not just drop by school and begin this conversation. Be sure to arrive at the scheduled meeting on time with the intent of keeping the conversation a positive learning exchange.

- At the meeting start with positive comments about the school and the teacher. Communicate your concern as clearly as possible without blame. Keep the focus on your children's academic and social-emotional needs. Come prepared to share specific examples related to your concerns.

- Be sure to express a willingness to help resolve the problem and work collaboratively toward a positive solution. Plan together to determine the responsibilities for you, your child, and the teacher. Determine a reasonable timeline for evaluating progress. After the conference, keep the lines of communication open and schedule a follow-up meeting.

Conclusion

School can be a very frustrating experience for gifted students with disabilities, their parents, and their teachers. As parents, you can play an important role in helping your children understand and learn to cope with their mixed abilities, to understand their own unique set of individual strengths, challenges, and interests, and to learn and apply strategies to build resilience. Through your actions, you can empower your children to overcome their disabilities and to persist through their frustration. Advocate for your children by working collaboratively with the school. In these ways, you can parent your twice-exceptional children through frustration to success.

Resources

Baum, S., & Owens, S. V. (2004). *To be gifted and learning disabled: Strategies for helping bright students with LD, ADHD, and more.* Mansfield Center, CT: Creative Learning Press.

Kay, K. (2000). *Uniquely gifted: Identifying and meeting the needs of twice-exceptional students.* Gilsum, NH: Avocus.

Strip, C. A., & Hirsch, G. (2000). *Helping gifted children soar: A practical guide for parents and teachers.* Scottsdale, AZ: Great Potential Press.

Webb, J. T., Amend, E. R., Webb, N. E., Goerss, J., Beljan, P., & Olenchak, F. R. (2004). *Misdiagnosis and dual diagnoses of gifted children an adults: ADHD, bipolar, OCD, Asperger's, depression, and other disorders.* Scottsdale, AZ: Great Potential Press.

Weinfeld, R., Barnes-Robinson, L., Jeweler, S., & Roffman Shevitz, B. (2006). *Smart kids with learning difficulties: Overcoming obstacles and realizing potential.* Waco, TX: Prufrock Press.

Chapter 40

Attention Deficit/Hyperactivity Disorder: A Difficult Diagnosis

by Sylvia Rimm

A READER from St. George, UT, writes: "My child has been diagnosed with attention-deficit-disorder, and I can't get anyone to really explain what this is. How do I know if the diagnosis is correct? What are the symptoms of this disorder? Does my son have to take drugs to control it?"

Many parents of gifted children who have school-related problems have been told by teachers that their children may have attention deficit disorders. Parents struggle with whether or not to ask physicians to provide medication for the problem and are not sure how to determine if their children truly have the disorder. The problem is exacerbated because the symptoms may be caused biochemically, environmentally, or both.

Teachers also are uncertain whether or not to suggest that an attention disorder may be at the root of a student's problems. Several teachers of gifted children report that high percentages (as much as 30%–50%) of children in their special classes receive medication for Attention Deficit/Hyperactivity Disorder (ADHD).

It is important for parents to know what symptoms of ADHD to look for because their ability to communicate observations will be important for diagnosis purposes. There are two types of ADHD: inattentive and hyperactive-impulsive. The characteristics of both types are listed in Figure 40.1. The greatest problem with the characteristics is that they also describe many typical children and many gifted children.

Characteristics of ADHD Inattentive Type

- Inattentiveness
- Forgetfulness
- Disorganization
- Carelessness
- Lack of follow through
- Easily distracted
- Poor listening
- Daydreaming

Characteristics of ADHD Hyperactive-Impulsive Type

- Fidgety
- Restless
- Overactive
- Excessively talkative
- Difficulty with waiting turns
- Intrusive (interrupts)
- Impulsive (talks or acts without thinking)

Figure 40.1. Characteristics of each type of ADHD.

As a matter of fact, some of them are typical of gifted children, so it is important not to make the mistake of assuming your children have ADHD unless:

- They show many of these symptoms.
- The symptoms are extreme.
- The symptoms began before age 7.
- The symptoms are present in more than one environment (e.g., home and school).

Actual diagnosis of this disorder should be made by a qualified and experienced professional. Psychologists, psychiatrists, pediatricians, or counselors are typically trained to make an ADHD diagnosis. Medication should not be used for diagnosis. Children without ADHD also may seem to have an improved attention span with medication but they should not be given it because of potential side effects. To compound the confusion, there is no definitive test for ADHD. Instead, observation checklists based on the characteristics of the disorder are administered to parents and teachers, and the results are reviewed by an appropriate mental health professional. It also is helpful to observe children in their school environment. When an objective professional compares a child's behavior to that of other children, and notices the positive and negative attention the child attracts, it can help to determine if the child's symptoms are caused biologically or environmentally.

Other Causes of ADHD-Like Symptoms

To determine if your child has a true attention deficit disorder, you have to be aware of other life events that may produce similar symptoms. These include allergies, inappropriate school curriculum (e.g., undiagnosed learning disabilities or lack of challenge); too much positive or negative attention at home or school; traumatic experiences at home (e.g., divorce, illnesses, accidents); extreme sibling rivalry; parents giving children too much power; or parents inconsistently applying family rules.

Some of the special characteristics of giftedness can be misinterpreted as ADHD behavior. Many gifted children have high energy and some seem to need little sleep. They can manage complexity and may be involved in more than one project at a time. Therefore, it may seem like they are inattentive because they can attend to so much at once. In addition, verbally gifted children often receive much attention for their verbosity, which encourages them to use continuous talk to attract attention. They may talk out of turn and talk too much. Also, the intellectual needs of gifted children often are not met in the regular classroom, which leads many gifted children to pay little attention to their lessons out of boredom.

You may wish to make some changes in your home environment before seeking professional help. Some changes you can make at home include:
- Structure your child's time positively.
- Encourage your child's interests.

- Be sure your child is sufficiently intellectually stimulated at home and school.
- Minimize roughhousing but provide appropriate, physically stimulating outlets like sports.
- Eliminate violent television and computer games.
- Communicate with and support the child's school.
- Avoid saying negative things in front of the child about him or her.
- Develop consistent household rules of conduct and discipline.
- Follow through firmly with appropriate consequences.

Next Steps

If the problems continue after observing your child's behavior and making changes in your home environment, you may need to consider medication or other treatment. Consult a mental health professional who will work with you, your child, and the school. Be sure the mental health professional has knowledge and experience in the field of attention deficit disorders and does not have a reputation for overdiagnosing the disorder.

If your child is diagnosed as having ADHD, he or she can be treated with behavioral psychotherapy and a stimulant medication such as Ritalin or Adderall. However, don't hurry to your doctors to ask for medication even if your child's characteristics match those on the list. Try behavioral changes first. Medications can have side effects such as sleeplessness and loss of appetite. There is no long-term research that finds that children's achievement improves with the use of medication. The medications should only be used with careful supervision by a physician. For some children who have severe symptoms, medication can be very helpful for control of both attention and impulsivity. Sometimes medication is only needed temporarily. For others it continues to be important through adulthood. It is important to have periodic monitoring. Remember, medication alone is not enough. You and your children also need to make some behavioral and environmental changes.

Suggestions for Teachers

Below are some suggestions for teachers to use with children who exhibit behavior problems or show symptoms of ADHD:

- *Use moderate praise words to encourage children when you find them behaving well.* The praise should be geared to the characteristics you are trying to encourage (e.g., gentle, kind, caring, sharing, good thinking, loving, good helper, persevering, good concentration, creative thinking). Extreme praise may be counterproductive.

- *Handle inappropriate behavior privately.* Overt negative comments will only trigger more negative behavior. It is not always possible to ignore or signal children privately without drawing negative attention, but it will be helpful in the long run.

- *Develop a "time-out" policy.* Explain to children how you plan to use the time-out when they are in a good frame of mind. You also can permit them to use time-out voluntarily if they feel they need a little time to themselves. Quietly escorting them to time-out will be appropriate if they are out of control. Be sure they understand that it is your way of helping them to get themselves under control and that it will not be for very long. If the child has hurt another, have him apologize to the child privately after time-out.

- *Use a sticker or star system to reward good days.* The stickers can be awarded at home where they can be placed on a calendar or in a sticker book so children can see their improvement. Again, this sticker system should be private with absolutely no class attention. Do not ask the class to help the child with his problems. It may make children's problems worse.

- *Using positive signals is another helpful way to encourage children's concentration.* Explain to the child that you are watching how well he is concentrating and paying attention. When you notice him working hard, you might wink your eye at him or scratch your head (pick one). Although no one else will know, he will know that you've noticed his good behavior. He will feel as if you are watching for his good behavior, and it should increase.

- *Be sure to provide appropriately challenging materials.* Gifted children are sometimes uneven in their abilities and may seem challenged part of the time but become bored when material they've learned long ago is retaught.

There is much that parents and teachers can do to help children with ADHD control their symptoms and outbursts. If medication becomes necessary, make sure that it is administered judiciously by a professional with experience treating ADHD.

Chapter 41

Parenting Gifted Children With ADHD

by Sidney M. Moon

O NE of the most neglected subpopulations of gifted students with multiple exceptionalities is gifted children with Attention Deficit/Hyperactivity Disorder (ADHD). I first became interested in gifted children with ADHD when one of my sons was diagnosed with ADHD in middle school. The diagnosis transformed my son's life. Behaviors, habits, and frustrations that had been inexplicable suddenly made sense to both my son and I. For example, we understood for the first time why he had so much difficulty staying in his seat at meal times and why he was underachieving in school. Perhaps more importantly, we had a direction for the development of coping strategies. Once my son understood the nature of his disorder, he was able to use his intelligence to develop strategies to overcome it. Over the next 6 years, he transformed himself into a well-adjusted, well-disciplined, and high-achieving college student with a large circle of friends.

My experience with my son was further reinforced in my family counseling practice where I specialized in working with families of gifted children. I found that most of the families who came to me for help had children with multiple exceptionalities and that the most frequent additional exceptionality was ADHD. As I worked with these families during a period of 10 years, I experienced firsthand their frustrations with both the behavioral effects of the disorder and the inability of schools to meet their child's needs.

To learn more about the characteristics of gifted children with ADHD, I worked with a colleague with expertise in ADHD to design a comparative case study. The purpose of our study was to compare the characteristics of three boys with both giftedness and ADHD to boys who had only one of the two exceptionalities. In other words, we compared gifted boys with ADHD to three gifted boys without ADHD and three boys with ADHD whose intelligence was in the average range. We focused our study on the learning characteristics of the students and their emotional, social, and family characteristics. We found that the gifted children in our study with ADHD were quite vulnerable to social-emotional adjustment problems. Their emotional difficulties included immaturity, emotionality, and struggles coping with the large gap between their delayed social-emotional development and their advanced cognitive development. Social problems included annoying and/or aggressive social behavior and difficulties handling peer rejection.

The social-emotional difficulties experienced by the boys with ADHD and giftedness in our study were judged by our research team to be more severe than those experienced by all three boys with ADHD alone and much more severe than those experienced by the other two boys with giftedness alone. The remaining gifted boy was experiencing social-emotional difficulties we attributed to a recent divorce and remarriage. To put it simply, the boys with giftedness and ADHD in our study were experiencing a lot of stress, as were their families.

Parenting strategies that seemed to help buffer the stress were different for participants who were intellectually gifted than for other participants. Parents of the gifted boys reported that their child was helped by one-on-one conversations about rules and the reasons for them, nurturing the child's creativity, and encouraging independence. Parents of the boys with average intelligence, on the other hand, reported that their children were helped by shared family activities such as fishing, wrestling, playing games, going for drives, or attending car shows. These differences may have been due to differences in stimulation preferences in the two groups. All of the boys with ADHD also needed higher than normal levels of stimulation for optimal functioning, which is typical of children with ADHD. However, the boys with

ADHD and average intelligence preferred concrete, sensory, and social stimulation (e.g., sports, building things, computers, group learning), whereas the intellectually gifted boys with ADHD preferred cognitive, language-based, and imaginative stimulation (e.g., learning, reading, creative dramatics).

Unfortunately, intellectual giftedness did not protect our participants from the problems associated with ADHD. Indeed, all six boys with ADHD had similar difficulties getting on track (organizing, attending to and following directions, starting the day, starting text-based assignments), staying on track (failing to sustain attention or work production, underachievement), and managing group work and homework. Such difficulties are typical in children with attention deficits and often appear to adults to represent lack of motivation when they really result from impairments in the brain circuits responsible for self-regulation. The boys with giftedness alone, on the other hand, liked school and had excellent attentional profiles, with the exception of one boy who was experiencing considerable family stress. In summary, boys with giftedness and ADHD in our study had difficulty succeeding academically and socially in classrooms designed for gifted students where most of their gifted peers had strong self-regulatory and social abilities.

The National Research Center on the Gifted and Talented commissioned Felice Kaufmann, Layne Kalbfleisch, and Xavier Castellanos to write a monograph answering the question "What do we really know about attention deficit disorders and gifted students?" Their monograph stressed that researchers have neglected this population of students so we don't yet know as much as we need to know to help them. What we do know is that it is vital to identify gifted children with ADHD early and accurately in order to maximize their potential and prevent them from being misunderstood by adults and themselves. They concluded their monograph with 10 recommendations for working with intellectually gifted children who have been identified by a comprehensive assessment as having ADHD.

The following five of their recommendations are particularly relevant to parents.

1. *Explore multiple perspectives in your pursuit of information about ADHD.* The literature on gifted children with ADHD is still

growing and very few school personnel are trained to work with them, so parents need to inform themselves. The best way to do this is to learn about the characteristics of giftedness and ADHD, noting which characteristics from each exceptionality seem relevant to your child (see resources at the end of this article).

2. *Become familiar with a variety of educational and behavioral strategies to determine which combinations might be effective for the individual child.* My own experience in working with gifted children with ADHD suggests that "what works" is very individualized. Therefore, parents and children need to be creative in thinking of possible coping strategies. This requires both knowledge of the workings of ADHD and a lot of experimentation to determine the strategies that will be successful for a particular child. For example, the need of the ADHD child for additional stimulation when working on routine tasks might be met by listening to music and/or watching television while working, taking frequent activity breaks, or trying to accomplish a certain amount of work before a 3-minute egg timer goes off. Parents can suggest some of these strategies and then encourage their child to try them on an experimental basis. Because all strategies tend to have a short shelf-life with this population (i.e., they stop working when the novelty wears off), the process may need to be repeated frequently.

3. *Be cautious about promises of "quick fixes"—whether behavioral, educational, or medical.* ADHD is a real disorder that cannot be "cured," only managed. There are no quick fixes. Persistence and patience are needed to help a child with ADHD overcome his or her disability.

4. *Be aware that individuals with ADHD have their greatest difficulties in the "output" stage of cognitive processing.* This recommendation points to one of the greatest frustrations experienced by these children and those who care about them. They can plan but they can't implement. They have the will but not the way. They set goals but can't achieve them. Their disorder affects their ability to self-regulate and to output what they know.

Parents need to understand that gifted children with ADHD may lag 2 to 4 years behind gifted children without the disorder in their ability to self-monitor, handle long-term projects, and keep track of their belongings. Parents can help by working with their child to identify "small steps" they can take to improve these abilities and by being patient with slow progress.

5. *Model and support the process of "knowing thyself."* This may be the most important recommendation for parents of gifted children with ADHD. To be successful in life, these children must come to know themselves very well. They must recognize and celebrate their strengths while finding ways to compensate for their weaknesses. Yet gaining self-knowledge is difficult for them due to the nature of their disorder. They need emotional support, accurate feedback, and positive modeling to understand and accept themselves.

In my experience, parents are absolutely crucial to the development of gifted children with ADHD. Parents know the whole child. They have observed their child's development and characteristics firsthand over many years. They are in the best position to provide the unconditional love and patient support that are so essential to these children. If you suspect that your child demonstrates both high ability and ADHD, don't assume that you have to proceed entirely on your own, or that the school will recognize the challenge easily. Do not hesitate to express your concerns to your child's teacher, principal, or counselor, or to make an appointment to discuss your child's behavior with the gifted education coordinator or special education director. Share with them the behavior that you are observing in your child, and ask for their assistance and support. The recommended resources at the end of this article provide a starting point for parents who want to learn more about ADHD in order to better understand and nurture their child, or who want to share information with concerned educators.

Resources

Books

Barkley, R. A. (2000). *Taking charge of ADHD: The complete, authoritative guide for parents* (Rev. ed.). New York, NY: Guilford.

Cohen, M. W. (1998). *The attention zone: A parents' guide to Attention Deficit/ Hyperactivity Disorder.* Washington, DC: Routledge.

Fowler, M. (2006). *Attention deficit disorders: Educator's manual* (2nd ed.). Fairfax, VA: Children and Adults with Attention Deficit Disorders.

Garber, S. W., Garber, M. D., & Spizman, R. F. (1996). *Beyond Ritalin: Facts about medication and other strategies for helping children, adolescents, and adults with attention deficit disorders.* New York, NY: Harper Perennial.

Iseman, J. S., Silverman, S. M., & Jeweler, S. (2010). *101 school success tools for students with ADHD.* Waco, TX: Prufrock Press.

Kaufmann, F., Kalbfleisch, M. L., & Castellanos, F. X. (2000). *Attention deficit disorders and gifted students: What do we really know?* (RM00146). Storrs: University of Connecticut, The National Research Center on the Gifted and Talented.

Reif, S. F. (1993). *How to reach and teach ADD/ADHD children: Practical strategies, and interventions for helping children with attention problems and hyperactivity.* West Nyack, NY: The Center for Applied Research in Education.

Silverman, S. M., Iseman, J. S., & Jeweler, S. (2009). *School success for kids with ADHD.* Waco, TX: Prufrock Press.

Websites

Attention Deficit Disorder Association—http://www.add.org

CHADD: Children and Adults with Attention Deficit/Hyperactivity Disorder— http://www.chadd.org

MentalHelp.Net—http://www.mentalhelp.net

National Institute of Mental Health—http://www.nimh.nih.gov/index.shtml

PART VIII

Social and Emotional Needs

by Maureen Neihart and Liang See Tan

RESEARCH findings show that the influence of home is greater than the school. A home environment can contribute to the growth of gifted and talented individuals by building mental energy and psychological resources that, in turn, enable gifted individuals to face challenges either in school or life. In this section, the authors examine the social and emotional needs of gifted children and the various roles parents and family play in meeting those needs. You may be surprised to learn that the phrase, "social and emotional needs of the gifted" is relatively new. It was first used around 1980 when a series of circumstances prompted a surge of renewed interest in the social and emotional development of high-ability children. In the collection of chapters that follow, you will take a tour through some of the major themes and guiding questions that have dominated the literature during the past 30 years.

All of the chapters build on a foundational understanding that the environment plays a pivotal but complex role in nurturing children's gifts and talents. We identified several themes among these chapters. The themes include the ways a gifted child's uneven development (asynchrony) impacts parenting, characteristics of gifted children that

411

are sometimes a concern (e.g., perfectionism, high sensitivity), gender-specific strategies, and the importance of parents modeling the behaviors and attitudes that they want to develop in their children.

The chapters in this section have been divided into eight loose categories: general issues of social-emotional development with chapters by Beth Andrews and Henry J. Nicols and Susan Baum; asynchronous development, featuring the Joan Franklin Smutny chapter; gender, with chapters contributed by Sally Reis, Thomas Hébert, and Leighann Pennington; a chapter by Sylvia Rimm on underachievement; social responsibility chapters by Joseph S. Renzulli and his colleagues, Rachel E. Sytsma and Robin M. Schader, and Barbara A. Lewis; a look at depression and suicide by Andrea Dawn Frazier and Tracy L. Cross; chapters on counseling by Jean Sunde Peterson and Andrew Mahoney; and finally, a chapter on perfectionism by Michael Pyryt. The chapters also cross these boundaries to cover various aspects of social-emotional development, as discussed below.

Three of the chapters provide broad frameworks for parenting gifted children but from different viewpoints. In his chapter on "Developing Giftedness for a Better World," Renzulli and his associates identify six factors that impact giftedness: optimism, courage, sensitivity to human concerns, physical/mental energy, vision/sense of destiny, and romance with a topic of discipline. These complex elements support cognitive growth such as academic achievement, research skills, creativity, and problem-solving skills. Mahoney offers a conceptual map that includes four components—validation, affirmation, affiliation, and affinity—and explains how parents can answer a series of four questions to guide them in creating a "good fit" for their child. Peterson looks at the parallel development of parents and children and discusses how parents can model effective coping behaviors in their children. These authors recommend practical steps parents can take to effectively meet the social and emotional needs of their gifted children. All of them stress the value and need of parental modeling, particularly when it comes to serving others, and appropriate risk taking.

Four of the chapters in this collection explore topics of common concern to parents: stress, depression/suicide, underachievement, and perfectionism. For instance, in their chapter on "High Achievers—

Actively Engaged but Secretly Stressed," Nicols and Baum describe physiological and psychological manifestations of stress as high achievers striving for excellence. Popular psychologist Sylvia Rimm explains how well-meaning overempowerment can lead to underachievement in some families, and Michael Pyryt offers parents five broad strategies they can adopt to help their children make the most of their perfectionism. Finally, Frazier and Cross clarify the facts about gifted children and suicide, stressing that the evidence doesn't suggest gifted children have any greater risk and cautioning parents to not expect extremes in behavior as the norm for gifted children.

Differences in gifted boys' and girls' social and emotional development also are frequent themes across many of the chapters in this collection. Hébert's chapter about enhancing communication between fathers and their talented sons, for example, points out that the heightened sensitivity and emotional intensity so characteristic of gifted individuals can be potentially frightening and even painful for gifted boys if they lack appropriate channels for understanding, expressing, and sharing these feelings. Pennington advocates writing as a means to develop identity and self-actualization in boys. She emphasizes that writing is also an expressive outlet that benefits gifted boys' social and emotional well-being, as well as promotes critical and independent thinking skills.

Reis highlights the struggles and dilemmas that gifted and talented girls faced growing up in her chapter, "Overcoming Barriers to Girls' Talent Development." The internal barriers she identifies include abilities, talents, perfectionism, attributing success to luck rather than ability, poor peer choices, and a tendency to be overly self-critical. External barriers she describes include decisions about relationships and familial duty and caring. Although both Hébert and Pennington bring to our attention the need to develop talented boys to express and communicate feelings, Reis points out that bright girls are constantly struggling in their female role and living in the dilemmas of balancing personal achievement and social expectations.

Frequently, the authors mention taking action as an effective way to combat the fears or worries gifted children may have about complex social or environmental issues. Although school supports the growth of cognitive attributes, parents should not leave the growth of their bright children solely in the hand of the schools. Parents who take the time to enjoy learning with their children also reap the rewards of their effort and perseverance. Hébert and Lewis, for instance, both discuss the role volunteering can play in reducing a child's anxiety, promoting empathy, and in channeling a heightened sensitivity and advanced moral understanding into compassion and service for others. They each include numerous practical ideas for how parents can get started. Smutny and Andrews take different approaches to a common concern parents of gifted children have: how to help gifted children cope with the emotional impact of their advanced understanding and insight about themselves and the world around them and their deep need for a life purpose. Smutny examines the issue broadly, stressing the potential for building resilience and courage, while Andrews focuses more sharply on how gifted children may cope with traumatic events they hear about or are exposed to directly.

Because there are many issues raised by the authors, reflect upon the following questions to guide your thoughts as you read this section:

1. What comments or scenarios mentioned in these chapters resonate the most with your personal experience?
2. What are the strengths, weaknesses, and learning profiles of your children?
3. How do you learn together as a family? What are you modeling?
4. Do you think the authors' recommendations are good for all children? What is it about gifted children in particular that makes the authors' suggestions relevant and useful?
5. In what ways did the chapters affirm what you are already doing with and for your children? Are there any cautions you think you need to heed? What additional steps recommended by the authors can you take to strengthen your children's resilience and develop their talents?

Some gaps remain in our understanding of the social, emotional, and cognitive development of gifted children. One question that remains unanswered in the literature has to do with developmental differences observed in gifted children. We still don't know whether these differences are true qualitative differences or merely an expression of accelerated development. If we were to compare a group of gifted 10-year-olds with a group of average ability 12- or 13-year-olds, for example, would we find that they are more similar than different? Or would we observe characteristics in the gifted children that are not present in the older children? A second question has to do with gender differences. Do boys and girls face similar stressors at home? We know from numerous studies that boys and girls have very different experiences in school and in life, but what about in the home? Do differences persist there as well? Are there gender differences in the definition of success? How do we help gifted children succeed who do not have ideal parenting practices at home? There also continues to be a great lack of understanding regarding cultural differences in the development of gifted children. Yet we know from the literature that enormous differences sometimes exist among gifted children from low-income and high-income families and among children from various cultural groups.

Chapter 42

Raising Bright Children in a Scary World

by Beth Andrews

Bloody images of a school shooting flashed across national news as parents, families, and friends grieved over the tragedy at Virginia Tech in 2007. No matter how hard we try to protect our children, no place seems safe or exempt from violence. So, how do we help our children cope in a capricious, unpredictable, and sometimes very dangerous world? And how do we cope with being a parent in such a scary world?

Sometimes I wish my daughter wasn't quite so smart. She hears and pays attention to things in the media long before she is emotionally ready to deal with what they mean. I had to stop listening to the news in the car when she was 3 because she would quiz me endlessly about every news story and why the people did what they did. That was fine . . . unless the news stories were about rape or murder or war. Then she would worry about the victims, and about whether she was next.

We were living one mile from a local suburban high school when two students walked in with machine guns and opened fire on the student body. They killed 10 students, one teacher, and then themselves. Many more were severely injured, and some were permanently disabled. My daughter was 4 at the time.

My cousins had attended this high school several years before the tragedy. It was the kind of upper middle class neighborhood where parents move to make sure their children have a good education and are safe from the violence of the inner city. Kids grow up there participating in soccer and Little League, and in the summer they all swim at the neighborhood pool together. People know their neighbors and watch each other's kids grow up. My cousins knew the teacher who was killed—he had been their coach. My aunt was a friend of the school librarian and the principal.

I was at work when I heard the news. Everyone just needed to hold his or her children close that day. I left early, picked my daughter up at day care, and began the drive home. Traffic is usually bad in big cities, but on this day it was worse than usual. Many of the streets were blocked off, and there was a constant drone of sirens. The drive home was interminable. Of course, she had endless questions about why there were so many police cars and fire trucks.

I tried to shield her from too much news coverage, but it was impossible. It was all anyone ever talked about. A whole community was devastated and struggling to understand. Understand what? No one was even sure what there was to understand. How does something like this happen and no one sees it coming?

The entire youth group from our church was in the school when it happened, and some of them were hospitalized. All of them were traumatized. The parents were in shock for a long time, as was the whole community. I'm glad I wasn't the minister that Sunday. How do you preach a sermon about such devastation? What can you say that makes any sense?

As the days and weeks went by, counselors and other community members volunteered their time to help the 2,000 kids who were in the building that terrible day. Many of them had been hiding anywhere they could find, desperately praying for their lives. Most had lost friends, and some even siblings. I felt guilty about not helping, but I had a 4-year-old to think about.

She had lots of questions. Most of them hurt to answer, partly because there was a keen awareness for every parent in the community that it could have been their child who had died. We'd see a police car and she'd ask, "Mommy, is that policeman going to shoot me?" "No, honey," I'd answer. "The policemen are there to help us and keep us safe." But I had doubts about whether I really believed what I was saying. Certainly, no one had been able to keep these kids safe.

One day, she said, "Mommy, if those bad guys come to my day care, I'm going to hide under the table and tell all my friends to hide, too." I felt as if a knife had stabbed me, but I had to answer calmly.

I tried to reassure her. "Well, honey, if they came to your day care, they couldn't get in. Remember, it's locked."

"But what if they had a key?"

"They couldn't get a key. No one would give them one."

"But what if they broke the window and got in?"

"Well, then, the staff would call the police and they would come and protect you."

"What if they didn't get there soon enough?"

The questions went on and on. Finally, with no other way to reassure her, I said, "Honey, those bad guys can't come to your day care because they are dead, too."

She looked puzzled. "So, how did they die?"

"Am I really going to have to explain suicide to a 4-year-old?" I thought.

I took a deep breath, and said, "Well, they shot themselves."

Now she looked even more puzzled. "But why would they do that?"

"Because they were sick in the head," I explained. "The important part is that you are safe." That seemed to satisfy her for the moment, but it felt like a hollow promise.

The trouble is, I can't really promise that she will be safe. Events such as this have shattered any illusions we might have held that the world is a safe and predictable place that includes devastating hurricanes, tornadoes, and tsunamis. Even worse, we live in a world where people fly airplanes into high-rise buildings, trying to kill as many people as they can, or blow up a building knowing that there is a day care center in the basement. Yet in spite of our anxieties, we have to find ways to cope and to help our children flourish.

How We Cope (or Don't!) as Adults

Following a traumatic event, some adults will experience what mental health professionals call Posttraumatic Stress Disorder (PTSD).

This is essentially a normal reaction to an abnormal event in which the person is physically harmed, perceives that he or she may be harmed, or witnesses someone else being harmed. Examples of events that can trigger this include natural disasters, life-threatening car accidents, being a victim of a violent crime or witnessing it, war, rape, domestic violence, and childhood physical or sexual abuse. The American Psychological Association estimates that approximately 3.6% of adults ages 18–54 experience enough symptoms to be diagnosed with PTSD in any given year. Symptoms of PTSD can show up even months or years later, and typically include some of the following:

- nightmares, which may lead to insomnia;
- flashbacks—suddenly acting or feeling that you are back in the traumatic situation;
- feeling numb or flooded with feelings;
- becoming panicked when faced with "triggers"—sights, sounds, or smells that are reminders of the trauma;
- exaggerated "startle response"—being jumpy and easily startled;
- feeling detached or distant from others, withdrawing;
- "hyper-vigilance"—being on guard or scanning the environment for danger;
- difficulty concentrating;
- irritability or explosive anger;
- avoiding people or situations that are reminders of the trauma;
- losing interest in activities that used to be fun;
- thoughts about the trauma that intrude when you are trying to concentrate on something else;
- being unable to think about the future or acting as if there is no future;
- feeling guilty for your actions during the trauma or because you survived when others did not; and
- sadness, grief, or depression about what happened.

The degree of reaction depends on a number of factors including the duration and severity of the trauma, the strength of our support systems, and whether we have experienced other past traumas that may be reactivated by the current event. It also matters whether it was a natural or human-caused disaster. Generally human-caused traumas are worse, especially if someone caused them we thought we could trust.

Two months after the terrorist attacks on September 11, a full 17% of the adult population in the United States experienced enough symptoms to be diagnosed with PTSD, whether or not they were anywhere near New York City at the time. Over the next 2 years, there was a 49% increase in the number of suicide attempts in the U.S. due to the chronic stress we experienced as a nation. Five years later in 2006, a National Mental Health Association study found that 50% of all Americans and 65% of all parents in the U.S. remained fearful about the threat of terrorism. Obviously even adults are very affected by traumatic events, both individually and collectively as a society.

Most intriguing, however, is the fact that the majority of adults (and children) who experience a trauma do not develop PTSD. This concept has been labeled "resilience." In their book *Promoting Student Resiliency*, Kris Bosworth and Garry Walz defined resilience as "the ability to succeed in the face of adversity . . . the process of self-righting and growth . . . the capacity to meet challenges and become more capable as a result of those experiences." Robert Brooks and Sam Goldstein in *Raising Resilient Children* further described it as,

> the inner strength to deal competently and successfully, day after day, with the challenges and demands [encountered]. . . . Resilience embraces the ability . . . to deal more effectively with stress and pressure, to cope with everyday challenges, to bounce back from disappointments, adversity, and trauma, to develop clear and realistic goals, to solve problems, to relate comfortably with others, and to treat oneself and others with respect.

In other words, it is more than just survival. It is the ability to learn, grow, and become a better person as a result of the trauma, to somehow use this painful experience for good in the long run.

The Impact of Traumatic Events on Children

Of course, we have to start by differentiating between children who are victimized by or directly witness traumatic events and those who just experience them through the media. There is a continuum to the risk of problems based on the amount of exposure, but even children not living in a community where violence or another trauma occurs are affected. Degree of impact also depends on the child's age and developmental level, temperament, awareness, and general sensitivity to outside events.

Adults and children alike are probably more affected by traumatic events today than they were a generation ago. With Internet and satellite TV coverage of news events, information is more immediate and coverage more graphic. The Persian Gulf War in 1991 was the first to have battle scenes broadcast instantaneously around the world and then replayed 24 hours a day. Young children watching these news reports cannot cognitively differentiate between something happening halfway around the world and something posing an immediate danger to them and their family.

According to Lorna Knox, in her 2004 book, *Scary News*, we are bombarded constantly with more and more information than we were even 10 or 20 years ago. The end result is that news events feel more personal and evoke emotions at a faster pace than ever before. This may be a contributing factor to the increased rates of depression in children and adolescents in recent years.

Kids worry much more than we realize. For example, a study cited in Paul Foxman's book *The Worried Child: Recognizing Anxiety in Children and Helping Them Heal* showed that 71% of all eighth and ninth graders worry about being shot or stabbed at school. This much emotional material even for adults can become overwhelming, let alone for children who do not yet have the skills or emotional maturity to handle it.

Lastly, numerous studies show that children who are exposed to too much violence at an early age can become desensitized to it. This can happen whether the violence is in the home, in the neighborhood or school, or with violent TV and video games. We would do well as parents to pay close attention to monitoring what our children are exposed to.

Are Gifted Children More Susceptible?

Research is limited in this area, but it stands to reason that many, if not most, gifted children may worry more because they are more aware than others of the world around them. They may intellectually understand all of the possibilities and implications of a situation they see or hear on the news and yet not be at a developmental stage where they are ready to cope with the information emotionally. Our kids may seem mature enough to handle certain situations because they can reason as if they were older. Don't let that fool you. They still need us as adults to protect them from situations they are not emotionally ready to handle.

Two other factors come into play here. First, according to Lesley Sword in "Parenting Emotionally Intense Gifted Children," gifted children often have a heightened sensitivity and are more intense emotionally than other kids. This is part of their giftedness and a wonderful asset, but it also can be anxiety provoking and painful for the child (and frustrating for the parent!). They can be much more affected emotionally by the events around them.

Secondly, we parents may carry emotional intensity, heightened awareness, and resulting anxiety with us. Our kids watch us and follow our lead. They also may intuitively sense, and even act out, our feelings. I call my daughter my "little mirror." We need to learn healthy ways to express our feelings so that we can model this behavior rather than intensifying our children's anxiety.

Helping Children Cope With Scary Events

In *Scary News*, Knox discussed ways to help children cope with what they hear and experience in the world. The hope is to do more than minimize the damage done by this exposure to world events: "We can give our children the skills to cope with the scary news and have a life filled with light, hope, joy, and appreciation." The bottom line, she said, is to teach kids to make decisions out of love rather than fear. This happens first and foremost by giving them reliable, loving, and secure relationships with their parents and other adults, and by providing a positive, nurturing environment. In turn, this helps them feel safe and confident when faced with anxiety-provoking situations.

Younger children are just not ready developmentally to watch media coverage of traumatic events in the same way that they are not ready for a horror movie. They are not yet able to separate fact from fiction, put things into perspective, or understand that there is no direct danger to them. Therapists found, for example, that young children who watched media images of the twin towers falling on September 11 believed that every time they saw it again, it was happening again. Even in cases where they might be directly affected (e.g., their parent is deployed to a war zone), they do not need to be frightened unnecessarily. They should not be allowed to watch TV news or experience other media images without close parental supervision.

At any age, Knox suggested carefully examining whether the information is unavoidable and necessary, whether it provides an opportunity for growth, and whether your child is ready for it. At age 4, my daughter was not ready for what she saw and heard but it was so pervasive that exposure to the event was unavoidable. I sheltered her from the news as much as possible, then talked with her about what she did hear. In fact, her most vivid memory of the event is of me pulling her away from the TV!

According to Knox, it is wise to refrain from discussing adult topics when children might be listening in, to provide comfort and show affection in stressful times, and to keep routines in place. Talk with children about their fears directly, giving them facts and reassurance. Lastly, communicate to children that we can all learn and grow from each experience, whether it be positive or negative. We can choose to become stronger and wiser as a result.

Talking with children about the fact that the world isn't a perfect place is important. There is a struggle between good and evil, and bad things do happen. Good also can come out of an evil situation. Most children's movies have a theme along these lines, which can be used as a starting point for discussion. In doing so, however, we need to be cautious to use age-appropriate language, keeping in mind the child's developmental level. We need to use "honesty with restraint." That is, tell the truth and answer their questions but without giving a lot of details for which they may not be ready.

In a disaster or other situation of trauma, adults usually want to do something to help. They donate food, clothing, and money. They volunteer their time or expertise in whatever way they can. This helps them feel as if they are contributing and wards off helplessness and hopelessness. Children are no different. In doing something to help the victims of a trauma, they feel as if they are important and contributing. They also learn an important value—the importance of reaching out to help others. As parents, we can help them find a way to help—for example, contributing part of their allowance, drawing pictures and cards for victims or rescue workers, or helping deliver food and clothing.

How Much to Protect

Most aware and caring parents these days struggle with the balance between vigilantly protecting our children from harm versus not wanting to be overprotective or discourage kids from experiencing the world. We are much more aware of the dangers awaiting our children in the world than at any time in the past. Twenty years ago there was no such thing as an Internet sex predator. Drugs were less prevalent at such an early age. School shootings were not at such a large scale nor were they national news. It would have been unthinkable to watch an execution live on the computer. The world is changing and we must change with it. So, how do we as parents teach our children to be aware and cautious without scaring them too much or making them constantly anxious?

There is no easy answer, no formula to follow. We face this same question with each new situation:

- "Yes, I know your friend's mother lets her stay home alone, but I do not believe that you are old enough."

- "No, you may not go to your friend's house unless I know the parents."
- "You may ride your bicycle but only on this street where I can see you and only with a helmet."
- "You may no longer play with this friend because he thinks it is funny to lie, steal, and hit you."
- "I know you are angry about it, but I will monitor what websites you visit and not let you e-mail with people you don't know."

Talk with other parents who share your values and whose opinions you trust. But above all, trust your gut. If it feels unsafe, it probably is—err on the side of safety. Don't be afraid to say no just because other kids are allowed to do something. Foxman suggested that we teach children about high-risk situations (e.g., Internet child molesters and how they work), but this must be balanced with reassuring kids that although there are real dangers to look out for, in many cases the chances are low of something bad happening.

Strengths Our Children Have That Can Help

Bright children have strengths that can be used to help them cope. First, they have a higher reasoning ability than many other children. They are able to understand concepts at an earlier age and are more verbal and able to discuss their thoughts and feelings. This can be used to give them an edge on understanding community or world events.

Second, you are concerned enough to read this so we know they have at least one caring and involved parent or other adult in their life. This love and security is probably the most important factor in building resilience. Even if they go through a trauma, they will be much more capable of bouncing back if they know you are there to support them.

Last, their emotional sensitivity gives them a greater capacity for empathy and understanding of the importance of justice. As parents, we can further emphasize the importance of having compassion for and giving to others. We can teach them that they have a responsibility to make the world a better place. We can give them the tools to stand up for what is right, help others, and create hope. Our children are the leaders of tomorrow, with the capacity to change the world. As we guide them in how to use their strengths, they can and will make a difference.

Resources

Books for Children

Crist, J. (2004). *What to do when you're scared and worried: A guide for kids.* Minneapolis, MN: Free Spirit.

Holmes, M. (2000). *A terrible thing happened: A story for children who have witnessed violence or trauma.* Washington, DC: Magination Press.

Shuman, C. (2003). *Jenny is scared! When sad things happen in the world.* Washington, DC: Magination Press.

Resources for Parents and Teachers

American Red Cross. (2001). *Facing fear curriculum.* Washington, DC: Author.

American Red Cross, & Federal Emergency Management Agency. (1998). *Helping children cope with disaster.* Washington, DC: Author.

Andrews, B. (2006). *Coping with post traumatic stress disorder.* Hawthorne, NY: Sunburst Visual Media.

Andrews, B. (2005). *Lifemap to coping with anxiety.* Hawthorne, NY: Bureau for At-Risk Youth.

DeWolfe, D. (n.d.) *Helping children cope with a traumatic event.* Washington, DC: American Red Cross. Retrieved from http://www.helpstartshere. org/kids-and-families/family-safety/parents-and-terrorism.html

La Greca, A., Silverman, W. K., Vernberg, E. M., & Roberts, M. C. (Eds.). (2002). *Helping children cope with disasters and terrorism.* Washington, DC: American Psychological Association.

Matthews, D., & Foster, J. (2005). *Being smart about gifted children: A guide for parents and educators.* Scottsdale, AZ: Great Potential Press.

Zucker, B. (2008). *Anxiety-free kids: An interactive guide for parents and children.* Waco, TX: Prufrock Press.

Websites

American Academy of Child & Adolescent Psychiatry—http://www.aacap.org
American Psychological Association—http://www.apa.org/helpcenter
MentalHelp.Net—http://www.mentalhelp.net
National Child Traumatic Stress Network—http://www.nctsn.org
National Institute of Mental Health—http://www.nimh.nih.gov
Raising Resilient Children—http://www.raisingresilientkids.com

References

American Psychological Association. (2006). *The effects of trauma do not have to last a lifetime.* Washington, DC: Author.

Bosworth, K., & Walz, G. (2005). *Promoting student resiliency.* Alexandria, VA: American Counseling Association Foundation.

Brooks, R., & Goldstein, S. (2001). *Raising resilient children.* New York, NY: McGraw-Hill Books.

Foxman, P. (2004). *The worried child: Recognizing anxiety in children and helping them heal.* Alameda, CA: Hunter House.

Knox, L. (2004). *Scary news: 12 ways to raise joyful children when the headlines are full of fear.* Nevada City, CA: Crystal Clarity Publishers.

National Mental Health Association. (2006). *Coping with tragedy: The fifth anniversary of 9/11.* Alexandria, VA: Author.

Sword, L. (2006). *Parenting emotionally intense gifted children.* Retrieved from http://talentdevelop.com/articles/ParentingEIGC.html

Chapter 43

High Achievers—Actively Engaged but Secretly Stressed: Keys to Helping Youngsters With Stress Reduction

by Henry J. Nicols and Susan Baum

"My daughter was just elected to student council and has been admitted to three Advanced Placement courses. Now she is trying out for the school play. I know she will be disappointed if she doesn't get a leading role."

"My son is annoyed. The school is offering moot court competitions at the same time as basketball. Now he will have to make a choice. I am considering calling the guidance counselor to see if the times can be rescheduled."

"I am trying to schedule a time for my daughter to take SAT prep course. If she doesn't score above 1,200, I don't know what we can do."

Do these comments sound familiar? Is your son or daughter overscheduled? Is your child experiencing the negative consequences of too much stress? We know that stress is an important and necessary part of life. It helps us reach our peak performance, enjoy the highs of life, and protects us from some disasters. However, when too many stressors overwhelm us in our lives, there can be both physical and emotional manifestations.

Many bright adolescents are earning top grades and are actively involved in a variety of activities. Ostensibly they appear healthy and happy. But for some, their productivity causes them to be secretly stressed. We use the term hidden stress syndrome to describe the subtle but problematic stress that many bright youngsters are experiencing, especially during adolescence. In general, they may seem to be happy, goal directed, and reaping academic rewards for their efforts. However, upon closer investigation, a different picture emerges. Today, we are seeing youngsters with physiological symptoms, generalized feelings of anxiety, and a sense of urgency about college admission. Many of these manifestations of stress had their genesis much earlier when the youngsters were in elementary school.

We know that gifted children are particularly susceptible to stress for many reasons. Their high ability and perception that they must achieve encourage them to bite off much more than they can chew. Inadvertently, the adults in their world have contributed to the problem. You have provided many opportunities for your children to develop their talents as a means to assure them a better-than-average chance to succeed in a competitive world. In so doing parents and teachers alike may have become a part of the problem, not the solution.

Over the past 20 years, numerous studies have examined the social and emotional issues underlying the manifestations of stress in bright children. Judy Galbraith and Jim Delisle's *Gifted Kids Survival Guides* describe some of the complaints of gifted youngsters. Among them were the lack of challenge in school, inappropriate peer group, and expectations by adults for the children to perform perfectly.

Partially in reaction to those issues, parents have created and sought out talent development activities for their gifted youngsters. They have encouraged interaction with friends with similar interests and abilities. Schools, too, have provided an enriched environment with more challenging curricula and exciting afterschool programs. Summer programs at universities as well as outstanding, and often competitive, extracurricular activities in the arts, athletics, debate, writing, and mock trial competitions are just a few of the activities that are available to bright, motivated students. Many secondary schools offer accelerated math and science courses, Advanced Placement classes, and the International Baccalaureate program, as well as community service and other independent study opportunities.

The problem for some high-potential youngsters is not the lack of challenging opportunities, but the students' lack of skill in making appropriate choices. Parents and teachers have been somewhat remiss in teaching gifted youngsters how to make choices, manage their time, or identify their passions. In fact, due to the competitive nature of their social setting or environment, and parents' desire to have bright children accepted at the most prestigious universities, some students begin to harbor the belief that doing more is in their best interest. Growing up in today's world is very much different than it was just a generation ago. Child development specialists Laurence Coleman and Michael Sanders call attention to the fact that the social milieu has a profound effect on the adjustment of youth. The expectations placed on bright youngsters in today's competitive society potentially place these youngsters at risk of the negative effects of stress. Adolescence is an especially trying time for children as they begin to establish their own identities. They test limits, challenge parents, and explore possibilities. The choices they make are influenced by the social context in which they live. For bright and talented children the choices today often are overwhelming.

What Stresses Today's Gifted and Talented Adolescents?

During the past year we had the pleasure of conducting a series of focus groups with high-ability students in middle and high school about their perceptions of the stress in their lives. The results offer some new insight into the lives of adolescents today and confirm their lack of ability to manage stress. As you might have suspected, gifted students recognize that they are experiencing significant negative stress. School is chief among their stressors. Students worry about their grades and parental reactions. Middle school students fear disappointing their parents, while high school students often believe that grades lower than an "A" jeopardize college acceptance. These students typically are enrolled in all honors or high-level classes; choosing a less demanding course or one based on interest rather than rigor is not an option in their minds. Students feel that they needed to be actively involved in the arts, athletics, and academics in order to be admitted to the college of their choice. For these capable youngsters, high school is the time to build an impressive resume based often on quantity rather than quality of experience. Their interests or passions played a small role in decision making. Interestingly, even though the students feel they had to be involved in sports to maintain the image of the well-rounded student, many said that participating in sports caused considerable stress. Most of these students play at least one competitive sport and report feeling stressed by their coaches' expectations for winning. They fear letting down their coach or team.

Instead of providing safety or a respite from the stresses of the day, friends and relationships offer another source of stress. Many of these bright youngsters are very sensitive and have high expectations for friendships. They worry about disappointing their friends or being disappointed themselves. Trust and loyalty are major issues for them. Because students are overwhelmed with academics and extracurricular activities, they often sacrifice things they value and know are important to their physical well-being. They unanimously admit that they do not have enough time to sleep or eat. Sleep often seems to be the only opportunity for flexibility and is expendable ("I need to do extra homework, I sleep less."). Enjoying time with family, having fun with friends, or just hanging out is high on their wish lists, but often beyond reasonable expectation.

Even in elementary school, children are often overscheduled with little time to amuse themselves, develop their imagination, or dream about the future and their role in it. Little time is available for reading for pleasure, not for an assignment, or creating for the sake of creating.

How Do Our Children Deal With Stress?

We discovered that children might be as overwhelmed by stress as adults. Youngsters have learned inappropriate coping skills from their adult role models. The students talk of feeling angry or sad. But instead of identifying and prioritizing tasks and then tackling the tasks at hand, they often will talk to friends for hours on the phone or watch television to escape. Others simply give up eating and sleeping to get their tasks done. One boy explained that he felt that every hour had to be filled or he would be wasting time.

Some students described feeling physically ill. Their symptoms often included head- and stomachaches. Several students described experiencing tremors. Some talked about crying and generally having difficulty communicating their feelings. They find it especially difficult to communicate these symptoms to adults. Others described feeling irritated and having a difficult time falling asleep. Younger children who feel stressed often spend considerable time with the school nurse complaining of some type of ailment. A principal described her alarm at the increasing number of physical illnesses of youngsters in her district. She described a fourth grader who has recently been diagnosed with ulcers: "He worries about everything."

How Can We Help? Seven Strategies for Stress Management!

Stress is an integral and important part of life. It helps us to achieve more, perform better, and fulfill great expectations. Unmanaged stress often is cited as a major factor contributing to disease and death in adults.

Adults must work to prevent stress from negatively affecting youngsters today. Parents can have a major role in helping their children deal appropriately with the stress in their lives. We have found the following strategies very useful in working with both adults and children, and they may help you understand what causes stress for your youngsters and improve their ability to manage it. (An additional benefit is that you may decrease your own stress as well.)

The first six strategies describe long-term investments that can be used to help create a less stressful lifestyle. The earlier you start practicing these strategies the more you can prevent your children from developing inappropriate levels of anxiety. The last strategy involves techniques for dealing with especially stressful moments. These techniques can help to diffuse short-term, immediate stress and to make the most of a challenging moment.

1. Help Your Children to Identify Their Values, Hopes, and Dreams so That They Live a Life Consistent With Their Values and Goals

Share with them lessons that you have learned about your goals, how you find meaning in life, and how you decide what matters most. Children often report school as a significant stressor because of the way they are encouraged to believe their lives depend on their daily performance. A student told us during a focus group, "It is important to stay up late studying. One bad grade can ruin your life!"

Do you believe that? More importantly, does your son or daughter believe that? Will success in life be contingent upon receiving all A's or taking every honors course? The reality may be that, if there is too much emphasis on grades, students may be pressured beyond what is reasonable and lose sight of what is important. Teen suicide statistics show that, tragically, some children do believe a single failure can lead to a "ruined life." Consequently, paying for that failure with their life becomes an option.

2. Create Opportunities to Identify and Explore the Issues With Your Children

Do you take the time to talk with your sons or daughters about their lives? Consider discussing with them who they are and who they dream of becoming. Too often conversations with children focus on what they accomplish rather than how they feel, what they think, and what they want and need. Your verbal interactions with them are powerful indicators of what your interest is in their lives. The expectation that they will win your praise only if they produce is detrimental to their adjustment and your relationship. One young man we interviewed described his dream of becoming a philosophy professor but instead will apply to business school to please his parents. What message are you giving your child?

3. Use Family Meetings to Discuss Issues

Meeting together allows all members of the family to participate in decision making. When children feel their opinions are valued, they are more likely to talk about what is bothering them. Use a symbol to assure active listening and participation (e.g., we use a heart-shaped pillow). Only the person with the pillow may speak, and until the pillow is relinquished, the possessor has the exclusive right to speak. Everyone gets a turn with the pillow until all have had the chance to say what is on their minds. While making decisions at these meetings, try using Creative Problem Solving—a natural, flexible process that makes solving problems and prioritizing goals constructive and enjoyable, rather than stressful. Many materials are available about this framework for both children and adults. For more information, consult the resources at the end of this article.

4. Establish Weekly "Walk and Talks"

Walking briskly outdoors in the fresh air is healthy in and of itself. This habit can be developed into a lifelong practice. We know that physical activity such as walking not only benefits health but also reduces the negative chemical effects of stress, while at the same time contributes to relationship building. When was the last time you walked? When was the last time you walked holding hands with someone you love? Sound corny? Try it. It works!

5. Create Balance in Your Life

We all need balance in our lives. Balance should include recreation, exercise, and well-balanced diet. Without that balance, stress can become overwhelming. The students we spoke to often skip meals and sleep to complete tasks they believed of greater priority. One young woman remarked, "After completing school assignments, afterschool activities, and homework who has time for fun or sleep?" We asked her when she is happiest. She answered, "I am happiest when I ride my horse and can just be myself."

Her peers agreed, "Having time alone to reflect is wonderful. My favorite time is waiting alone for the school bus. I think and dream. Everything seems possible."

Help your youngster value recreational down time by modeling it for them. Do you have a balance in your life? Most adults model inappropriate stress management behaviors. How about you? Do you have time for fun? Do you take time to do what matters most? Every day?

As Steven Covey describes in *7 Habits of Highly Effective People*, every task in your life can fall into one of four quadrants (see Figure 43.1). Quadrant 1 contains items that are "Important and Urgent." Quadrant 2 lists things that are "Important and Not Urgent." Quadrant 3 includes items that are "Not Important and Urgent." Quadrant 4 describes those things that are "Not Important and Not Urgent."

6. Encourage Your Children to Have a Creative Outlet

Some people engage in creative activities because they find joy in the performance. When people are creating, they are lost in the moment. Stress disappears. Mihaly Csikszentmihalyi, a developmental psychologist who studies creativity and happiness, describes these experiences as being in a "state of flow." What creative activity does your child love for its own sake? Perhaps it is dance, photography, building with LEGOs®, sketching, or writing poetry. Supporting children in pursuing what they love is the single best way that we can help them have a balanced life. During stressful moments or days, taking an hour and playing the piano or writing a poem will have a positive effect on reducing stress.

The strategies briefly described thus far explain long-term investments for creating a less stressful lifestyle. They take time and practice, but will pay healthy dividends. The next strategy describes techniques

Q-1 Important and Urgent	Q-2 Important and Not Urgent
Family crisis	Planning
Project due now	Recreation
Medical emergencies	Relationship building
Studying for tomorrow's test	Doing what matters most
Q-3 Not Important and Urgent	**Q-4 Not Important and Not Urgent**
Most e-mail	TV
Many meetings	Roaming around at the mall
Most telephone calls	Surfing the net
Many tasks with no priority	Endless phone calls

Have members of the family create their own chart by filling in a typical day's activities. Figure out where each of you spends most of your time. Have you considered the effects of spending a majority of time in each of the four quadrants? There are negative and positive effects as summarized below.

Q-1 Important and Urgent	Q-2 Important and Not Urgent
High stress and anxiety	Improved relationships
Risk of heart & other diseases	Doing what matters most to you
(Yes, even our children are getting ulcers,	Planning reduces time in Q-1 & Q-3
tics, and tremors.)	Recreation allows for RE-CREATION
Premature death	Living a life that meets your values and fulfills
Stress on relationships	your goals
Increased incident of drug use	
Q-3 Not Important and Urgent	**Q-4 Not Important and Not Urgent**
The body cannot tell the difference between	Lack of exercise
something "important and urgent" and	Poor relationships
something "not important and urgent."	Becoming a couch potato
The health effects are the same as in Q-1	Weight and health problems
	Underachievement

How do you then choose to spend your time? Where will you get the time to do what matters most? Below are some strategies to maximize your opportunities!

Q-1 Important and Urgent	Q-2 Important and Not Urgent
Do this NOW!	Maximizing time in Q-2, such as planning, reduces the time spent in Q-1 & Q-3 and gives you the time to do what is most important to you.
Q-3 Not Important and Urgent	**Q-4 Not Important and Not Urgent**
Identify	Eliminate activities that are truly a waste of time
Delegate	or reassign the activities that help you to relax
Eliminate	and enjoy true recreational opportunities you identified in Q-2.

Figure 43.1. Four quadrants for life tasks.

to diffuse the discomfort of stressful moments. We refer to them as stress busters.

7. Teach and Model the Use of Stress Busters

We admit that there are times when the demand of the moment can be overwhelming, calling for an instant stress buster guaranteed to help manage the moment. Try the following:

Deep breathing. A typical breath uses only about 60% of the capacity of the lungs. During stressful times deep, focused breathing where the breath is held for just a matter of seconds can instantly lower the blood pressure, slow the pulse, and help keep things in perspective. Focus on the breathing, think of the muscles being used, and try to use the abdominal muscles. An easy way to learn abdominal muscle breathing is to lie flat on your back on the floor, place a heavy book on your stomach, and focus on the muscles used to breathe while moving the book up and down.

Disassociation (sometimes called visualization). Being able to mentally create a nonstressful situation is a favorite stress management technique of soldiers, mountain climbers, and others who need to reduce the stress of the moment by focusing on another time and place. For example, while climbing Mount Rainier and stuck for 48 hours during a storm with 70 mph winds and near-zero temperatures, a climber describes disassociating to the Grand Canyon and the hot dessert. While crossing the Kaibab Plateau in temperatures of more than 100 degrees carrying a 50-pound pack, the same climber disassociated to vanilla milkshakes. Disassociation is easy to learn. Focus on where you would choose to be. Go there. We know that the body cannot tell the difference between an experience that is real and one that is vividly imagined. So, think where you would choose to be! Accept no excuse; go there!

Finding someone to talk to. Remember a burden shared is a burden lightened. Just having a friend, a counselor, an advisor—someone who is trusted to share the burden—can be reassuring. Thinking that there is no one who would listen can be dangerous, forcing us to carry on alone.

Encourage your child to have a trusted person with whom he can share the many challenges and burdens when he is feeling especially tense.

Neck rolls. Head and neck rolls are an easy to learn, effective, and instant stress buster. Begin slowly and easily without quick movements and without straining. Tilt the head back, tilt the head forward touching the chin to the chest, gently roll the head 360 degrees clockwise, then repeat counter clockwise. Repeat the entire process for six repetitions.

A Final Word

Stress is an important and necessary part of our lives. But when it becomes overwhelming it can have powerful negative effects. Inappropriate stress management, or simply too much stress, may lead to depression, disease, premature death, relationship failures, drug use, and, in extreme cases, suicide. Remember that you might be a poor role model for stress management and inadvertently underestimate and elevate the level of stress in your children. To help children alleviate stress, begin by modeling healthy habits and making decisions based on your values and passions. As you improve your management of unhealthy stress, you will help your children learn to cope with even the most stressful moments. In short, by modeling a lifestyle in which you control stress rather than letting it control you, you will help both you and your child to live longer, more productive, and happier lives.

Resources

Books

Covey, S. (1998). *The 7 habits of highly effective teens: The ultimate teenage success guide.* New York, NY: Simon & Schuster.

Covey, S. R. (1989). *The 7 habits of highly effective people: Restoring the character ethic.* New York, NY: Simon & Schuster.

Davis, M., Robbins, M., Eshelman, M., & McKay, M. (1998). *Relaxation and stress reduction workbook.* Oakland, CA: New Harbinger.

Peterson, J. (1993). *Talk with teens about self and stress.* Minneapolis, MN: Free Spirit.

Peterson, J. (1995). *Talk with teens about feelings, family, relationships and the future.* Minneapolis, MN: Free Spirit.

Romain T., & Verdick, E. (2000). *Stress can really get on your nerves.* Minneapolis, MN: Free Spirit.

Treffinger, D. J., Isaksen, S. G., & Stead-Dorval, K. B. (2006). *Creative problem solving: An introduction* (4th ed.). Waco, TX: Prufrock Press.

Websites

The American Institute of Stress—http://www.stress.org
Center for Creative Learning—http://www.creativelearning.com
The Creative Problem Solving Group-Buffalo—http://www.cpsb.com

"Why Am I Here? What Makes the World so Unfair?" Reaching Out to the Questing Gifted Child

by Joan Franklin Smutny

RECEIVED a call from a father who said that his 9-year-old son liked to discuss the nature of time. Was there always time? If it depends on the movement of the planets, then would it stop if they reversed course? He was particularly eager to discuss the possibility of life before birth, as his father noted:

> I used to think that this was because he played with a friend whose family is Buddhist, but when I asked, "Harry, do you mean you wonder if you were here before?" he would say, "No, not here, but somewhere. I just know I was somewhere else." And then he would argue that if time had to do with moving planets then why couldn't he have existed somewhere that was outside of that? He would put on his pouty, you-should-know-better look and say, "If there's something after death as you told me when Pop [his hamster] died, then why not before too?" I couldn't answer of course. I also had the distinct impression that he was only telling me a fraction of what was going on in his head. How do we deal with these kinds of questions?

Another child I know—a gifted middle schooler—wanted to talk to her parents about the inferior status of animals in human society. This fourth grader had read some rather dense, complex books on animals and conservation, trying to understand why people treated other species as beneath them. As her mother shared,

> My husband and I were a bit taken aback when out of the blue our daughter said, "You know, I'm probably going to end up a misanthrope." I said, "A misanthrope? When did you learn that word?" She just rolled her eyes with an exaggerated sigh and said, "If most people in the world don't like animals that much and only see them as playthings or meat to eat or whatever, I'm not going to like people very much and therefore I'll be . . . well . . . alone in this world." I tried to assure her that there are, in fact, a lot of people who care about animals. But she just looked off into the distance and continued, "If it's because people have more brains or something, then what about really disabled people? Do they lose their rights and get locked in cages and abused if they can't think as good as . . . like . . . a monkey who's extra smart? No. The monkey would still be in the cage. So it's got to be prejudice against nonhumans." Anna has a really hard time dealing with cruelty, especially toward animals. I wish we could find ways of helping her through this.

The "Questing" Gifted Child

The following list is intended to aid parents in recognizing the quest of their own children. Although not all gifted young people engage in such a quest—searching and probing complex issues in great depth—many highly sensitive and intuitive learners do. They have a tendency to be:

- interested in philosophical questions far in advance of others their age;

- paralyzed by the intensity of their feelings in the presence of injustice, cruelty, or self-centeredness;
- inspired by a sense of the wholeness of life (encompassing all beings and the universe) and feeling part of this large whole;
- subject to an acute sense of vulnerability in the world due to feeling "different" from peers and to difficult experiences in school;
- profoundly affected by daily experience and inclined to plumb its meaning to the depths;
- possessed of a highly developed moral understanding and strong convictions about fundamental principles (such as the right to a fair trial);
- acutely intuitive about human and animal behavior;
- deeply drawn toward the creative, artistic, and the imaginative;
- interested in unexplained phenomena—UFOs, telepathic abilities, near-death experiences, or visions of the future;
- highly sensitive and compassionate toward others, particularly toward those who are mistreated, troubled, or unhappy; and
- able to take strong, courageous stands about ethical issues based on well-reasoned arguments for doing so and in spite of opposition.

Because of their advanced abilities, a number of gifted students achieve an extraordinary level of awareness and insight about themselves and the world around them. The following are some comments made by these children to their parents and/or teachers:

When I walk in a room, I can feel what everyone there is feeling. If someone is sad, I feel it. If kids notice the stain on my sweater or my dorky shoes, I feel that. If they don't like the teacher, I feel that, too, and then I feel bad for the teacher who doesn't know it. Sometimes I think I'm just crazy and imagining all this, but then someone will come up to me and say something that proves I was right.—Sixth grader

I once overheard my parents talking with their friends about how kids think they're the center of the universe. Are they nuts? I'm a teeny tiny speck floating in the cosmos. It's totally overwhelming!—Fifth grader

Where do "I" end and "You" begin?—First grader

If what we think affects what we see, then are all the scientists in the world going to have to redo their experiments? Are we living in our own dream?—Third grader

Nature always keeps me sane. When I watch a spider weaving a web, I relax. I can tell he's not worried.—Seventh grader

Facing the Wall

Children with intuitive sensibilities and probing minds often are ushered into this awareness without the emotional maturity or life experience to cope with it. Particularly noticeable among young gifted children, the phenomenon known as "asynchrony" makes them seem like a 25-year-old in metaphysical understanding and a 6-year-old in emotional maturity. A 7-year-old talks about the nature of consciousness at one moment and weeps over a missing toy the next. A 10-year-old asks if humans "can evolve into a kinder species than the 'moral Neanderthals' they are now" while watching *SpongeBob SquarePants* on cable television.

At older ages, they continue the struggle to make sense of experiences and insights they can hardly understand. Essential to this inner conflict is the fact that their accelerated moral development bumps up against the world outside them—the confusing behaviors of people in different settings (e.g., double standards, lack of authenticity, hypocrisy, ignorance of complexity), the shallowness of some aspects of popular culture, and the illogical nature of certain customs and/or rules. In cases where they have no one to talk to, no words to put to the sensibilities they feel, and no strategies for working with them, gifted young people have few options at their disposal. They can rebel, keep their thoughts to themselves, or withdraw from those around them. Sensing something within themselves that they cannot articulate (yet cannot deny either), these children awaken to the sad reality that others do not share this awareness. At that moment, they realize they are alone.

At School

It is in the context of school where these promising children most keenly experience a conflict, a struggle due largely to the invisible inner world that schools do not normally recognize. Because schools cannot nurture what they cannot see, these children experience a lack of nourishment on a deep level, even though they often don't know what is missing. Over time, they feel more and more invisible, less engaged, less alive. Adult guidance that could help them communicate, understand, and give shape to their inner world rarely exists in school because of the one-sided emphasis on academic growth as a thing separate from the realm of character, sensibility, and intuition.

A young girl who paints the "spirit face" of animals and people discovers, with a jolt, that the other kids have no idea what she's doing. "You know," she explains, "there is the face that we see with our eyes and then there is the other one." She shows pictures of her cat on four different days with the second face painted over the first like an otherworldly being. There is no response. The child immediately senses the gulf between what she sees and the physical here-and-now world of her classmates.

For these intuitive gifted children, the "invisible" domain affects their whole being—the way they learn, love, connect to the world, and form relationships. It is a sad day when they discover that their peers don't stare out the window at the pigeons and wonder if being a bird would improve the feeling of life. They don't concern themselves with the concept of compassion for animals and how this relates to living in harmony with all life. They don't wonder if they could "see" their deceased grandparents by changing their state of mind. When these children fully awaken to the fact that those around them do not occupy or even see the same realm as they do, they may decide to let that domain go.

At Home

Gifted children with these sensibilities either flourish in families that understand them on a deep level or they revolt in families that do not. Parents who enforce their own ideas, philosophies, and visions on their gifted children without regard to their unique personality, intelligence, and sensibility can cause harm. It is critically important to understand the difference between empowering a child to discover his own calling in life and imposing (consciously or unconsciously) their own calling on the child.

> Writing haikus was the only thing that gave me peace. When I lived in Japan I was good in math and everyone said I would be a mathematician like my father. Back then, I loved math because numbers gave me a sense of order and security in the world. When we moved to this country, I was 10 and I remember being shocked to discover how much culture influences personality. I would lie in bed at night wondering if the "I" who existed before could even survive in America and what did this mean? It spurred on a deep awakening in me. Is being a person a myth? Are we just energy that gets shaped differently as we move from culture to culture? Is there an essence that is me? The haikus started during this time. They helped me explore questions about the nature of identity. My parents didn't understand what was happening and, of course, how could I explain myself? Every spare moment, I wrote haikus. I looked for myself in the haikus. I'm still writing them, still searching for my elusive self on little scraps of paper.—Gifted adult, remembering his childhood

Even the most well-meaning parents can miss the signs of the questing child. This can happen in a variety of ways. In the above example, the family's effort to adapt to life in America and the parents' investment in the child's academic success make them less aware of the child's soul struggling to find its voice in the new world. Religious tradition also can influence parental response. A mother or father may close down certain lines of questioning in order to keep the child on the "straight path" and protect her from losing the guidance and strength she needs in life. This also happens among many immigrant families, who become deeply invested in preserving the religious traditions in their young people as a way of resisting amalgamation into mainstream American culture. In many cases where the child has no freedom to question beliefs or religious ideas, he will maintain the outward appearance of a believer (so as not to disappoint his parents), while inside he continues his search alone.

Lack of adult awareness is at the root of many problems facing these young seekers. Without intending to, we marginalize the profound experiences of our children and dismiss the rich, invisible world where their deepest thinking takes place. Less in tune with the invisible realm, discounting it in so many inadvertent and unconscious ways, we little realize how this makes them feel estranged and isolated. They look to us for connection and what they find are parents who cannot see or give a name to the world they know so intimately. "Who are you talking to now?" we might ask a child engaged in lively debate with an imaginary being, the only recipient of his theories about parallel universes. "Ohhhhh, I don't know about that" we may say carelessly when our child earnestly asks if we can make a special trip to visit an aunt she "senses" needs special help. "Can't we at least call her?" she asks, almost desperate. "Oh, of course we can, no problem!" we say lightly, trying to cajole her out of her growing fear for her aunt.

The Fork in the Road

In order to really belong to their families, friends, and community, many gifted students feel they have to make a choice between their sensibility and the more material sense of living and being that surrounds them. But, becoming more like the rest of the world carries a high price—alienation from the most precious part of their sensibility. They act in one of two ways: They either pretend to be like everyone else and keep their questioning to themselves or they decide that the domain of feeling is unrealistic and silly—a thing to outgrow. Whatever the choice, most of these gifted people experience a profound loss.

> As a child, I can remember feeling so close to nature, so close to my love for painting and for the divine—what Rachel Carson called the "sense of wonder." All of that dwindled away. I can't remember the day or the event that made this happen. I think that, as a kid who performed well academically, I got pulled in other directions and bit-by-bit, the demands and concerns over grades and success and getting ahead chipped away at my more philosophical side until I just let it go. I remember telling myself that I had to get my priorities straight and there were other more pressing and practical things to do. And in the distraction and bustle of school and research and work, I stopped hearing my own voice and over time, I felt less and less connected to anything. It was only after bottoming out completely that I realized I had lost myself somehow. My own voice actually stopped speaking, even in the silence. Now, interestingly, I'm returning to the rich, mystical work of my childhood.—Ph.D. candidate

A Window for the Questing Mind

Over the years, I have come across the shared wisdom and advice of researchers, counselors, parents, and gifted children on how to respond to the "quest" of young people for a deeper understanding of the world.

Express in the stories you tell an empathy with, openness to, and understanding of their inner searching and struggles. Express genuine interest in the thoughts and feelings of your children, however incidental, odd, or hypersensitive they may seem. A particularly effective approach is to share your childhood stories about the things that concerned you—what thoughts came to you in the silence of the night, what conclusions you arrived at, and how you found a sense of inner peace. Children find this kind of sharing enormously reassuring and instructive. They feel understood at the deepest level and can find guideposts for their own journey.

Show them that you genuinely care what they think and feel. Inquire about their projects and thought processes; ask what led them to ask certain questions. When a sudden change has occurred in the family (e.g., divorce, new baby, change of address, loss of a beloved relative or pet), try to discover how your child is processing this change. The same principle applies to national or international crises such as war or a tsunami. Express to the child your own interest in and openness to their thoughts and questions about any subject.

Be Open in Discussing Complex Moral or Metaphysical Questions

Try not to express any sense of finality on a subject that children find troubling. Overly simple answers to complex subjects—the reason for criminal behavior, the possibilities of life beyond the grave, the lack of kindness in some kids at school, the nature of time, the purpose of life—will only push them away. Being intuitive, they will detect that they've hit a nerve and either retreat from the adults or pretend to agree. It's better to support a child's own process of discovery, sharing personal philosophies without any need to resolve every issue or close down the questioning. When adults say, "I can see why you would think and feel that way, but here's another way to look at this question . . .", the child feels that he has someone to talk to, someone who understands and honors his quest for meaning. Sharing personal convictions or philosophies in this fashion helps the child explore his own experiences, ideas, and intuited knowledge and enables parents to fulfill their unique role in his quest.

Help Them Achieve a Sense of Purpose

Most gifted children express a deeply felt need for a life purpose—a reason for being. As parents, you can facilitate this process by discovering the things that mean the most to them and then nurturing these things (e.g., passions, goals, dreams) in as many ways as possible. Consider the question: What can I do to give my child a vision of her future as a botanist/archeologist/lawyer/zoologist/astronaut? What resources (human and material) do I need? Here are some possibilities to consider:

- volunteer/community service opportunities that give your child an experience of making a difference doing something he loves (e.g., removing invasive species of flora from a forest preserve);
- biographies of eminent people (in the form of books and documentaries) that clearly show the characteristics (e.g., persistence, determination, resiliency, sense of humor) that led to significant achievement in their chosen field;
- inspiring mentors and/or coaches who can give him personal attention and encouragement, and model certain behaviors (e.g., work habits, skills, approaches, attitudes) that enable him to face difficulties and make significant progress.

Building a vision for the future—a vision that comes from the child's deeply felt values, convictions, and interests—will help the child navigate around the obstacles in his path.

Bear Witness to Acts of Bravery and a Resiliency of Spirit

Celebrate your children whenever they cope with a difficult situation well. This tells them that you recognize the hardship they faced and are proud of them for not abandoning what they most value, even under peer pressure. I know a parent who took her son out for dinner as a way of honoring his forbearance during a difficult group project and for his success in making fairness a standard for their collaborative work. When we bear witness to the beauty and bravery of our children's character, they feel strengthened to embrace these qualities in themselves.

When a teacher I know saw one of her gifted students comfort an unpopular child (even though this brought him a lot of grief from peers), she took him aside and thanked him in private. In the months ahead, she would remind him of this incident whenever he became nervous or held himself back. Even in his adulthood, he would remember her saying, "You're a brave soul, Jeremy, and you can call on it whenever you need it." In this and many other ways, children gain strength by valuing what really matters to them and by living their most cherished ideals. "To thine own self be true" should be a constant guide to gifted children.

Celebrate Curiosity and Discovery

Help gifted children engage in larger-than-life issues with a sense of joy and adventure. Share insights, experiences, and quotes from a wide variety of thinkers (past and present), all speaking to the subject of what they have discovered about living and how they approach their challenges. Present the quest for beauty, artistry, philosophy of nature, the purpose for being in the world, compassion for animals, the wholeness of all life, and so forth as a series of adventures and insights, each leading to new questions that lead to further discoveries. Again, share your own conclusions about life and how you came to them. Instill the hope of finding more answers, but also the delight in the unknown as the place of future learning.

Einstein offered excellent advice:

The important thing is not to stop questioning. Curiosity has its own reason for existing. One cannot help but be in awe when he contemplates the mysteries of eternity, of life, of the marvelous structure of reality. It is enough if one tries merely to comprehend a little of this mystery every day. Never lose a holy curiosity. (See more quotes by Einstein at http://www. simpletoremember.com/vitals/einstein.htm.)

Give Them Mentors, Teachers, and Coaches Who Are Respectful of Their Unique Sensibilities

Gifted children on an inner quest thrive on the kind of close personal attention that mentors and specialized teachers or coaches provide. You yourself may be one of them. Good mentors are able not only to guide exceptional ability in specific areas but also to help these children understand themselves better. An art teacher has a child combine sketches, painting, and collage to access her ideas. A martial arts teacher helps a withdrawn, often intimidated, gifted child find an inner stabilizing power. A writing coach creates exercises to free the spirit of an urban gifted child, trying to find his place in the world.

Hear the voice of Jarrel, a seventh grader from Chicago:

Standing, standing
is where I stand.
Sitting, sitting;
I think I'm lost.
There, there
is far away.
Walking, walking,
toward my goal.
My life, life,
I grasp, I hold.
Running, running,
far away.
I've got to get
away from here.
Hoping, hoping,
for a new day.
I always want, want,
what I can't have.
Asking, asking,
for what will never come.
I cry, cry,
to my pillow at night.
Choke, choking.
I'm sorry.
I got nervous.
Finally, finally,

windows have to show me
that the sky is still clear.

Concluding Thoughts

Gifted children advanced in moral and character development, inspired by visions and possessed of a wisdom beyond their years have the ability to impart a higher level of consciousness to whatever field they choose. To minister solely to their academic ability or to treat their intellect as separate from the hopes, feelings, and aspirations that move it is a disservice to the gifted child. Certainly, we can do no less than feed the heart that hungers to belong, hold on to the hand that reaches for support, and strengthen the steps of an intuitive explorer on a quest for a wider horizon.

Resources

Dabrowski, K. (1979/1994). The heroism of sensitivity (E. Hyzy-Sirzelecka, Trans.) *Advanced Development, 6,* 87–92.

Gross, M. (1998). The "me" behind the mask: Intellectually gifted students and the search for identity. *Roeper Review, 20,* 167–173.

Gross, M. (2003). *Exceptionally gifted children* (2nd ed.). New York, NY: Routledge.

Hillman, J. (1996). *The soul's code: In search of character and calling.* New York, NY: Warner Books.

Hollingworth, L. S. (1942). *Children above 180 IQ Stanford-Binet: Origin and development.* Yonkers-on-Hudson, NY: World Book.

Lovecky, D. V. (1997). Identity development in gifted children: Moral sensitivity. *Roeper Review, 20,* 90–94.

Lovecky, D. V. (1998). Spiritual sensitivity in gifted children. *Roeper Review, 20,* 178–183.

Sisk, D. S., & Torrance, E. P. (2001). *Spiritual intelligence: Developing higher consciousness.* Buffalo, NY: Creative Education Foundation Press.

Smutny, J. F. (2001). *Stand up for your gifted child: How to make the most of kids' strengths at school and at home.* Minneapolis, MN: Free Spirit.

Tolan, S. (1998). The learning conditions: Moral asynchrony and the isolated self. *Roeper Review, 20,* 211–214.

Webb, J. T., Meckstroth, E. A., & Tolan, S. S. (1989). *Guiding the gifted child.* Scottsdale, AZ: Great Potential Press.

Chapter 45

Overcoming Barriers to Girls' Talent Development

by Sally M. Reis

WHY do some talented females achieve and gain promi-
nence or eminence while others who had as much or
more potential fail to achieve the dreams they had as
young girls? Why do some gifted girls begin to underachieve in school, and when does the underachievement begin? Most
important, what can parents do to prevent underachievement in their
daughters and to encourage the development of their gifts and talents?
These and many other questions surrounding achievement and talent
development in girls and women were the basis for almost 20 years of
research that I have conducted on talented females.

More than 20 years ago, my interests became more personal when I
became the parent of first one and later two young girls. I have watched
with growing interest how the issues about which I have written affect
my own daughters. These issues involve the external barriers, as well as
personality factors that researchers know are the reasons many girls and
women either cannot or do not realize their potential. Of course, not
all women establish the same priorities or make the same decisions, but
commonalities do exist in many of the talented females I have studied.

Talented girls and women struggle with dilemmas about abilities
and talents. They also grapple with relationships or duty and caring
(putting the needs of others first) as opposed to developing personal
talents and/or personal interests, and religious and social issues.

External Barriers

The importance of environmental variables on the development of gifted and talented females cannot be overstated. Almost from birth, females find themselves in a world of limiting stereotypes and barriers to achievement. Research has identified external barriers that seem to negatively influence the development of talents and gifts in some gifted girls and women. External barriers can result from family and environmental issues such as socialization and stereotyping at home, school, and in society. Two major external barriers are the messages that parents may inadvertently send their daughters and the negative or stereotypical societal messages about the importance of appearance and the roles held by women and men.

Parental Messages

Parental attitudes often vary toward having and raising girls as opposed to boys. Children may learn the behaviors of their sex at an early age and display particular behavior patterns and play preferences even during preschool.

My research indicates that the primary mixed messages gifted and talented girls receive emanate from the interaction of family variables, their parents' relationship, and their parents' expectations that their daughters display certain types of manners and behaviors. Mothers seem to have a particular influence on their gifted daughters; talented girls with career-oriented mothers tended to develop a variety of talents and interests early in life and feel less conflict about growing up and becoming independent, autonomous women.

Paying too much attention to stereotypic manners and behaviors in childhood can negatively affect a talented girl's attitudes and her ability to question and speak out. "Don't interrupt," "don't ask so many questions," "don't raise your hand so much," "don't be so aggressive," "don't be so bold," and "show respect for your elders"—smart girls hear these admonishments and the first seeds of passivity are planted, eventually resulting in a young woman who doesn't ask questions, doesn't raise her hand, and gives up speaking out in class.

Too much attention paid to "minding manners" and being polite and "ladylike" may conflict with characteristics that are necessary for girls with high potential to evolve into successful women who make a difference in the world. In order to evolve into successful women, girls need to challenge convention, to question authority, and to speak out about things that need change. Determination, commitment, assertiveness, and the ability to control their own lives—characteristics all associated with talented women who have achieved eminence—directly conflict with what some parents encourage as good and appropriate manners in their daughters.

The strict code of manners taught to some daughters and sons are, of course, influenced by the cultures in which we live. Although not wanting to eliminate what is unique to each diverse culture, a discussion of some of the issues related to strict implementation of a code of manners and behavior for girls (as well as boys) is warranted. Although I am not advocating that we raise daughters who are rude or discourteous, I advocate that we consider raising daughters who speak out, say no, and challenge authority when necessary.

From the time she was barely old enough to talk, I have enjoyed watching the growth and development of a young girl in our church. We have a children's message each week and all of the children who are in fourth grade or younger go to the front of the church where they listen to a special message. This young girl delighted me and the rest of the congregation on a weekly basis, often calling out funny responses to our minister's questions. Her verbal creativity and outgoing personality never failed to make all of us smile. One day after she had answered two or three questions, I overheard her mother reprimand her, explaining that she had, once again, monopolized the conversation and brought attention to herself. Too many parents squelch their daughters' enthusiasm and spirit under the guise of manners.

Some of the passion and the excitement that gifted children feel simply bubbles to the surface; discouraging this passion may very well influence later behaviors and attitudes. I often urge parents to try to channel the overexcitability, determination, willfulness, or stubbornness they find in their gifted daughters to something positive such as social action or improving some aspect of life. Girls can apply energy to sports, hobbies, music lessons, or any personal-interest area.

Stereotyping

Like a camera in the brain, each time a child has an experience a snapshot is embedded in her experiential base. Millions of snapshots produce attitudes that in turn, affect actions. Stereotypes abound in our society, from shampoo commercials and newspaper ads to the teen magazines our daughters read. Newspapers and news shows on television regularly feature photographs and stories about men in positions of authority. Children's books, television shows, and textbooks all present more men than women, and when women are presented, their physical appearances are usually stressed.

Each time a young girl turns on the television, reaches for a magazine, and participates in or overhears a conversation between friends, she is in the process of experiencing and being influenced by her social surroundings. The process begins at birth and continues throughout life; the effects are pervasive and overwhelming. Attitudes and opinions about what girls should look and act like come from family and friends, from observations throughout life, television and other media, and from print materials including books, magazines, and textbooks. For the last decade or two, researchers and educators have made suggestions for ways to eliminate gender stereotypes that impede gifted females from realizing their potential. However, we have yet to make the widespread, comprehensive commitment necessary to reduce the social pressures that affect talent development in girls.

Aware of all of the socializing incidents that affect young girls, my husband and I made a conscious attempt from the day both of our daughters were born to provide an equitable and fair environment for them. We tried to expose them to female role models, both in life and through nonfiction and fiction literature. We drove a fair distance to take them to a female dentist. They had medical visits with females. My friends sometimes teased me about my mission to have my daughters know the names of Rosa Parks, Rachel Carson, Marie Curie, Hypatia, and other accomplished women. We bought books about female doctors, scientists, and lawyers, and I was satisfied with my efforts. My husband and I share household tasks and participate equally in caring for our daughters.

One afternoon when we picked up our then 6-year-old daughter after school, she sat in the back of the car and sighed loudly—a signal we had come to understand as her way of telling us something was bothering her. As I was driving, my husband turned around and asked, "What's the matter, Sara?"

She paused and said, "I wish I was a boy."

My husband's face became incredulous as he turned to her, "Why on Earth would you want to be a boy, Sara?"

She responded, "They just get to do more!" She told us about a number of specific incidents in her classroom that had led her to this conclusion. It became clear that she was reacting to the environment in her school and classroom, and a long conversation with her classroom teacher indicated that Sara's observations were on target. Her teacher explained to us that the boys tried to monopolize the computer in the classroom, spoke out more in class, and constantly competed for more of her time and attention. Despite her efforts, Sara's teacher reported to me that she had begun to notice some of the girls becoming quieter. Even when she had tried to establish "girl only time" on the computer and some of the other equipment in the classroom, she found the girls giving up their computer time to their male friends who seemed to cajole the girls into additional time. Despite our efforts to provide role models and equity for our daughters at home and to limit television time and exposure to negative print materials, we were struck head-on with their encounters in the world outside of our home.

Although that incident occurred years ago, daily reminders of stereotyping continue to occur in our lives. At 12 years old, Sara asked if she could buy a copy of the teen magazine, *YM* (*Young and Modern*). "Please Mom," she said, "all of my friends are reading this magazine. Can I get a copy?" On the cover of the magazine was the photograph of a very slim, beautiful, young teenage girl. I read with amazement the bullets of some of the stories inside: "Total Love Guide: 100 Guys Dish the New Rules," "Kiss and Be Kissed: 26 Pucker-Up Pointers," "Dazzle Him: Hottest Date Clothes Ever," "Buff Your Bod: The Rock

Goddess Way," and "Beauty Blitz and Major Makeovers: 10 Hot New Looks—Find the One For You."

We did buy the magazine, primarily as a way of discussing gender stereotyping, and we later wrote a letter to the editor about the content of the articles. Parents must be aware of what their daughters are reading, watching, and learning about and continue to try to expose them to appropriate literature, role models, and learning experiences. A number of resources are included at the end of this article.

Internal Barriers

Numerous internal barriers affect talent development in gifted girls. They include dilemmas about abilities and talents, perfectionism, attributing success to luck rather than ability, poor choices of peers, and a tendency to be overly self-critical. I discuss one of these barriers in greater depth below.

Hiding Abilities, Doubting Abilities, and Feeling Different

Thomas Buescher, a psychologist who studied gifted adolescent boys and girls a decade ago, found that while 15% of boys hide their ability in school, 65% of girls consistently hide their talents. Buescher found that boys sought ways that they could be recognized for their abilities in areas like athletics, student council, and honors classes, while girls did not. My interviews have consistently found that young girls do not want to be considered different from their friends and same-age peers. A tendency exists for many females, regardless of age, to try to minimize their differences because both young girls and older women have a greater need to be accepted and a need to associate with people who are like them.

Defying the crowd is the last thing that many girls and women seek to accomplish. If girls either feel different or are different, most want to minimize differences through quiet work, avoiding calling attention to themselves. Parental influences, such as teaching daughters to be modest or polite, seem to compound this issue. In many interviews, gifted girls explained that they did not like to share the news of a high grade or a special accomplishment because it would seem as if they were bragging.

In one especially poignant interview I learned why Jenny, a gifted first grader who was reading at a fourth-grade level, was hiding her reading ability from her teacher. When I spoke to Jenny, I asked her pointedly if she was trying to hide the fact that she was an excellent reader from her teacher or her friends. She paused momentarily before answering, "Both." She then explained that she did not want to hurt her friends' feelings who were not yet reading and did not want to appear different either to her teacher or her friends. She also explained that it seemed like she was showing off if she read "bigger, harder books than anybody else in the class." To solve this problem, Jenny was paired for reading instruction and free reading time with a first grader from another class who read at a similar level.

For many girls, however, the problem is more difficult as they become older and their talents and gifts set them apart from their peers and friends. If the school environment is one in which academics take a backseat to athletics or which is somewhat anti-intellectual, the issue may be exacerbated. Parents must become actively involved in helping their daughters recognize and believe that they have talents and abilities that are valued as well as helping them to develop them.

Summary: What Girls and Parents Should Do

Gifted young females should explore careers, further their education, and plan and pursue professional opportunities that will challenge their intellect as well as fit into their personal plans for the future. With their daughters, parents should explore and discuss the personality issues and personal choices facing talented girls and women. Personality development is intricate and complex. What one young girl regards as an impossible obstacle another may regard as an intriguing challenge. Many of the women I interviewed were negatively influenced by their parents' lack of support for their career preferences so they changed their career plans; a much smaller percentage of women were so angry that their parents tried to steer them away from their dreams that they rebelled and became eminent in their selected areas of endeavor. Persistence, determination, and inner will are vital characteristics that gifted females must develop throughout their lives. Exploring how and when they develop these characteristics will help parents guide their daughters in these journeys.

Gifted and talented girls should:

- be exposed through personal contact and the media to female role models and mentors who have successfully balanced career and family;
- develop independence and intellectual risk-taking as well as an understanding of sex-role stereotyping and cultural biases;
- be involved in career counseling at an early age, be exposed to a wide variety of career options, and learn the value of planning for the future;
- become involved in leadership roles and extracurricular activities;
- learn various communication styles;
- learn to question, speak out, and take action;
- learn from mistakes and try again;
- discuss with other girls in supportive settings issues related to gender, success, and academic goals; and
- identify a dream for important work and develop a plan to make that dream come true.

Parents should:

- become assertive advocates for their daughter's interests and talents;
- maintain a proactive, supportive role to support their daughter's interests;
- encourage humor and positive risk taking;
- provide career encouragement and planning;
- identify role models in literature and in life;
- provide extensive experiences in museums, travel, and interaction with adults;
- foster independence and an inclination for creative action;
- encourage independent decision making;

- withhold criticism and never make fun of appearance or weight—parents should not focus on their daughter's appearance as it sends negative messages about what is most important;
- encourage participation in sports, competition, and extracurricular activities—teach daughters that everybody loses sometimes;
- monitor television viewing and media exposure—watch out for magazines that primarily stress appearance and beauty; and
- stay in close touch with the child's teachers and guidance counselors and closely monitor their academic decisions.

Resources

Books

Cooney, R. P. J. (2005). *The times and triumphs of American women*. Elizabeth, NJ: American Graphic.

Cowen, L., & Wexler, J. (1998). *Daughters & mothers: A celebration*. Philadelphia, PA: Running Press.

Websites

Girls for Change—http://www.girlsforachange.org

National Girls Collaborative Project—http://www.ngcproject.org/index.cfm

National Women's History Project—http://www.nwhp.org

National Women's Hall of Fame—http://www.greatwomen.org

Chapter 46

Man to Man: Building Channels of Communication Between Fathers and Their Talented Sons

by Thomas P. Hébert

MY brother is the proud father of three talented boys. I enjoyed spending time with my nephews Michael, Daniel, and Brian during a holiday visit with my family. I gained some valuable insights from my brother and his sons as I watched all three boys express their emotional feelings differently. Michael, the oldest son, informed his father during breakfast of his worry that his best friend might transfer to a private school. For Michael, this meant they would no longer be walking to school in the morning, a time recognized by his family as valuable because it was then that the two friends "talked about important stuff." Brian, my youngest nephew, spent an active day playing hockey with his older brothers and building a snowman with his dad, and later ended his day watching television with the family affectionately cuddled in his father's lap. Daniel, the second son, is different from his verbally expressive older brother and his demonstrative younger brother. Known for resisting hugs and kisses from relatives, he remained the strong, stoic type throughout our weekend together. When his grandparents asked questions, he smiled his usual warm smile, shrugged his shoulders nonchalantly, and did not offer much information about his school experiences or his adventures with his neighborhood friends.

My observations of the different ways my nephews communicated their feelings led me to ask some questions regarding how talented young men express their emotional feelings differently. Why do my nephews Michael and Brian operate differently from their stoic brother Daniel? Why does one brother share his personal worries and another openly express his emotions, while another remains private and tight lipped? I celebrate the fact that Michael and Brian are able to express and to communicate their feelings openly with their family; however, I realize that my nephew Daniel is perhaps more typical of most young men today. Since that holiday weekend with my brother and his three boys, I have questioned how fathers can assist their sons' emotional development. I have come to believe that fathers can serve as communicative role models by initiating and facilitating conversations with their sons. They also can organize father and son activities that allow for communication and work to design home environments where father and son communication is authentic and meaningful.

Why Do Some Young Men Have Difficulty Communicating Their Feelings?

Researchers and clinicians have offered explanations for why some males in our society have difficulty in expressing their emotions. Dan Kindlon and Michael Thompson, child psychologists and the authors of the 1999 book *Raising Cain: Protecting the Emotional Life of Boys,* maintained that our culture's assignment of relationship work to women has turned emotions into a disregarded "second language" for men. As a result many men have limited awareness of their feelings or the feelings of others. Not having learned from their own fathers, they find it difficult to express the love they do feel for their sons. Kindlon and Thompson indicated that fathers are forced to fall back on what they have been taught to do with other men—"compete, control, or criticize." The problem often begins early in a young man's life. William Pollack, a clinical professor of psychiatry at Harvard Medical School, conducted extensive interviews in a nationwide study of young and adolescent boys. In his 2000 book *Real Boys' Voices*, he concluded that boys and young men are not receiving the consistent attention, empathy, and support they need.

Pollack noted, "We've developed a culture in which too often boys only feel comfortable communicating a small portion of their feelings and experiences." In *Real Boys' Voices*, a teenager named Graham who participated in the research described the problem poignantly, "I have a big group of friends and we're all pretty comfortable with one another . . . . But we never talk about our feelings unless something is *really* up." Graham also shared his view of why he think this occurs as he explained, "Perhaps it's because their dads raised them not to need anyone else's help, and because of that they don't realize they need help even if they do." Graham described how young men need to be able to say, "I've got a problem. I can't handle this myself. I need to get it off my chest."

The Problem Also Includes Difficulty Communicating Feelings About Dad

Graham's insightful comments are helpful because they shed light on an important issue: Perhaps boys have difficulty sharing their feelings with friends because they have had little or no practice communicating with their fathers. Ralph Keyes, author of the 1999 book *Sons on Fathers: A Book of Men's Writing*, interviewed men about their fathers and collected written reflections by sons about their fathers. One man who wrote for Keyes explained the problem of emotionally distant fathers when he described his relationship with his dad by saying, "There was always a stiffness in the air between us as if we were both guests at a party, and the host had gone off without introducing us." Keyes pointed out that feelings for his father can be a man's strongest, yet these feelings are seldom expressed. He noted, "Athletes never mouth 'Hi Dad!' to TV cameras. Few men tell me that they ever say 'I love you,' to their fathers, no matter how much they want to." Keyes reminded boys that their fathers are also sons, and they should take the initiative in expressing their feelings for their dads. He encouraged young men to search for a "common ground" with their fathers. He wrote, "Are you experiencing some of the same things he went through? Do you have fond memories of time spent together? Say so."

Why Is This Problem Especially Important for Talented Males?

All young men may need help in learning to deal with their emotionality and communicate their feelings; however, very intelligent boys especially need appropriate outlets for expressing their feelings because of their advanced psychological development. Dr. Linda Silverman, a child psychologist, indicated that among intelligent young people there is a high correlation between intellectual giftedness and heightened sensitivity. Many talented boys experience an abundance of emotional energy, sensitivity, and strong compassion for others. According to Silverman, the greatest support fathers can give their highly able sons is an appreciation of their heightened sensitivity. For these young men, feeling everything more deeply than others may be painful and frightening; therefore, it is important that dads help their sons understand that their feelings are normal for highly intelligent youngsters and teach them ways of expressing their emotions appropriately. Building healthy channels of communication between a talented young man and his father is a great way to begin.

Along with heightened sensitivity and emotional intensity, gifted young men often have deep concerns regarding societal issues. It is not unusual for gifted boys to worry about social injustice, hunger, poverty, homelessness, or the troubled environment. Their sensitivity to these issues may not be valued by other young men their age. Because these issues may seem overwhelming to a serious, sensitive young man, he will need the support of a parent who understands why he worries, appreciates his sensitivity, communicates with him about his concerns, and assists him in addressing the societal issues that are troubling him. Healthy channels of communication between father and son will provide an outlet for intelligent young men to discuss their concerns.

Consider Activities to Engage in Conversation With Your Son

If sons are to begin healthy conversations with their fathers, they will need a home environment that allows them to feel comfortable holding those conversations. Creating that safe environment requires dad approaching this challenge creatively. To accomplish this, fathers should consider an important lesson I learned as an educator. As an enrichment teacher, I attended a workshop on methods to address the affective needs of high-ability students. One of the strategies I transferred back to my middle school classroom was "temperature taking." This is an activity in which the students ranked how they were feeling that day on a scale of 1 to 10 with 1 indicating their temperature was very low, and they were having a difficult time, and 10 representing a high temperature consistent with how "high" they were feeling about life in general. I began each class session with this activity and noted that the girls had no difficulty taking their temperatures and describing in detail what kind of day they were having. With arms folded, the boys consistently reported that their temperatures were "5" and when asked to elaborate, they remained silent and chose to "pass." After several days, Greg approached me after class and announced, "Mr. Hébert, if you won't stop doing this touchy-feely stuff every day, I'm going to get my schedule changed and drop this class!" As we discussed his concerns, I realized Greg thought I'd gone overboard with the affective activities, and he wanted his hour in the enrichment classroom to involve more intellectually rigorous activities. I assured Greg that we would soon begin on a presidential mock election, and I'd keep his feelings in mind as I planned instruction.

Weeks later, Greg and the other boys in the class were painting election campaign posters and banners. I grabbed a paintbrush and joined them. As we painted, I learned of Greg's concerns about the unfair way in which his wrestling coach was treating athletes. Greg also shared a problem he was having with his father and the frustration he felt with his older brother whom he viewed as "really smart but a slacker in school." The other young men in the group also disclosed important issues in their personal lives. This comfortable conversation came from the same students who only weeks before had refused to open up in the temperature-taking activity! Their involvement in an enjoyable activity apparently allowed them to feel more comfortable while talking about serious issues.

My realization of the importance of holding conversations with young men while engaged in activities should help to enlighten fathers. Bill Beausay, author of the 1998 book *Teenage Boys*, agreed that in order to provoke meaningful conversations with boys, fathers need to get in the habit of conducting them while engaged in something enjoyable together. Beausay described an afternoon at home with his teenage son's friends "hanging out," basically being bored. He suggested some activities that they arrogantly turned down, but when he went outside and starting shooting baskets by himself, the gang joined him. Beausay was surprised as he described,

> What amazed me most was that as soon as they entered the court, they wouldn't stop talking. They were so open during the game that they answered questions about their families, girl problems, and money woes. I actually thought for a minute that I'd invented a new kind of therapy: basketball analysis!

What Beausay had actually done was discover what I learned from Greg and his friends: adolescent males seldom discuss things. Talking is something they do while having fun.

Beausay's insights are helpful. If fathers want to get close to their sons and help them unload their worries or share the highlights of their day at school, dads will want to consider doing things together with their boys. In today's hectic American household, that may mean housework or washing and waxing the family car. Whether a father is teaching his son how to cook chili for dinner or how to get a really good shine on the linoleum kitchen floor, these are the times when a son will begin to tell his father about his problems with algebra or the attractive young woman who is aggravating him in study hall. Steven Biddulph, author of 2004's *Raising Boys*, wrote,

Quite seriously, doing work with your son—teaching him the tricks of doing it well, how to be fast and efficient and happy on making life cleaner and tidier—is a way that a parent and child can enjoy each other, have good long talks, and pass on all kinds of wisdom.

Fathers Model How They Express Their Feelings

Sons learn about feelings by watching their fathers and other men. Boys need to see that fathers have emotions. Dads can share their fears, say they are upset, and even cry. Boys are trying to match their inner feelings with outer ways of behaving and need their fathers to show them how this is done. In a letter written to Steve Biddulph, one man shared the importance of fathers modeling appropriate emotionality when he wrote of his experience losing a friend to cancer. His letter read:

I put the phone down and began to fight back the tears. I walked into the living room thinking: "Is this OK? Is this how I want my son to see me?" The answer came back: "Of course, it's good that he sees me like this." I asked my wife for a hug, and stood there holding her and sobbing. I felt my son's approach and then his hand on my shoulder; he was comforting me! It was wonderful. Perhaps seeing me like that will mean that, when he needs to, he also will have access to the sweet release of tears. I don't want him to be bottled up and volcanic when he meets the inevitable griefs of life.

Are You Really Listening?

Not only do fathers need to be good models for their sons, they also need to be good listeners. A father listening to his son will do more to improve their relationship than anything he could say. Young men cannot always divulge their real thoughts, opinions, and fears because they aren't always sure what they are, so fathers need to just listen to them.

Beausay assured fathers that they can allow their sons to be wrong in their thinking and how they feel about issues, allow them to struggle with the feelings, allow them to struggle with expressing their feelings, and if necessary, allow them to struggle for an extended amount of time. A father must realize that his son's willingness to communicate with his dad about himself and his life is more important than dad's ability to appear worldly to his son. Fathers need to listen without speaking, to listen with their hearts.

Fathers who want to help their sons develop into emotionally healthy young men need ways to help them create home environments where father and son conversations are authentic and their sons feel comfortable expressing their emotions. In addition, mothers who are raising sons on their own also may want to examine how men communicate and apply methods of father-son communication to their situations. Let's consider a few strategies to assist in opening channels of communication with talented young men.

Try Writing Him a Letter

Tucked away in my closet is a collection of letters I've received from my father over the years. He wrote a number of them to me when I faced important decisions in my life. He wrote others when I experienced major disappointments. The supportive and loving handwritten messages from my father are something I continue to cherish. In this age of electronic mail and cell phones, many of us have forgotten about the beauty of a handwritten letter. Letter writing is a thoughtful method of communication more fathers should consider. If a father has a concern about his son, wants to compliment him, or wants to provide him encouragement, delivering that message with feelings expressed in writing can be powerful. A dad can mail the letter to his son, tuck it between the pages of his favorite magazine, surprise him with it in his school bookbag, or even deliver it in person. A dad shouldn't worry that his son won't read the letter. A young man's curiosity will overcome any resistance to reading a letter from his dad, and a father's sincere effort to communicate his feelings will certainly connect with his son. The letter will provide a young man with privacy and time to process through the message delivered by his father, enabling him to sort through his feelings when he's ready, and allowing his dad's letter to influence his thinking. Take it from me: My father's did.

Share a Movie

Beausay also suggested that if fathers really want to spend quality time with their sons, discover how they view the world, and explore their new interests, it may be wise to consider tubs of popcorn at the local cinema. A father attending a movie with his son is participating in a teenager's ritual, and doing it for the purpose of finding discussion topics is smart. Big screen actors like Denzel Washington, Tom Cruise, or Al Pacino can easily furnish hours of father and son conversation. Movies can provide dads and their sons with stimulating talk about characters in conflict. Films can deliver great lessons in morality that fathers and sons can digest together. Films that appeal to a son may be filled with teenage characters struggling with angst or making major decisions in life, providing fathers with rich topics for healthy discussion. Movies also can serve as a source of great art for both father and son to appreciate as well as outrageous exploitation they may both want to condemn. By attending movies together, fathers will be building an inventory of thought-provoking topics to trigger great conversations with their sons.

Share a New Sport or Hobby; Enjoy an Excursion Together

Some dads will readily admit they have always wanted to start a collection or begin photography as a hobby but haven't taken the time to explore the possibilities. Others confess that they have been wanting to learn rollerblading but haven't found the courage. Fathers may want to consider sharing new sports or hobbies with their sons. As a father and son stumble and slide together down the neighborhood's sidewalks or share the excitement of developing their first roll of black-and-white film in the darkroom, they are bound to enjoy many hours of good conversation. Imagine how much they will learn about each other as they explore new ways of having fun together. Through these experiences working together on a shared interest, fathers will enjoy many hours of meaningful conversation with their sons that will make important memories for the two men for years to come.

Fathers also may want to consider a father and son weekend away. Dads may want to explore new hiking trails with their boys. Some fathers may prefer investigating a museum with their sons. Others may want to suggest taking a canoe trip. Some men would delight in taking a camping trip with their sons. The healthy conversations that evolve late at night around an open campfire would be worth all of the hard work involved in carrying out such an excursion. Nothing brings a father and son closer than an adventure they plan and share together.

Share a Son's Concern Through a Father-Son Project

Because gifted young men frequently express concerns about serious societal issues, fathers may want to consider becoming involved with their sons in addressing these concerns through community action projects. For example, fathers and sons might enjoy volunteering in a local homeless shelter, running a marathon to raise money for cancer research, or working on a construction team to build a home with Habitat for Humanity. Such projects will allow fathers and sons not only to discuss the troubling societal concerns but also to take action on these concerns and share a common feeling of accomplishment.

Take Your Son to Work With You

One of my fondest childhood memories is an overnight trip I took with my own father many years ago. It was mid-August, and I was bored with summer and could not keep myself entertained until school started in the fall. My dad noticed this and suggested that I accompany him to work. My father was a wholesale electrical, hardware, and plumbing supply salesman, and every other week his job required that he conduct an overnight trip through several New England states, meeting with contractors and providing them with the materials they needed to conduct their businesses. As a 12-year-old, I had heard my father share many stories of his customers at the dinner table, and I suddenly had the opportunity to meet many of the interesting "characters" my father had entertained us with in his stories of the road.

Having packed my overnight suitcase and a hefty supply of my favorite comic books, I enjoyed the quality time on the road with my father as we traveled from one small town to another. During that trip I learned a great deal about the man I called "Dad." I had the opportunity to watch my father interact with his customers, men who shared their business trials and tribulations and the joys and tragedies of their personal lives. I saw my father's strong interpersonal skills in action and admired his ability to make his clients feel important. His natural way of expressing his concern for their well-being and the success of their companies was obviously one reason my father was so successful as a salesman. Although neither my father nor I realized it at the time, he provided me with a model of how a man shares his emotions appropriately in a professional setting, an important lesson I value today. My father's lesson is one many more fathers could share with their sons. Consider taking your son to work and allow him to watch you interact with the important individuals in your professional world. What better model can an intelligent young man ask for than his own father?

Boys Without Fathers Present

With the high percentage of families today without fathers present in the home, many women in this country face the challenge of raising boys on their own. Single mothers should feel encouraged by the words of Ann Caron, author of 1995's *Strong Mothers, Strong Sons*. She wrote, "An adolescent boy wants his mother to believe in him, to be committed to him and to provide the support he needs to successfully maneuver through adolescence." In her research, Caron found that communication between mother and son may be different from father and son, but most boys enjoy talking with their mothers. Because appropriate modeling of masculinity is important to talented young men, mothers raising boys on their own may want to consider finding opportunities for their sons to spend time engaged in activities with male relatives, neighbors, coaches, religious leaders, or mentors. However, Caron's guidance should encourage single moms as she advised, "Remember talking is not the only way to form close bonds. Enjoy being with him."

Summing Up . . .

My nephews have helped me to understand how each boy is unique in his way of dealing with his emotions and being comfortable communicating his feelings. Students like Greg have also helped me to realize the importance of creating supportive environments for young men to talk about what's going on in their lives. We want talented young men to have a healthy array of options to express their emotionality and develop their masculinity appropriately. Dedicated fathers who are part of the emotional fabric of their families can best teach their sons these options. With fathers modeling healthy masculine behavior and working to build channels of communication with their sons, families of talented young men will benefit from healthy father and son relationships as the men enjoy meaningful conversations man to man, heart to heart.

Resources

Gurian, M., & Stevens, K. (2007). *The minds of boys: Saving our sons from falling behind in school and life*. New York, NY: Jossey-Bass.

Neu, T. W., & Weinfeld, R. (2006). *Helping boys succeed in school*. Waco, TX: Prufrock Press.

Tyre, P. (2009). *The trouble with boys: A surprising report card on our sons, their problems at school, and what parents and educators must do*. New York, NY: Three Rivers Press.

References

Beausay, B. (1998). *Teenage boys: Surviving and enjoying these extraordinary years.* Colorado Springs, CO: WaterBrook Press.

Biddulph, S. (2004). *Raising boys: Why boys are different—and how to help them become happy and well-balanced men.* Berkeley, CA: Celestial Arts.

Caron, A. (1995). *Strong mothers, strong sons: Raising the next generation of men.* New York, NY: HarperCollins.

Keyes, R. (1993). *Sons on fathers: A book of men's writings.* New York, NY: Perennial.

Kindlon, D., & Thompson, M. (1999). *Raising Cain: Protecting the emotional life of boys.* New York, NY: Ballantine.

Pollack, W. (2000). *Real boys' voices.* New York, NY: Random House.

Chapter 47

Engaging Gifted Boys in Reading and Writing

by Leighann Pennington

Unlikely Candidates

The Skateboarder: The required wardrobe is black skinny jeans, skater shoes, and a black Volcom T-shirt. His appearance suggests a rebel rather than candidate for reading a poem written in the voice of an adorable puppy.

The Math Genius: He is the stereotypical math genius, with black-rimmed glasses slipping down his nose. Although his most voracious interest is in the realm of numbers, he comes to class willing to give writing a try. How did this boy fall in love with reading and writing poetry?

The Slacker: When the school year began, he bragged that he'd never read an entire book straight through before. Now he is making grand pronouncements like: "Writing with a structured assignment is like a geometry painting, but free-writing is like an abstract painting," and commenting that he feels "intellectual and grown-up."

The Class Clown: And finally, the one who "acts up," throwing erasers and pencils around the classroom—yet now he's writing imaginative extra-credit journal entries about how aliens prevented him from doing his homework.

The boys above are real kids, ages 10–13. Maybe your son is one of these boys, or maybe he's all of them? These boys are interested in many things: action movies, math equations, the latest iPod, sports, comedy videos on YouTube, comic books, skateboarding, sci-fi, surfing the Internet, the newest cell phones, and acquiring friends on MySpace and Facebook. Now they're interested in reading and writing, too.

Hmmm . . . as a parent, you may wonder, "What happened here? And how can I recreate this experience to help my son to actually like (maybe even love) reading and especially writing?" Parents often ask me: "How can my son improve his writing? How can I engage my child in reading?" As parents and teachers, we don't want underdeveloped verbal skills to become a barrier to success. In order to achieve eminence in any field today, reading and writing are integral. Academic careers will run smoother when reading and writing aren't painful experiences, but appealing ones.

Let's begin by discussing why writing is important, especially for gifted boys, and factors that influence their disenchantment with writing. The methods included in this article can support and challenge them. Also included are creative tips to help you create experiences at home to positively promote writing and influence your son's experiences at school.

Why Gifted Boys Need Writing

Often writing is not an end in itself. It is not only an academic skill, but a route to developing identity and self-actualization. Gifted boys who are frustrated by a prevailing spirit of competition in academics, sports, and peer relationships may find an expressive outlet in writing that will benefit their social and emotional well-being along with their academic writing, and critical and independent thinking skills. For some boys, writing fiction, poetry, or a song allows for the expression of feelings, alleviation of isolation, or a connection to others. Finding out who you are and determining how you can influence the world around you is an empowering experience, especially for socially and politically aware gifted boys.

Connect Writing to Your Child's Specific Interests

Gifted boys may avoid writing because they are simply more passionate about a particular area of interest. Like many gifted students, they often pursue these interests exclusively with intense focus. Some common interests include: astronomy, inventing, mathematics, dinosaurs, comic book heroes, architecture, or even designing computer programs and video games. What is your son's obsession of the moment? The key is to use these outside interests as an entry point into reading and writing.

The Power of Parents

The influence parents have on their son's desire to write cannot be overestimated. In *Real Boys' Voices* (Pollack, 2000), teenager Caleb wrote:

> Writing is hard because you never know if something is good or if it's just a waste of time. But it's really nice when people encourage you and ask to see your work as soon as it's done. My mom encourages me . . .

In their 1993 study of talented teenagers, Csikszentmihalyi and colleagues related the significance of parental influence and support to developing talent:

> The connection between family members is an instance of integration, or the stable condition whereby the individuals feel a sense of consistency and support. Differentiation refers to the fact that members are encouraged to develop their individuality by seeking out new challenges and opportunities.

Writing together is a way to integrate and differentiate, connect, and communicate with your child, while supporting the process of individuation and developing varied talents.

Creative Methods for Encouraging Writing

The following are ways to encourage writing at home and to discover why your son may be disengaged with writing at school and intervene.

The Handwriting Dilemma

Your son may have messy, even unintelligible handwriting. A teacher's emphasis on neatness and spelling during writing assignments may turn students off to writing by hindering the flow of ideas. The first step is getting the ideas out.

One way to get these ideas out is to allow typing at home instead of writing only by hand. Simply sitting in front of the computer, which kids associate with games, chatting, music, and Web surfing, will encourage boys to associate writing with fun. For example, a current events written response assignment in my sixth-grade social studies class was met with a groan from the boys—at first. Their view changed when they found out they could type the assignment, which led to students rushing to the computer lab, *The New York Times Upfront* magazines open, typing out their thoughtful analyses of complex and informative articles about the space satellite Sputnik, legal debates, and child soldiers in Africa.

Too Much? Or Not Enough?

Are the writing assignments at school too structured or not structured enough? Ask the teacher for specific criteria, such as a rubric, which will determine how your child's work is graded. Broach the topic that some writing assignments could be ungraded, such as journaling and free-writing, allowing for more freedom and less anxiety relating to the final product.

Bor-ing?!

Are the writing assignments your child receives at school boring or uninspiring? Ask the teacher if students can choose from among a range of options or make up their own writing topic every so often, as long as it meets the intent of the assignment. Allow your son to express himself and draw and write in the genres he enjoys reading, such as comics, fantasy, anime, or science fiction.

Eliminate Writer's Block

Is your son thinking too hard before putting pen to paper? Get those ideas out! Map out a story using concept maps, a comic book, or picture sequence. Discuss ideas first. You can jot down his ideas as he talks, which then can be easily converted into an outline.

Understand Writing Anxiety

Sit down and write with your child—you might experience the same fears and paralyzing emotions that prevent your child from writing and gain insights into the writing process. Ask your child why he doesn't like to write. Answers could range from the process of handwriting ("My hand hurts!") to frustration at the mismatch between mental and physical processing speed ("I can't get my ideas out fast enough—my hand moves too slow.").

Break It Down

If the scope of a project seems too overwhelming, break it down into smaller pieces, focusing only on the first sentence. Sometimes when the beginning is intimidating, it is helpful to start in the middle or at the end.

Draw It Out

Drawing a picture to go along with writing, which is common in elementary school, can still be inspiring for writers in later grades. The excitement of "I get to draw a picture!" distracts from the intimidation a writing assignment may conjure.

Promoting Writing at Home

Short Assignments

- Write a page in the voice of a favorite character from books or movies. Imitate Donkey from *Shrek* or Holden Caulfield from *The Catcher in the Rye*. Watch a section of the movie or read aloud from a book to set the stage for inspiration. Many great writers were inspired by the creative work of others.
- Love sports? Write commentary (funny or serious) for a game on TV, using an "announcer voice." Support your son by participating, whether writing lines or reading aloud.
- Send in an article or letter to the editor of a favorite magazine.
- Discussing politics is always lively and controversial. Write a list of questions, interview people, or pretend to be news anchors covering the presidential debates or members of a roundtable discussion on CNN.
- Write jokes and deliver them on "stage" in the living room.

A Hero's Journey

Chances are your son loves comic books, superhero movies, or the TV show *Heroes*, all of which are based on a hero's journey. Together, write a traditional hero story, using the elements of a traditional hero tale. The hero leaves his typical life, is called to adventure, goes out into the wild, overcomes obstacles, makes mistakes, and recognizes his flaws. Ensure that the hero has a tragic flaw that leads to his downfall, and that the character achieves catharsis, where he realizes his flaw led to his tragic ending. Begin by discussing how this played out in a movie like *Spider-Man 3*. This step-by-step structure will make writing a story more manageable, but the varied elements will challenge gifted boys.

Cinematherapy

Watch the movie *Finding Forrester* and discuss the dilemma the main character experiences among sports, the way peers view him, and his interest in writing. Read books that also are movies, such as *Bridge to Terabithia, Because of Winn-Dixie, Tuck Everlasting, The Golden Compass, The Chronicles of Narnia, A Series of Unfortunate Events*, or the *Harry Potter* series. Discuss and write about the similarities and differences between the book and movie in detail.

Plug Into Technology

- Build a free website together to publish your child's writing. Google Page Creator is attractive and easy to use.
- Choose a topic in which your son is an expert, such as dinosaurs, baseball, or astronomy. Create or edit a current Wikipedia entry.
- Supervise your child in keeping a blog, an online journal, where he can rant about annoying things, tell funny stories about what happened that day, or share favorite quotes, music, ideas, and reviews of last night's TV shows with friends. Entries can be set to "private" or "friends only" to protect his privacy.
- Build a "Soundtrack of My Life" iTunes playlist. Write a list of songs that would be on the soundtrack and why they're included.
- Use a tape recorder or record short videos on a digital camera. Have your son tell the story to emphasize that writing is not just about putting a pen to paper, but the act of storytelling, sharing stories in a communal way.
- Listen to a comedian on CD, or watch one on TV or on YouTube, and then write a comedy monologue. Act out, tape record, or digitally record and play it on the computer or post

it on a YouTube profile for friends to see. If he posts online, be sure to access privacy settings, so only a select few people can watch the video.

Family Fun Night: Not Just Board Games Anymore

- Act out stories your child wrote with family or friends.
- Play word games together like Scattergories, SCRABBLE™, Catch Phrase, or Boggle.
- Make up a new board game and write out the rules and creative background information for the game.
- Create a trading card game, like Pokémon or Dungeons and Dragons, and make up the rules and playing cards with drawings on the front and descriptions on the back.
- Add snacks—food always makes things better. Your son can write advertisements for his favorite snacks. Go out for pizza, ice cream, or sushi and then write reviews of the food or restaurant. Try new flavors in order to describe them. List words on the back of a business card or napkin. Write on unconventional materials—sometimes a big, blank white page can be scary and seems like too much space to fill.

Conclusion

Through these activities, you will get to know your son better and have fun—exercising creativity while he becomes a better writer. When writing is transformed from a lonely or isolating activity into a way to relate to peers and have fun with friends and family, it will be a lot more enjoyable for everyone!

Resources

Books and Articles for Parents

Heydt, S. (2004). Dear diary: Don't be alarmed . . . I'm a boy. *Gifted Child Today, 27*(3), 16–25.

Kerr, B., & Cohn, S. (2001). *Smart boys: Talent, manhood, and the search for meaning.* Scottsdale, AZ: Great Potential Press.

Kindlon, D., & Thompson, M. (1999). *Raising Cain: Protecting the emotional lives of our boys.* New York, NY: Ballantine.

Neihart, M., Reis, S. M., Robinson, N. M., & Moon, S. M. (Eds.). (2002). *The social and emotional development of gifted children: What do we know?* Waco, TX: Prufrock Press.

Odean, K. (1998). *Great books for boys.* New York, NY: Ballantine.

Pollack, W. S. (1998). *Real boys: Rescuing our sons from the myths of boyhood.* New York, NY: Holt.

Scieszka, J. (2008). *Guys write for guys read: Boys' favorite authors write about being boys.* New York, NY: Viking.

Silverman, L. K. (Ed.). (1993). *Counseling the gifted and talented.* Denver, CO: Love.

Books for Boys

Alex Rider series by Anthony Horowitz

Artemis Fowl series by Eoin Colfer

Eragon by Christopher Paolini

The Golden Compass—His Dark Materials Trilogy by Philip Pullman

Guys Write for Guys Read edited by Jon Scieszka

Harry Potter series by J. K. Rowling

Hatchet and entire *Brian* series by Gary Paulsen

Island Boyz by Graham Salisbury

The Invention of Hugo Cabret by Brian Selznick

Lord of the Rings by J. R. R. Tolkien

The Pendragon series by D. J. MacHale

The Redwall series by Brian Jacques

A Wrinkle in Time and companions by Madeleine L'Engle

Websites

Guys Read—http://www.guysread.com
Hoagies Gifted Education Page Gender Issues—http://www.hoagiesgifted.org/
gender.htm

References

Csikszentmihalyi, M., Rathunde, K., & Whalen, S. (1993). *Talented teenagers: The roots of success and failure.* New York, NY: Cambridge University Press.
Pollack, W. S. (2000). *Real boys' voices.* New York, NY: Random House.

When Overempowerment Yields Underachievement— Strategies to Adjust

by Sylvia Rimm

A T the 2006 National Association for Gifted Children conference in Charlotte, NC, I was honored to have the opportunity to give a keynote address. My presentation was based on findings from my clinical experiences in preventing and reversing underachievement of gifted children and my recent research with middle school children. Because many parents are unable to attend our national meetings, I'd like to share a summary of my presentation with you, emphasizing what I believe parents can do to prevent overempowerment and underachievement in their own gifted children.

Underachievement Is Not a Mystery

There has been considerable research on the underachievement of gifted children, and there are many teaching, parenting, and mentoring strategies that have been proven to be effective in helping to reverse underachievement and motivate gifted children. Because underachievement is learned behavior, it can be unlearned. Underachieving is a bad habit of avoiding effort, but habits can be changed, and motivation can be fostered, taught, and encouraged. Despite the success of various approaches, it's important for parents to realize that it's rarely easy to

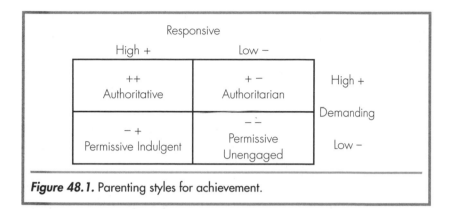

Figure 48.1. Parenting styles for achievement.

reverse underachievement because children, circumstances, families, and classroom environments are all complex.

Classic Good Parenting

Classic studies of family environments that led children to high achievement involved parents who were both responsive and demanding. In her research, for example, Baumrind (see Figure 48.1) labeled this kind of appropriate parenting as *authoritative* parenting, which she contrasted with *authoritarian* parenting, which she described as nonresponsive, but also demanding, or *permissive indulgent* parenting that was responsive, but not demanding (neither of which was effective for fostering children's achievement in school). Most obviously permissive, *unengaged* parenting also did not foster achievement. Classrooms that are responsive to children's intellectual, social, and emotional needs also lead to high achievement. For gifted children, appropriately challenging curriculum is an important component of responsiveness to academic needs.

The V of Love

The V of Love for raising and teaching children is a "common sense" description that fits well with the conception of authoritative parenting.

Parents set the limiting walls of the V, but increase power, freedom, choices, and responsibilities between the walls of the V as children develop and mature. Thus young children are at the base of the V and are given few choices, power, freedom, and responsibilities that match their small size. Childhood and adolescence can be relatively smooth if children are only gradually empowered. If parents don't expand the limiting walls of the V, children are overcontrolled and have little opportunity to become independently motivated. Authoritarian parents don't expand the walls of the V.

Parents of gifted children may easily fall into the trap of permissive indulgent parenting as envisioned in an inverted V. The verbal precocity and adult-sounding reasoning or very high IQ scores of high-ability students may tempt parents to "adultize" them early and assume they are more capable of decision making than their maturity allows. When the V is inverted, children are given power, choices, and freedom too early and often make poor decisions that worry their parents. Parents, too late, attempt to set limits for these powerful children. Ordinary limits cause them to become angry, depressed, and rebellious because they feel powerless relative to the power they experienced too early. They are overempowered and have developed a habit of complete control. Accustomed to making all of their own decisions, these powerful children resent parents or teachers who guide them differently from their own preferences. They are offended by criticism, become defensive, argue only to prove they are right, and underachieve to assert that teachers and parents are wrong. The following letter from a mother of a profoundly gifted child provides an example of an overempowered, strong-willed child.

> I have a 7-year-old daughter who is a major challenge for me. How do you deal with an overconfident child who wants to change the world right now? I think my daughter is profoundly gifted. I homeschooled her until this year when she requested that I put her in "regular" school like "normal kids," so I did. She's in first grade, but could easily be in third or fourth grade. The school just completed an assessment, and I will get the results next month.

My daughter feels she shouldn't have to go to school or be homeschooled, and she should just be left alone to pursue her own ideas and inventions. She's very angry with me for "wasting her time doing baby stuff" at school. She loves her friends and the social aspect of school, but feels school is beneath her. Her teacher is a wonderful, certified teacher of gifted, but my daughter has recently become disrespectful to her because she caught her teacher making a mistake about something.

My daughter constantly begs me to convert our garage into a science lab so she can do experiments to find a cure for cancer. She packed her suitcase and ran away from home recently. She got to the end of the street before I convinced her to come back. She said I didn't understand and appreciate her desire to be a famous scientist today—not in the future.

I'm very distressed about this and don't know what to do. Have you seen these types of kids before? What's the best way to handle them and how do I handle her anger with me?

The Pressures of Giftedness

A great problem for gifted children is that the very same pressures of giftedness can lead to either high achievement motivation or to underachievement. These opposite expressions of similar life occurrences puzzle parents and teachers. Consider that children with extraordinary vocabulary, unusual thinking, and rapidly developing skills often are surrounded by adults who praise them or describe them to others with words like perfect, brilliant, extraordinary, spectacular, genius, or the conviction that they will surely cure cancer. Those innocent but extravagant descriptors set values and expectations for children in the family and in the classroom.

For some children who have appropriate school and home environments, these words will inspire them to set high goals and work hard toward those goals. They will learn to enjoy the learning and discovery process as they mature. For other children, they will internalize these goals as impossible pressures, be disappointed in themselves, fear risking effort, and will invest considerable energy in protecting their fragile self-concepts for fear that if they made an effort, it would only prove that they aren't as intelligent or extraordinary as people assumed. I refer to this second group of underachieving children as "dethroned" children because their personalities and behaviors change so dramatically from a childhood where they were overpraised and overempowered.

Dethronement

The most difficult hazard of overempowerment is "dethronement." When another sibling is born or if the overempowered child isn't recognized as special in the classroom, he or she may feel irrationally and extraordinarily rejected. Dethroned children exhibit negativity, anger, aggressiveness, or sadness. They may readily be labeled depressed, anxious, or as having Attention Deficit/Hyperactive Disorder (ADHD). Their personalities change dramatically and they may literally "shut down" to learning.

Dethroned children may try to run their families, their teachers, and other students, and they may argue incessantly to "outsmart" adults. Their parents often refer to them as "lawyers." Victory in an argument temporarily restores their throne. As these children trap adults into the battles, parents and teachers find themselves losing their tempers. Teachers and parents, offended by such powerful children, try to "put them in their places." Adults respond to these oppositional, offensive children with a big no permanently engraved on their foreheads. "Unfair," the children argue, undaunted. They believe that no one understands them, and indeed few people do.

Dethronement may happen any time in life briefly, or it may become long lasting. It truly seems like an altered state and a dramatic change in the child. Read the following stories about Patrick and Laura for examples of dethronement at home and at school.

Patrick's Story

Patrick, a first "miracle" child born to a couple in their late 30s, was a delightful, bright baby and toddler, and by age 3 was reading fluently. His parents enrolled him in preschool, coincidentally, at about the same time his brother was born. At first Patrick was excited about going to school; however, whenever he was expected to join in with other children for a group activity, he resisted and remained alone. The teachers permitted him time for adjustment, but then they insisted that Patrick join the class. Patrick ran away from school. The school officials asked his mother to take him home on the days he ran away. Patrick ran away multiple times, so the school asked that Patrick wait a year before entering their school again because they believed him to be immature. Patrick repeated the problem at a second preschool and was dismissed again.

At home, Patrick did well with playmates and was very kind and sweet to his baby brother. He continued to love to play imaginatively and read and did math prodigiously. His "dethronement" wasn't obvious.

Patrick's play evaluation session at Family Achievement Clinic yielded the secret of his dethronement. He placed his mom and dad and himself inside the playhouse as he explained that his little brother could not come in and must stay outside. When I suggested that mom and dad would be sad without his brother, he sulked and said, "That's OK if they're sad. I don't care."

When Patrick ran away from his summer camp, we shortened his morning temporarily and explained that if he had a bad day, he would be timed-out in his room at home with his door closed. If he had a good day, he earned a sticker and some special one-to-one time with his mom or dad. He needed to experience only one closed-door time-out before he realized that running away would not bring his sought after parent attention. We gradually lengthened his day at camp. In his mother's words, "I have my old Patrick back again." The more positive adjustment continued when Patrick enrolled in his third preschool where his excellent skills were put to use and social needs were met appropriately.

Laura's Story

Laura came to the clinic after her junior year in high school. Her school history showed her to be a perfect A student throughout elementary school. In middle school she earned a few B's. She ended her freshman year in high school with a 3.7 average. During her sophomore year, she studied less and occasionally missed assignments. Her grade point average decreased further. She told her father that it made no sense to study if she couldn't earn A's. Her second semester, junior year, grade point average was 3.0. With F's on her report card, a 4-year college might no longer be an option for Laura. Laura's peer group had changed from students who were planning to attend college to those who might never attend and used alcohol and drugs.

Laura's "dethronement" at home had caused problems for many years. As a first child, first grandchild, and first niece, she was initially the designated "queen." Laura was not happy about the eventual addition of three brothers whom she bossed mercilessly. Her personality changed. Temper tantrums were common when plans didn't work as Laura wanted them to, and her tantrums were effective for many years in giving her control of the household. She manipulated her father against her mother, making her mother feel powerless, as Laura and her dad blamed her mother for being too controlling. Laura's mother withdrew and concentrated her parenting energies on her sons.

Laura didn't want to see a therapist and was angry, oppositional, and not forthcoming in answers about her dilemma. When I asked whether her concern that she couldn't get A's had caused her to stop doing her work, she admitted that had happened in her sophomore year, but denied it was continuing to affect her now. She claimed she was confident that she could again earn grades to get her into college, although she had no idea about what she'd like to do as a career. She told me that she'd like most to be "a good person" and that was her only important goal. In response to my question, she said she was like neither parent and claimed neither understood her. She chose a friend as a role model who she said had a mother who was understanding. She denied use of alcohol or drugs, but did not make eye contact with me as she voiced that denial. When I asked what she might wish for if I were a fairy godmother and could grant her three wishes, her first wish was to be able to control all people, her second for a million dollars, and her third for a guaranteed successful career.

Laura was accustomed to control. Laura's first dethronement at home took place when her brother was born. Her second dethronement happened gradually in middle school and more dramatically after her first year in high school. Laura could no longer manipulate her angry father. She felt rejected and turned to a negative boyfriend for comfort, love, and sexual activity.

Laura's progress is precarious, but she has separated from her negative peer group. Her grades are back to mostly A's, with just one C+. Her mom and dad are united, and her relationship with both parents has improved.

Research on Overempowerment

In my survey of 5,400 middle grade children for my book, *Growing Up Too Fast: The Rimm Report on the Secret World of America's Middle Schoolers,* I found that middle grade children today are growing up in environments more similar to what their parents experienced in high school and beyond. The media have prematurely sexualized them. By third grade, 15% worried a lot about popularity with the opposite sex, and a similar percentage worried that their parents didn't understand them. In earlier generations, such worries were reserved for adolescence. For third graders at that time, their priorities were pleasing parents and teachers and playing with children of their own gender. Popularity wasn't even a word in their vocabulary. In our clinic, when young, gifted children are tested and asked to pronounce the word condemn, the most frequent mispronunciation is condom, and even small children have wished for "sexy" clothes.

In focus groups with gifted fifth through eighth graders, the children indicated they believed they had already made an average of two thirds of the decisions in their lives. When I asked if they thought their parents permitted them enough of their own decision making, most were not contented. Among the fifth graders, more than half (55%)

were unsatisfied, and by eighth grade, 90% of the students believed they should have more power. Here are examples of what they had to say:

- "My parents won't listen to me. My dad thinks I should be treated differently just because I'm a kid. I want the same treatment as my parents."—Fifth-grade boy
- "I think parents can help us make some decisions, but if we want to make them ourselves, they should just accept that and let us do it."—Seventh-grade girl
- "My parents trust my judgment. They might give me some ideas, but I make 90% of the decisions."—Seventh-grade boy

What Parents Can Do to Preserve Early Adolescence

In addition to raising children in responsive environments where parents set clear limits as in the V of Love, there's much that parents can do to help preserve a healthy childhood. My research found that children with good family relationships, less TV and movie watching, and more involvement in interests and extracurricular activities were less likely to be caught up in high-risk behaviors like drinking alcohol, doing drugs, and promiscuous sexual involvement. Youngsters who described their family relationships as above average also were less likely to be quite as worried about being pretty and popular. That isn't to say they didn't care about these peer issues, but family support and engagement in positive activities were extremely helpful. Families who find time to work, play, laugh, and talk together help preserve healthy childhoods. Of course, you knew that already, but with such busy lives, many of us may need reminders.

Reversing Dethronement and Underachievement

In my book, *Why Bright Kids Get Poor Grades and What You Can Do About It,* I proposed a trifocal model in which parents and teachers together could select from many approaches to reverse their children's or students' underachievement when it has been caused by psychological dethronement.

Reversing Underachievement Alliance

Ally with the child privately about motivations and pressures.
Listen to what the child has to say.
Learn what the child is thinking.
Invite opportunities for recognition of child's strengths.
Add challenging and interesting curriculum and activities.
Nurture relationships with respectful and appropriate role models.
Create specific consequences, firmly and reasonably, if the child doesn't
  meet expectations.
Emphasize effort, independence, realistic expectations, and ways strengths
  can be used to cope with problems.

Figure 48.2. Reversing underachievement alliance acrostic.

Readings with solutions are included at the end of this chapter and the Reversing Underachievement Alliance acrostic (see Figure 48.2) summarizes important steps to restoring a dethroned child to achievement.

It is important to realize that sometimes the reversal of underachievement is almost immediate, particularly among younger children. Other times, the reversal takes extraordinary patience and seems like a "two steps forward, one step backward" process. For many underachievers, reversing that powerless feeling of dethronement results in intense and passionate achievement. It's almost like "awakening a sleeping giant." For Patrick at age 4, his mother described the change as having her old Patrick back again; while for Laura, her success is not yet entirely clear. Adults who retrospectively recall the reversal of their child's underachievement often report—a mentor, a teacher, or a partner who believed in them.

Resilience

Most parents tell me that they want happy, achieving lifestyles for their gifted children. They hope their children will find careers that tap their talents and interests, balanced with relationships that help them to feel happy and fulfilled. Most parents also understand that those goals are not easy to achieve. Successful gifted children will face many struggles and failure experiences. Their ultimate success will often depend on whether their lives have taught them resilience.

Dr. Robert Sapolsky, professor of biology and neurology at Stanford University and author of the book, *Why Zebras Don't Get Ulcers*, discussed how difficult experiences serve to inoculate people and increase their resilience. Thus, with small stresses children learn to cope and "vaccinate" themselves to cope better with the larger stresses that life is likely to deliver. If we, as parents, overindulge, overprotect, or overempower our children, we may be withholding the vaccination that can lead them to resilience.

Parents, You Are Very Important to Your Children

No parent is perfect, and, indeed, children remember their childhood very differently from how parents remember parenting them. The mistakes you believe you've made may be forgotten by your children, and what you believe were successful efforts may not even be valued by them. In my interviews with hundreds of successful women, the women recalled their parents' messages and guidance, even as they remembered occasionally protesting with rolled-back eyes during adolescence. In my clinical work with underachievers, parents have returned to share stories of how their grown children thanked them later for setting the very limits these children had rebelled against in adolescence. As you parent your gifted children, consider that your responsibility is not to be sure they're happy every day and every hour, but to prepare them for the resilience, achievement, and balance in relationships they will require to launch happy adult lives. If you parent with foresight, their small unhappinesses may vaccinate them with the resilience they'll require. Here's a final story to think about.

A Nerdy, Smart Boy

A long time ago, in the post-Sputnik years when gifted programming was new and was targeted toward science and mathematics, we lived in northwestern, rural New Jersey. My new husband was a graduate student working on his master's degree in dairy genetics, and I had just graduated from college and was substitute teaching, hoping to get my first real teaching job.

Our only neighbors were my husband's major professor, Bob Mather, his wife, Martha, who was an elementary school teacher, and their two children, John and Janet. We would visit back and forth, and Martha told me about the importance of the new ability grouping for gifted children. Bob was interested in astronomy and had gotten a telescope so that he and his middle school children could explore the star-studded sky that only a rural area provides.

The children didn't have many friends and spent a lot of time learning, working, and having fun with their family. I never heard the parents describe their children as brilliant, extraordinary, or even gifted, although they did consider them smart. John, particularly, seemed shy and definitely in the "nerd" category. In his later words, he was a "nerd" even before others had coined the word.

Astronomy became John's love. John went to a public, rural school in a very small school district and chose a small college, Swarthmore, because he considered it "to be respectable to be a 'nerd' there." He went on to do graduate work in astronomy at the University of California, Berkeley. At a time when many college students were busy being hippies or protesting, he graduated with a 4.0 average.

John took a job with NASA. That's what post-Sputnik gifted education was all about, no surprises there, but here's the surprise! That shy, timid, nerdy kid, John C. Mather, was later awarded the Nobel Prize in Physics for his work on the COBE (Cosmic Background Explorer) satellite that helped cement the Big Bang Theory of the universe and can be regarded as "the starting point for cosmology as a precision science" (Mather & Boslough, 1998). Most parents can't count on raising their gifted children to Nobel Prize status. John's parents didn't expect to, either. But perhaps if we can inspire our gifted children to become engaged in their interests, to work hard, and to be resilient enough to endure "nerdhood," they, too, may make meaningful contributions.

Resources

Baum, S., Renzulli, J., & Hébert, T. (1995). *The prism metaphor: A new paradigm for reversing underachievement*. Storrs: University of Connecticut, The National Research Center on the Gifted and Talented.

Baumrind, D. (1966). Effects of authoritative control on child behavior. *Child Development, 37,* 887–907.

Baumrind, D. (1991). Parenting styles and adolescent development. In R. Lerner, A. Petersen, & J. Brooks-Gunn (Eds.), *Encyclopedia of adolescence* (pp. 746–758). New York, NY: Garland.

Cod, C. (1992). *Motivating underachievers: 172 strategies for success*. Beavercreek, OH: Creative Learning Consultants.

Mather, J. C., & Boslough, J. (1998). *The very first light: The true inside story of the scientific journey back to the dawn of the universe*. New York, NY: Basic Books.

Reis, S. M., & McCoach, D. B. (2002). Underachievement in gifted students. In M. Neihart, S. M. Reis, N. M. Robinson, & S. M. Moon (Eds.), *The social and emotional development of gifted children: What do we know?* (pp. 81–92). Waco, TX: Prufrock Press.

Rimm, S. (1995). *Why bright kids get poor grades and what you can do about it*. New York, NY: Crown.

Rimm, S. (2005). *Growing up too fast: The Rimm report on the secret world of America's middle schoolers*. New York, NY: Rodale.

Sapolsky, R (2004). *Why zebras don't get ulcers* (3rd ed.). New York, NY: Henry Holt.

Siegle, D. (2004). *Understanding underachievement*. Storrs: University of Connecticut, The National Research Center on the Gifted and Talented.

Siegle, D., Reis, S. M., McCoach, D. B., Mann, R., Green, M., & Schreiber, F. (2002). *Intervention strategies for improving academic achievement* [CD]. Storrs: University of Connecticut, The National Research Center on the Gifted and Talented.

Developing Giftedness for a Better World

by Joseph S. Renzulli, Rachel E. Sytsma, and Robin M. Schader

Changing the World . . . One Step at a Time

As a third grader, Ryan was proud to read the local paper, sometimes sitting right alongside his father. One evening he saw an article reporting an extremely large increase in fines for littering, which led to his questions about why there needed to be fines for littering when it wasn't a big deal to simply put trash where it belongs. Ryan's father asked him if he had ever been too lazy to find a garbage can, or if he had seen his friends carelessly throw things down, and Ryan became a bit defensive. "Well, maybe once or twice, but no big deal," he answered. "Well," said his father, "what if everyone had the same attitude you do about trash? After all, one or two pieces of trash still add up. I'll bet the fine is being increased because it costs so much to hire people to clean up other people's mess."

The conversation continued into dinner. Ryan's parents speculated that young kids, with all their energy, might be able to contribute substantially to the welfare of their small town by actively becoming involved in this issue. Two days later, Ryan came home from school with the gem of an idea. What if he and his friends could pick up trash alongside the road to school on the coming Saturday? That first day, the four boys collected six bags of trash. One of the mothers sent a letter to the editor about their contribution, and soon others in school became involved. A local restaurant contributed free hamburgers for the kids who joined the next "trash day," and parents joined as "flaggers" for traffic safety.

For many years, our definition of giftedness has been based on the interaction of three characteristics: above-average (but not necessarily superior) ability, creativity, and task commitment. In other words, high ability is not enough to explain giftedness. It also takes an intensity and focus in a certain area, along with the willingness to try new ideas or look at something with a different perspective. Gifted behaviors occur when these three components intersect, and this happens in some people (not all people) at certain times (not all times), and under certain circumstances (not all circumstances). We only recently began to turn our attention to understanding more fully the sources of these gifted behaviors and, more importantly, the ways in which people use their gifts and talents in a constructive and positive way. Why did Ryan contribute time and energy to a socially responsible project that would make life better in his community? Can a better understanding of people who use their gifts for the greater good help us create conditions that expand the number of people who willingly contribute to the growth of both social and economic capital? How can parents provide opportunities so their children develop their abilities in responsible ways?

Social Capital and Gifted Education

Financial and intellectual capital are well-known forces that drive the economy and generate professional advancement, wealth production, and highly valued material assets—all important to a capitalistic economic system. Social capital, on the other hand, consists of intangible assets that address the collective needs and problems of individuals and communities. Continual investments in social capital benefit everyone, communities and individuals alike, because they help create the values, norms, and networks that constitute the bedrock of social trust.

What is perhaps most striking when examining the commentary of leading scholars about economic capital versus social capital is that investments in both types of national assets are necessary for greater prosperity and improved physical and mental health, as well as a society that honors freedom, happiness, justice, civic participation, and the dignity of a diverse population. Robert Putnam, for example, pointed out that historically the aggregation of social capital has contributed to economic development. He found that widespread social trust, participation in group activities, and cooperation created conditions for both good government and prosperity. Tracing the roots of investments in social capital to medieval times, Putnam concluded that communities did not become civil because they were rich, but rather became rich because they were civil.

Over the latter half of the 20th century, however, striking evidence indicates a marked decline in social capital in Western culture. Surveys show decreases over the last few decades in voter turnout and political participation, membership in service clubs, church-related groups, parent-teacher associations, unions, and fraternal groups.

Past research on gifted individuals has tried to address the difference between high-ability persons who use their intellectual, motivational, and creative assets in ways that lead to outstanding manifestations of creative productivity (such as Edison with the electric light bulb or the Wright Brothers with the airplane) and those gifted individuals with similar or perhaps even more considerable assets who do not achieve high levels of accomplishment. Perhaps the more important question when thinking about the production of social capital is: "What causes some people to mobilize their interpersonal, political, ethical, and moral senses in such ways that they place human concerns and the common good above materialism, ego enhancement, and self-indulgence?"

Operation Houndstooth

In an effort to promote gifted leadership for a new century we believe that the definition of giftedness should be expanded to include several traits that characterize persons who have had a profound impact on the improvement of society. In order to accomplish that goal, we developed a research project called Operation Houndstooth, which has two major phases. The first phase of the project includes clarifying definitions while identifying, adapting, and constructing assessment procedures to extend our understanding of six important factors that emerged from a comprehensive review of the literature and a series of surveys given to high school students. The six components are described in Figure 49.1.

Our research has already shown that Houndstooth components can be found in diverse groups and across age levels. A major assumption underlying this project is that all the components defined in our background research can be modified under certain circumstances. Thus, the second phase consists of a series of experimental studies to determine how we might promote the types of behavior defined within those six components.

The word "Houndstooth" refers to the complex background pattern of interwoven factors that have an impact on gifted behaviors. Consider how the warp and woof of cloth provide strength and pattern. Like threads, gifted behaviors do not exist in isolation, but develop within particular situations. Operation Houndstooth was created to investigate which factors contribute to the positive use of personal assets.

It is important for parents to consider possible ingredients for giftedness and creative productivity if they are to help their children develop their potential. We can find many theories and anecdotal accounts of high achievers that call attention to different components and conditions for exceptional accomplishment; yet it is still unclear why certain persons have devoted their lives and considerable talents to improving the human condition. What contributes to the creation of persons such as Nelson Mandela, Rachel Carson, or Mother Teresa?

The positive psychology movement, championed by Martin E. P. Seligman and Mihaly Csikszentmihalyi, focuses on the enhancement of what is good in life, and the investigation of human strengths and virtues. The goal is for social science to become a positive force in the advancement of the highest qualities of civic and personal life.

Operation Houndstooth results from the coupling of this movement's tenets with a continuing search for key components that give rise to socially constructive giftedness, especially in young people. We know these components can have a positive impact on the development

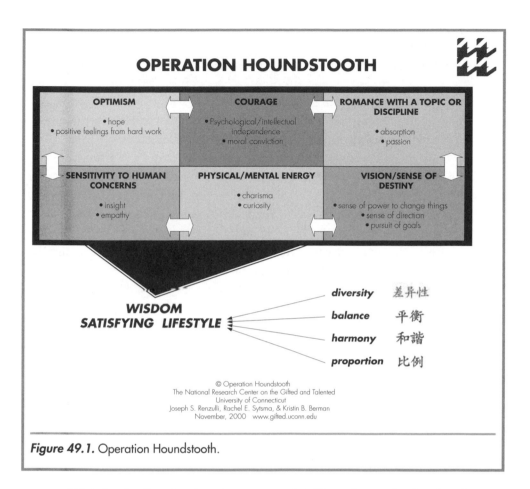

Figure 49.1. Operation Houndstooth.

of high levels of motivation, interpersonal skills, and organizational and management skills. In addition, we believe Houndstooth components support the growth of cognitive attributes such as academic achievement, research skills, creativity, and problem-solving skills.

Before discussing how we can create learning environments that nurture Houndstooth characteristics, we should acknowledge a few cautions when considering how to instill those traits in young people. Simply telling children about these more complex capacities doesn't work—you can't teach or preach vision or sense of destiny. We also should emphasize voluntary student participation in programs and projects designed to promote the characteristics and behaviors identified in Operation Houndstooth. Student-initiated service is more powerful and engaging than required community service or forcing uncommitted young people to participate in projects based on someone else's values.

How then can we promote the capacities represented in Houndstooth? We suggest that the answer lies in providing young people with ways to: (a) examine their individual abilities, interests, and learning styles; (b) explore areas of potential involvement based on existing or developing interests; (c) find opportunities, resources, and encouragement for firsthand investigative or creative experiences within their chosen areas of interest; and (d) become involved in ways they can see positive traits being modeled by adults. Parents can take a proactive role in making this happen.

Early characteristics of gifted children that may indicate interest in socially constructive work include:

- observations of "fairness" at school,
- a strong sense of right and wrong,
- sensitivity to the feelings of others, and
- strong awareness of the needs of others.

Examining Abilities, Interests, and Learning Styles

The best examples of positive behaviors identified in the Houndstooth research have resulted from children who have a good picture of who they are as students, and how they learn best. Although academic strengths are usually obvious and well documented through regular school programs, information about interests, learning styles, thinking styles, and preference for various modes of expression comes from thoughtful conversations over time between parents, their children, and other involved adults. Guided discussions with your children about important topics can provide insights into how, where, why, at what times, and under what conditions each child is best able to learn. At the same time, the exploration of preferences can help establish a respect for individual differences. For example, it is likely you and your child will find that your learning profiles are not the same, yet you both have found ways to absorb information as well as "show what you know." We use a document called the Total Talent Portfolio (TTP) to collect this information. The TTP includes several kinds of information about a person, including:

- academic strengths,
- general and specific areas of interest,
- learning style preferences,
- learning environment preferences,
- thinking style preferences, and
- preferred style of expression.

Exploring Areas of Potential Involvement

Houndstooth capacities develop when students become passionately involved in an area of personal choice. The best way to promote such involvement is to expose young people to dynamic experiences within their general area(s) of interest. Parents who are familiar with what their child likes to do outside of school can help stimulate their child's curiosity about a variety of topics. The 2003 book *Child's Play: Enriching Your Child's Interests*, by Monica Cardoza, explains how activities outside of school can be good starting points for developing interests. The author suggests that, if your child enjoys a particular activity, it will be wise to explore it in all its detail, looking into its offshoots or variations. For example, if your child studies ballet, you might encourage her or him to research other forms of dance, to read about the history of dance, or to study famous dancers, costumes, or music.

Another way to encourage in-depth involvement is by visiting places where creative activity is taking place. Business offices, film and television studios, research laboratories, publishing houses, artists' studios, and backstage visits to theaters are just a few examples of places where you can take your child to see creative people at work. Once again, understanding your child's interests and learning styles helps you become more effective in focusing and stimulating interests. In the vignette at the beginning of this article, Ryan's father was aware that his son loved the challenge of finding many different solutions to a problem and then figuring out what would work best. The two of them spent most of dinnertime talking about "trash" (e.g., fines, recycling, waste facilities, machines).

Participation in lively discussions about controversial issues, events, books, and media presentations is another way to stimulate opportunities for intensive follow-up. Listening to a house guest talk about his passion for sustainable agriculture/aquaculture in Third World countries recently motivated two high school students to contact an organization that provides materials and training for rooftop gardens in Mexico City. As a result, one of them spent a summer working with families and then, upon returning home, the two friends began a club to train other students in their city in specialized gardening techniques.

Children who talk about work in which they are interested often have "stars in their eyes." They frequently recount clever and creative ways in which they overcome obstacles. For example, one young musician who had organized groups of other musicians to play in rural elementary schools talked about arriving at a school without a tuned piano and having to adjust the program to include awareness of sound quality and the joy of beautiful music, rather than focus the performance on pieces that included the unplayable piano. As a result, a young student at that school sought out a piano tuner, learned about his craft, and collected funds to have the school piano tuned on a regular schedule so the whole student body would benefit. The main message should always be: "Find an interest and get involved." Being a gifted contributor is not a spectator sport!

Providing Opportunities

Parents who see emerging interests in their children and then spend time learning about what excites their curiosity can offer opportunities for the development of those interests. For example, when a father first learned of his son's concern for homeless children, he included his son in a Rotary Club lunch meeting about famine. Later the two of them watched a documentary on national poverty. As his son continued to ask questions, this father sought out more and more ways to help his son learn. He clipped relevant articles from newspapers and magazines, and even sent letters with clippings when his job took him away from home. He commented on conversations he heard at work, and openly encouraged his son's burgeoning interest.

Becoming Involved Oneself

The best role models for good works are parents. The father described above, an accountant, signed up as a regular volunteer right alongside his son at a local soup kitchen. As a team, they have now created a schedule and organized a committee to collect donations from restaurants around town that can then be used for soup kitchen lunches. In these cases, two underlying themes are "we can make things happen" and "we can instigate positive change." Perhaps the most important outcome is the sheer enjoyment along with learning problem-solving skills that children can glean from addressing issues outside the realm of conventional classroom subjects.

How Can Parents Help Encourage Houndstooth Characteristics?

- Discuss, brainstorm, and explore little ways to help make a difference.
- Search out biographies of people who have made a difference (see http://www.achievement.org).
- Bring up topics such as "What is fairness?" in conversations with your child.
- Help scaffold and build your child's interest by searching out opportunities, finding resources, and helping him or her meet and work with appropriate people (adults and other students).
- Read or watch the news together and discuss current events (not focusing on negatives or seemingly hopeless situations).

Are the Goals of Operation Houndstooth Realistic?

If, as studies have shown, self-interest has replaced some of the values that created a more socially conscious early America, and if the negative trends of young people's overindulgences and disassociations are growing, then we must ask if there is a role that parents and schools can play in gently influencing future citizens, and especially future leaders, toward a value system that assumes greater responsibility for the production of social capital. In spite of our best efforts to identify students for special programs, it is still difficult to predict who will be our most gifted future contributors to our world. So far as the work on Operation Houndstooth is concerned, the possibility exists that by expanding our conception of giftedness beyond traditional high-scoring test takers and good lesson learners, we will find as rich a source of high potential young people in the broad and diverse populations of nonselected students as we find in students traditionally selected for gifted programs.

Understanding how positive human attributes develop is especially important because it will help us direct the educational and environmental experiences we provide for the potentially gifted and talented young people who will be in a position to shape both the values and the actions of this new century. Although the whole notion of changing the big picture seems awesome and overwhelming, the words of Margaret Mead remind us that it can be done: "Never doubt that a small group of thoughtful, committed citizens can change the world . . . indeed, it is the only thing that ever does."

Parents have the opportunity—and the responsibility—to interact with their children in positive and future-oriented ways. Perhaps one of the most important things we can do for our children is to empower them to shape their own futures. In so doing, we will instill in them the motivation to help create a better society, or even a better world.

Resources

Burns, D., Purcell, J., & Schader, R. M. (September, 1999). Parents, teachers, and the talent portfolio: Making curriculum modification and differentiation a reality, *Parenting for High Potential*, 6–7, 30.

Purcell, J. H., & Renzulli, J. S. (1998). *Total talent portfolio: A systematic plan to identify and nurture gifts and talents.* Mansfield Center, CT: Creative Learning Press.

Rogers, K. B. (2001). *Re-forming gifted education: Matching the program to the child.* Scottsdale, AZ: Great Potential Press.

Seligman, M. E. P., & Csikszentmihalyi, M. (2000). Positive psychology. *American Psychologist, 55,* 5–14.

References

Cardoza, M. M. (2003). *Child's play: Enhancing your child's interests, from rocket science to rock climbing, stamp collecting to sculpture.* New York, NY: Citadel Press.

Putnam, R. (1993). *Making democracy work: Civic traditions in modern Italy.* Princeton, NJ: Princeton University Press.

Putnam, R. (1995). Bowling alone: America's declining social capital. *Journal of Democracy, 6,* 65–78.

Chapter 50

Getting Your Child Involved in Volunteering

by Barbara A. Lewis

Elephants are big. Second graders are small, but the size difference didn't look like a hurdle to a group of feisty 7-year-olds at Vidya Elementary School in Petaluma, CA. Their teacher, Diana Lightman, introduced the kids to their giant-sized friends in class, but it was one of the parents who took over after their teacher tucked the elephant unit away in a file cabinet.

When Steve Quirt's son, Mark, cried into his pillow one night because he loved elephants so much, Steve picked up on his son's intense interest and decided to do something about it. Steve, Mark, and some of Mark's friends started a club for elephants. The kids chose to call themselves FOWL (Friends of Wildlife) and continued to meet through high school. In the process they saved many elephants in Africa, Asia, and the U.S. that would have been destroyed without their fundraising efforts. The FOWLers were responsible for more than 1,000 letters being mailed to Washington, DC, that helped bring about the ivory ban in 1990.

Aside from the contribution to the natural world, the FOWLers' self-confidence soared in leadership positions and in their personal lives. Their achievement in school increased as well. A key factor in their success might be explained by counselor and educator, Linda Silverman: "Service is a *need* of the gifted. When gifted children find their paths of service, they experience a deep sense of fulfillment, as if there is a reason that they are here."

Service can provide a vehicle for kids to develop "successful intelligence," what Robert Sternberg describes as the ability to succeed in life and to make contributions. Service also can help kids develop their cognitive abilities such as reasoning and being able to analyze problems around them. By learning to understand and to care for other things, children also can expand their emotional intelligence.

Research has shown that kids involved in service increase their social responsibility and have more positive attitudes toward adults and others, enhanced self-esteem, growth in moral and ego development, complex thinking, and mastery of skills. Service has even helped kids raise math and reading scores and reduce drug use among their peers.

One criticism sometimes voiced against allowing children to get involved in this type of problem solving (i.e., volunteer service) is that it might frighten children as they become more aware of problems. However, children are bombarded with problems in comic strips, on TV, in the newspaper, in books they read, and in watching life itself. Often they feel helpless.

Contrary to feeling helpless, volunteering can help reduce the amount of anxiety a child experiences. Reports from both the Wisconsin Center for Environmental Education and Washington State University found that kids aren't overwhelmed with worries when they are participating in the solutions. They believe problems can be solved and that they can help solve them. The researchers found that children who took action to protect the environment had higher feelings of self-esteem and control over their lives.

Fostering a Desire to Serve

What can you, as a parent, do to foster in your children a desire to serve?

- *Set an example.* Children might not jump into service projects unless they have seen their parents serving. When parents serve others by taking soup to a sick neighbor or by raking leaves, they should allow their children to help. It can be messy. Children spill soup and redistribute leaves across raked grass, but the development of the child is more important than the service rendered by the child.

- *Encourage and reward service at home.* When your child picks up his or her socks and puts them in the hamper, you might say, "Thank you, you have helped you and me, and now I'll help you." By labeling kind behaviors as service, your child can begin to understand that service is a valued and rewarded behavior. By offering to do something nice in return, your child begins to learn the concept of showing gratitude as a return of service.

- *Take time for night-time talk.* Lie down with your child when he goes to bed. Talk about the events of the day in your child's life. Ask him about the best things, the worst things, what made him mad or happy, what was funny. If your child is reluctant to share, you might try offering some of your own childhood experiences, including an emphasis on how you solved some problem. As your child begins to open up to you, refrain from judging or giving solutions. When your child mentions a problem, you might ask, "What did you do to solve it?" or "What do you think you will do from now on?" Congratulate your child on his good thinking.

- *Discover the interests of your child.* Parents who expose their children to a variety of interests through reading, playing together, and taking excursions often can uncover the talents and passions of their children. These are obvious things to do, but it shouldn't stop with uncovering your child's interests. When Steve Quirt discovered his second grader's intense interest in elephants, he guided and extended his son's interests into making a contribution.

- *Take scavenger hunts for problems.* When a parent takes a walk with a child, it might be turned into a problem-solving session. This should not be confused with a doomsday, everything-is-wrong session. It should be upbeat and positive with an emphasis on solution finding. For example, you might say: "There are some gum wrappers on the street. I wonder how they got there? What should we do?" Scavenger hunts provide suspense for kids and can lead them into service through removing litter, planting trees, raking leaves, shoveling walks, helping seniors or others in need, helping animals, and so on.

- *Plan a family service project.* Brainstorm problems with your children. Who needs what? Look at different categories such as family members (grandparents, cousins, aunts, uncles), neighbors, seniors, homeless, orphans, schools, neighborhood or home safety, environment, and others. Keep asking questions to encourage creative thinking. Write down all of their answers. You can let your children vote on one project, or you can direct them to a project.

Once your children decide on a project, allow them to brainstorm solutions. Write down all answers, even wild and crazy ones. Then discuss which solutions seem like the best ones to do. Allow the children to select which parts they want to be in charge. You can make a chart with each person's responsibilities. Check them off as they are done and award a service badge or other reward.

- *Encourage service opportunities in school.* Visit your child's teacher. Find out what the class is studying and offer to extend this unit into a service project. School service projects that are attached to learning can be both encouraged and funded by the federal government through the Corporation for National and Community Service, "Learn and Serve." For example, suppose your child's teacher plans to prepare a unit on the history of your state or community. Students could extend that knowledge base to a service project by collecting stories of what grandparents or seniors remember of the community, compiling the stories in a book, and contributing their book to the school library or local historical society.

- *Outside of school, families can join a church or faith community or other service organization that provides opportunities for youth and adult services.* Encourage your child to join clubs, summer camps, or other community youth organizations. The scouting program invites service through merit badge requirements. Boys' and Girls' Clubs, 4-H, and other youth organizations also encourage service. If you volunteer in your child's club experience, you can ensure the kids' participation in service experiences. Additionally, universities or summer education extension programs often provide opportunities for youth service.

- *At home, practice table talk, TV news talk, and book talk.* Simply discussing issues with your children at the dinner table can encourage their interest in service. This activity will be a more valuable experience if you ask them their opinions on topics and often will generate all kinds of ideas for service. For example, you might be watching the news on TV together when you hear that one third of the children in your community are not immunized against childhood diseases. Ask you child's opinion. Then say, "Is there something you could do to help?" This could result in your child making a flyer and passing it around the neighborhood to announce locations and times where kids can be immunized for free. It might result in your child writing a jingle on getting immunized and sending it to a local radio station or drawing a poster and getting permission to hang it in a grocery store or other building.

Setting Up a Project

- *Brainstorm with your child possible problems that need solving.* Determine his or her interests and concerns.
- *Brainstorm solutions with your child.* Allow your child to choose his or her own solutions.
- *Direct your child's interests by asking questions so that they come up with the answers.* For example, a child might see a stray cat or dog. You might ask, "Do you know how you can tell that an animal doesn't have a home?" You might then discuss the physical appearance of the animal and even some instructions on not petting stray animals and why. Then you might ask something such as, "What could we do about it?" It might lead the child to call the humane society to find homes for abandoned pets or to provide a better habitat for cats. Or it

might be something as simple as taking care of the neighbor's family cat when they go out of town.

- *Refrain from judgment, from being the expert.* Allow your child to discover answers. The more leadership experience you allow your child in directing his or her own volunteer service, the more growth you will see.

- *Be a good facilitator.* This means that you might call an organization ahead of time to lay the foundation for your child's phone call to volunteer. Set up a certain time when your child can call and talk with a specific person. You also can find out ahead of time the kinds of things your child might do to volunteer. Then allow your child to think of the same ideas by asking questions, or let your child express his or her own ideas.

- *Always keep the veto power.* Obviously, if your child chooses to paint over graffiti in a dark, crime-infested alley in the worst section of town, you have the right to say, "No way!" But you also might redirect his or her interest into a safer activity such as asking the police to act as chaperones as your child paints over graffiti, starting a graffiti awareness campaign at school, or organizing a graffiti removal activity at school.

- *Help your child brainstorm a list of things to do to accomplish the service.* Number them in order of importance.

- *Help your child research up-to-date information about his or her volunteer interests.* Your child can conduct interviews, make telephone calls, and look on the Internet and at other sources.

- *Help your child seek the appropriate permissions and background information he or she needs before setting out.* For example, before kids decide to make chocolate marble cupcakes for the seniors in a retirement or nursing home, they better find out if there are any food allergies or if the home allows such things.

- *Try to remove the major obstacles.* Is there anyone who might not want your child volunteering? If your child wants to clean up a junky lot, it would be important to find out how neighbors feel and who owns the land so that your child can get their responses. Most people want to help children, but they might not like being taken by surprise.

- *Relax and have fun.* Remove pressure and enjoy the experience with your child.
- *When the project is done, discuss the experience with your child.* How does he or she feel about it? Would your child do it again? What might he or she do differently? To help your child reflect on the volunteer experience, encourage him or her to record the experience in a journal or on videotape, write a poem, or draw a picture. This step is important because it will help your child find meaning in what he or she does.
- *Celebrate your child's success.* Go out to dinner, go sledding, have a water balloon fight, buy a book, or take off your shoes and walk in the mud together.

Resources

Learn and Serve America—http://www.learnandserve.gov
International Service Learning—http://www.islonline.org
National Service-Learning Partnership—http://www.service-learningpartnership.
  org/sitc/PageServer
Volunteer Match—http://www.volunteermatch.org

Chapter 51

Debunking the Myths of Suicide in Gifted Children

by Andrea Dawn Frazier and Tracy L. Cross

POPULAR culture perpetuates myths that people with gifts and talents are more susceptible than others to psychological distress. This is readily evident in movies such as *Little Man Tate* or *Searching for Bobby Fischer*. One such myth is that talented and gifted people burn too bright to live long lives. Yet, published research up to this point has not proven this to be the case. Likewise, suicide in gifted youth is relatively unstudied and/or misunderstood. That being said, what can you do? The good news is that you can take proactive steps in working to safeguard your son or daughter against the dangers of despair so dire that she or he ultimately is successful in completing suicide. Although suicide can be difficult to talk about, this is our attempt to provide you the educative tools necessary to engage your child and the communities surrounding your child in an important conversation of this nature.

Surprisingly, children as young as 5 have been successful in taking their lives. Out of 100,000 young people between the ages of 15 and 24, approximately 10 will be successful in committing suicide. Moreover, the American Association of Suicidology (http://www.suicidology.org) estimates that for every successful suicide, there are 25 unsuccessful attempts. Suicide rates among adolescents and young adults (individuals aged 15–24) increased more than 240% between 1950 and 1995. Currently, suicide is the third leading cause of death in adolescents.

That being said, suicide rates within this population have been decreasing consistently since 1994.

Terms and Definitions

Suicidal behavior is best understood as at least four categories of behaviors. The first group of behaviors exists under the umbrella *suicide ideation*. Individuals who are ideators spend considerable time thinking of killing themselves. Those who are *gesturors* make attempts on their life, although they are not serious attempts. People are considered *attemptors* when they make serious but unsuccessful attempts to take their life. Finally, individuals who are successful are labeled *completers*.

Although these definitions may give one the idea that suicide is a process that is linear, this is, in fact, far from the case. Researchers who study suicide, or suicidologists, believe that one must ideate about suicide before attempting it. However, ideation does not necessarily lead to gesturing. Some go as far as gesturing and then stop. Others make serious attempts on their life and stop there.

Finally, you have those individuals who are successful in taking their lives. The rates at which adolescents ideate, gesture, and attempt to take their life are not known at this time. Much of the data currently reported only focuses on children who were successful in completing suicide. Suffice it to say, although it may seem that teens are on a runaway train when it comes to suicide, they can make the decision to get off.

What We Know About Gifted Youth and Suicide

At present, suicidology, or the study of suicide, does not have a great deal to say concerning suicide among gifted youth. This is in part due to the invisibility of giftedness in many school settings and an inability to fix on a consistent definition for "giftedness." Current numbers concerning suicide in teens do not comment on whether students were gifted. Moreover, data are generally collected after a suicide attempt has been completed. Often, the information about the young person is too sensitive for researchers to gain access to it.

Some researchers have made unsubstantiated claims that certain characteristics surrounding giftedness could make adolescents predisposed to suicide. These characteristics include becoming totally absorbed in school work, feeling the need to be perfect, and being extremely isolated from peers because the child is an introvert and/or awkward socially.

On the other hand, researchers including Tracy L. Cross, Karyn Gust-Brey, P. Bonny Ball, and Jerrell Cassady have not found that young people with gifts and talents have more suicidal ideation than their non-gifted peers. Cross and his colleagues would temper this with the following sober conclusions about suicide among gifted and talented youth:

- Adolescents are committing suicide; therefore, gifted adolescents are committing suicide.
- The rate of suicide has increased over the past four decades for the general population of adolescents within the context of an overall increase across all groups; therefore, it is reasonable to conclude that the incidence of suicide among gifted adolescents has increased over the past decade, keeping in mind that there are no definitive data available on the subject.
- Given the limited data available, we cannot ascertain whether the incidence of suicide among gifted adolescents is different than its incidence in the general population of adolescents.

Thus, when it comes to identifying risk factors for suicide in gifted teens, the prudent path would be to examine risk factors for suicide in the general population.

Risk Factors for Suicide in Gifted Youth

Activists with the Suicide Prevention Action Network USA (http://www.spanusa.org) contend that 90% of all suicide cases are due to depression or some other psychological disorder. The National Mental Health Association puts that number between 30% and 70%. The common denominator between these groups is the understanding that depression and the presence of other psychiatric disorders like manic depression or bipolarism play a large role in whether or not young people will consider suicide.

Something to keep in mind is the fact that depression comes in many different guises in children. It is only in late adolescence and early adulthood that depression expresses itself in ways that have been traditionally portrayed; thus, it is at this time that a young person may be more prone to considering suicide as a means of ending his or her forlornness. In adolescence, suicide ideation is anger and emotional pain turned inward. In younger children, anger is expressed more overtly; therefore, it should be extremes in anger that should serve as warning signs for depression. This includes rebellion and a strident defense of personal autonomy in the middle adolescent years, and, for preadolescents, anger is coupled with being muddled or mercurial. Essentially, preteens and teens should not stay within a narrow realm of emotional expression. Please resist the temptation to go along with conventional wisdom and see extremes in behavior as typical of gifted youth. They are not.

Some further risks associated with depression are drug and alcohol use (in the attempt to self-medicate) and a family history of suicide or other psychological disorders. Likewise, teens who are in constant trouble with the law or who are in other ways troubled are more prone to consider suicide. In fact, troubled adolescents are between 33% and 61% more likely to commit suicide than their untroubled peers. Finally, if a young person has weathered a loss in the family; if someone close to her or him successfully commits suicide; if she or he identifies as gay, lesbian, bisexual, or transgendered; if there is easy access to dangerous weapons; or if there has been an emphasis on suicide in the media, these are red flags for suicide ideation.

Theories About Suicide

It is a natural inclination to look toward a tomorrow, to foresee the future. Thus, it is no easy feat to lose the will to live. Suicidal people are waging a war within themselves concerning whether it is worthwhile to see another day. Several researchers have theorized about how people traverse this ambiguous path about living.

Those who support a cognitive explanation for suicide can allege that young people who do not have adequate problem-solving skills and face agonizing dilemmas begin to feel hopeless. Children caught in this way of thinking begin to see suicide as the only real alternative to which they have access. Researchers in support of contemporary psychodynamic theory suggest that people attempt suicide as a means of escaping conflict and mental stress. Finally, researchers who advance an existential theory for suicide contend that young people consider suicide when they feel their life lacks meaning. This lack of meaning can cause teens to feel useless, hopeless, and depressed.

The Suicide Trajectory Model by Judith Stillion and Eugene McDowell condensed the previous conversation concerning potential risks into four risk factor categories. Biological factors are risk factors like depression or a family history of suicide. Psychological risk factors deal with issues like low self-esteem and a sense of hopelessness. Cognitive risk factors are factors like poor problem solving and rigid thinking. Environment factors center on risk factors like the presence of lethal weapons and events that happen in the life of the family collectively or the child individually. Stillion and McDowell contended that the level of an interaction among these four categories of factors determines whether or not a young person will attempt suicide.

Warning Signs That an Adolescent May Be Suicidal

Warning signs are a bit different from risk factors. Risk factors highlight the areas in a young person's life that may make him or her prone to considering suicide as a viable option. The activists with the Suicide Prevention Action Network USA have created the following list of behaviors that are the overt signals that a young person may—at the bare minimum—be ideating about suicide:

- talks about committing suicide;
- has trouble eating or sleeping;
- experiences drastic changes in behavior;

- withdraws from friends and/or social activities;
- loses interest in hobbies, work, and school;
- makes out a will and final arrangements;
- gives away prized possessions;
- has attempted suicide in the past;
- takes unnecessary risks;
- has had recent severe losses;
- is preoccupied with death and dying;
- loses interest in personal appearance; and
- increases the use of alcohol or drugs.

Please bear in mind two things. Firstly, exhibiting one of these warning signs is not enough to point to a child ideating about suicide. It would be irresponsible to say, for example, that taking more risks means that a young person is considering suicide. However, if you see an adolescent exhibiting several of these characteristics, it is time for you to intervene.

Secondly, this is not an exhaustive list. It would be dangerous to say that a youth has not thought about suicide at all in the absence of any of these signs. We are all unique beings. There will never be a list that captures our complexity. So, you as a parent must be on your guard and be prepared to take action.

What Can You Do?

More often than not, people will work to communicate their sorrow to the outside world. Hence, it is vital you recognize the language symptomatic of suicide and intervene. How would you do that, you ask? Quite simply, you have to talk about suicide.

And this is where it gets hard, because suicide is a difficult thing to talk about. For a variety of reasons, be it religious beliefs, cultural mores, or personal reluctance, many of us are hesitant to delve into this grey area. However, our willingness to move past our boundaries and take this great personal gamble can make all the difference in the world.

Please rest assured of one thing. Having an honest conversation, or several, exploring thoughts concerning suicide does not make this act more attractive. The way to begin is to ask your child whether she or he has thought about suicide. If your child confirms that suicide has been on his or her mind, ask if he or she has a plan. These two questions can let you know what your son or daughter is thinking and the immediacy of danger. Use direct language, and be prepared to hear unpleasant things with as much of a calm demeanor as you can muster. Once you have ascertained that your child is, in fact, considering suicide, with all speed find a professional who can help your son or daughter through this tenuous time. Stay this course despite any opposition you might meet. Finally, do not discount the observations of others. A teacher or best friend sees different sides to your child on a regular basis. They are full of very valuable insight.

To conclude, due to a lack of any published research stating that suicide is a different phenomenon for gifted youth, we can rely on the prevailing means of identifying and treating gifted and talented children who are ideating about suicide. Enlist the aid of professionals and peers to provide safe environments for and identify the mental health needs of your child in particular and young people in general. Communication and intervening in a young person's life is the best defense we have for preventing loss of life to suicide. So, when in doubt, act.

Resources

Books and Articles

Cassady, J. C., & Cross, T. L. (2006). A factorial representation of suicidal ideation among academically gifted adolescents. *Journal for the Education of the Gifted, 29,* 290–304.

Cohen, L. M., & Frydenberg, E. (2006). *Coping for capable kids: Strategies for parents, teachers, and students* (Rev. ed.). Waco, TX: Prufrock Press.

Cross, T. L. (2008). Suicide. In C. M. Callahan & J. Plucker (Eds.), *Critical issue and practices in gifted education: What the research says* (pp. 629–640). Waco, TX: Prufrock Press.

Kitano, M. K., & Lewis, R. B. (2005). Resilience and coping: Implications for gifted children and youth at risk. *Roeper Review, 27,* 200–205.

Neihart, M. (2006). Dimensions of underachievement, difficult contexts, and perceptions of self-achievement/affiliation conflicts in gifted adolescents. *Roeper Review, 28,* 203–209.

Websites

American Association of Suicidology—http://www.suicidology.org
Mental Health America—http://www.nmha.org
Suicide Prevention Action Network USA—http://www.spanusa.org

References

Cross, T. L., Gust-Brey, K., & Ball, P. B. (2002). A psychological autopsy of the suicide of an academically gifted student: Researchers' and parents' perspectives. *Gifted Child Quarterly, 46,* 247–264.

Chapter 52

A Counselor's Perspective on Parenting for High Potential

by Jean Sunde Peterson

ATIE was in a discussion group geared to the social and emotional concerns in her school's program for the gifted and talented. She summarized her experiences in writing at the end of her senior year:

> Although I'm not very open, hearing other kids talk opened my eyes that some things I'm going through are things other people struggle with, too. Discussion group has benefited me more than you can ever know. When we discussed stress and its effect early in the year, and you mentioned eating disorders, I realized I had a problem. My parents still don't know. It took me 3 months to ask for help, but through my interaction with the kids in the group, and knowing that not everyone will turn away from me because of it, I was able to at least accept myself, instead of hurting myself more.

Katie subsequently did inform her parents, and she received help. She had learned that concerns could be discussed and that others, too, were wrestling with stress.

High ability certainly does not preclude burdensome stress, of course. Besides experiencing the usually manageable stressors related to relationships and responsibilities, students may feel under siege or hypercritically examined in particular environments. Certainly there are gifted individuals who are bullied, demeaned, or traumatized, or who feel great disappointment, despair, or pressure to perform. There are a multitude of potential stressors, as any parent knows. Life events and circumstances may result in loss of trust, innocence, or a secure childhood, and there may be other losses as well. They or close friends may relocate and close relatives or pets may die. Siblings or parents or gifted students themselves may have severe disabilities and illnesses. Gifted children and adolescents are not exempt from stressful life events. In fact, simply having exceptional abilities can be stressful some or much of the time.

The sensitivity and intensity that have been associated with high ability may exacerbate difficulties associated with these circumstances and events. Even "normal development" can dramatically unsettle those who are bright and capable. Rebounding from traumatic experiences may be especially complex and intense in gifted individuals, although various dimensions of their intellect also may contribute to resilience.

Unfortunately, in programs for gifted students, social and emotional development usually receives less emphasis, if any at all, than does academic or talent development. Even parents may forget that their bright and productive children need and deserve guidance in regard to social and emotional development. I will argue here, from a counselor's perspective, that affective concerns of the gifted should not be discounted either at school or at home, and I will emphasize what parents can do to enhance the development of their children in nonacademic areas. However, I will begin with some context and perspectives concerning child, parent, and family development.

Developmental Tasks and Stressors

This article is based on a rich trove of information contributed by gifted students themselves. For several years, I led weekly small-group discussions with gifted middle and high school students, involving more than 100 students each year. These groups were semistructured, with a focus each week, usually associated with a developmental task. Often a brief paper-and-pencil activity introduced the topic for the day. Groups discussed areas such as sibling and peer relationships and developing social competence, identity, direction, and eventual separate-but-connected differentiation from family. They did not just "hang out" in the groups, and, because of the structure, no group members dominated the discussions. With no pressure to participate, several shy students attended regularly and comfortably without offering much verbally. Group members taught me about their concerns, some of which I will discuss before offering some suggestions about parenting high-potential children.

These students had impressive strengths: intellectual agility, keen insights, unique ways of thinking, creative talent, leadership skills, and athletic ability. Although these strengths were usually advantageous, they sometimes also contributed to "burdens," including heavy expectations from themselves and others. For some, those expectations afforded little room to take reasonable social or academic risks. In addition, sometimes their strengths exacted a social price in their complex interpersonal world. At various developmental junctures they examined their internal and external worlds (their inner thoughts and feelings and their external behavior, activities, and relationships).

Most important, their strengths and sense of differentness had kept many of them from accepting that they and their age peers were all dealing with developmental challenges—and that, in spite of their own intellectual or other strengths, they and their classmates had much in common developmentally. At the same time, adults' preoccupation with their achievement and productivity suggested to some that social and emotional development was not worthy of discussion, as one group member expressed in writing:

> In school no one teaches us anything about what most kids are thinking about all the time—relationships. It's sad to think we have no classes or places where we can discuss that. We need to learn how to deal with people, not just words and numbers.

Gifted adolescents are especially prone to wrestling silently with developmental stress, but our discussions revealed many stressors. One male remarked at the end of his group experience, "You end up talking about things you kind of wanted to, but never could." A female wrote, "Sometimes when I don't know what to do with myself, it helps just to talk."

The gifted students in these groups seemed to believe that only individuals with a level of ability similar to theirs were able to understand and be trusted. Yet even with able peers they may not communicate concerns unless a safe context is created. They also may not be able to articulate their concerns. The students I worked with appreciated having a safe place to "practice" articulating developmental stressors.

Sensitivities and Intensities

It may be helpful to consider the impact of exceptional ability on development. High ability normally provides a certain amount of control over one's surroundings. Verbal ability, for example, can help to explain, convince, excuse, and manipulate. General intelligence helps to understand one's environment. However, developmental transitions may challenge that sense of control. For example, the complexities of puberty and sexuality, relationships, and new environments may seem overwhelming at times. Having many choices and multiple talents also may be burdensome, especially when seeking a perfect decision about college and career, for example. Even entering kindergarten, moving from a small to a larger school, changing from having one teacher to having more than one, going to a summer camp, or entering high school may be formidable challenges for individuals who respond to life in extremely sensitive ways. Life's transitions involve change, and change involves leaving something behind, perhaps with unrecognized grief responses. At times, parents need to step back and consider the transitions their children are experiencing. Then they can help their children make sense of the experiences.

Parallel Development: Child and Family

Everyone in a family is developing simultaneously, of course, including each parent, stepparent, or guardian. Each family member's development affects other family members and family dynamics in general. Each must adjust to all others in the family. For example, Son begins high school and experiences a growth spurt; Older Daughter is a precocious, physically mature seventh grader; and Younger Daughter begins kindergarten at an older age than her classmates because of the age requirement in the state they just moved from. Dad, already frustrated with the job he just moved to, considers starting his own business. Mom, with all children now in school, considers finding a job, but worries that she will need to be flexible to attend periodically to the deteriorating health of her mother, who has diabetes, in a distant city. Each family member represents a place on the continuum of development across the lifespan.

Some individuals and families are not nimble in making developmental adjustments. Adults, for instance, may experience unsettling anxiety upon entering midlife, facing employment decisions and transitions, losing a parent to death, being aware of health concerns, or anticipating retirement. At the same time, their children are experiencing unique, and sometimes extended, developmental moments. The developing family also may be preparing to launch an oldest or youngest child into the next stage— kindergarten, adolescence, college, or marriage, for instance. Conscientious, education-oriented, economically successful families may experience as much trouble with developmental transitions as do families who lack leadership and organization—or even more. Developmental shifts can feel out of control to families who are used to being organized and successful. Parenting is only one of several aspects of family life that must be adjusted accordingly.

Parents Themselves

Parents' own issues can affect their parenting. Uncomfortable memories about loneliness, shyness, academic or social "failure," bullying, traumatic losses, or family moves might contribute to anxiety as their children enter the years where they themselves experienced problems. Similarly, parents may anticipate positive experiences for their children, based on their own school successes or relationships with peers and teachers. Such memories may mean ready support for the system, but also may mean that parents cannot relate to their children's interpersonal or academic difficulties at school.

When one or both parents are immoderately absorbed in their children's lives, children may feel pressure to perform and meet parents' needs, and they may not be encouraged to explore their own identity or interests. Parents need to recognize that their own and their children's strengths differ. They also need to set good boundaries with their children, recognizing where their child's responsibility begins and where their own ends, in the interest of allowing enough autonomy for healthy growth and appropriate differentiation. Knowing when to encourage a child to solve problems independently with peers, teachers, siblings, coaches, or employers, for instance, can contribute to a sense of confidence and competence in the child. Knowing when not to rescue a child who forgets to bring something to school has the same potential.

On the other hand, bright and talented children can be given too much deferential treatment. Parents, awed by their gifted child's adult-like wisdom, might even rely on the child to make major family decisions. Young gifted children may assume heavy household responsibilities—because they are so capable. In some situations, parents behave as if their children were their peers, confidants, or even parents. Although the children may seem to function well in these roles, not being able to trust adults to be reliable, competent, and adult-like during stressful times may contribute to insecurity. Parents can forget that adult-like children still need comfort, nurturing, and guidance. When parents assume appropriate parental roles, children are free to act their age, feel secure, and eventually move comfortably into adulthood.

Suggestions for Parents

From their parents, the students in my discussion groups wanted calm attention and support, uninterrupted communication, respect, and sensitivity to feelings. They wanted parents who were not distracted, constantly evaluative, condemning, or absent. They wanted to feel OK. Based on these themes, and other experiences as a counselor of gifted individuals and their families, I offer the following suggestions to parents of gifted children and adolescents.

Communicating Unconditional Love and Acceptance

Wise parents help their children to know that being loved does not depend on performance. They are valued for being, not just doing, even though the children find satisfaction in accomplishments and feel their parents' pride. Their achievements are not central to their parents' self-esteem and do not need to be compensation for their parents' pasts. Their parents have enough of a life of their own not to be dependent on, or to overvalue, their children's accomplishments.

Listening—Really Listening

Nonjudgmental listening is one way to convey unconditional acceptance. It may be as important in parenting as providing material comforts or accessing enrichment activities. Listening helps parents to enter the child's world. It invites, rather than squelches, communication. In addition, a good listener learns from the speaker, who becomes teacher. Listening also models crucial relationship skills. Active listening is hard work and takes energy, commitment, concentration, and poise. It means paying attention to words and feelings. If a problem is being presented, a good listener avoids rushing in to fix the problem with advice or solutions. Statements (e.g., "I'll bet that was frustrating" or "So, he sort of shocked you") take precedence over questions, which tend to control conversation. Good listeners also use open-ended questions (e.g., "How did you accomplish that?" or "What should I understand about this?") instead of closed questions, which generate yes/no responses (often beginning with Do/Did, Is/Was/Were, or Have/Had, such as "Did you tell her?" or "Were you wearing your jacket?" or "Have you done your homework?"). They invite elaboration (e.g., "Tell me what happened"), and avoid "Why" questions (e.g., "Why didn't you just tell him?"), which may provoke defensiveness. They recognize that often a child just needs a listener, and they make themselves available for that.

Supporting the Trip, Not Just the Destination

Wise parents support process, not just products. They give feedback about effort, creativity, and investment and are interested in their children's experiences and insights during the process, not just at the end of projects, reports, or tests. In order not to contribute to preoccupation with external evaluation, they encourage activities that are not graded—even in the form of parental praise. They model a process-orientation themselves, enjoying the trip, not just the destination, when doing their own projects, job assignments, or midlife transitions.

Taking Note of Negative Messages

I have listened to adolescents tell about parents' strong messages, both positive and negative. Actually, I have heard more about the negative messages, because they are loudest. The sensitivities present in many gifted children help parental messages to have thunderous impact. For example, perfectionistic children may increase their self-critical tendencies in response to their parents' evaluation and criticism, which can mask parental feelings and concerns, including love, fear, and protection. Unfortunately, demeaning, critical language is used to control children in some homes.

Changing the language used with children—perhaps altering cross-generational patterns—can improve household climate and lessen stress in children. When achievement is the only topic of conversation, a child is likely to perceive that personal worth depends on achievement. By contrast, children who sense that they are loved foremost and sufficiently as son or daughter will not be paralyzed by fears that they will be disowned for poor performance. Parental love will be understood as unconditional—not dependent on grades, awards, or perfect behavior. Parents can say, "I'm so glad you're my daughter/son" or "I'm so glad you were born" or "I love you—you don't have to do anything to have my love." Parents also can say, when their children return from school, "Tell me about your day," instead of "Did you get an A on the test?"

Modeling Effective Coping With Stress

Children learn how to cope with stress partly through observation. When parents respond to stress by being irritable and critical, having a foul temper, chronically condemning the boss, or running away through work, substance abuse, withdrawal, depression, or other absence, these behaviors serve as powerful lessons for the developing child. Children benefit when parents model unambiguous expression of feelings (e.g., "I've been feeling sad about Grandma's situation lately" or "I feel like crying when I think about that" or "I'm angry about what happened"), rather than translating sadness into anger, for instance, or anger into sadness, irritability, stubbornness, manipulation, or passive-aggressive inaction.

Parents are wise when they demonstrate that feelings do not have to be denied or displaced. They validate their children's feelings with comments like "I can see you're sad (or angry, stressed, frustrated) about that." They communicate that it is acceptable to feel and that feelings do not last forever and are survivable, although practice may be required for coping effectively with them. Going through feelings gives children important experience with feeling. However, when feelings interfere with functioning or are potentially life-threatening, whether for parents or for children, counseling and possibly medication are recommended.

Gifted children, because of others' preoccupation with "reaching their potential," may not be encouraged to "just play." Children are fortunate when parents make sure that they do not forget how to play.

Modeling Independence, Risk, and Dealing With Mistakes

Wise parents model appropriate risk-taking, including venturing into territory where competence is not yet established, such as signing up for language classes, hanging wallpaper, building an arbor, or installing a bathroom fixture. When something does not work out as planned, or mistakes are made, they are kind to themselves (e.g., "Oops. Guess I goofed"). They give their children permission to explore—and make mistakes (e.g., "Give it a try. It's OK if it doesn't work out"). Children benefit when allowed to solve problems on their own. Making choices and even stumbling are important educational experiences that contribute to resilience and self-confidence. When parents overfunction, doing for their children what the children could do for themselves, the latter may learn to be dependent, fear failure, and avoid taking appropriate risks. Concerned parents, wanting to protect the self-esteem of their talented children and to ensure success, can easily fall into these patterns. Even overscheduling children may take away opportunities to learn to conquer boredom themselves and organize their own lives. Wise parents recognize when they are arranging activities for their children to meet their own needs, instead of their children's.

Modeling Respect for Others, Including Institutions

Parents convey attitudes about the future work world, as well as the present school world, in their everyday comments. Those who disparage their workplace, authority figures, community institutions, and the school system should not be surprised when their children are cynical about work, school, and the system. It is important to help gifted children understand the system. They can be anthropologists, observing and drawing conclusions about how their school functions and how children relate to one another and to teachers. Just as children can be helped to appreciate and interact with diversity, so, too, can frustrated students be helped to understand that teaching a classroom of students with wide-ranging abilities is not an easy task for teachers. Parents also can raise their children's awareness that there are many kinds of intelligence, including some they may not have themselves. Maybe they should visit the industrial technology area at school.

Parents can help their children figure out how to advocate for themselves, including how to thank teachers who are helpful. Because children and adolescents need to have the school system work for them, parents can encourage them to use their intelligence to figure out how to get what they need from the school system. When parents need to intercede for their children, they are wise and discreet. When families and children "shoot themselves in the foot" by being disrespectful of teachers and administrators, their needs are not met, and they have then sacrificed themselves to the institution.

Not Being a Needy Parent

Nurturing children, setting appropriate limits, and providing stable leadership all require poise and focus. Parents who are emotionally needy themselves may have difficulty focusing on their children's needs. In fact, children may find themselves meeting a parent's emotional needs, rather than vice versa. Wise parents know that it is not unusual for their children to be angry with them at times. Not having their own self-esteem dependent on their children's affirmation helps parents to remain composed when anger is directed at them. Parents can validate anger as a legitimate, important feeling and encourage appropriate and acceptable expression and resolution of it, such as through talking, writing, physical activity, or structured conflict mediation. Those strategies are usually much more effective, long term, and less harmful to relationships than dealing with anger indirectly or with tantrums.

Encouraging Them to Talk With Someone

All parents probably hope that their children will talk to them when in crisis. Unfortunately, even in the best of situations, circumstances may create doubt about parents' ability to understand. Wise parents anticipate this and encourage talking to someone—a school counselor, a teacher, a coach, someone in the clergy, or a grandparent, for example. Such permission might save a life.

Recognizing Strengths

Wise parents are alert to moments when they can genuinely affirm their children's strengths, not in a general or superficial cheerleading fashion, but rather in the form of credible statements about specific strengths (e.g., "You have good people skills" or "I appreciated your flexibility when we changed our plans"). Intelligence, which researchers have found to be an important factor of resilience, can be noted, as well as interpersonal skills, curiosity, insightfulness, tolerance for ambiguity, concern for others, and perseverance. Children pay attention to their parents' definitions of them, and genuine comments about strengths are remembered.

Conclusion

Parents and educators should, of course, be alert to situations that warrant seeking help from a mental health counselor, clinical social worker, marriage and family therapist, clinical or counseling psychologist, or psychiatrist. That action would be appropriate and perhaps urgent when a gifted child or adolescent displays symptoms of depression, an eating disorder, Posttraumatic Stress Disorder, or obsessive-compulsive disorder, for example. A good guideline is to seek help when situations or behaviors interfere with living effectively. The following might reflect problems that require professional attention, depending on frequency, duration, and severity:

- isolation, withdrawal, avoidance, anxiety;
- aggression, impulsivity;
- somatic complaints;
- mood disturbances;
- difficulty forming or maintaining relationships;
- low tolerance of frustration;
- unusual apathy, sadness, hopelessness;
- dramatic changes in sleeping, eating;
- inability to concentrate; and
- repetitive behaviors, such as washing, checking, ordering.

Problems related to life events, perfectionism, interpersonal difficulties, developmental transitions, or school behavior also might warrant the attention of a mental health professional. Parents need only to ask the questions and provide information; they can leave assessment to the mental health providers. Their cooperation, including respect for the counselor-client relationship and possibly being involved in the treatment plan, will be important in the healing process.

School counselors can offer options and referral resources as well as short-term counseling, because they are trained counselors as well as developmental guidance specialists. In fact, school counselors might provide a positive initial counseling experience, in a familiar environment, that paves the way for further work with mental health providers outside of the school setting. Parents should be aware that one school counselor may be responsible for more than 500 students and may not be able to sustain regular counseling over an extended period of time.

According to current literature, gifted individuals are probably no more likely than the rest of the population to need interventions for social and emotional concerns. Nevertheless, these concerns deserve attention. Parents can advocate for an affective dimension in their school's program for gifted students, most easily and efficiently delivered in the form of regular small-group discussions focusing on child and adolescent development. Programs also can sponsor periodic group workshops with an engaging mental health professional, and gifted education teachers and school counselors can cofacilitate large- and small-group discussions. As a result of these activities, behaviors and feelings associated with giftedness may be normalized, and school counselors also can become more familiar with the concerns of gifted youth.

Parents can likewise contribute to the mental health of their children by heeding the points presented in this article. Parents are the most crucial social and emotional support system for gifted youth. When social and emotional concerns are deemed as worthy of discussion as academic and talent concerns, parents help to prepare their children for present and future relationships and help them to maintain emotional balance as well.

Resources

Johnson, K. (2001). Integrating an affective component in the curriculum for gifted and talented students. *Gifted Child Today, 24*(4), 14–18.

Lovecky, D. (1992). Exploring social and emotional aspects of giftedness in children. *Roeper Review, 15,* 18–25.

Neihart, M., Reis, S. M., Robinson, N. M., & Moon, S. M. (Eds.). (2002). *The social and emotional development of gifted children: What do we know?* Waco, TX: Prufrock Press.

Peterson, J. S. (1995). *Talk with teens about feelings, family, relationships, and the future: 50 guided discussions for school and counseling groups.* Minneapolis, MN: Free Spirit.

Peterson, J. S. (1998). The burdens of capability. *Reclaiming Children and Youth, 6,* 194–198.

Strop, J. (2000). The affective side of gifted students' development: Do we need to teach students intrapersonal and interpersonal skills? *Understanding Our Gifted, 12*(4), 16–17.

Goodness of Fit:
The Challenge of Parenting
Gifted Children

by Andrew Mahoney

A s a counselor and family therapist who has spent more than 20 years working with gifted and talented children and their families, I was excited when asked to discuss the challenge of parenting the gifted. I was reintroduced to how complex and substantial the challenge is of parenting the gifted child. In my practice I provide counsel and support to parents daily. What the parent brings is a host of differentiated needs, issues, and struggles that can't quite be solved with marginal everyday solutions or a quick fix. Parenting a gifted child requires the same level of differentiation as we can hope to find educating or counseling the gifted.

Defining and understanding the challenge of parenting the gifted is a daunting charge. With such an array of issues, where a parent begins can be a challenge. Some parents want to let go and hope for the best, while others may cling to their fears and overmanage their child's life. Reaching a balance is complex. The parents in this case may benefit from a differentiated model tailored to their child.

The Gifted Identity Formation Model

The Gifted Identity Formation Model (GIFM) was developed with this process in mind. This differentiation model is designed for parents, counselors, and individuals to address the complex needs of the gifted. Presented here are sections of the model to conceptualize and explore the challenge of parenting the gifted and provide practical means to address the challenge. The basis of the model is to provide a framework to assist in meeting the differentiated needs, what I have termed a goodness of fit, a term borrowed from the research literature. The challenge comes into play when a parent has to find the right fit to meet the exceptionality of a gifted child. Goodness of fit results when there is a match between the differentiated needs of an individual and what is provided or available to meet those needs, leading to a fulfilled potential and content self.

The four constructs in GIFM are validation, affirmation, affiliation, and affinity. I refer to these as the underpinnings or processes involved in meeting needs and forming one's identity. In this case we are exploring gifted identity and creating a goodness of fit.

Validation

Validation is the process of corroborating exactly what giftedness is for the child, knowing more specifically how the child is gifted, and what vulnerabilities come along with that giftedness. So, to have a valid self as gifted, whose needs are met, requires knowledge and assessment that is more than just an IQ score or having a label attached. This is a critical piece for parents, to have an appropriate view or complete profile of the child's giftedness. This may involve extensive testing and assessment and an ongoing process of recognizing your child's uniqueness. Validation is the first step in meeting needs.

Affirmation

Affirmation is the process that involves the challenge, effort, and enrichment (e.g., acceleration programs, advanced study, mentoring relationships) of the child. This approach fits with the child's gifts and takes into account the vulnerabilities associated with his giftedness. This also could be referred to as a matched challenge.

Affiliation

Affiliation involves the need for belonging, how gifted children find others of like mind, nature, or ability. This is a critical struggle for many gifted children and is relevant to meeting educational needs.

Affinity

The last construct, affinity, is the child's purpose or calling in life. This is not the parents' desire for what the child should do with his or her gifts or others' expectations, but the child's affinity (i.e., also referred to as purpose, calling, or will to meaning). Meeting affinity is about what engages the child to meet needs and fulfill self. Affinity also is important in understanding what motivates a gifted child.

In order to conceptualize this challenge and use the four constructs listed above, I have synthesized some of the critical and more frequent needs of the parent of the gifted in the form of four questions. Each of these questions parallels the constructs. These questions were formulated based on the research literature, my extensive experience working with parents, and from an analysis of hundreds of collected questions from presentations I have delivered to thousands of parents of the gifted (at every parent presentation I ask parents to write down their critical questions that brought them to hear me speak. I have collected these questions over the years and identified issues that are central to parents of the gifted).

Applying the Constructs

How does a parent reconcile having expectations that are appropriate, while at the same time matching the expectations the child does or doesn't have regarding the process of developing his or her own self as a gifted individual? (Validation)

This reconciliation is a two-part process involving an appropriate validation of how your child is gifted and then understanding your child's perception of being gifted. In validating your child's giftedness, you are taking the first and most critical step to meeting his needs. For parents, validation involves reading literature about giftedness, and possibly seeking consultation. For the gifted child, validation includes formal assessment and testing conducted by a trained neuropsychologist or psychologist (with experience testing gifted children), and appropriate educational experiences. These steps can ease parental anxieties and guide parenting intervention.

Validation is an involved and ongoing process. Gifted children develop differently (asynchrony of development) and often do not follow a normal trajectory. Rigidly fixed perceptions about your child's giftedness may lead to not meeting his or her complex needs. Many parents will acknowledge giftedness in their child and then never revisit what that means as their child grows. I have repeatedly seen parents of gifted adolescents who have held the exact same perception of the child's abilities since they were preschoolers. This type of fixed view often leads to the conflicts involving expectation.

The second part of the validation process involves a child's own perception and expectations regarding giftedness. This awareness will vary greatly for each child. When a gifted child does not have an appropriate validation of self as gifted, her expectations will not match her needs. Validation therefore is critical in self-advocacy. It is imperative that the child explores what giftedness is and understands his strengths or vulnerabilities in relation to his giftedness. A reconciliation of expectations comes from a process of validation that is comprehensive and addresses the differentiated nature of your child's giftedness, along with an awareness of your child's perceptions of giftedness. Reconciliation now occurs through an appropriate process of validation, providing expectations that fit with the nature of your child's giftedness.

How do parents provide the right mix of stimulation, challenge, and effort without feeling as though they are overburdening or accelerating their child too far or not enough? (Affirmation)

Refer back first to the construct of validation. Do you have an accurate and realistic view of your child's learning and developmental profile?

Once this is established, a parent can begin the process of providing the right mix of enrichment, acceleration, and accommodation to support that challenge. You also must explore what is available to your child and work toward creating an experience with a goodness of fit. Focus on finding opportunities or offering to help provide support and resources. In many cases there will be struggle; however, the approach taken can make a big difference. First, accept the realities of the situation and view them as an opportunity rather than a challenge or a struggle.

The affirmation process involves finding both an appropriately challenging curriculum and enriching activities, and identifying subtleties in your child's abilities. For example, the gifted child with undiagnosed executive functioning problems or learning disabilities may demonstrate the clear need for acceleration, but once receiving that provision can fail miserably. This typically happens because the appropriate assessments were not provided, so the framework needed for that child to take advantage of the acccleration was thwarted. This also can occur due to the denial that gifted children can be vulnerable, asynchronous in development, or possess learning problems or disabilities.

When communicating with teachers and institutions, the goal should be to create alliances rather than build adversarial relationships that can lead to negative perceptions. I caution parents on a regular basis that society still grapples with gifted education, a discipline that has yet to evolve into a complete discipline and matriculate through the educational system as a whole.

How does a parent assist his or her child with feeling a sense of belonging without trying to make the child fit in? (Affiliation)

The whole idea of fitting in is one that really challenges parents, because there is this desire to have your child feel accepted, have friends and be social, all of which are understandable goals. Unfortunately, the intense need on the part of the parent to have this occur can seriously compromise who your child is and where he or she will actually find affiliations. The norm is to use chronological age as a guide; for the gifted child this is not, and should not be the case. I have seen many parents hold very ingrained beliefs about their children needing to be with chronological peers. This can be one of the hardest ideas of differentiation to grasp. This also is the area where parents believe the child will suffer the most ridicule and alienation for his or her difference, so the need to fix the problem becomes heightened and intensified. For many gifted children, the solution will not be as simple as being in a gifted program, although that is a crucial piece to meeting affiliation needs, as well as for learning. Some gifted children need their parents to create affiliations for them, connecting through other means such as searching out parents with similar children who also are seeking connection. This takes intention and effort; I remind parents who are working on this that being gifted often brings the necessity to think outside the box to solve problems and get results.

How do parents motivate a child without compromising the child's innate purpose and desires by projecting their own agendas or those of the external world? (Affinity)

The challenge here involves you as the parent exploring the values you hold about affinity, purpose, and calling in life for your gifted child. In meeting affinity needs, understanding your expectations and values is critical. I ask that parents explore their deep ingrained values about giftedness and what they feel that means for them relative to who their child is and the child's sense of purpose or calling. Examine for yourself where that value or expectation comes from in your life. Ask yourself, does my belief match my child's belief about purpose? Be careful not to confuse your own unmet affinity needs with your child's. I can assure you that if you are asking your child to be someone he is not, he will let you know in his own way. I also ask that parents explore the idea that just because the child has a gift or multiple gifts does not mean that the cultivation of that specific gift(s) is going to fulfill his purpose.

Thus, who your child becomes is about who he is and the purpose within him, not necessarily who you want or think he should be. This is not to say you should not influence your child or instill values. A crucial method for helping a child develop a sense of purpose lies in how well you as a parent fulfill your own calling(s). Another means is to assess early in your child's life the interests she pursues and the experiences where motivation is present. I believe that meeting one's affinity in life is directly linked to motivation. So, when a child appears lazy or unmotivated, it may be a sign that purpose or affinity is being unmet or not cultivated in the goodness of fit.

As you may know, or can imagine, the challenge of parenting the gifted child is an exceptional one. The approach I have presented here is just one way to begin the process in finding a helpful means. Remember, finding that goodness of fit involves looking beyond the norm and differentiating for your child in the ways discussed through validation, affirmation, affiliation, and affinity. Please take the time to seek out as many of the resources available, tailoring your parenting experience in a manner that fulfills both your experience and your child's giftedness.

Resources

Books and Articles

Lovecky, D. V. (2004). *Different minds: Gifted children with AD/HD, Asperger syndrome, and other learning deficits.* New York, NY: Jessica Kingsley.

Mahoncy, A. S. (1997). In search of gifted identity: From abstract concept to workable counseling constructs. *Roeper Review, 20,* 222–227.

Mahoney, A. S., Martin, D., & Martin, M. (2007). Gifted identity formation: A therapeutic model for counseling gifted children and adolescents. In S. Mendaglio & J. S. Peterson (Eds.), *Models of counseling gifted children, adolescents, and young adults* (pp. 199–227). Waco, TX: Prufrock Press.

McCoach, D. B., Thomas, J. K., Bray, M. A., & Siegle, D. (2001). Best practices in the identification of gifted students with learning disabilities. *Psychology in the Schools, 38,* 403–411.

Websites

Hoagies' Gifted Education Page—http://www.hoagiesgifted.org
National Association for Gifted Children—http://www.nagc.org
Supporting Emotional Needs of the Gifted—http://www.sengifted.org

Chapter 54

Helping Gifted Students Cope With Perfectionism

by Michael C. Pyryt

Does your child pay more attention to mistakes than to correct answers?

Does your child set unrealistic expectations for his or her work?

Is your child dissatisfied with a grade of A instead of A+?

Does your child focus on unmet goals instead of enjoying current accomplishments?

Does your child get extremely upset when anything in life doesn't work perfectly?

Perfectionism

I F you answered "yes" to any of these questions, your child may be at risk for becoming an unhealthy perfectionist. There is a fine line between striving to reach high standards of excellence and feeling self-defeated through the inability to reach unrealistic expectations of perfection. When that line is crossed, the perfectionistic tendencies become disabling. Others use perfectionism only when referring to the negative aspects of the syndrome. In schools, perfectionism can lead to underachievement. Outside of school, serious health problems are associated with perfectionism including abdominal pain, alcoholism, anorexia, bulimia, chronic depression, and obsessive-compulsive personality disorders. The problem of perfectionism is so prevalent among university students that many university counseling centers offer workshops on overcoming perfectionism.

Perfectionism also can be thought of as a way of thinking. One aspect of perfectionistic thinking is dichotomous (all or none) thinking, in which a child believes that a project is either perfect or it is worthless. Sally, a 10-year-old, creates a science fair report that is among the best in her class. She comes home crying and tears the report up because the teacher found one typo in a 6-page report. Another component of perfectionistic thinking is transforming desires (wants) into demands (musts). Joe, an 11th grader, wants to do well on the mathematics portion of the SAT. This desire gets changed into believing that he must make an 800 (a perfect score) or he will feel like a failure. A third element of perfectionistic thinking is focusing on unmet goals and challenges rather than savoring successes. Ann, a sixth grader, has read 9 of 10 short stories for her language arts project. Ann is likely to complete the project before anyone else in the class and 2 weeks before the project is due. Rather than feeling good about her excellent progress, Ann remains highly anxious because she still has one short story to read.

Perfectionists tend to come in many packages. Some perfectionists are intense and demanding from birth. They are never satisfied with their accomplishments and feel inadequate because there is room for improvement. For others, perfectionism is a learned behavior influenced by critical parents or teachers who verbalize when a child makes a 90% statements along the lines of, "That's nice, what happened on the other 10%?" Some children expect everything they do to be perfect and everyone around them to treat them perfectly. These children want to have perfect breakfasts, perfect interactions on the playground, perfect feedback from teachers, and perfect performance on assignments and tests. Unless everything is perfect, they are disappointed. Others may only demand perfection when it comes to school work. Generally, the first signs of perfectionism will be evident in how children respond to competition ("I must be the best!") and how they respond to compliments ("It's nice of you to say that but I should have done much better."). For those who struggle with perfectionism, it is a lifelong challenge. However, I believe that people can learn to cope effectively with perfectionistic tendencies.

As children struggle with perfectionism, parents may wonder, "Should I get professional help from a counselor or psychologist?" It really depends on the degree of perfectionism and the extent to which perfectionist tendencies are leading to other problems: obsessive-compulsive disorder, panic attacks, eating disorders, or depression. Parents might want to begin by discussing their observations about their child's perfectionist tendencies with the child's teacher. They might say, "Paul seems to be having a hard time doing your science fair project because it's not going to be perfect. Is there a way that we can work together to support and help him move forward?"

Perfectionism and Giftedness

Among educators of the gifted, the link between giftedness and perfectionism is clearly established. The tendency toward perfectionism commonly appears as an item on rating scales and checklists used by parents and teachers to nominate potentially gifted students. Articles on counseling needs of the gifted routinely mention perfectionism as a risk for gifted students. There are two major concerns about perfectionism for gifted students: underachievement and emotional turmoil. Perfectionistic tendencies make some gifted students vulnerable for underachievement because they do not submit work unless it is perfect. As a result, they may receive poor or failing marks. In terms of emotional stress, perfectionism is seen to cause feelings of worthlessness and depression when gifted individuals fail to live up to unrealistic expectations.

Research suggests that the relationship between perfectionism and giftedness may not be as strong as the gifted education community believes. Few differences were found between academic talent search participants and average-ability comparison groups. Talent search participants tended to exhibit healthy perfectionism marked by high personal standards and organization. There is enough evidence from case study research, however, to suggest that some gifted students may be prone to perfectionism.

Coping With Perfectionism

Coping with perfectionism involves changing one's thinking from "It's never going to be good enough so why bother" to "I'm happy that I took the opportunity to challenge myself and learn new things. My next project will be even better." The following sections highlight some key concepts that perfectionistic students need to internalize. Suggestions for helping parents instill these ideas in gifted students follow.

1. Don't Take It Personally

From kindergarten upward, children tend to equate the evaluations they receive on their assignments as indications of their self-worth. The grade of A may become a stamp of approval for the student. A poor grade represents a disconfirmation of a child's brightness. (For a perfectionist, a grade of A- might be perceived as a poor grade). Each test, assignment, and project becomes another situation that puts the self-concept at risk. Some children avoid this threat to their self-worth by procrastinating. The work that is eventually submitted only reflects a small commitment of their time. The evaluation of their work, even if negative, has little impact on their feelings of self-worth because the children can rationalize the poor evaluation with lack of effort. Parents may reinforce this equating of self-worth with achievement by spending time criticizing children for their mistakes rather than acknowledging their successes ("I see that you made a 95 on the spelling quiz. What happened on the other five words?"). Students need to learn to separate their self-worth from their products. They need to learn that the evaluation simply reflects the extent to which their work matches the criteria used for grading. If students are frustrated when they don't receive the highest marks on a project, parents should allow their children to express these feelings. After a "cooling period," a parent might begin a discussion by asking to see the "rubric" or evaluation criteria used. (Students should be able to produce the rubric because it is now common practice for teachers to provide the rubric as part of the assignment). With the rubric in hand, parents can discuss with their children how the content of their project matched the evaluation criteria. Parents can support their children by focusing first on the content that meets the criteria. Children might identify one thing to improve upon when a new project is assigned.

2. Know When to Quit

I just did an Internet search using the term perfectionism and the Google search engine. There were 856,000 links to the term. If I explored the information in each link for only 10 minutes per link before attempting to write this paper, I might be ready to begin in 10 years. I need to be selective in my choice of sources. Gifted students need to know that whatever topic they pick for a project, they will find more possible references available than they can possibly manage to acquire and read in the time allotted. Parents can help gifted students develop skills in determining which available resources will be the most useful and accessible for them. This simple example highlights only one of the steps in completing a project. Perfectionistic students may need assistance getting closure at each step of the project. Parents can help children become more effective in making progress toward program completion by routinely having discussions on the expectations for the project. Parents can assist their children by asking questions about the parameters of the project (minimum and maximum length, number of references, expected financial costs). Parents also can help children develop monitoring skills to check that their projects fall within the expected parameters.

3. Match the Time Commitment to the Value of Assignments

Perfectionistic students need to learn that if they want to earn the highest grades they should put the most effort into the assignments or components that count the most. In my courses, I might give 5-page essay assignments worth 10% each and one 25-page research paper worth 50% of the term grade. I hope that my students are spending five times the amount of their course effort on their research paper than on any one of the essay assignments. Perfectionistic students have a hard time grasping this concept and often spend inordinate amounts of time on simple projects by greatly extending the scope of the project. Within any given project, the various components often have unequal weightings. Parents can help children express their understanding of the weightings of the different parts of the assignment and how they have addressed each part.

4. Set Goals and Focus on Improvement

The attainment of excellence typically occurs as a result of small incremental improvements over time rather than quantum leaps. It's helpful to set goals and work toward their achievement. An excellent example of the successful use of goal setting is the story of John Naber. In 1972, Naber watched Mark Spitz triumph at the Munich Olympics winning seven gold medals, one of which was in the 100-meter backstroke, Naber's specialty. Naber envisioned himself winning gold at the 1976 Olympics in Montreal. Naber believed that he would have to improve his time by 4 seconds to achieve this feat. Given the brevity of the 100-meter race, a 4-second improvement would be a remarkable accomplishment. Through goal setting, Naber realized that he had 4 years to achieve his goal, so only needed to improve 1 second per year. Because Naber swam every day, he only needed to improve 1/365 of a second per day. Because Naber swam twice a day, he only needed to improve 1/730 of a second per workout. Naber dedicated himself to such incremental improvements in performance each day and stood on the podium as the gold medalist in the 100-meter backstroke in the 1976 Olympics. Parents can help students generate goals, determine the steps needed to accomplish the goals, develop an action plan for achieving their goals, and monitoring attainment toward the goal. The acronym SMART (Specific, Measurable, Achievable, Realistic, and Timeframe-provided) can be used to facilitate the goal-setting process.

5. Study the Lives of Eminent People

A 12-year-old perfectionistic student might win a state science fair and still be disappointed that the project is not the theory of relativity. The 12-year-old student needs to know that Einstein didn't produce the theory of relativity at 12, either. In fact, at 12, Einstein's potential greatness was masked by poor school performance. Einstein tested 20 theories before he properly formulated the equations for the theory of relativity. Gifted students can learn many lessons from studying the lives of eminent people by reading biographies and autobiographies, or simply watching a television program such as *Biography*. One basic lesson to learn is that the path to success is not a simple, linear one. Barriers such as rejection, illness, economic misfortunes, and relationship issues can make it difficult for an individual to achieve and maintain success.

One of the key factors is being able to persevere in the face of obstacles. Another lesson is that great effort is required. Edison observed that genius is 1% inspiration and 99% perspiration. The image of Michelangelo, lying on his back for several years painting the ceiling of the Sistine Chapel, is a testament to his commitment. A third lesson is that revision/refinement is part of the process. Books that can be found in bookstores and libraries have undergone revisions and rewriting before publication. It's unrealistic to think that the first draft will be perfect or publishable. Parents can encourage students to share their first draft with peers, siblings, and themselves so that the students can get feedback for potential revisions. A fourth lesson to be learned is that failure can be constructive. Jonathan Salk's polio vaccine was not perfect in its first distillation. Medicines undergo a rigorous process of experimentation and refinement before they are put on the market. Rather than viewing the poor performance of a potential drug in a clinical trial as a cause for despair, the successful scientist will try another compound in hopes of success. Parents might help students organize their biographical investigations by examining the barriers (e.g., physical, economic, cultural, psychological, and sociological) that eminent people faced and the strategies and qualities they used to overcome the barriers.

6. Enjoy the Journey

Some perfectionistic students expect everything in their lives to be perfect every day. This unrealistic expectation will inevitably lead to frustration when it is not met. Daily frustration can lead to depression, which in turn may lead to counseling and perhaps treatment with drugs. An alternative is to take a different perspective. If your child is constantly frustrated by the way the world is compared to the ideal of how it ought to be, celebrate the fact that he or she has high ideals. Try to help your child move forward each day to reduce the discrepancy. A first step is to help him or her find an activity that will help the child feel as if he or she is making a difference in the world (e.g., volunteering with a United Way agency, collecting pledges for a charitable cause, writing persuasive editorials about injustices in the community).

Perfectionists also focus on unmet goals rather than savoring and enjoying accomplishments. An Olympic swimmer should be satisfied winning the gold medal and not be crushed if the time didn't merit a world record. Another swimmer who achieves a personal best should enjoy the accomplishment even if he or she does not win a medal.

Because the perfectionist's life can be very stressful, perfectionistic individuals need to find hobbies and pursuits that can bring joy. Whether it's jogging or Tai Chi, playing bridge or solitaire, or listening to symphonies or rock bands, active engagement in avocational interests can be psychologically and physically rewarding. Parents can help their children identify and nurture extracurricular interests that can serve as positive forces in their lifelong journeys.

Resources

Adderholdt, M. R., & Goldberg, M. R. (1999). *Perfectionism: What's bad about being too good?* Minneapolis, MN: Free Spirit.

Adelson, J. L., & Wilson, H. E. (2009). *Letting go of perfect: Overcoming perfectionism in kids.* Waco, TX: Prufrock Press.

Delisle, J. R., & Galbraith, J. (2002). *When gifted kids don't have all the answers: How to meet their social and emotional needs.* Minneapolis, MN: Free Spirit.

Galbraith, J. (2009). *The gifted kids' survival guide for ages 10 and under* (3rd ed.). Minneapolis, MN: Free Spirit.

Galbraith, J., & Delisle, J. R. (1996). *The gifted kids' survival guide: A teen handbook* (Rev. ed.). Minneapolis, MN: Free Spirit.

Greenspon, T. (2001). *Freeing our families from perfectionism.* Minneapolis, MN: Free Spirit.

Heacox, D. (1991). *Up from underachievement.* Minneapolis, MN: Free Spirit.

Hipp, E. (1995). *Fighting invisible tigers: A stress management guide for teens* (Rev. ed.). Minneapolis, MN: Free Spirit.

Parker, W. D. (2000). Healthy perfectionism in the gifted. *Journal of Secondary Gifted Education, 34,* 173–182.

Parker, W. D., & Mills, C. (1996). The incidence of perfectionism in gifted students. *Gifted Child Quarterly, 40,* 194–199.

Schuler, P. A., Ferbenzer, I., O'Leary, N., Popova, L., Delou, C. M. C., & Limont, W. (2003). Perfectionism: International case studies. *Gifted and Talented International, 18,* 67–75.

Troxclair, D. (1999, December). Recognizing perfectionism in gifted children. *Parenting for High Potential,* 18–21.

Walker, S. Y. (2002). *The survival guide for parents of gifted kids: How to understand, live with, and stick up for your gifted child.* Minneapolis, MN: Free Spirit.

Zucker, B. (2008). *Anxiety-free kids: An interactive guide for parents and children.* Waco, TX: Prufrock Press.

About the Editors

Jennifer L. Jolly, Ph.D., received her doctorate in educational psychology with a concentrate in gifted education from Baylor University. Currently she is assistant professor in elementary and gifted education at Louisiana State University. Her research interests include the history of gifted education and parents of gifted children. She is the current editor-in-chief of NAGC's *Parenting for High Potential* (*PHP*) and secretary of the CEC's The Association for the Gifted (TAG) board.

Donald J. Treffinger, Ph.D., is president of the Center for Creative Learning, Inc., in Sarasota, FL, and is an internationally known researcher, writer, teacher, and presenter in the area of creativity and gifted and talented education. He holds a Ph.D. from Cornell University, and in June 2009 received an honorary Doctor of Laws degree from the University of Winnipeg. He has authored or coauthored more than 60 books and monographs and 350 articles. Don has served as editor of *Gifted Child Quarterly* (*GCQ*) and, from 2000–2007 was editor-in-chief of *Parenting for High Potential*. He is currently a member of the *GCQ* Editorial Advisory Board.

Tracy Ford Inman, M.A.Ed., is associate director of The Center for Gifted Studies at Western Kentucky University and current chair of the *PHP* Editorial Advisory Board. She has taught at the high school and collegiate levels, as well as in summer programs for gifted and talented youth. In addition to writing and cowriting several articles, Tracy has coauthored two books with Dr. Julia Links Roberts. She is currently working on an Ed.D.

Joan Franklin Smutny, Ph.D., is founder and director of the Center for Gifted at National-Louis University. Each year, she directs programs for thousands of gifted children throughout the Chicago area, and regularly offers workshops for parent groups and organizations. Joan has authored, coauthored, and edited many books on gifted education, including *Stand Up for Your Gifted Child* and *Acceleration for Gifted Learners, K–5*.

About the Authors

Edward R. Amend, Psy.D., is a practicing clinical psychologist in Lexington, KY, and Cincinnati, OH, offering services focused on the social-emotional and educational needs of gifted and talented youth, adults, and their families. He provides evaluations, therapy, and discussion groups, and also offers consultation and training for professionals. Ed is coauthor of two award-winning books: *A Parent's Guide to Gifted Children* and *Misdiagnosis and Dual Diagnoses of Gifted Children and Adults*. He has served on the board of directors of Supporting Emotional Needs of the Gifted (SENG), as president of the Kentucky Association for Gifted Education, and as a consultant to the Davidson Institute for Talent Development.

Beth Andrews, LCSW, LAC, is a program supervisor at Spanish Peaks Mental Health Center in Pueblo, CO. She is the author of two children's self-help books, *Why Are You So Sad?: A Child's Book About Parental Depression* and *I Miss You! A Military Kid's Book About Deployment,* and her story, "Bedtime Battles" appears in *Cup of Comfort for Single Mothers.* She has published numerous booklets as well as articles for *Counselor,* the *Journal of Divorce and Remarriage,* and the *National Mental Health Self-Help Clearinghouse.*

Susan Baum, Ph.D., is professor at the College of New Rochelle and is involved in a variety of projects addressing the needs of gifted students.

Sherry S. Bragg, M.A., is a doctoral student in educational psychology and the coordinator of the Super Saturday program at Purdue University. She also is the solo parent of seven children.

Catherine M. Brighton, Ph.D., is associate professor at the University of Virginia, a principal investigator on Project Parallax, which aims to develop talent in underrepresented elementary students in the science, technology, engineering, and math (STEM) areas, and the director of the University of Virginia Institutes on Academic Diversity. Her research interests include factors that support and inhibit teacher change and school reform initiatives; differentiating curriculum, instruction, and assessment; and qualitative methodologies. She was recognized by NAGC in 2005 with the Early Leader award.

Karen Burke, Ed.D., is professor in Instructional Leadership Doctoral Program, Western Connecticut State University. She was the recipient of the 2009 Connecticut State University Board of Trustees Faculty Research Award. Karen's research with learning styles has extended to staff development programs conducted in the United States and more than 20 other countries. These research projects subsequently led to more than 40 scholarly publications in educational journals and edited books.

Vicki Caruana is an educational consultant in the Tampa Bay area and produces a newsletter, "Homeschoolers Online," and a website to help Florida homeschoolers get connected.

Barbara Clark, Ed.D., is a professor emerita at California State University, Los Angeles. She is the author of *Growing Up Gifted*, a text in gifted education now in its seventh edition, and other books and articles in numerous professional journals. Barbara is a past president of the World Council for Gifted and Talented Children, past president of NAGC, and a past president of the California Association for the Gifted. Barbara has presented major addresses and workshops at conferences and in school districts throughout the world.

Richard M. Clouse, M.D., is a family practitioner and assistant clinical professor at the University of Louisville/Glasgow Family Practice Residency in Glasgow, KY.

Nancy A. Cook is a gifted programming specialist in New York's Williamsville-Central School District.

Carolyn R. Cooper, Ph.D., is a seasoned administrator in the field of educating high-potential students. She has taught gifted and talented students at the elementary, junior high, middle school, and high school levels as well as teachers of high-potential youngsters. Active in the National Association for Gifted Children since 1982, Carolyn advises both public and private schools on educating students of high ability, makes presentations to parent groups, and writes regularly for quarterly publications including *Parenting for High Potential*.

Courtney Crim, Ed.D., is an assistant professor at Trinity University. She has a doctorate in curriculum and instruction with an emphasis in gifted education from the University of Houston and a Masters of Arts in Teaching from Trinity University. She has 15 years teaching experience at the elementary and higher education levels. Her research interests focus on the connection between differentiation and how this philosophy relates to the classroom as well as professional development design for both preservice and in-service teachers. Specifically, this line of research intersects the practice of differentiated instruction across learning environments.

Tracy L. Cross, Ph.D., holds an endowed chair, Jody and Layton Smith Professor of Psychology and Gifted Education, and is the executive director of the Center for Gifted Education at The College of William and Mary. Previously he served Ball State University as the George and Frances Ball Distinguished Professor of Psychology and Gifted Studies, the executive director of the Center for Gifted Studies and Talent Development, as well as the Institute for Research on the Psychology of the Gifted Students. He has edited five journals in the field of gifted studies and is the current editor of the *Journal for the Education of the Gifted*. He was recently given the Lifetime Achievement Award from the MENSA Education and Research Foundation.

Michelle Davis, M.Ed., is the director of ABCs for Life Success and Special Needs Advocacy, in Washington, DC, delivering expert evaluation and consulting services to educators, families, and schools. Her *Special Needs Advocacy Resource Book* forms the curriculum for her Special Needs Advocacy Training Institute.

Arlene R. DeVries, M.S.E., has served on the boards of NAGC, SENG, Iowa Talented and Gifted, and *PHP*. After retiring as a gifted consultant with the Des Moines Public Schools, she is now a private consultant in gifted education. She is coauthor of *Gifted Parent Groups: The SENG Model* and *A Parent's Guide to Gifted Children*.

Deborah Douglas served as the gifted education coordinator for the Manitowoc (WI) Public School District for 15 years. As a board member and president-elect of the Wisconsin Association for Talented and Gifted, she consults and advocates for gifted adolescents in the Upper Midwest.

Rita Dunn, Ed.D., was professor, Division of Administrative and Instructional Leadership, and director, Center for the Study of Learning and Teaching Styles at St. John's University in New York.

Andrea Dawn Frazier, Ph.D., received her doctorate in educational psychology from Ball State University in 2009. While earning her doctorate, she edited the *Journal for the Education of the Gifted*, one of the premier journals in the field of gifted education. Before moving to Muncie, IN, to complete her degree, she worked for 7 years at the Illinois Mathematics and Science Academy, a residential school for gifted and talented students in math, science, and technology. Her research interests encompass inequality in schooling for girls and students of color.

Michael Freedman, Ed.D., is assistant professor of science education in the Graduate School of Education at Fordham University.

James J. Gallagher, Ph.D., is senior scientist emeritus and former director of the Frank Porter Graham (FPG) Child Development Institute at the University of North Carolina at Chapel Hill. He has been with FPG since 1970. Gallagher is an internationally recognized early childhood development expert.

Thomas P. Hébert, Ph.D., is a professor in the Department of Educational Psychology and Instructional Technology at the University of Georgia where he teaches graduate courses in gifted education and qualitative research methods. His research interests include the social and emotional development of gifted students, gifted culturally diverse students, and counseling issues faced by gifted males.

John Houtz, Ph.D., is professor of educational psychology and former associate dean for Academic Affairs in the Graduate School of Education at Fordham University.

Sue Jeweler spent her 30-year career in Maryland's Montgomery County Public Schools (MCPS) teaching elementary school; training student teachers from area universities; training teachers in conflict-resolution strategies, gifted and talented instruction, differentiation, and accommodation strategies; and in writing conflict resolution and social studies curricula. Sue has been a consultant to the Kennedy Center, the Smithsonian Institute, National Geographic, Berns & Kay, and Street Law. She has coauthored two educational kits, more than

30 books, and numerous articles for journals and magazines. She has received many awards, including the prestigious *Washington Post* Agnes Meyer Outstanding Teaching Award.

Julia Johnston, M.A., has coauthored three books with Mary Kay Shanley. Julia is a freelance journalist with more than 20 years of experience writing for newspapers and magazines. She also has served as a writing consultant coach at Drake Law School. She taught in juvenile shelters and lock-up facilities; volunteered in her district's first writing center program; and advocated, along with Mary Kay, a weighted-grade system for the high school. Julia earned a bachelor's degree from University of Maryland-College Park, and a master's in journalism and teaching certification from Drake University in Des Moines, IA.

Barbara A. Lewis is an award-winning author and teacher. Her students worked to clean up hazardous waste, fight crime, initiate six laws in the Utah legislature, and more. Barbara has been featured in *Newsweek, The Wall Street Journal, The Congressional Record, Family Circle,* and *CBS World News.* She has written numerous articles and authored several books including *The Kid's Guide to Social Action, The Kid's Guide to Service Projects, Kids With Courage, What Do You Stand For?, The Survival Guide for Teachers of Gifted Kids,* and *The Teen Guide to Global Action.*

Andrew Mahoney, M.S., L.P.C., is a counselor and marriage and family therapist specializing in the gifted and talented population. He also is director of The Counseling Practice of Andrew S. Mahoney, a counseling and consulting center for the gifted and talented in Chicago and Pittsburgh.

Ken McCluskey, Ph.D., dean and professor of education at the University of Winnipeg, has had 25 years experience as a school psychologist, special educator, and administrator in the public school system. A recipient of major program development, creativity, and publication awards from the Canadian Council for Exceptional Children, the International Centre for Innovation in Education, the World Council for Gifted and Talented Children, and Reclaiming Youth International (along with his institution's teaching, research, and community service awards), Ken has written more than 100 professional articles and chapters, and is the author, coauthor, or editor of 15 books, including *Lost Prizes: Talent Development and Problem Solving with At-Risk Populations* and *Understanding ADHD: Our Personal Journey.*

Sidney M. Moon, Ph.D., is a professor of Gifted, Creative, and Talented Studies and associate dean for learning and engagement in the College of Education at Purdue University. She has been involved in the field of gifted, creative, and talented studies for more than 25 years. In that time, she has contributed more than 75 books, articles, and chapters to the field. Her most recent book is *The Handbook of Secondary Gifted Education.* Sidney is active in NAGC where she has served as chair of the Research and Evaluation Division, a member of the Board of Directors, and chair of the Bylaws Committee. Currently, she is the association editor for NAGC. Her research interests include talent development in the STEM disciplines, underserved populations of gifted students, and personal talent development.

Diane Nash is an educator, writer, and consultant from Snyder, NY, and coauthor of *The Mentor Kit.*

Maureen Neihart, Psy.D., is a licensed clinical child psychologist and associate professor of psychological studies at the National Institute of Education at Nanyang Technological University in Singapore. She is a former member of the Board of Directors of NAGC and a contributing editor to *Gifted Child Quarterly, Roeper Review,* and *Journal for the Education of the Gifted.*

Henry J. Nicols is the director of system support for Bassett Healthcare in Cooperstown, NY, and is completing a book on children and stress in the international community.

Ben Paris is a tutor, a former curriculum director for Kaplan Test Prep, and a designer of award-winning online test preparation courses. He also is a member of the national advisory board of the California Learning Strategies Center (http://www.learningstrategiescenter.com), a think tank for parents of gifted students.

Jeanne L. Paynter, Ed.D., is the state specialist for gifted and talented education at the Maryland State Department of Education.

Leighann Pennington, M.Ed., currently teaches sixth grade at TVT Community Day School in Irvine, CA. She graduated from Miami University with a bachelor's degree in English/creative writing and a M.Ed. in educational psychology/gifted education from the University of Virginia. She also teaches at Johns Hopkins University's Center for Talented Youth.

Jean Sunde Peterson, Ph.D., professor and director of school counselor preparation at Purdue University, is a former gifted education teacher. Based on her extensive research and counseling experience with gifted youth and their families, she conducts workshops related to their development. She is author of *The Essential Guide to Talking With Gifted Teens* and *Gifted at Risk: Poetic Profiles* and coeditor of *Models of Counseling Gifted Children, Adolescents, and Young Adults*. She is a member of the Board of Directors of NAGC and a past chair of the Counseling and Guidance Network.

Michael C. Pyryt, Ed.M., was professor at the Centre for Gifted Education at the University of Calgary in Calgary, Alberta, Canada.

Diana Reeves, M.Ed., is a parent member on the NAGC Board of Directors and is chairperson of the Massachusetts Association for Gifted Education. She holds a B.S. from the University of Wisconsin, a M.Ed. from Boston University, and a Sixth Year Degree from the University of Connecticut. Diana has served as a state education specialist for gifted education and as a consultant for school systems and parent groups throughout New England. She has taught students at every level and presently teaches third grade at The Gordon School in East Providence, RI. While alternating a wide variety of hats, Diana always wears her dancing shoes.

Sally M. Reis, Ph.D., is a Board of Trustees Distinguished Professor and the past department head of the Educational Psychology Department at the University of Connecticut where she also serves as a principal investigator for the National Research Center on the Gifted and Talented. She has authored or coauthored more than 250 articles, books, book chapters, monographs and technical reports including *The Schoolwide Enrichment Model*, *The Secondary Triad Model*, and *Work Left Undone*: *Choices and Compromises of Talented Females*. A past president of NAGC, she recently was honored with the highest award in her field as the Distinguished Scholar of NAGC and named a fellow of the American Psychological Association.

Joseph S. Renzulli, Ed.D., is director of the National Research Center on the Gifted and Talented at the Neag School of Education at the University of Connecticut. His most recent work is a book for parents coauthored with Dr. Sally Reis entitled *Light Up Your Child's Mind*, and an Internet-based program that uses computer technology to identify student strengths and match highly engaging enrichment resources to each individual's profile. Information about the program can be found at http://www.renzullilearning.com. Joe recently received the Harold W. McGraw, Jr. Prize for innovative contributions to education.

Sylvia Rimm, Ph.D., is a psychologist, directs the Family Achievement Clinic in Ohio, and specializes in working with gifted children. She also is a clinical professor at Case School of Medicine. Sylvia speaks and publishes internationally on parenting, giftedness, creativity, and underachievement. Among her many books are *How to Parent So Children Will Learn*, *Why Bright Kids Get Poor Grades*, and *Education of the Gifted and Talented*. Sylvia was a longtime contributor to NBC's *Today*, hosted *Family Talk* on public radio, and served on the Board of Directors of NAGC. She is a syndicated newspaper columnist with Creators Syndicate.

Lisa Rivero, M.A., is a homeschool and gifted education advocate and author of *Gifted Education Comes Home: A Case for Self-Directed Homeschooling* and *Creative Home Schooling for Gifted Children: A Resource Guide*. She and her husband homeschool their 10-year-old son in Glendale, WI.

Rebecca Robbins is an attorney, a freelance writer, and a parent advocate for gifted education in Bloomington, IN.

Julia Link Roberts, Ed.D., is the Mahurin Professor of Gifted Studies at Western Kentucky University. She is the executive director of The Center for Gifted Studies and the Carol Martin Gatton Academy of Mathematics and Science in Kentucky. Julia is a member of the Executive Committee of the World Council for Gifted and Talented Children and a board member of The Association for the Gifted and the Kentucky Association for Gifted Education. Julia received the first David W. Belin NAGC Award for Advocacy. She is coauthor with Tracy Ford Inman of *Strategies for Differentiating Instruction: Best*

Practices for the Classroom and *Assessing Differentiated Student Products: A Protocol for Development and Evaluation.*

Ann Robinson, Ph.D., is professor of education and founding director of the Center for Gifted Education at the University of Arkansas at Little Rock. She is a former editor of *Gifted Child Quarterly*, and is the president of the National Association for Gifted Children. She is the coauthor of *Best Practices in Gifted Education: An Evidence-Based Guide.*

Robin M. Schader, Ph.D., is NAGC's Parent Resource Advisor. She completed her Ph.D. at the Neag School of Education at the University of Connecticut where her research explored parental influence in talent development, particularly musicians, athletes, and young adults with disabilities. Her recent work focuses on developing effective collaboration between home and school, creating community awareness for the needs of high-ability learners, and, most importantly, finding educational alternatives for gifted children.

Stephen T. Schroth, Ph.D., earned his degree in educational psychology and gifted education from the University of Virginia. He serves as an assistant professor of educational studies at Knox College in Galesburg, IL, before which he worked as a classroom teacher, literacy coach, and gifted coordinator for a decade in the Los Angeles Unified School District. With Jason A. Helfer, Stephen is the recipient of the 2008 MENSA Education and Research Foundation Award for Excellence in Research. Recent publications include "Identifying Gifted Students: Educators' Beliefs Regarding Various Processes and Procedures" in the *Journal for the Education of the Gifted* (with Jason Helfer).

Mary Kay Shanley has written six books in addition to coauthoring three books with Julia Johnston. She is a public speaker and conducts writing workshops, including the prestigious University of Iowa Summer Writing Festival and the annual Women and Memoir Writing Retreat. A member for 10 years of the Iowa Talented and Gifted State Board of Directors, she also is a recipient of its Distinguished Service Award. She earned degrees in journalism and political science from Creighton University in Omaha, NE.

Robert J. Sternberg, Ph.D., is dean of the School of Arts and Sciences and professor of psychology and education at Tufts University.

He is president of the International Association for Cognitive Education and Psychology and president-elect of the Federation of Associations of Behavioral and Brain Sciences. Robert is a past winner of NAGC's E. Paul Torrance Award and its Distinguished Scholar Award.

Robert D. Strom, Ph.D., began his career as a secondary teacher in Detroit and St. Paul, MN. He is a professor of Advanced Studies in Learning, Technology and Psychology at Arizona State University. Bob's recent books are *Adolescents in the Internet Age* and *Parenting Young Children: The Internet, Television, Play, and Reading.* He has received three Fulbright Research Awards at University of Stockholm, Sweden; Canberra University, Australia; and University of the Philippines. His published instruments include the online Teamwork Skills Inventory for adolescents and adults and the Parent Success Indicator for parents and adolescents.

Rachel E. Sytsma, Ph.D., is assistant professor in education at Calvin College in Grand Rapids, MI. She also is program coordinator for the National Science Foundation grant TRIAGE. She served as a staff member at The National Research Center on the Gifted and Talented and the Neag School of Education at the University of Connecticut.

Liang See Tan, M.S.Ed., is presently a lecturer at the National Institute of Education, Nanyang Technological University, Singapore. Her interests focus on arts education, differentiated curriculum and instruction, talent development, learning, and engagement. Prior to her current position, she taught 16 years in high school and spearheaded programs for the gifted and talented.

Carol Ann Tomlinson, Ed.D., is William Clay Parrish, Jr. Professor and chair of Educational Leadership, Foundations and Policy at the University of Virginia's Curry School of Education. She is a past president of NAGC.

Beverly A. Trail, Ed.D., is a twice-exceptional consultant, trainer, researcher, and author. She has 22 years experience as a gifted resource teacher, district twice-exceptional consultant, and district gifted education coordinator. As an independent consultant for Colorado Department of Education, she was contracted to develop a twice-exceptional resource guide and conduct statewide workshops. Currently, she teaches gifted education courses at Regis University. Beverly's qualifications include an endorsement as a Gifted Education Specialist, a M.A. in gifted education, and a doctorate in special education. Her book, *The Twice-Exceptional Gifted Child*, will be published by Prufrock Press.

Joyce VanTassel-Baska, Ed.D., is professor emerita and former director of the Center for Gifted Education at The College of William and Mary in Williamsburg, VA.

Sandra Warren is a long-time gifted and talented parent advocate and author of books for children and adults. She is a former editor of NAGC's Parent Division Newsletter.

James T. Webb, Ph.D., has been recognized as one of the 25 most influential psychologists nationally on gifted education. Jim, who established SENG (Supporting Emotional Needs of the Gifted), has served on the board of directors of NAGC and was president of the American Association of Gifted Children. He is the lead author of five books and several DVDs about gifted children, including the award-winning books *A Parent's Guide to Gifted Children* and *Misdiagnosis and Dual Diagnoses of Gifted Children and Adults: ADHD, Bipolar, OCD, Asperger's, Depression, and Other Disorders*.

Rich Weinfeld, M.S., is currently the director of the Weinfeld Education Group, LLC, which provides advocacy to parents of students with learning challenges, trains parents and staff on educational topics, and offers consultation to school systems.

Janet Whitley, Ph.D., is a retired professor from Tarleton State University but still teaches part time. She is a Certified Learning Styles Trainer.

Carol V. Wittig, M.S., is an associate of the Center for Creative Learning in Sarasota, FL, and a former gifted programming specialist in the Williamsville, NY, Central School District.

List of Article
Publication Dates

"No Child Is Just Born Gifted: Creating and Developing Unlimited Potential" originally appeared in the March 1997 issue of *Parenting for High Potential*. Copyright ©1997 by National Association for Gifted Children.

"Developing Your Child's Successful Intelligence" originally appeared in the June 1997 issue of *Parenting for High Potential*. Copyright ©1997 by National Association for Gifted Children.

"Why Gifted Children May Not Test Well" originally appeared in the March 2009 issue of *Parenting for High Potential*. Copyright ©2009 by National Association for Gifted Children.

"A Glossary of Terms Used in Educational Assessment" originally appeared in the March 2004 issue of *Parenting for High Potential*. Copyright ©2004 by National Association for Gifted Children.

"Self-Regulated Learning and Academically Talented Students" originally appeared in the December 2004 issue of *Parenting for High Potential*. Copyright ©2004 by National Association for Gifted Children.

"What Do You Know About Learning Style? A Guide for Parents of Gifted Children" originally appeared in the June 2000 issue of *Parenting for High Potential*. Copyright ©2000 by National Association for Gifted Children.

"The Importance of Being Early: A Case for Preschool Enrichment" originally appeared in the March 2000 issue of *Parenting for High Potential*. Copyright ©2000 by National Association for Gifted Children.

"Too Busy to Play?" originally appeared in the March 2002 issue of *Parenting for High Potential*. Copyright ©2002 by National Association for Gifted Children.

"Growing Up Too Fast—and Gifted" originally appeared in the March 2006 issue of *Parenting for High Potential*. Copyright ©2006 by National Association for Gifted Children.

"Creating Successful Middle School Partnerships: A Parent's Perspective" originally appeared in the June 2005 issue of *Parenting for High Potential*. Copyright ©2005 by National Association for Gifted Children.

"College Planning With Gifted Children: Start Early" originally appeared in the December 1998 issue of *Parenting for High Potential*. Copyright ©1998 by National Association for Gifted Children.

"Real Fears of Incoming First-Year College Students: What Parents Can Do" originally appeared in the March 2009 issue of *Parenting for High Potential*. Copyright ©2009 by National Association for Gifted Children.

"Nurturing an Awareness and Acceptance of Diversity in Our Gifted Children" originally appeared in the March 2005 issue of *Parenting for High Potential*. Copyright ©2005 by National Association for Gifted Children.

"Looking for Gifts in All the 'Wrong' Places" originally appeared in the December 2005 issue of *Parenting for High Potential*. Copyright ©2005 by National Association for Gifted Children.